Compatriots or Competitors?

WRITING WALES IN ENGLISH

CREW series of Critical and Scholarly Studies
General Editors: Kirsti Bohata and Daniel G. Williams (*CREW*, Swansea University)

This *CREW* series is dedicated to Emyr Humphreys, a major figure in the literary culture of modern Wales, a founding patron of the *Centre for Research into the English Literature and Language of Wales*. Grateful thanks are due to the late Richard Dynevor for making this series possible.

Other titles in the series
Stephen Knight, *A Hundred Years of Fiction* (978-0-7083-1846-1)
Barbara Prys-Williams, *Twentieth-Century Autobiography* (978-0-7083-1891-1)
Kirsti Bohata, *Postcolonialism Revisited* (978-0-7083-1892-8)
Chris Wigginton, *Modernism from the Margins* (978-0-7083-1927-7)
Linden Peach, *Contemporary Irish and Welsh Women's Fiction* (978-0-7083-1998-7)
Sarah Prescott, *Eighteenth-Century Writing from Wales: Bards and Britons* (978-0-7083-2053-2)
Hywel Dix, *After Raymond Williams: Cultural Materialism and the Break-Up of Britain* (978-0-7083-2153-9)
Matthew Jarvis, *Welsh Environments in Contemporary Welsh Poetry* (978-0-7083-2152-2)
Harri Garrod Roberts, *Embodying Identity: Representations of the Body in Welsh Literature* (978-0-7083-2169-0)
Diane Green, *Emyr Humphreys: A Postcolonial Novelist* (978-0-7083-2217-8)
M. Wynn Thomas, *In the Shadow of the Pulpit: Literature and Nonconformist Wales* (978-0-7083-2225-3)
Linden Peach, *The Fiction of Emyr Humphreys: Contemporary Critical Perspectives* (978-0-7083-2216-1)
Daniel Westover, *R. S. Thomas: A Stylistic Biography* (978-0-7083-2413-4)
Jasmine Donahaye, *Whose People? Wales, Israel, Palestine* (978-0-7083-2483-7)
Judy Kendall, *Edward Thomas: The Origins of His Poetry* (978-0-7083-2403-5)
Damian Walford Davies, *Cartographies of Culture: New Geographies of Welsh Writing in English* (978-0-7083-2476-9)
Daniel G. Williams, *Black Skin, Blue Books: African Americans and Wales 1845–1945* (978-0-7083-1987-1)
Andrew Webb, *Edward Thomas and World Literary Studies: Wales, Anglocentrism and English Literature* (978-0-7083-2622-0)
Alyce von Rothkirch, *J. O. Francis, realist drama and ethics: Culture, place and nation* (978-1-7831-6070-9)
Rhian Barfoot, *Liberating Dylan Thomas: Rescuing a Poet from Psycho-Sexual Servitude* (978-1-7831-6184-3)
Daniel G. Williams, *Wales Unchained: Literature, Politics and Identity in the American Century* (978-1-7831-6212-3)
M. Wynn Thomas, *The Nations of Wales 1890–1914* (978-1-78316-837-8)
Richard McLauchlan, *Saturday's Silence: R. S. Thomas and Paschal Reading* (978-1-7831-6920-7)
Bethan M. Jenkins, *Between Wales and England: Anglophone Welsh Writing of the Eighteenth Century* (978-1-7868-3029-6)
M. Wynn Thomas, *All that is Wales: The Collected Essays of M. Wynn Thomas* (978-1-7868-3088-3)
Laura Wainwright, *New Territories in Modernism: Anglophone Welsh Writing, 1930–1949* (978-1-7868-3217-7)
Siriol McAvoy, *Locating Lynette Roberts: 'Always Observant and Slightly Obscure'* (978-1-7868-3382-2)
Linden Peach, *Pacifism, Peace and Modern Welsh Writing* (978-1-7868-3402-7)
Kieron Smith, *John Ormond's Organic Mosaic* (978-1-7868-3488-1)
Georgia Burdett and Sarah Morse (eds), *Fight and Flight: Essays on Ron Berry* (978-1-7868-3528-4)
M. Wynn Thomas, *Eutopia: Studies in Cultural Euro-Welshness, 1850–1980* (978-1-78683-614-4)
Linden Peach, *Animals, Animality and Controversy in Modern Welsh Literature and Culture* (978-1-78683-937-4)

Compatriots or Competitors?

Welsh, Scottish, English and Northern Irish Writing and Brexit in Comparative Contexts

WRITING WALES IN ENGLISH

Hywel Dix

UNIVERSITY OF WALES PRESS
2022

© Hywel Dix, 2022

All rights reserved. No part of this book may be reproduced in any material form (including photocopying or storing it in any medium by electronic means and whether or not transiently or incidentally to some other use of this publication) without the written permission of the copyright owner. Applications for the copyright owner's written permission to reproduce any part of this publication should be addressed to the University of Wales Press, University Registry, King Edward VII Avenue, Cardiff CF10 3NS.

www.uwp.co.uk

British Library CIP Data
A catalogue record for this book is available from the British Library.

ISBN: 978-1-78683-934-3
e-ISBN: 978-1-78683-935-0

The right of Hywel Dix to be identified as author of this work has been asserted in accordance with sections 77 and 79 of the Copyright, Designs and Patents Act 1988.

THE ASSOCIATION FOR
WELSH WRITING IN ENGLISH
CYMDEITHAS LLÊN SAESNEG CYMRU

Typeset by Marie Doherty
Printed by CPI Antony Rowe, Melksham

Contents

Series Editors' Preface		vii
Acknowledgements		xi
List of Illustrations		xiii
Introduction: Compatriots or Competitors?		1
1	From Counter-Culture to Creative Industries	19
2	The Cultural Capital of Capitals of Culture	63
3	Imaging Northern Europe: British Varieties of Nordic Noir	109
4	Aspiration by Proxy: National Book Awards in International Markets	167
5	Brexit and Beyond	229
Afterword: Brexit and Coronavirus		283
References		289
Index		311

Series Editors' Preface

The aim of this series, since its founding in 2004 by Professor M. Wynn Thomas, is to publish scholarly and critical work by established specialists and younger scholars that reflects the richness and variety of the English-language literature of modern Wales. The studies published so far have amply demonstrated that concepts, models and discourses current in the best contemporary studies can illuminate aspects of Welsh culture, and have also foregrounded the potential of the Welsh example to draw attention to themes that are often neglected or marginalised in anglophone cultural studies. The series defines and explores that which distinguishes Wales's anglophone literature, challenges critics to develop methods and approaches adequate to the task of interpreting Welsh culture, and invites its readers to locate the process of writing Wales in English within comparative and transnational contexts.

Professor Kirsti Bohata and Professor Daniel G. Williams

Founding Editor: Professor M. Wynn Thomas (2004–15)

CREW (*Centre for Research into the English Literature and Language of Wales*)
Swansea University

*For Rosie, a true Welsh European.
I am writing this while listening to you sing
and you fill my heart with joy.*

Acknowledgements

Much of this work was written during the coronavirus lockdown of 2020 when the kinds of informal discussions with colleagues through which researchers often develop their thinking were not easily available. Nevertheless, Chloé Ashbridge, Tabitha Baker, Eva Burke, Berit Glanz, Bethan Jenkins, Kristian Shaw, Katerina Strani, Claire Squires, Jakob Stougaard-Nielsen, Jeff Wallace and Candida Yates were generous enough to read early drafts of some of these chapters, giving me helpful feedback and answering detailed questions. Although the interpretations put forward here are of course my own, I am humbled by how much effort this must have taken during a very difficult period and would like to express my deep thanks for their valuable contribution, which seems to me the best kind of academic citizenship.

List of Illustrations

FIGURE 1	The Sex Pistols, *God Save the Queen*, 1977. Michael Kemp/Alamy Stock Photo	20
FIGURE 2	Geri Halliwell's Union Jack Dress, 1997. PA Images/Alamy Stock Photo	20
FIGURE 3	Tony Blair and Noel Gallagher, 10 Downing Street, 1997. REUTERS/Alamy Stock Photo	43
FIGURE 4	Shirley Bassey, Opening of the Welsh Assembly, 1999. Trinity Mirror/Mirrorpix/Alamy Stock Photo	59

Introduction: Compatriots or Competitors?

> **It's Scotland's Oil**
> *– SNP slogan, 1974*
>
> **Hope over Hate**
> *– Bill Clinton on the Good Friday Agreement in Northern Ireland, 1998*
>
> **Don't break up this family of nations**
> *– David Cameron on 2014 Scottish referendum*
>
> **Parity with Scotland**
> *– Plaid Cymru Election Pledge, 2015*
>
> **English Votes for English Laws**
> *– New procedure introduced into the House of Commons, 2015*
>
> **Take Back Control**
> *– Campaign slogan, Vote Leave, 2016*

More than forty years have passed since the publication of *The Break-up of Britain* by Tom Nairn in 1977 and it is over a generation since key texts by Eric Hobsbawm (1983), Linda Colley (1992) and Robert Crawford (1992) identified the relationship between cultural production and constructions of Britishness during the imperial period. Beginning with the premise that the intervening decades have been ones of fundamental change in British cultures, this book argues that a new approach is needed to conceptualise the relationship between literature, politics and society in each of the four nations of the United Kingdom in a more fluid way, taking account of the constitutional and cultural changes of recent years, especially Brexit. It suggests that the central dynamic of that relationship is a dialectical interplay between ongoing manifestations of Unionist politics at the British centre and simultaneous expressions of different kinds of nationalism in all four of the nations of the UK which have the effect of putting that same Unionism in active question.

One of the effects of this dialectical relationship between Unionism and counter-unionist nationalisms is that nations and nationalist movements that might be expected to take a strong interest in each other as potential sources on which alternatives to the Union might be modelled, or even to collaborate with each other in the development of such alternatives, have for the most part failed to do so and instead have tended to disseminate a sense of their own fundamental uniqueness compared to both the Union itself and to the other nations within it. This situation has meant that emerging forms of nationalism in each of the nations of Britain have been more likely to model themselves on other nations and movements overseas than on any of the other British varieties of nationalism; and this in turn has contributed to determining both the nature that the varieties of nationalist movements have taken and the means by which the cultures in each of the nations have been constructed and conceptualised as national. More specifically, political and cultural engagement with debates over Britain's membership of the European Union, both in the lead up to the 2016 referendum and during the subsequent protracted process of Britain's withdrawal from the EU throughout 2016–20, have done more than anything else since political devolution in the 1990s to intensify feelings of cultural and political difference between the nations. This has resulted in a dynamic of potential comradeship among them being hampered by varying degrees of competition between them, so that competition itself – for greater degrees of political, economic and cultural capital – has become an unspoken feature of the relationship.

Although a great deal of research has already been published about the legal, economic and political aspects of the UK's withdrawal from the European Union, there has been significantly less critical consideration of the cultural implications: very little scholarly analysis has identified specific forms of cultural production that pre-empted and possibly even precipitated the Brexit decision and little critical research has been conducted either into cultural responses to it or into how forms of cultural production are likely to be affected and changed by it in the future. On the other hand, much of the legal and political discourse surrounding Brexit has drawn attention to the fact that Brexit has widened political differences between the different nations of the UK. Supplementing existing political and legal discussion with cultural analysis, this book will argue that those political differences both inform and are informed by corresponding cultural developments. In doing so, it will activate what Raymond Williams once referred to as two 'related but distinguishable' ways of defining the concept of *representation* (1989, 261): one political and the other cultural.

TWO DEFINITIONS OF REPRESENTATION

A key insight developed by Williams in the 1970s was that how we develop political perspectives and orientations on the world is underpinned by our cultural experiences of it; and that how we learn to form culturally specific value judgements is critically informed by the infusion of political ideology; so that the relationship between culture and politics is fundamentally dialectical and mutually informing. The name Williams gave to the process of analysing how the former relates to the latter and vice versa is cultural materialism and it is the principal method of this book. But if politics and culture are theoretically intertwined they are also pragmatically and analytically distinct and this practical distinction accounts for the fact that new forms of representation have emerged in the different nations of Britain in both politics and culture over the same period.

In politics the Scottish National Party (SNP)'s 1974 electoral slogan 'It's Scotland's Oil' (in reference to the discovery of oil in the North Sea) was directed against the perception that Scottish natural resources were being used to prop up the British state during a period of extreme financial instability, especially in England; it has symbolised the idea favoured by Scottish nationalists that only an independent Scotland can ensure a distribution of Scotland's natural resources in a way that benefits the Scottish people ever since. But if there was a gap (real or perceived) between economic priorities in Scotland and England, a comparable gap was also starting to be perceived from within Wales with regard to Scotland. The so-called Barnett formula, the mechanism by which budgets are allocated to the devolved national governments, had allocated more public money per capita to the people of Scotland than to the people of Wales, and the Scottish Parliament had had greater powers than the Welsh Assembly, including tax-raising powers and hence higher levels of budgetary control. Although the Welsh Assembly had gained higher powers after 2011, reflected in the shift in name from National Assembly to Assembly Government and then simply Welsh Government, the differences in levels of economic and political authority compared to Scotland remained, giving rise to the Welsh nationalist political party Plaid Cymru's call for forms of political representation that would lessen the disparity. Thus, they campaigned in the 2015 general election campaign under the slogan: Parity with Scotland.

In fact, anticipating the electorate turning against the Liberal Democrat leader Nick Clegg for creating the Tory–Lib Dem coalition government of 2010–15, the SNP leader Nicola Sturgeon clearly felt there was a possibility that her party would replace the Liberal Democrats as the third largest party in Britain, and that she might thus be in the position of kingmaker. In the 2015 televised leadership debates she was therefore careful to speak in the measured tones of a stateswoman capable of addressing the people of the UK as a whole. By contrast, there was never any chance that Plaid Cymru would hold the balance of power between the largest electoral parties at Westminster: even the most successful of imaginable outcomes for them would have been a return of four or five MPs out of a total of 650. Knowing this to be the case, Plaid Cymru leader Leanne Wood used the debates to address the people of Wales specifically.

In the event, neither held the balance of power. The 2015 election returned the first majority Conservative government since 1997 and led directly to David Cameron's decision to hold the 2016 referendum on Europe primarily (he thought) as a way of unifying the party by being able to tell the Eurosceptics they had been heard on the one hand, but that the majority of the party did not share their views (on the other). Having failed to foresee the outcome of the referendum, Cameron was replaced by Theresa May who, in a comparable miscalculation, held another general election in 2017 which ostensibly aimed to establish her own mandate, but actually led to her all-but losing her parliamentary majority. As a result, she became dependent on reaching an electoral agreement with Ulster's Democratic Unionist Party (DUP), which brought Northern Ireland to its high noon of UK-wide political influence, and achieving for Northern Ireland in Westminster what Sturgeon and Wood could only dream of. In exchange for the parliamentary support of Arlene Foster's DUP, May committed to allocate an extra billion pounds beyond what had already been budgeted to Northern Ireland over the next two years, as well as other additional concessions such as maintaining spending in agriculture, defence and state pensions at a time when these were all being cut in other parts of the UK (Hunt, 2017). Although Foster's influence waned after May's replacement by Johnson, Johnson's eventual Brexit trade deal nevertheless created the possibility of what his Secretary of State for Northern Ireland, Brandon Lewis, referred to as a 'competitive advantage' for Northern Ireland in attracting investment and enterprise compared to all other parts of the UK, because businesses based there retained the ability to trade with the EU (BBC, 2021).

To some extent the jockeying of Sturgeon, Wood and Foster for influence first with Cameron and subsequently both May and Johnson exemplifies the dynamic of built-in competition for access to forms of political representation which is paradigmatic of the current relationship between the different nations of the UK. But this is more clearly highlighted by the fact that political devolution in Northern Ireland, Scotland and Wales had given rise to a growing perception of asymmetrical devolution in England and a growing call for England to gain its own equivalent form of political representation. This was initially articulated in the campaign for an English parliament but reached fuller expression in the implementation in the House of Commons between 2015 and 2021 of the parliamentary procedure of English Votes for English Laws, whereby only members representing English constituencies could vote on matters that were deemed by the speaker to apply only to England (as opposed to the UK as a whole).

It is hard to imagine a starker example of the structurally fostered ethos of competition between the nations of the United Kingdom, as opposed to their ongoing comradely partnership with each other, than English Votes for English Laws. Political devolution had been created not only to address national aspirations in Scotland and Wales and the Troubles in Northern Ireland but also to redress real historical inequalities for which there were simply no directly comparable equivalents in England. Yet in the process of catching up with them,

English Votes for English laws in fact surpassed them: there had never been a practice of Scottish (or Welsh) votes for Scottish (or Welsh) laws in Westminster; and if there had been, arguably the entire process of devolution would have been redundant. Accepting that devolution had created the need for an equivalent form of political representation in England, the only way in which this could equitably have been achieved would have been through the establishment of a separate body for England thereby putting English politics on the same footing as those in all three of the other nations. The failure to do this, and instead the establishment of the English Votes for English Laws procedure, allowed members representing English constituencies more power both than members of the Scottish and Welsh governments and than Westminster MPs representing Scottish or Welsh constituencies precisely because those roles are disaggregated whereas in England they were not. In the light of the increasing political differences between the nations it is becoming more and more difficult to see how having the same members represent Britain in Parliament on some matters but only England on others when this was not possible for Northern Irish, Scottish or Welsh members could fail to be anything other than a conflict of interest.

It is in the context of this conflict, and a newly hegemonic Englishness dominating the electoral politics of the United Kingdom, that Brexit is best understood. This is partly because both the implementation of English Votes for English Laws in 2015 and the 2016 European referendum were politically calculated moves on the part of the Conservative Party designed to short-circuit devolution and shore up the party's electoral position. But it is also the result of a number of factors that transcend party politics. Scott Hames has shown that the victory for the 'Better Together' (i.e. 'no') campaign in Scotland's 2014 independence referendum, led by former New Labour Prime Minister Gordon Brown, actively 'reversed' the logic on which political devolution was based (2015, n.p.). As a unionist policy aimed at providing a certain level of self-government while forestalling the demand for full independence, devolution had offered to put England, Northern Ireland, Scotland and Wales on an approximately equal footing without the need to break up the overall family of nations. Yet it also had the effect of disavowing the possibility of a fully federal British state. For this reason, as Hames goes on to show in a subsequent paper, the result of the 2016 EU vote took to an even further extreme the undoing of the logic of devolution by undermining the allusion of equal footing that it had created because the outcome in England was able to 'change the union's cultural and political meaning' without regard to what was happening in the other nations (2020, n.p.).

In another work again, *The Literary Politics of Scottish Devolution: Voice, Class, Nation* (2019), Hames draws attention to the role played by literature in elaborating and disseminating the 'dream' of nationhood in Scotland and this is where forms of political representation start to relate literary, artistic and cultural ones. It has of course become something of a commonplace that contemporary Scottish literature is an important bearer of national aspirations – indeed, the literature has been inculcated with those aspirations even in cases of work by authors such as James Kelman whose primary terms of reference are not the Scottish 'nation'. Robert Crawford (1992) argued that the discipline of English literature owes its existence to the aftermath of the 1707 Act of Union, when aspiring members of Scotland's political class practised elocution in order to make themselves better understood among their counterparts in London. Murray Pittock (2003) concurs, seeing in the establishment of the academic study of rhetoric and *belles lettres* the forerunner of the field that subsequently became known as English literature, and in Scottish professor Hugh Blair 'arguably the first chair in literature' in the world (235). Building on the ideas of Crawford and Pittock, Michael Gardiner sees English Literature as inherently British and unionist, while Cairns Craig (1999) and Monica Germanà (2014) both situate distinctively Scottish forms of writing in the last quarter of the twentieth century in the context of growing claims for political autonomy.

Within contemporary British literatures, the association of literature with nationhood has not been limited to Scotland. It has, for example, been explored in Wales in M. Wynn Thomas's collection *Welsh Writing in English* (2003) and Jane Aaron and Chris Williams's volume *Postcolonial Wales* (2005); in Northern Ireland in Fiona McCann, *A poetics of dissensus: confronting violence in contemporary prose writing from the North of Ireland* (2014) and Elizabeth Crooke and Thomas Maguire's collection *Heritage after Conflict: Northern Ireland* (2018); and (more latterly) in England by Mark Perryman's *Imagined Nation: England After Britain* (2008), Michael Gardiner's *The Return of England in English Literature* (2012) and Claire Westall and Michael Gardiner's *Literature of an Independent England*: *Revisions of England, Englishness and English Literature* (2013).

What none of these studies do, however, is take a comparative approach. That is, none has yet synthesised, compared or evaluated different cultural articulations of nationhood in each case. Linden Peach argues in *Contemporary Irish and Welsh Women's Fiction* (2008) that owing to the historic association of church or chapel with patriarchal authority, female writers in Ireland and Wales have adopted a 'pagan perspective' with regard to those structures (184). But that is a subtly different argument from one that associates culture with nationhood – indeed, one that is almost antithetical to it. There is a brief chapter about cultural connections between Scotland and Ireland, again partly on religious grounds, in Berthold Schoene's *Edinburgh Companion to Contemporary Scottish Literature* (2007), but given the volume's opening emphasis on 'cosmopolitan' Scottishness (7), the neglect of potentially rich linkages between Scotland and Welsh and Irish culture (let alone English) seems positively wilful, as does their absence from Michael Gardiner, Graeme Macdonald and Niall O'Gallagher's collection *Scottish Literature and Postcolonial Literature: Comparative Texts and Critical Perspectives* (2011).

And what of the relationship between any of them and Europe? Writing in *Imagined Communities* in 1983, Benedict Anderson suggested that one of the challenges for supranational political entities was that unlike individual nations, which have at least some degree of organic connection to their people, bureaucratic units are neither grounded in them nor enjoy the same degree of emotional investment from them: 'market zones, "natural"-geographic or politico-administrative, do not create attachments. Who will willingly die for Comecon or the EEC?' (53). This succinct summary of the difficulty involved in gaining popular assent for transnational political entities of an essentially corporate nature perhaps contrasts with the argument of Crawford's *Bannockburns: Scottish Independence and Literary Imagination, 1314–2014* that in William Wallace and Robert the Bruce, Scottish history provided the popular imagination with icons around whom emotional attachment has been cultivated by seven centuries of literary representation. Naturally these have changed over time, emphasising less the militaristic element and more the commitment to comradeship and solidarity, so that whereas Anderson saw the fact that no one would risk their lives for the cause of the EEC (the forerunner of the European Union) as an indicator of weakness and lack of buy-in, Murray Pittock suggests 'one of the positive things that can be said for Scottish nationalism' is that 'not one person died or was killed for it in the course of the twentieth century' (277). But still the overall challenge remains: human beings feel less emotional affinity with committee structures than with the places and relationships – that is, the nations – where they live.

Thus, for example, whereas Linda Colley has shown how much cultural effort went into constructing and defining the terms *Britain* and *Britons* in an aspirational way in the years after 1707, there has never been anything like the same cultural elucidation either of what it means to be European or of what Europe collectively might stand for. In fact, the near absence of collective narratives of Europe might be one of the biggest challenges of all for the future of the European Union: neither Richard Bellamy, Dario Castiglione and Jo Shaw's collection *Making European Citizens: Civic Inclusion in a Transnational Context* (2006) nor Willem Maas's monograph on *Creating European Citizens* (2007) contains a single chapter that even considers what a culturally articulated feeling of Europeanness might look like. The contrast with the cultural definition of *Britons* during the imperial period – or in another context, with the extremely high cultural investment in defining *Americans* in the period since 1945 – could hardly be stronger.

COMPATRIOTS OR COMPETITORS?

That political scientists tend not to say very much about culture is maybe not surprising, and in any case the fact that Bellamy's and Maas's books do not discuss creative or artistic expressions of a common European culture does not necessarily mean that no such expressions occurred. But as will be shown in the case of the European Capitals of Culture programme in Chapter Two and the discussion of European book prizes in Chapter Four, where these have happened they have tended to be highly paternalistic in character, taking a predominantly top-down approach to the dissemination of culture. This is at odds with other modes of cultural production over the past decade, some of which in Britain have variously anticipated, pre-empted and contributed to, or questioned and contested, Britain's departure from the European Union. At the same time, the key argument that will be developed over the following chapters is that those different forms of cultural engagement with the Brexit debate over the period 2010–20 have exposed cultural differences between the different nations of Britain.

The opening chapter will identify and discuss one of the key cultural developments in Britain during the years since 1979: the fact that during the 1970s and 1980s, the dominant ideology of capitalism spawned a very rich and vibrant counter-culture in music, film, television and writing, whereas by the end of the millennium the political establishment had been very successful in incorporating cultural movements into its own ideology and hence in undermining the capacity for culture to operate as an effective site for political resistance. This explains why the 1970s produced such subcultural movements as punk and heavy metal, whereas the 1990s produced Britpop and the Spice Girls.

Looking at the development first of the heritage industry in the 1980s, then of the cultural industries in the 1990s and finally of the creative industries since 2000, it will argue that the loosening of counter-cultural affiliations and the increased incorporation of the creative industries into the mainstream of political and economic power has had the effect of altering the nature of cultural production itself. Accordingly, this key transition from the 1980s to the 2000s provides a necessary context and starting point for a comparative discussion of contemporary British cultures. Thus, for example, the paradigmatic example of Britpop is *Trainspotting*, which by dint of existing in the form of a novel, play, film adaptation and popular music soundtrack was variously positioned either as a symptomatic expression of British creativity or as a distinctively Scottish one. Likewise, the Welsh variant of Britpop – Cool Cymru – was hailed at the time as an expression of increasing Welsh confidence in the years around political self-determination, and the Welsh film *Twin Town* was again variously constructed as a typical British film or a specifically Welsh one, and often, in the latter case, expressly as Wales's 'version' of *Trainspotting*. While none of these claims or counter-claims can be considered finally true or untrue in themselves, the chapter will explore how the case of Britpop, coming right in the midst of the transition from counter-cultures to creative industries, reveals two important conflicts: (1) between expressions of Britishness and expressions of counter-British nationhood; and (2) between the different national cultures that exist in Britain. Varying forms of those conflicts, it will suggest, have then been played out in a number of different areas of cultural life around the UK since then.

One of the points to emerge from this discussion is the instrumental use to which culture has increasingly been put across Britain in order to contribute to an agenda of urban regeneration and social inclusion. These things will be explored further in Chapter Two, which considers the relationship between two accolades that have contributed to the process of using culture for urban regeneration: European Capital of Culture (1985+) and UK City of Culture (2009+). Although there is already a wealth of research on these things (especially the former), it has mostly been carried out from within the disciplines of tourism or urban planning, focusing on the effects achieved in one individual city or another by hosting the relevant cultural festival. Very little comparative research has been carried out into the experiences of different capitals of culture; and almost none has been carried out from within arts or cultural disciplines, making it difficult to evaluate the artistic content of any of them. Moreover, relatively little research has been carried out into the dynamics of the bidding process; or into the characteristics of successful bids; or most critically of all into the weaknesses of unsuccessful candidates. This chapter therefore proposes to treat the bids for these accolades as specific forms of writing and to subject them to detailed critical comparative analysis.

Beginning with a discussion of Glasgow and Dublin as European City (subsequently, Capital) of Culture in 1990 and 1991, it will argue that this year-long cultural festival, like other so-called 'Big' events such as the Olympic Games, has become a key mechanism by which cities attempt to achieve various forms of economic regeneration; social mobility; and international visibility. For this reason, it has become an attractive event for cities to host, with the candidature process itself increasingly competitive and bidding alone often costing millions of pounds (or euros). In turn, city councils are unable to commit to such an outlay unless they can be guaranteed some kind of return on their investment. But this is only possible if the bids themselves are structured in such a way that the perceived benefits can be achieved whether or not the bid itself is successful. These 'benefits' vary from economic factors such as job creation, external investment and tourist dollars to softer social gains such as empowering communities through the development of a participatory culture, or creating a new image for a particular region in the eyes of the world. Although close inspection will reveal a high degree of conflict over the definition of public good in this context (and especially a high level of class-based critique), the event itself was seen as so desirable that by the time of the UK's next hosting of European Capital of Culture in 2008 it was highly competitive: during the host city selection phase in 2001–3, twelve rival bids were whittled down via a pre-selection process to a shortlist of six. Close analysis of the successful bid (Liverpool) and some of the unsuccessful ones (Cardiff, Belfast, Newcastle, Bristol) will make it possible to explore closely the ideological battles over definition of the public good which accompanied these decisions; and also the structuring dynamic itself whereby bid teams could leverage some of the 'gains' even if they were ultimately unsuccessful.

Having discovered through its management of the bidding process in 2001–3 for European Capital of Culture 2008 that each city could make key gains even if they didn't win the eventual right to host the festival, the UK Department for Culture, Media and Sport discovered during the 2008 event itself that since the UK's turn to host it only happened once every fifteen to eighteen years, the economic and social impact gained by doing so is quite limited. This realisation was the starting point for the idea of UK City of Culture, a new cultural festival which was launched the following year (2009) and first hosted by Derry/Londonderry in 2013. After exploring the contribution made by the 2013 event to forms of post-conflict public heritage in Northern Ireland, the chapter will argue that the process of using culture to achieve both urban regeneration and social empowerment fully accords with the practice of using the creative industries for social and economic ends discussed in Chapter One. It will then go on to explore the bidding process for the second UK City of Culture, 2017 (in which Hull held off rivals from Leicester, Swansea and Dundee). Finally, it will draw attention to the fact that the next iteration of UK City of Culture (2021) coincided in time with what was due to be the run-up to the UK's next turn to host European Capital of Culture (2023). However, in the light of the UK Referendum on membership of the European Union in 2016, the right to host European Capital of Culture 2023 was withdrawn from the UK, causing some of the cities that had already started to invest in bids for it to bring their bids forward and apply instead for UK City of Culture 2021. This means that bid teams around the UK had in effect learnt from Liverpool 2008: (a) that it was possible to have the 'benefits' associated with the European Capital of Culture accolade whether or not they actually won it; and (b) that they could access the socio-economic goals pursued through instrumentalising the arts and culture without participating in the European festival at all. One of the great ironies to emerge from this discussion is that the European Capital of Culture offers to promote closer transnational integration through cultural activity, but does so in an explicitly competitive way that sets cities against each other and militates against a sense of easy alliance. As a result, the chapter will conclude, the UK City of Culture appears in retrospect to be a secessionist movement with regard to the European Capital of Culture. Moreover, it too pits both cities and nations within the union against each other in the increasingly competitive sphere of cultural production.

Having argued in Chapter Two that UK City of Culture should be seen as an early cultural precursor to Britain's break with the European Union, Chapter Three will suggest a different context for the same process. Specifically, it considers the position of Nordic noir television in Britain and aims to plot an important historical trajectory in which the surge of interest in this genre should be understood. The chapter will argue that the Nordic nations have not always been viewed from within Britain as the most enthusiastic participants in cultural and political union at a wider European level, so that the increased presence of Nordic noir television in Britain during the period 2011–21 has given rise to the dissemination of a Northern European image pool which is distinct from the popular conception of the rest of Europe and so underpins the process by which Britain can be pictured outside the European Union.

There are a number of important caveats here. First of all, no suggestion is made that the Nordic nations are any less European than the other nations of Europe; merely that they have not been perceived as the major players in European integration. Secondly, there is no direct cause-and-effect relationship between what people see on television and how they behave in their daily life (let alone their voting behaviour) so that to present the relative popularity of Nordic noir as a root cause of Brexit seems like a methodological blind alley. Thirdly, repeated studies have shown that the majority audience for Nordic noir (and indeed most foreign-language drama in subtitled translation) is university educated and middle-class – the same demographic that was most likely to oppose Brexit. For this reason, and fourthly, the analysis is concerned not so much with audience studies or with the reception of the genre as with its mere presence in Britain. Although the argument cannot be stated any more determinedly than this, it is possible to suggest that at the levels of visual imagery and the semiotic imaginary the presence of Nordic noir in Britain contributed to the formation of the symbolic terrain on which the route to Brexit would eventually be mapped out.

After making this point, the second half of Chapter Three will identify a number of Nordic noir-inspired series, or post-Nordic noirs, produced more recently in Britain. Partly because of the distinctive settings of these series and partly also because of the involvement of different national and regional companies in their production, the chapter will suggest that British post-Nordic 'noirs' *Shetland* (Scotland), *The Fall* (Northern Ireland), *Y Gwyll/Hinterland*, *Craith/Hidden* (both Wales), and *Wallander* and *The Tunnel* (both England) participate in solidifying particular aspects of cultural specificity in each of the nations of the United Kingdom. In the process they display a simultaneous feeling of similarity to and distinction from each other. Overall, therefore, just as the presence of the Nordic genre in Britain creates a certain cultural context for the path towards Brexit, so too those British post-Nordic noirs should be understood in the context of the dialectical relationship between continuing commitment to the British union and the assertion of individual national differences.

The conclusion of Chapter Three represents something of a pivot in the book. Having explored a series of cultural precursors to Brexit in Chapters One to Three, Chapters Four and Five explore some of the literary responses to it. If the atmosphere of competition between cultural producers in the different nations of Britain was discernible in varieties of Britpop, the bidding for UK City of Culture, and the different varieties of post-Nordic noir before Brexit, then this competitive (indeed, at times antagonistic) relationship has been even more explicit in its wake. Chapter Four will explore the implications of this conflictual relationship between the cultural production of the different nations of the UK in another area of cultural life that has become increasingly competitive over time, that of national book prizes. It will argue that the European Economic Community's commitment to opening up free markets created the conditions in which national book awards participate, so that their histories reveal a dialectical interplay between expressing national cultures and looking beyond the limits of the nation. National book awards offer to assert distinctive local or national voices on the one hand; but are also involved in transnational networks of production and reception in which the commitment to nationhood as such is downplayed, on the other.

In Britain this tension is evident in the case of the Booker Prize. However, the situation is complicated because although the Booker

Prize is not explicitly billed as an 'English' national prize, it has often been treated that way by critics, journalists and writers. This conflation, the chapter will argue, has been common in many other areas of everyday life in Britain, and frustration with it is perhaps one reason why since 1982 the Saltire Society has annually awarded the separate accolade of Scottish Book of the Year; and why the Arts Council of Wales established its own Wales Book of the Year in 1992. In situating these two developments within the wider trajectory of national cultural evolution in each place, the chapter will argue that one reason for the belatedness of a national book of the year prize in Wales is that Wales already had the longest-running literary prize in Britain, the Chairing of the Bard at the National Eisteddfod, and that the latter intersects with Wales Book of the Year in the construction of Wales's particular literary culture in various ways. Wales Book of the Year has helped to give greater prominence to the field of Welsh writing as a whole than it had before, and a knock-on effect of this prominence is that Welsh writers have been long- or shortlisted for other British and international awards since 1992 more often than was the case before that time. In other words, the national Book of the Year award in Wales is not merely an indicator but also a positive driver of Welsh cultural production.

A further irony to emerge from the discussion of book prizes in the different nations of Britain is that conferring prizes explicitly billed as national is an act of laying claim (in some cases, of reclamation) which brings the lauded writers and works inside the parameters of the particular national culture whether or not the writers in question compartmentalise their work along national lines or even conceive of it as belonging to that particular nation. In these cases, the material practice of awarding literary prizes is thus assimilated to the tools of nation building. Moreover, part of how nationalist movements in Scotland and Wales have constructed their cultures as national has been through cathecting values such as diversity, transnational solidarity, interculturalism and cosmopolitanism as integral aspects of the nascent national cultures. However, the cultural politics of Brexit has presented various challenges to these forms of self-imagination in those nations, challenges that have had the effect of provoking a renewed commitment to them. Through analysis of the national book prizes awarded in each nation in the years surrounding the European referendum (2015–20), the chapter will argue that the awards reveal how those components of the national cultures have been re-articulated – both to contest Britain's withdrawal from Europe, and as a means by which cultural leaders in Scotland and Wales reaffirmed their solidarity with other European nations.

However, there is the key difference that, in Scotland, the majority of voters had voted to remain in the European Union so that the intellectuals who expressed this preference accorded with the outlook of the population more generally and could be considered examples of organic intellectuals in Gramsci's sense. Although a discernible majority of Welsh intellectuals were in favour of remaining in the European Union, their mood was not replicated by the majority of the Welsh population, which in fact voted to leave. Thus, in the aftermath of the referendum it has been difficult for intellectuals in Wales to lay claim to the same degree of organic connection to the people as those in Scotland, which is why the process of Britain withdrawing from the European Union has created a different feeling of crisis in Wales from that in Scotland. The only way to square these positions appears to be to consider the possibility that the Scottish people voted remain as a protest against Westminster politics, whereas those in Wales voted the opposite – for the same reason.

The chapter will conclude by considering the case of Northern Ireland, which has no national book prize. Drawing on research into recent post-conflict cultural practices there, and focusing on the building of new forms of public memory and collective culture, the chapter will argue that the absence of book prizes accords with an overall process of downplaying controversial or contested elements of Northern Ireland's culture and history and emphasising instead opportunities for common participation in a shared culture. This process has been an important hallmark of Northern Irish society since the Good Friday Agreement of 1998, and one that accords with Derry/Londonderry's hosting of UK City of Culture in 2013 discussed in Chapter Two (but, as will be shown, the surface commitment to avoiding controversy itself is by no means an ideologically neutral one).

Although there is no national book award, there has been one winner each from Northern Ireland for both the Nobel Prize for Literature (Seamus Heaney) and the Booker Prize (Anna Burns). Close examination of these writers and, more importantly, of the ways in which they were presented within the prize discourse that laid claim to them, will demonstrate how both awards accord with the post-conflict logic that characterises the society as a whole. Moreover, exploring the conditions in which these awards were conferred will reveal that many of the same predicaments discussed above in the cases of Scotland and Wales pertain in different ways to Northern Ireland: the conflation of England with Britain in the structures of the Booker prize; the need to decouple these things from each other; and the dialectical relationship that exists between the local and the global in the adumbration of literary prize culture.

Finally, the key argument to be presented in Chapter Five is that the period since 2016 has seen the emergence of a discernible sub-genre in contemporary British fiction: the Brexit novel. In a sense, all literature after Brexit belongs to this genre, since Brexit will affect every aspect of life. However, owing to the protracted nature of the process itself, many of the fictional portrayals of it were written in the period between 2015 and 2020, *before* Britain had in fact left the European Union. For this reason, they refer forward to a subsequent period when the UK's withdrawal is imagined to have taken place. In other words, BrexLit is anticipatory in nature and defined by what it is looking towards, rather than what it comes after. In this sense, it bucks many recent definitions of contemporary culture such as those of Agamben, Deleuze, Nancy and Luckhurst, for whom the contemporary is defined by a sense of afterwardsness. By moving away from this definition of the contemporary and looking forward rather than back, BrexLit thus unwittingly chimes in with the feeling of a symbolic new start which was actively propagated by the Brexiteers, even though many of the novelists in question are actively critical of it. Northern Irish novelists, by contrast, have been remarkably silent on the matter of Brexit, although the chapter will argue that Brexit is an unspoken presence in key works by Eimear McBride and Nick Laird, works which can be situated in the general practice of avoiding controversy in the service of building post-conflict cultures in Northern Ireland over the past twenty years.

Through a discussion of work by Scottish writers A. L. Kennedy and Ali Smith; English writers Sarah Hall, Jonathan Coe, Linda Grant, Ian McEwan, Amanda Craig, Bernadine Evaristo, and Alan Kent; and the work of Welsh writers Robert Minhinnick and Niall Griffiths, the chapter will argue that novelistic portrayals tend to associate opposition to Brexit with a progressive world view in other areas of social and cultural life such as gay rights; pacifism; animal welfare; immigration and multiculturalism; and climate change. By contrast, the fictional portrayals tend to associate support for Brexit with reactionary political views in all of these other areas. Moreover, and overwhelmingly, the novelists associate pro-European attitudes with characters based in middle-class communities in metropolitan areas (especially London), and anti-European sentiment with rural areas (the frequency with which Cornwall is portrayed in this way is striking).

These tendencies mean that the Brexit novel genre fails to interrogate the assumption of entrenched divisions between an educated metropolitan elite and a backwards-looking hinterland on which much rhetoric in favour of Brexit depended, creating a sense of entrapment and revealing the extent to which the dominant ideology set and determined the terms of debate in advance. Unable to transform those terms, the Brexit novel genre ends up repeating the polarisation of opinion and related simplistic dichotomies on which they are based. This is evident in the various ways in which it constructs and depicts diverse regional settings – which it again polarises, thereby exacerbating 'national' and 'regional' differences as opposed to merely reflecting them. The chapter will conclude that only Niall Griffiths's *Broken Ghost* is capable of thinking beyond these parameters, deploying a range of linguistic strategies for moving the portrayal of Brexit Britain beyond the binary categories of Leave/Remain; Us/Them on which it had been based, and so hinting at a possible future beyond these confines.

1

FROM COUNTER-CULTURE TO CREATIVE INDUSTRIES

INTRODUCTION

On 27 May 1977 punk band the Sex Pistols released their second single 'God Save the Queen'. Its celebrated cover artwork featured an image of Queen Elizabeth II, whose Silver Jubilee was due to be celebrated in a riverside pageant in London later that Summer. Her eyes and mouth are defaced, with the name of the band and the song superimposed over the top in a collage of different newspaper-style fonts giving the impression of a ransom note or threatening message. In some versions of the record cover, this image itself is ironically framed by a rippling British flag as if to hint at a disjunction between the glorious values it enshrines and the alternative experiences of British life that are documented in the song (see Figure 1).

On 24 February 1997 pop singer Geri Halliwell wore a Union Jack dress while performing with her group the Spice Girls at the Brit Awards music ceremony. The edginess and air of menace that characterise the Sex Pistols' release have disappeared. Instead, the dress and Halliwell's performance in it evince an air of cultured ease, a feeling of being completely at home in the world of commercial culture and establishment aesthetics. This comfort is accompanied by an aggressive pride in the flag and therefore implicitly in the country to which it refers. There is no feeling of irony at all. (See Figure 2.)

What do these two performances tell us about the changes in British culture between those dates?

FIGURE 1: The Sex Pistols, *God Save the Queen*, 1977.
Michael Kemp/Alamy Stock Photo

FIGURE 2: Geri Halliwell's Union Jack Dress, 1997.
PA Images/Alamy Stock Photo

This chapter will situate the transition from punk to Britpop and Cool Britannia within a wider series of transformations in British society. Beginning with an overview of the subcultures that arose out of the social conflicts of the 1970s, it will identify punk as both a manifestation of and a response to those conflicts, briefly articulating a moment of anti-establishment subversion before surrendering its oppositional potential in the face of a reassertion of the strength of state and capitalist forces. The main argument to be made is that the highly polarised political currents of the 1970s and early 1980s created a space in which a rich counter-cultural creative work that both expressed and participated in the political conflicts of the broader society could thrive. By contrast, as the dominant ideology of the 1980s became more and more corporate, previously prominent alternative ideas became ground down so that the space for subversion was squeezed out. This erosion explains why although it continued – and continues – to exist, punk rapidly lost its subversive potential after the 1970s. It also accounts for the fact that the late 1970s gave rise to a genuinely anti-authoritarian aesthetic like that of the Sex Pistols, whereas the 1990s stimulated the politically toothless music of Britpop – and its more anodyne variant, Cool Britannia.

As the chapter will go on to show, a key context for this transition is the gradual replacement in Britain of manufacturing by the creative industries as a key pillar of the economy and hence of the political structure. Drawing on Robert Hewison's account of the conversion of disused factories, mills and industrial estates into visitor centres, museums and galleries, the middle part of the chapter will identify the birth of the heritage industry as a forerunner of what would subsequently become the cultural (and later creative) industries. That is, in the face of the decline of Britain's heavy industries, culture itself become a key export commodity in an increasingly global market place. But, by definition, if culture was the site of capitalist expansion, it could not also easily function as a site of resistance or opposition to it. Thus, there was a steady incorporation of previously oppositional forms of cultural expression into the very areas to which they had been opposed: the state, mass media, big business; and the period 1977–97 saw the gradual mainstreaming and disarming of previously avant-garde forms of expression. The apotheosis of this process came when two of the main protagonists in the Britpop movement, Damon Albarn and Noel Gallagher, each met prime-minister-in-waiting Tony Blair at the Houses of Parliament in 1995 to advise him on how music could be used to harness the youth vote. Where once music had been fundamentally opposed to government and authority, now it had indirectly become a part of the political scene.

The flowering of Britpop did not only coincide in time with the emergence of Blair's third-way politics but is actively related to it. The second half of the chapter will argue that the same is true of its relationship to one of the flagship New Labour policies of the period: political devolution in the different nations as a means of appeasing separatist movements in them and so retaining political power at the centre. In fact, the relationship between devolution and Britpop is manifest in various ways. For example, a key position in the Britpop firmament is occupied by the film *Trainspotting* (1996), partly because the novel on which it is based has often been cited as an example of Scottish national cultural distinctiveness in the years around devolution and partly because the film itself plays down that same element of Scottish difference, especially through its Britpop soundtrack. Comparable claims have been made in Wales of Kevin Allen's film *Twin Town* (1997) and of the relative outpouring of work by a number of artists and musicians such as The Manic Street Preachers, Catatonia, Super Furry Animals and Stereophonics in the 1990s.[1] On one hand these have been seen as the expression of a slowly reawakening nation starting to rediscover its voice; but it is arguable that their involvement in the wider world of Britpop undermines that possibility of national difference on the other.

Meanwhile, Northern Ireland's most prominent engagement with the music and aesthetics of Britpop occurred in a highly belated way, through their inclusion in the Channel 4 television series *Derry Girls* (2018–22), which used them as a way of mediating common adolescent behaviours such as dancing, music and parties in its retrospective portrayal of Ulster's gradual movement away from the political Troubles. The peace process is generally seen as the main achievement of New Labour and because the forms of heritage and creative industries that have flourished in Northern Ireland since then typically adumbrate shared experiences rather than divisive or controversial ones, it is logical that the series uses Britpop as a means of structuring apparently universal themes like dating and coming of age precisely in order to downplay political and cultural differences between different members of the community. One ironic effect of this is that in *Derry Girls*' use of Britpop Northern Irish difference from mainstream British culture ends up being underplayed, even though the series loudly heralds it.

Thus, in the forms of Britpop we find in Scotland, Wales and Northern Ireland since devolution, the main dynamic is one of tension between expressing national distinctiveness and continuing inclusion in the British whole. How variations on this dynamic play out varies significantly in each case. What is interesting, however, is that although there have been numerous accounts of the local variations of Britpop within each nation, there have been far fewer analyses of the structural relationship this tension creates between them. Addressing this gap, the chapter will conclude by exploring the implications raised by the political moment of British devolution in the 1990s for the newly emergent dynamic of competition between nations whose national cultures nevertheless remain in some form of solidarity with each other.

SUBCULTURES REVISITED

In hindsight, two publications are absolutely essential in any consideration of the emergence of subcultures in Britain in the 1970s. Stuart Hall and Tony Jefferson's *Resistance Through Rituals: Youth subcultures in post-war Britain* (1975) was a multi-authored volume of articles edited for the Centre for Contemporary Cultural Studies at the University of Birmingham. Dick Hebdige, who was one of the contributors to *Resistance Through Rituals*, expanded his own contribution in the subsequent monograph *Subculture: The Meaning of Style* (1979).

In their opening chapter, Hall and Jefferson explore how the post-war period was characterised by a growth in youth cultures. They found that the political consensus of the post-war period failed to address the material aspirations of the working-class population, especially young working-class men, who became alienated from the political establishment as a result. Subcultures then arose as specifically working-class forms of youth culture which were oppositional to the bourgeois political settlement and its dominant ideology in post-war Britain. This is the context in which the growth of punk should be understood because as Matthew Worley (2014) would later say, 'punk typically purports to provide a voice or means of expression for the disenfranchised, marginalised and disaffected' (2).

If punk was a movement in which members of the working-class population were involved in the authentic production of their own forms of cultural expression, this suggests that it was more than just a musical movement, and certainly more than a musical genre, and was a way of expressing political dissatisfaction in different media. Thus, Herbert Pimlott (2014) uses Raymond Williams's insight into ideological conflicts to extend the range of cultural practices and signifying forms grouped together under the category of punk: 'Political ephemera in this period, however, includes more than disposable literature; it includes a range of media, from graffiti long since painted over ... to faded fly-posters and poorly photocopied zines, which retain the structure of feeling in typeface, layout, words, phrases and symbols' (277). He then interprets those forms of expression as emergent or politically oppositional in Williams's sense to argue that they revealed 'an emergent structure of feeling of a subaltern social class' (269). Michelle Liptrot (2014) concurs, arguing that because it expressed sentiments that were suspicious of large-scale forms of commerce, punk should be seen 'as a form of cultural resistance that is fundamentally counter-hegemonic' (236).

But if punk was able to identify the contradictions between the post-war consensus and working-class aspiration, it was not necessarily able to resolve them. As a result, Hall and Jefferson identify punk as a form of subversion that occurred at the mainly symbolic level, 'magically' resolving the contradictions which remained hidden or unsolved in the dominant culture (32). More specifically, members of each subculture made specific stylistic choices in dress, music, and language that, when taken collectively, provided a distinct code which enabled the subculture to cohere as a group and therefore in ritualised form provided a strategy by which young working-class men could negotiate the challenges of their collective existence. For the same reason, the stylistic elements of subcultures had two contradictory and potentially paradoxical functions: one to provide a form of cohesive culture capable of cementing the group together and constituting it as a collective entity with which its members could collectively identify; and the other to communicate separation from, distaste for, and sometimes hostility towards other social groups and corresponding forms of culture perceived to be antagonistic to it. Or as Hall and Jefferson put it, 'the symbolic use of things to consolidate and express an internal coherence was, in the same moment, a kind of implied opposition to (where it was not an active and conscious contradiction of) *other groups against* which its activity was defined' (55–6, emphasis in original).

In a sense, Hall and Jefferson's identification of the paradox whereby a subculture is only able create communicational bonds between its members at the same time that it communicates distance from other groups and so fractures social unity was the starting point for Dick Hebdige's analysis of the aesthetic elements of subcultures in his follow-up study, *Subculture: The Meaning of Style* (1979). To explain how subcultures were able to do these two things at once, Hebdige sought to identify what precise conjuncture of specific elements gave rise to them in the first place. Drawing on the work of Phil Cohen he identified the main stylistic elements as dress, dance, argot and music, which were then treated as forms of signification in a communicational chain. But the point is that the objects associated with subcultures (the smart working-class suits of the skinheads; the motorbikes of the mods; the boots, safety pins and swastikas of punk) do not communicate because of any inherent properties in the objects themselves; they do so in a relational sense. This means that their meanings are not stable or inert and are amenable to redefinition and change. Therefore, drawing on the work of Julia Kristeva, Hebdige argues that the objects cherished by members of different subcultures become mobilised, displayed and deployed in new social contexts which have the effect of opening them up to new and oppositional interpretations. That is, rather than participating in an act of 'signification' whose meaning is always already determined in advance, their use in altered contexts symbolically opens up such objects to the active creation of new meanings or 'signifiance' (124). This distinction between *signification* and *signifiance* tells us that stylistically chosen objects communicate meaning both within the subcultures and from within them towards the outside world; but what they signify has actively to be created in a relational (which often turns out to be a politically oppositional) way.

To decode the sociological meaning of everyday objects as they were taken up within subcultures and hence read them from a semiotic perspective, Hebdige next introduced a new term to his discussion: the anthropological concept of *bricolage*. In a chapter on bricolage in *Resistance Through Rituals*, John Clarke had already applied the concept to a discussion of subcultures because it appears to describe the process whereby members attach themselves to particular items that already exist in the wider society and then combine them together in new combinations. In the process, they endow them with new meaning so that they come to mean new things and signify in new ways. As Clarke says: 'There's no point in it, if the new assemblage looks exactly like, carries exactly the same message as, that previously existing' (178). This suggests that the new meanings are ironically rooted in the older, in a complex dialectic.

In the 1970s, this everyday war on conventional lifestyles through objects recodified as elements in a semiotic language of resistance was most evident in the rituals of punk and its characteristic dress, dance, music, performance, language and ritual. Hebdige treats Vivienne Westwood's description of punk clothing and accessories as 'confrontation dressing' as an example of this language (107). Even aesthetic choices such as the cut-up script and typeface of the cover for the record *God Save the Queen*, drawing on the style of graffiti and of ransom notes, were part of it. Another example he gives is the paradoxical consistency with which punks adopted the motif of the swastika – not because they wanted to express Nazi ideology (they opposed the National Front) but because they wanted to shock the mainstream by adopting a symbol now detached from its original context but simultaneously retaining its prior associations in the eyes of an outside observer. In other words, the swastika was used in punk to communicate nothingness because in a period of failed working-class aspiration the expectation of nothingness was punks' everyday experience of the world.

Hebdige's emphasis on signifying practice means he attributed less meaning to the finished product of subcultural bricolage than to the relational process of its assemblage, which might be more or less oppositional in any given case. His interest was not to assert the richness of the subculture as artistic practice in an abstract aesthetic way, but to think about how 'the interest of works of art lies in the ways in which they explore and modify the codes which they seem to be using' (129). This open dialectic makes possible the creation, adoption and adaptation of specific subcultural styles whereby specifically assembled items of bricolage are transported between a set of polarities (parent/youth; bourgeois/working-class; punk/teddy boy; straight culture/subculture) and transformed into new elements in a semiotic language of subversion. 'Subcultures are therefore expressive forms but what they express is, in the last instance, a fundamental tension between those in power and those condemned to subordinate positions and second-class lives' (132).

Overall, Hebdige emphasised that analysis of subcultures should focus on the moment of potential transformation rather than on the objects associated with them. Yet it was a potential that remained largely unfulfilled. The conventional account of punk's demise, as put forward by Hall and Jefferson in *Resistance Through Rituals*, is that its rebellion failed because, like that of all subcultures, it was pitched at the symbolic level rather than practical experience. In other words, the problem of a subordinate class position could be experienced and even articulated but not resolved through purely symbolic means: 'There is no "sub-cultural career" for the working-class lad, no "solution" in the sub-cultural milieu, for problems posed by the key structuring experiences of the class' (Hall and Jefferson, 47). Given that subcultures could not change real material conditions, when they addressed the problematics of class experience they reproduced gaps between real negotiations and symbolically displaced resolutions. That is, they solved in an only 'imaginary' way problems that at the concrete material level, 'remain unresolved' (ibid.).

In *Subculture*, however, Hebdige puts forward a different reason for the blunting of punk's subversive potential: its growing (and sincere) association with Rock Against Racism in opposition to the growing National Front. In fact, identifying this as a contributory factor in punk's demise feels somewhat tragic because punk's relationship with a number of Afro-Caribbean subcultures created opportunities for genuinely intercultural activities at a time when these were rare in British cities and when the atomisation and ghettoisation of different cultures was much more common. This intercultural influence is reflected in the forms of music produced both by white working-class members of punk subcultures and Afro-Caribbean ones so that the influence of ska, reggae and two-tone can be discerned in punk and vice versa. However, this association of different subcultures belied certain tensions and contradictions between them, most notably in the fact that urban black youth cultures had access to the symbolic resources of both another place (Jamaica or Ethiopia) and another time (the pre-diasporic past), neither of which were available to white youth. Owing to this difference, punk became endowed with what Hebdige calls a 'petrified' quality (69) because it was forever arrested in the frozen dialectic of black and white which was incapable of renewal on any other terms and so remained 'imprisoned within its own irreducible antimonies' (70).

If inability to transcend the dialectics of race and the restriction of its rebellion to the realm of the symbolic are two reasons why punk ultimately lost its subversive power, there is also a third: namely, its incorporation into the dominant culture. This is the stage at which the dominant culture succeeds in divesting the subculture of its ideological challenge to authority. In *Resistance Through Rituals* John Clarke identified two ways in which this can happen: *diffusion* and *defusion*. Diffusion occurs when access to a subculture is extended and popularised so that it is taken up by a greater number of people. Almost by definition, this results in a broadening of the base so that the distinctiveness of the subculture, what it is about the subculture that poses a threat to straight society, becomes defused because in effect it has become a part of that society. Indeed, Hebdige found that the incorporation of punk into the mainstream after 1978 took two distinctive forms: the commodity form and the ideological form. Ideologically, this involved the labelling and redefinition of so-called deviant behaviour by dominant groups such as the police, judiciary, media and other gate keepers of culture. In turn, this ideological labelling and definition brought forth two common means for defusing the subcultural threat posed by punk. These were either to trivialise and domesticate its properties; or to transform its props into meaningless exotica, pure objects. But then those same objects, stripped of their raw political signification, became amenable to be taken up and marketed via the commodity form.

Thus, when *Cosmopolitan* magazine ran a special issue on punk fashion in 1977 entitled 'To shock is chic', this 'presaged the subculture's imminent demise' because '[y]outh cultural styles may begin by issuing symbolic challenges, but they must inevitably end by establishing new sets of conventions; by creating new commodities, new industries or rejuvenating old ones' (Hebdige, 96). By this point, far from expressing a significant challenge to the ruling order, punk had unwittingly become a recognisable feature of daily culture, and the space from which it could speak in the voice of subcultural dissent had disappeared. This collapse of the distance between politics and economics on the one hand and politically engaged forms of subcultural practice on the other would squeeze out counter-cultural voices throughout the 1980s and pave the way for a newly quiescent integration of politics and culture in the 1990s, as the following sections will explore.

THE RISE OF THE CREATIVE INDUSTRIES

So far, this chapter has concentrated on the nexus of social, economic, demographic and cultural changes that took place in Britain between the 1950s and the 1970s and the subcultures that emerged out of the feeling of crisis that those changes produced. But if those subcultures arose as means of symbolically articulating forms of opposition to the dominant, mainstream or what Hebdige terms 'straight' culture, the questions that have not yet been answered are wherein this mainstream itself chiefly resided and what were its principal characteristics. In effect, these are the questions that Robert Hewison set out to answer in his landmark study *The Heritage Industry: Britain in a Climate of Decline* (1987). In it, Hewison explored the historical process by which manufacturing and heavy industry in Britain declined throughout the 1960s and 1970s and were gradually replaced by organisations such as museums, arts centres, cultural organisations and other institutions ostensibly dedicated to preserving the nation's heritage. His characterisation of the dominant culture that emerged out of the nascent heritage industries can then be expressed in one word: nostalgia. And this nostalgic tendency in turn had a deeply ideological tendency because not only did it offer to use the past as a means of distracting from various social, economic and political crises in the present but worse, it posited a situation in which all the best creative work in Britain was always already concluded in advance, as if no new visions for the country or its people could ever be created, thereby foreclosing on the possibility that the post-war social settlement could ever be changed in the present or beyond.

Although Hewison is a historian rather than a sociologist like Hebdige or Hall and his focus is quite different from theirs, the 'no future' generation proclaimed by the Sex Pistols and emblematic of punk subcultures can thus be seen as the direct flip side of the tendency towards nostalgia that was evident in the main infrastructural developments in Britain in the period in question: the replacement of industry by heritage as a result of a downturn in Britain's economic power. Hewison identified a whole series of symptoms of this prevailing climate of decline, seeing it in things as diverse as the altered urban landscape brought about by the construction (and later abandonment) of high-rise estates; the encroachment of urbanisation into the countryside; the destruction of forests and hedgerows by mega farms; the closure of railway stations and lines; increases in the amount of land that was derelict; and finally in the perceived failures by the 1980s of the welfare state.

To some extent physical changes in the built environment were seen as the price to pay for an increased standard of prosperity that compensated for the earlier depression of the 1930s and for the UK's loss of status internationally after decolonisation. But whereas the immediate post-war period had been characterised by an atmosphere of renewal and modernisation, by the 1970s change was taking place in a less optimistic mood. This is the context in which the nostalgic impulse arose. For example, in a discussion of the recently opened Wigan Heritage Centre, Hewison identifies an irony whereby it seems to make a virtue out of the fact that Orwell's famous book lambasted the harsh social and economic conditions created in the region by industrialisation, because it at least made it famous and so made the place potentially marketable as a leisure destination after all the real industry had gone. And Wigan was not the only example: writing in 1987 he found forty-one other heritage centres around the country and almost four thousand museums, half of which had opened since 1970, while the listing of ancient buildings was also continuing apace. Noting both that there were more visitors to museums and galleries than either to performing arts or even the cinema and that they received more state funding than the live arts, he suggested that 'since the Second World War, nostalgia has become a dominant characteristic' (1987, 28).

As the Wigan Heritage Centre shows, the periods for which we are encouraged to feel most nostalgia (the Victorian era, the roaring 20s) are often periods of social disturbance. Yet in the nostalgic re-presentation of those periods troubling elements are generally filtered out and downplayed as if to create a feeling of a harmonious social structure to which we could all imagine ourselves belonging. Hewison thus argues that nostalgia is not the same as true recall, but 'supplies the deep links that identify a particular generation' since 'nationally it is the source of binding social myths' (1987, 46). The queen's silver jubilee in 1977 and the 1981 royal wedding were stage managed enactments of tribal loyalty; and Margaret Thatcher made all sorts of appeal to nostalgia during the 1983 election and 1984 miners' strike. As such, Hewison considers it an inherently conservative mechanism because, although the impulse to nostalgia is understandable at times of turbulent change, if we dwell too much on the past, we lose any sense of the present or of a possible new future. 'The question then is not whether or not we should preserve the past, but what kind of past we have chosen to preserve, and what that has done to our present' (ibid.).

Having identified nostalgia as a dominant and reactionary ideology in Britain as the 1970s gave way to the 1980s, Hewison then goes on to explore its institutional embodiments in a range of different organisations. He takes the rise of the discipline of industrial archaeology to be symptomatic of that ideology, because it bespeaks the impulse to keep preserved aspects and artefacts from the industrial past that are now obsolete. When those artefacts are preserved in museums and visitor centres, they also have the effect of preserving in symbolic form the social structure of earlier periods when industrial society had had the effect of creating a strongly stratified class structure, while also mystifying that same stratification in the name of unity or national culture. On the site of the former Beamish colliery in the North East of England, a mock-up of the colliery was so authentically recreated that the only thing that looked incongruous were the visitors. Yet this picture postcard version of the past was being created at a time of widespread closures in industry and significant unemployment in the region, causing Hewison to conclude that 'while this charming world was being created, the life of the North East was being destroyed' (1987, 95). In other words, although nostalgia is comforting at times of change, when museums of the past are a growth industry, they are a sign not of vitality but of decline.

Of course, the opening of museums and galleries per se need not mean this. In some ways these institutions have taken on the old social and symbolic public functions of social cohesion once supplied by church and state. But Hewison's point is that museums interpret the present to itself. This is why some of the world's most impressive new museums are museums of modern art such as the Pompidou centre in Paris or Staatsgalerie in Stuttgart. As interpreters in and of the present, gallerists and museum directors have become the new high priests of the world because they play a crucial mediating role in the creation and dissemination of social meaning. The things they make exist in the form of images and ideas, events and performances just as much as in the form of material objects and artefacts. But although often intangible, they also carry considerable symbolic value in creating legitimacy for certain kinds of work or certain kinds of life and either by accident or design denying it to others. For this reason, when the heritage industry emerged in the 1970s and 1980s in the way

Hewison describes, the museums and visitor centres it created were carriers not just of the past but of profoundly ideological ideas about how we should live in the present, ideas which they in fact helped to shape and direct. As the dominant characteristic of public culture at the time, the positive premium placed on nostalgia by the heritage industry thus wielded considerable symbolic power over real political developments and in fact was created to arrest both symbolically and economically the sense of a nation in decline and unable to cope with change. Thus, what was ideologically problematic about an arts and cultural policy – a heritage industry – too obsessed with the past was that this backwards-facing focus made it difficult for newness, dynamism and confident forms of expression in the present and future. 'The heritage industry presents a history that stifles, but above all, a history that is *over*' (1987, 141, emphasis in original). In other words, the morbid fascination with (a selected version of) the past that had become a dominant characteristic of British public life cultivated a feeling that Britain, its people and its culture were all things of the past rather than subjects involved in a still active and evolving process of growth and self-expression.

* * *

In a chapter of *The Heritage Industry* analysing the Arts Council of Great Britain (which has subsequently been devolved into the national arts councils of each nation, and re-branded in a variety of ways in each), Hewison identifies it as the primary mechanism by which state funding was made available for artistic and cultural work throughout the 1980s and early 1990s. At the same time, he argues that since it reported directly to the government, its members were highly political appointments. The funding decisions they made offered themselves as neutral or objective but were based more on partisan affiliations and various vested interests than any discernible strategy. Given that its committees functioned through the manufacturing of consensus on any given decision, its institutional structure often militated against emerging, oppositional or new forms of creative work which would require taking on the weight of inherited tradition. As a result, the Arts Council after 1979 systematically violated the 'arm's length' principle by which it ostensibly kept political decisions out of cultural policy and instead allowed the former to infuse the latter (1987, 110).

In effect, Conservative Richard Luce as Minister for the Arts (1985–90) and William Rees-Mogg as chairman of the Arts Council

(1982–9) each saw it as their mission to reduce state funding for the arts and encourage greater levels of private sponsorship. But Hewison points out that private sponsorship could turn out to be a covert means of state (and hence political) patronage: partly through matched funding schemes between public and private partnerships; and partly through the prestige that could be 'sold' to commercial sponsors such as tobacco companies and arms manufacturers seeking to enhance their images. Moreover, it would be naïve in the extreme to think that corporate sponsors would not expect to have some say in what kind of work got commissioned and produced, with the effect of militating against anything edgy or challenging.

The supplanting of state funding by private investment for the arts came about in a period when the Conservative government had closed down the Greater London Council and six other metropolitan councils even though these were among some of the biggest state-funders of the arts at local level around the country. As chairman of the Arts Council, Rees-Mogg engineered a situation whereby not only was he now more influential in decision making than the council members, but the existence of the council enabled the government to abdicate any responsibility for funding the arts by taking on the role as the chief organisation by which state money was provided to them. As a result, Hewison argues that the arts were transformed into commodities to be consumed rather than dynamic experiences to inspire or engage. In tandem with this marketisation, a whole new economic language became associated with artistic activity such that audiences ceased to be 'lovers' of the arts as such, and became instead 'customers' for a market (1987, 128–9). The real shift therefore was from a state policy that valued the arts in and for themselves and their innate properties, towards a policy whereby the arts were valued (like any other commodity) in mainly economic terms: 'Thus, although the Conservative government since 1979 has done more to politicise the management of the arts than any previous administration, and the arts have been recruited for purely economic purposes, they nonetheless retain a low priority as independent expressions of culture' (1987, 118).

At the time of Luce's appointment in 1985, Britain had not had a dedicated arts minister since the 1960s and the Tories had been somewhat against the idea of establishing one because they associated it with Labour interference in wealth and patronage. The decision to do so enabled them to determine the parameters of public arts policy and therefore determine the scope and make-up of the field. Moreover, the choice of terminology used in the process is somewhat revealing of the ideological conflicts of the period: 'arts' having implications of a highbrow or elite set of activities in contrast to the more inclusive and also arguably more contemporary concept of 'culture'. When the post of Minister for the Arts was replaced by that of Secretary of State for National Heritage following the Conservatives' victory under John Major in the 1992 general election, this combined the reactionary tendencies of the heritage industry with the politicised decision making of the Arts Council. It would, however, be misleading to create the impression of a fundamental difference between Conservative and Labour policies with regards to culture and the arts. Hewison points out that, having identified the economic fillip that the newly emerging cultural industries could bring, the Labour party pledged to create forty thousand new jobs in the arts during the 1987 general election campaign, thereby revealing a subtle form of continuity in arts policy between the parties. When New Labour finally gained office in 1997 it established its own Department of Culture, modelled on that of National Heritage which preceded it, therefore continuing and modifying – as opposed to fundamentally rejecting – the economic instrumentalisation of culture that had started with the Tories.

In his more recent book, *Cultural Capital: The Rise and Fall of Creative Britain* (2014), Hewison sees the shift in nomenclature from 'arts' and 'heritage' to 'culture' as a posthumous victory for Raymond Williams and other advocates of 1960s-style cultural studies. The book's cultural analysis picks up where *The Heritage Industry* had ended, arguing that contemporary British culture is the product of a process that began with the de-industrialisation of the cities and the export of their functions overseas and with the turn to culture as an industry able to repurpose those places and people as contributors to cultural consumption and hence economic activity.

Hewison begins *Cultural Capital* by quoting a speech delivered by Tony Blair at Tate Modern in 2007, claiming that the previous ten years had been a golden age for culture in Britain. He notes that this was a highly appropriate setting since the process by which manufacturing was supplanted by the heritage industry reached its apotheosis in the conversion of a power station (that once produced electricity to drive machinery) into an art gallery (producing nothing). He also notes that this golden age speech was in fact the only speech ever given by Blair on the subject of the arts. The reality is that culture was driven by government in the hope of turning market failure into market success through a highly neo-liberal set of policies based on free market economics with little state regulation.

The main thrust of *Cultural Capital* is how Margaret Thatcher's so-called New Public Management of public services of the 1980s found a surprising degree of continuity in New Labour's third way in the late 1990s. The latter brought in a culture of inspection, targets and monitoring at every level of cultural policy, and despite the lauded devolution of political decision making to the different nations and regions of Britain, Blair was not really willing to give up control at the centre. With defeat of the referendum for a North Eastern assembly and Ken Livingstone beating the official New Labour candidate to become mayor of London, his real enthusiasm for regional democracy ended and he deferred to regional development agencies, whose aims, though ostensibly cultural, tended to be socio-economic. This had the effect that the role of the arts became further cemented as instruments of social and economic regeneration.

Like the Tory government that preceded it, New Labour was quite happy for commercial forces to play out in the cultural sphere and most people in the country seemed accepting of this too, mainly because most people tended not to engage with the elite/high arts, which also happened to be the ones most in need of large-scale revenue funding from the arts council and the Heritage Lottery Fund (which had been created when the National Lottery was introduced by John Major's administration). Hewison cites the example of a funding crisis at the Royal Opera as a clear example of the increasing instrumentalisation of the arts under New Labour: Chris Smith, the first Secretary of State in the newly created Department for Culture, Media and Sport (DCMS) was one of the few figures in Blair's cabinet with an interest in the arts for their own sake, but the funding crisis at the Royal Opera which erupted only two days into his ministry resulted in the need for a government bail-out that circumvented his department and left him unable to exert any real power. As a result, his new department depended on redefining culture in two ways: first, as economic commodity, demonstrating its worth by reckoning the financial contribution it made to the public realm; and, secondly, as a toolkit that could be put to the service of combating social exclusion, underdevelopment, inequality and even crime. With these developments, Hewison says, the 'creative industries' (2014, 28) were born.

New Labour's *Creative Industries Mapping Document* was launched in 1998, with a contingent focus on creativity – which had the capacity to offer new departures, on the one hand, while not being tied to anything tangible on the other. Part of the role of the creative industries as now defined was to combat social exclusion, especially poverty, and measures to achieve this now had to be built into all policies, with measurable targets and numerical measures of effectiveness. The Arts Council was distinctly unappreciative of being told what to do by central government with the result that it was the latter, through the DCMS, that took the lead in putting inclusivity on the agenda, with some emphasis on combating the social exclusion of members of ethnic minorities from participation in the arts. The real problem with this kind of instrumentalisation is that it required arts organisations to demonstrate how they were reducing social barriers and inequality in order to receive the revenue funding they needed to create artistic work (which was their real purpose); but the arts alone could not hope to address much bigger social and political issues such as these. Moreover, even where they moved to try and do so it was very hard for them to provide evidence that they had had any impact in the way the DCMS demanded – especially when it came to measuring intangible entities such as a growth in confidence, self-esteem, or levels of articulacy among participants in artistic projects.

In other words, just as 'heritage' was replaced by 'culture' in the early days of New Labour, so too *culture* was supplanted by *creative* as the new buzzword for the utilitarian approach to the arts under Blair. Hewison gives the example of Glasgow's hosting of European City of Culture in 1990 as an example of the overall policy of using the arts to stimulate economic growth and social transformation. When Chris Smith passed a new National Lottery Act making it easier for agencies to disburse funds directly to artists rather than organisations, the government was reluctant to trust individual artists and found it hard to record the shared economic benefit of such an approach, so it was reversed in 2005. Artists were not trusted as being the best people to understand what is needed in the creation of art; and instead, a raft of bureaucrats took centre stage.

What emerges from *Cultural Capital: The Rise and Fall of Creative Britain* is a sense of conflict between the government department; bodies such as the Arts Council and the Museums, Libraries and Archives Council (MLA); and the local organisations that they exist to serve and support. In many cases this becomes articulated as a battle between regional autonomy and central policy, as could be seen in the fate of Geraint Talfan Davies, Chair of the Welsh Arts Council. Before this became independent as the renamed Arts Council of Wales in 1994 it was officially a branch of the Arts Council of Great Britain, but in practice it had been allowed a good level of autonomy. After Welsh devolution in 1997, however, the Labour assembly government in Cardiff wanted to use the regeneration and inclusivity agendas to direct its operations in much the same way that London was directing Arts Council England. Davies complained of this violation of the arm's length principle which both politicised and instrumentalised the arts, and ended up resigning. It is ironic that someone who had spent his professional life campaigning for the cultural nationalism of Wales should have ended up losing his job as a result of it.

The main characteristics of Creative Britain, then, appear to have been the dialectic of distributed versus centralised leadership accompanied by the mobilisation of the creative industries to deliver both economic outputs and also social outcomes more broadly. These characteristics were carried forward throughout the New Labour period – especially, in Hewison's final example, in the fiasco of the Millennium Dome. Though officially billed as an opportunity to inspire and revitalise the entire nation, this was really a project aimed at regenerating a specific area, Greenwich, and so rival candidates bidding to host the flagship Millennium project in Birmingham, Derby and Stratford East had no real hope of success. Moreover, one of the members of the Millennium Commission was Michael Heseltine, who had driven the urban regeneration of the city of Liverpool through investment in its cultural infrastructure in the 1980s, so that there was an overall continuity of cultural policy. In fact, like the earlier manifestations of the heritage industry, the Dome itself was oddly content-less, saying little about Britain's history, and nothing about its imperial past. It was thus lacking in anything that might provoke controversy or dissent. In this, it displayed a cultural logic in common with that of one of the main cultural movements of the 1990s: Britpop.

BRITPOP INTO COOL BRITANNIA

Of the many books that have been written on the subject of Britpop, John Harris's *The Last Party: Britpop, Blair and the Demise of English Rock* (2003) is both the most detailed and the most critically evaluative. Rather than expressing either an unexamined enthusiasm for or an unmitigated critical mauling of the movement, Harris instead sets out to explore, analyse and assess the relationship between music and political change during the 1990s. His main argument is that both the period and the movement started off with a degree of innovation that had as much potential for political and an aesthetic transformation as anything in the 1960s, but that as a movement Britpop surrendered this transformative potential in response to political and economic developments and also as a result of the deleterious effects of taking heroin and cocaine. Hence whereas British music had long been counter-cultural and Britpop in the beginning was heir to that tradition, after 1995 its more challenging aspects fell away and by the end of the decade it seemed to strike the opposite note.

At the start of *The Last Party*, Harris charts the genealogy of the Britpop movement by arguing that, although the terms *subculture* and *counter-culture* are more commonly associated with the 1970s and the USA respectively, the ideology and ethos of Thatcherism provoked a cultural response, especially via music, that can properly be called counter-cultural. He tracks this counter-cultural emergence through the independent labels *Rough Trade*, *The Factory*, and finally *Creation*. He also draws attention to the *Red Wedge* group of musicians aligned to the Labour Party in the run up to the 1987 election in order to emphasise that the political commitments, and especially the cooperative spirit implied by the organisation of *Rough Trade*, could not necessarily be understood just by listening to the music and therefore that it was a broader 'movement' (8). However, he then identifies two key reasons why the indie movement was to fade by the end of the 1980s. First, although the ethos of indie labels was to eschew commercial success and reject private control of artists by their managers in favour of the development of communal networks and shared experiences, the reality was that large multimedia corporations started to acquire all alternative forms of production, thereby bringing what had aspired to remain outside the commercial world firmly within it. Secondly, Harris suggests that the emergence of the Acid House movement in the 1980s was a key reason for the decline of the indie counter-culture. Acid House was based around taking ecstasy, getting high and living in the moment through hedonistic, individual sensory perception and as such could hardly be considered a communal experience in the way the indie groups had wanted music to be; neither did it have a politically anti-establishment aesthetic.

Unlike the indie bands of the time, Acid House groups such as the Happy Mondays and Stone Roses did want commercial success, did want to be part of the cultural mainstream, did want to make private fortunes. They spawned lots of regional imitators, and the result of this was bound to have an effect on the kind of music that became mainstream. Moreover, as the 1980s gave way to the 1990s, a newly invigorated form of American regional rock music – grunge – was being successfully exported into Britain, where, divorced from the places and relationships in which it had arisen, its voices and messages ceased to have any local relevance. Thus, by the 1990s the role of music to be inherently counter-cultural, defining itself by what it existed in opposition to, no longer seemed to pertain and music became somewhat more self-interested and politically unengaged.

This is the situation in which, in Harris's account, Britpop arose, spearheaded by the triumvirate of bands encompassing Brett Anderson's Suede, Justine Frischmann's Elastica and Damon Albarn's Blur. Suede had their roots in 1970s rock rather than the indie tendencies of Blur, but both started to develop work in direct competition with American-dominated music. Despite its success in the UK, both felt that the grunge of Nirvana and their contemporaries spoke little to them or their lives and so encoded their work as an act of cultural reclamation, reconnecting with an English tradition that had been interrupted by grunge to the detriment of domestic creativity. In gigs and publicity throughout 1993 and especially via their second album *Modern Life is Rubbish* that same year, Albarn's Blur championed a return to musical forms that would tell stories of direct relevance to (predominantly English) lives, which he felt that grunge could never do.

In Harris's account, Britpop thus emerged through a dialectical relationship with the transatlantic music industry. Although the suicide of Nirvana's Kurt Cobain in 1994 appeared to leave free for Blur the cultural space that had been firmly occupied by grunge, it also had the effect of leaving the industry as a whole paralysed. Albarn suffered a mild form of depression which hindered Blur's creativity, and their record label Food Records was sold to EMI, thus relinquishing any claim to independence from the economic and commercial mainstream. Harris then cites the arrival of Matthew Bannister as controller of Radio One and his appointment of Steve Lamacq and Jo Whiley in key roles as evidence of a sea change that was starting to take place. These DJs heralded new musicians rather than the nostalgic ones which had long typified the BBC's musical programming, with the result that the next major Britpop band, Oasis, were given lots of airplay before even releasing a record. As they gained momentum throughout 1994, their tours and gigs increasingly became accompanied by reports of debauchery, even scandal, which appear to have helped cement them in the zeitgeist as potential bearers of a new anti-authoritarian aesthetic. Thus, by the end of 1994, Blur and Oasis were involved in a common attempt to supersede grunge, while their apparent comfort with commercial success moved them further away from the ideals of the indie movement.

One indicator Harris gives of the increasing commercial acumen of Blur and Oasis is their appearances at a growing number of awards ceremonies. When their singles 'Country House' and 'Roll with It' went head to head for number one in the Summer of 1995, the so-called Battle of the Bands was really a public relations exercise in which publicity and hence sales dramatically increased for both. It is therefore an example of Bourdieu's principle of how, in the field of cultural production, the normal structure of the economic world can be tactically reversed since there are no real losers in a game which, just by being played, upholds the principle on which it is based. Or as Harris puts it more succinctly, it was a 'win win' for everyone (235). Albarn in particular saw the battle as the fulfilment of his long-term mission to reclaim the musical sphere from American grunge. Meanwhile Noel Gallagher, who had already come face to face with then Leader of the Opposition Tony Blair at *Q* magazine's 1994 awards, was presented with an electric guitar by him at the 1995 annual general meeting of the British Phonographic Industry (BPI) – the umbrella group that included most record labels in the UK. According to Harris, this had the effect of ensuring that Blair, and through him New Labour, became 'included in the Britpop moment' (242).

By this time Labour had already had its own dalliance with rock music in the form of *Red Wedge*, spearheaded by Billy Bragg and Paul Weller. But this was wound up in 1988, in the wake of the disappointment of the 1987 general election, a time when 'the ideological ferocity of the Thatcher period was giving way to an altogether more apolitical climate' (153), of which the Stone Roses and Happy Mondays were the vanguard. Harris cites a *Red Wedge* pamphlet saying that the party had an insufficiently broad base, especially among younger people and diverse sections of the electorate, and had to change in order to become competitive again as an electoral force. In fact, one of the changes brought about in Blair's construction of New Labour was a different approach to using popular culture. Unlike the very unsubtle approach of *Red Wedge*, which had tried to harness music too directly to a political cause, the method of New Labour was subtle and indirect: a few meetings between musicians and politicians were accompanied by the occasional editorial or photograph in order to create a loose and symbolic affinity between them. Thus, for example, the political researcher Darren Kalynuk wooed Blur and hence the world of pop culture on behalf of Labour with the result that a meeting took place between its members and Tony Blair in John Prescott's office in 1995. When Oasis dominated the 1996 Brit Awards, there was Blair again, making a speech and being endorsed by Noel Gallagher in order to appear as a 'new hip politician' (Harris, 273).

The overall argument of *The Last Party: Britpop, Blair and the Demise of English Rock* is that the commercial waxing of Oasis represented the subversive waning of Suede, Blur and Elastica and hence the eclipse of Britpop's politically oppositional potential. Flushed with their success at the Brits, Oasis played two triumphant gigs at Maine Road, Manchester on 27 and 28 April 1996, at which Noel Gallagher first played his now-iconic Union Jack guitar. But whereas the Sex Pistols' use of the national flag in 1977 was both embittered and highly ironic, Oasis evinced neither of those feelings. Instead, they were both comfortable with sweeping commercial success and politically somewhat apathetic. As a result, Noel Gallagher's talent for crafting 'populist anthems' ended up characterising the 'rather lamentable legacy' of Britpop, which Harris says was 'the guiding of rock music away from dissent and experimentalism' (ibid.).

It may well be that the newly acquired insipidity of Oasis's music together with their increasing mass-market appeal were the very things that made them attractive bedfellows for New Labour. Certainly, the party sought to capitalise on the sense of cool and supposed cultural confidence associated with the band following the huge gigs at Maine Road and Knebworth. The hosting by England of the 1996 European Football Championships had a part to play in this process, because although its official song '3 Lions' (by the Lightning Seeds plus the comedians Frank Skinner and David Baddiel) was not musically part of the Britpop movement, 'it still pushed a lot of Britpop buttons' (Harris, 302) – notably in the fact that it was very clearly about English (as distinct from American) lives. When Blair alluded to the song and hence the movement in his party conference speech on 1 October 1996 ('eighteen years of hurt never stopped me dreaming: Labour's coming home'), he clearly ploughed the Britpop furrow. By 27 January 1997, sixty representatives of the music industry were meeting Blair in Parliament. As previously, New Labour did not directly orchestrate media interest, but did so in a subtle way that gradually rippled outwards.

According to Harris, it was Oasis's third album *Be Here Now* that signalled the end of Britpop's creative aspiration. It was produced in an atmosphere of 'neurotic control freakery' (336) whereby reviewers had to visit the *Creation* offices to listen to advance copies in a controlled environment and sign disclaimers promising not to play it to anyone else so that there was no risk of bootleg copies being made. This is a world away from the counter-culture of DIY Punk. Harris sees in the fact that Noel Gallagher's master copy arrived the morning after the 1997 general election evidence of a symbolic intersection between a political movement that had moved away from its origins and a musical one that had lost sight of its aspirations. Then – three weeks before the album's release – a celebrated photograph of Gallagher and his partner Meg Mathews attending a party hosted by the new Prime Minister Blair at 10 Downing Street was taken. Looking at the famous image of Blair and Gallagher, Harris wonders who was using whom: the politician who seemed swamped by superstar superficiality; or the musician whose very presence there 'spoke volumes about just how tamed his art form, once built on scattershot dissent, had become' (345). (See Figure 3.)

With Britpop in decline as a musical movement, it became much more quiescent and content-less. Robert Hewison has shown in *Cultural Capital: The Rise and Fall of Creative Britain* that, well before the 1997 election, New Labour had cultivated relationships with a wide range of cultural figures from a broad spectrum of the arts: Michael Grade, Alan Yentob, Peter Hall, Maurice Saatchi and Richard Eyre. These figures were influential in both commerce and culture and so played a key role in the reconfiguring of the arts with the wider fields of politics and economics that was taking place. In effect, it was among this group that Creative Britain was conceived and when *Vanity Fair* magazine first used the term 'Cool Britannia' (Harris, 328) it was referring to the world of fashion and celebrity rather than to music or politics, but nevertheless managed to shoehorn Blair into the cultural mood. Iconic images of Noel Gallagher's

FIGURE 3: Tony Blair and Noel Gallagher,
10 Downing Street, 1997.
REUTERS/Alamy Stock Photo

Union Jack guitar proliferated within the narrative of a confident country on the cusp of change. When that image was echoed by that of the Spice Girls and Geri Halliwell's Union Jack dress at the 1997 Brit Awards ceremony it became clear that Britpop had now been supplanted by something else.

In *The Last Party* Harris analyses the process by which, during 1997 and 1998, Cool Britannia took over as the politically exploiting arm of Britpop, which was effectively dead. This transition was operationalised by the publication by the think-tank Demos in Autumn 1997 of *Britain*™, a pamphlet that proposed using culture to re-brand Britain in the eyes of the world via the newly created Department for Culture, Media and Sport. At this time, Alan McGee of Creation records became an archetypal New Labour insider, causing Harris to note: 'Far from expressing any kind of dissent, in its new tamed state, the music seemed to be a manifestation of Mr Blair's beloved inclusivism. This was surely not the kind of future that either the punks, or the 1980s counter-culturalists who followed in their wake, had envisaged' (370). Where Britpop artists had set out to be the anti-establishment heirs to punk, it had been rebranded as Cool Britannia and had become a part of the establishment.

This politically fostered depoliticisation helps to explain why more than twenty years after the event, the music of Britpop enjoyed a belated and highly retrospective late outing when it was used repeatedly as the soundtrack to Lisa McGee's Northern Ireland-based television comedy series *Derry Girls* (2018–22). The connection between the political neutrality of Britpop and the series's own brand of conflict avoidance is pointed up in an iconic episode when the young female catholic character Clare goes to a party held by some protestant teenagers and to show a spirit of reconciliation with them wears a Union Jack dress which recalls that worn by Geri Halliwell at the Brit Awards. In reality, however, it was unlikely to have been countenanced by members of the Catholic community in the period when the series is set, the 1990s.

Philip Boland, Brendan Murtagh and Peter Shirlow have drawn attention to the fact that when the city of Derry/Londonderry became the inaugural UK City of Culture in 2013, its cultural programme was conspicuous for representing elements of Irish history from the remote or mythical past as opposed to those that have been politically contentious such as the plantation of Ulster in the seventeenth century or the more recent Troubles, and thereby performed a version of a shared, rather than an antagonistic, history. This negotiation of communal tensions resulted in a preference in the festival's programme for elements that were less likely to provoke animosity from within one section of the community with regard to another than those that were, and this in turn can be considered characteristic of forms of cultural expression that have evolved in Northern Ireland as it moves away from the sectarian conflicts of the past in the development of a post-conflict present and future.

Derry Girls trails in the wake of this process and broadly coheres to its logic. Roddy Flynn and Tony Tracy have described it as both 'the outstanding Irish screen hit' of 2018 and 'a comedy built around four young female leads in a context (the Northern Irish Troubles) not always associated with absurdist humour' (240). Although bomb scares, military searches, personal indignities and sectarian suspicion are daily realities for the girls in the series, these elements are converted into humour in a way that during the 1990s, when the painful memories of the Troubles were still recent, might have been harder to imagine. Even two decades later, with the peace process still at a relatively new and provisional stage of its creation, it seems the most comfortable way of representing the Troubles is through the comedic portrayal of experiences such as schooling, adolescence and first love that can be presented as universal, thereby again playing down fractious or potentially controversial elements that might divide the Northern Irish audience and hence its community. Eilis O'Hanlon identifies this downplaying of fissiparous elements when she notes that 'with one episode securing more than 600,000 viewers in Northern Ireland, a nearly 70% audience share' (2019), *Derry Girls* was able to speak to – and attract – far more viewers than the contemporary BBC Northern Ireland documentary series *The Troubles: A Secret History* (although even this, she notes, 'tries carefully' not to be 'polemical' in its depiction).

Given this emphasis on the avoidance of contentious elements, it is hard to agree with a suggestion made by Ilaria Villa that in 'this moment of uncertainty about what Brexit might mean for the Irish border, *Derry Girls* could be the perfect way to get a glimpse of what Northern Ireland was just a couple of decades ago' (318). Although the implications Brexit has on the peace process are significant (and will be explored in later chapters), the point is not so much that *Derry Girls* presents life in Ulster during the Troubles as it really was, as that it filters out and eviscerates the ordinary everyday experiences of living in a conflict society and converts them instead into an idealised, even a nostalgic, caricature of themselves. The music of Britpop, which was written during the period when *Derry Girls* is set, and which is notable for having sloughed off any form of political position-taking in order to maximise commercial success, is therefore an appropriate bearer of that nostalgic tendency.

TRAINSPOTTING CAUGHT IN THE MIDDLE

The transition from punk to Cool Britannia via Britpop represents a long but traceable decline in the capacity of British youth- and working-class cultures to interrogate, critique or transform the dominant ideology. If, as suggested above, Britpop represents the last gasp of a genuinely populist oppositional potential that was ultimately hollowed out and eviscerated to re-emerge in the much more anodyne forms of Cool Britannia, the fault line that connects both sides of the Britpop/Cool Britannia divide is straddled by one key work, Irvine Welsh's *Trainspotting* (1993). This is partly because the novel was adapted into not just one but two different stage versions, a film adaptation and twenty years later a sequel (*T2 Trainspotting*), with the soundtrack for the original film featuring music by Blur, Elastica, Pulp and Sleeper so that it is an instance of how, during its metamorphosis into Cool Britannia, Britpop became manifest in a wider variety of cultural forms and media than just popular music, and in the process also lost some of its original power. Of particular significance in the current discussion is how *Trainspotting*, and indeed Welsh, have subsequently been positioned at different points on the continuum that runs between counter-cultures and the economic and cultural mainstream. Modulating between these points involves at times rejecting concessions to more sanitised forms of consumer culture while at others finding agreeable accommodations with them. In other words, the *Trainspotting* phenomenon as a whole is notable because of how vividly it illustrates the general transition that has taken place in subcultures since the era of punk. Whereas Robert Morace (2001) notes that Irvine Welsh has variously been seen as a 'self-promoting entrepreneur' or a 'post-punk generational spokesperson' (13), the purpose of discussing it here is not to come down on one side or other of these apparent poles but to emphasise the dialectical relationship between them in order to evaluate the status and meaning of post-punk as depicted by *Trainspotting* and assess the extent to which the relationships it portrays can be considered examples of subcultures.

It is important to note that Welsh did not necessarily write *Trainspotting* in order to contribute explicitly to any nationalist agenda in Scotland, either political or cultural. However, writing in 1998 – that is, between the Scottish referendum of 1997 and the opening of its Parliament in 1999 – Christopher Whyte argued that in 'the absence of an elected political authority the task of representing the nation has been repeatedly devolved' to its writers (284). This task is in fact now very commonly remarked upon. Monica Germanà (2014) draws attention to the different ways in which 'the literary production of the Scottish 1980s' is characterised by a 'self-conscious interrogation of the alienated identity and marginal belonging of the Scottish self within Thatcherite Britain and an increasingly globalized political system' (52). Scott Hames (2019) has made a comparable point, drawing a distinction between the work of writers and cultural figures in keeping alive 'the dream' of Scottish self-representation between the two referendums of 1979 and 1997 and the 'grind' of slowly moving electoral politics (42).

Although Andrew Hook has dismissed Welsh's use of 'demotic Scots' as 'purely sensational' (2020), one of the ways in which *Trainspotting* took on the task of representing the Scottish people is through its mobilisation of Edinburgh vernacular speech. Of the novel's forty-three sections only four are narrated in standard English while the others are narrated by different characters in diverse accents and dialects. One of the effects of this is that language itself emerges as a de facto character in the novel. The text's overall feeling of linguistic richness evokes an intersubjective world in which the boundaries between one human being and another are relatively porous. For example, it is not clear if the old man who appears in the pub section is the same as the old man who participates in the section entitled 'Trainspotting at Leith Central Station' and who transpires to be Begbie's father; and whether either (or both) are the same as numerous other older men who traverse the text. This is partly because not all of the minor characters are named, and partly because certain characters appear to use different names (or different versions of their name) in different contexts. But it is also an effect of language, a device that forges connections between people by making it very hard to tell how many people are present at any given moment, or even when one person stops speaking and when another starts.

It has now become something of a commonplace that literary realism is a mode of writing that tends towards narrative closure which in turn is a form of ideological entrapment that ends up legitimating and reinforcing rather than interrogating the status quo. The social context in which Welsh was writing was one in which years of Thatcherite economics had had a devastating effect on working-class communities. As Britain was led away from its manufacturing past, the industrial cities bore much of the brunt of displacement and disaffection, with educational underachievement, unemployment and homelessness common. Thus, it is not surprising that Welsh was concerned to critique rather than endorse the dominant ideology of the period and Alan Freeman (1996) argues that he does this most effectively by 'pulling apart the conventions of realism' (257). Cairns Craig (1999), another of the writers who like Whyte have assimilated Welsh to a Scottish nationalist canon, saw a relationship between the uses of Edinburgh vernacular and a lament for the loss of traditional working-class life styles wrought by de-industrialisation and Thatcherism: 'like the empty shell of Leith Central Station' (which is long-closed), the use of dialect 'gestures to the lost community which dialect had represented in Scottish tradition and which has now been corrupted into fearful individualism' (97). Morace sees in Welsh's uncensored depiction of heroin users, junkies, prostitutes and criminals a literary form comparable to Bakhtin's carnivalesque: that is, the symbolic subversion of existing structures of legal, political and cultural authority. To the extent that this is true, his reading of *Trainspotting* feels closely aligned to the symbolic and stylistic subversion of authority associated with the youth subcultures of the 1970s, when Welsh was growing up. But Morace goes on:

> However, as Bakhtin realized and as a carnivalized text such as *Trainspotting* clearly implies, carnival depends upon the existence of an authentic folk culture and community without which carnival must itself degenerate, coming to exist solely in its negative aspect ... and ... resentment replaces regeneration. At this point, there is no affirmation of the person as a vital part of an organic community, only the triumph of the bourgeois self and the marketplace ethos of competitive individualism (34).

In the book, the act for which Renton is arrested and sent to counselling – stealing books – is oddly un-counter-cultural, given that his motivation for doing so is that he wants to read them (as opposed to such other counter-cultural activities as destroying them, defacing them or simply selling them to fuel the next drug hit). Moreover, in contrast to Spud who is sent to prison, Renton's apparent commitment to self-improvement through reading results in his being sentenced merely to therapy. Similarly, when he decides against admitting to Dianne's parents that he has been operating a complicated benefit fraud system he instead chooses to tell them he is an art gallerist, which as we know from Hewison was in the mid-1990s an occupation that could hardly be described as politically oppositional in any meaningful sense. The monologue that Welsh puts into Renton's mouth, in which he confesses to running his fraudulent syndicate, is one that draws attention both to corporate systems and complex managerial skills so that even this feels like a projection of the dominant consumerist culture rather than a rejection of it. And most notably of all, when he steals the gang's 'take' at the end of the novel and absconds to Amsterdam in order to escape the wrath of Begbie, this too underwrites an ethos of competitive individualism within the capitalist ideology rather than transforming it. Thus, Morace concludes:

If ... the British youth culture of teddy boys, mods and rockers, punks and ravers is 'traditionally tribal' and 'all about belonging', then much of what proves so disturbing about *Trainspotting* is the absence of nearly any benefit accruing from belonging to the Leith subculture (51).

This is the fundamental question that is foregrounded by the novel: where, if anywhere, is the space for symbolic subversion once occupied by subcultures? Morace responds to this question by suggesting that the heroin subculture remains but that unlike the forms of belonging generated through participation in the subcultures of the 1970s, no solidarity in collective action is enabled through it so that it becomes meaningless and ineffective. A more extreme response would be to suggest that these benefits do not accrue from the subculture because really *there is no subculture at all*. The people around Renton do not add up to any kind of actively constituted group in Hebdige's sense; they are just atomised individuals – as Renton says at several points.

This is because the world depicted by the novel has two different and contradictory impulses built into it as its precondition. The total absence of anything that can really be called belonging functions as an affirmation of what is missed. When this absence of intimacy is elevated from the individual to the collective plain it has the effect of gesturing towards forms of belonging, forms of community, which had by 1993 long since been dismantled. Thus, the relationships portrayed in the novel represent the last vestiges of the rich, symbolic and subversive subcultures of the 1970s. But by the time of *Trainspotting* those same subcultures have become evanescent and meaningless. The novel gestures towards them but never succeeds in fully embodying or actualising them so that the Leith heroin subculture feels more like an absent presence than a fully constituted and functioning social group. Thus, in an article analysing the characters of *Trainspotting* through the lens of Erving Goffman's (1963) sociological study of how certain individuals and groups come to be cast and stigmatised as abnormal, Alfonso Gutiérrez-Sibaja (2017) concludes: 'Even though their stigma brings them physically closer, they are the victims of a terrible isolation' (13).

That *Trainspotting* portrays the last throes of a once-rich subcultural history is further emphasised by David Higdon, who has drawn attention to the fact that Welsh brought his protagonists Renton, Rent Boy and Spud back as minor characters in his subsequent novel, *Glue* (2001). But Renton's return to Scotland is contingent on the fact that

Begbie remains safely behind bars and cannot threaten him, which means there is little more of interest that Welsh can say or do with the other characters:

> The protagonists of *Trainspotting*, now several years older, drift aimlessly through the world of *Glue*'s Terry Lawson, Carl Ewart, Billy Birrell, and Andrew Galloway, but as with most youth gangs in such novels, the foursome is isolated by age, school experience, and slang from Renton and the others, and, for many readers, will be set further apart because their angst is exhausted in nature. Rent Boy and Spud have shrunk in characterization, and the tone has changed (Higdon, 2004, 426).

One of the factors that had prompted the creation of subcultures in the 1960s and 1970s was a specific generational consciousness arising from the fact that several Education Acts had created a scenario where, more than at any other time in British history, teenagers spent the majority of their time with other people specifically the same age as themselves, rather than mixing across the age ranges. By the time of *Trainspotting* in 1993, active subcultures were being replaced by backwards-looking heritage industries, and counter-cultures were in the process of being usurped by the creative industries. *Glue* takes this process to an even greater stage in its depiction of the evanescence of whatever raw power Renton and the others might once have possessed.

If *Glue* illustrates this evanescence with regard to the earlier savage fury of *Trainspotting,* William C. Boles (2014) finds it taking place in the theatrical adaptations of the latter. In an essay that understands Welsh's forays into drama as part of the wider movement that briefly in the 1990s became known as In-Yer-Face Theatre, Boles compares Welsh to Mark Ravenhill, Sarah Kane, Jez Butterworth and Martin McDonagh: 'these young writers explored, in part, a disenfranchised youth culture' (35). Moreover, while the stage adaptation of *Trainspotting* existed in two different forms, one directed by Ian Brown and the other by Harry Gibson, Welsh wrote his next play, *You'll Have Had Your Hole* (which opened at the West Yorkshire Playhouse in 1998), directly for the theatre himself. However, Boles has drawn attention to the fact that its use of sexual violence cannot be assimilated to a wider thematic pattern or narrative trajectory, and thus finds that '*You'll Have Had Your Hole* turned out to be, perhaps, the biggest failure of not only Welsh's career, but also for the In-Yer-Face era' (39) because, unlike Sarah Kane's *Blasted* and Mark Ravenhill's *Shopping and Fucking*, 'Welsh fails to integrate the shocking action within the larger framework of his play' (43) so that sexual violence exists solely for shock value and 'elicits little emotional or intellectual investment from the audience' (45).

But it is in the film adaptation of *Trainspotting* that the travesty of subcultural political rebellion is most apparent. To some extent this is the result of the inherent difficulties involved in adapting a novel that does not really have a single protagonist or plotline into a format where those things are the norm. The screenwriters reassigned episodes from one character to another rather freely and also omitted episodes which could not be worked into the general tightening of focus onto Mark Renton, Sick Boy, Tommy, Spud and Begbie. Although it may not seem it on the surface, the language of *Trainspotting* the movie is somewhat closer to that of standard English than the novel, and, at the same time, the range of different Scottish dialects is much narrower and more limited. Given that its linguistic richness has been identified as both a strength of the novel and one of its key mechanisms for expressing an anti-establishment aesthetic, the corresponding linguistic impoverishment of the film cannot fail to undermine those things. It is very notable, for example, that the section 'Eating Out' which was left out of the film is the one where the novel's cultural politics takes on its most explicitly Scottish nationalist dimension. Although by and large Welsh avoids having his Leith stand in as a metonym for the nation as a whole, in 'Eating Out' the graphic and rebarbative revenge exacted by Kelly on four upper-class English restaurant customers for their perceived insensitivity to matters of national and cultural difference does gesture in this direction, so that its omission from the film downplays the question of Scottish difference.

David Higdon has suggested that the absence of another key section, 'Bad Blood', has a different effect. This section is about the revenge exacted by Dave on Alan Venters for having been the source of his girlfriend Donna's – and ultimately his own – HIV infection, and thereby foregrounds a cause of contemporary cultural anxiety that was decidedly uncommercial. Indeed, in Alan Sinfield's analysis of the adaptation of the text from 'subcultural novel' to 'mainstream film', Sinfield has drawn attention to how powerfully the latter is able to incorporate, absorb and profit from dissent (2004, xxxix). Morace likewise highlights the very different cultural politics of the two texts, notably in the film's suppression of racism, sexism, domestic violence and sectarian conflict, and also in the problematic way in which the film '"solves" the novel's AIDS problem by a sleight of acronymic wits, substituting MTV style for HIV substance' (84).

Patrick McGavin (1996) has argued that one effect of the novel's loose structure, eschewing of causality and continual switching between different characters' monologues is that we are 'inside their heads rather than [as in the film version] watching them on the screen' (39). The altered perspective between book and film therefore has the effect of transforming the characters into objects to be watched, even surveyed, by a distant and somewhat more judgemental observer. In other words, the film undermines the radical aesthetic challenges posed by the novel to the dominant ideology of the time, which as we have seen was based on a combination of nostalgia and heritage, and in fact assimilated it to those things. Like other films from the Cool Britannia era such as *The Full Monty* (1997) and *Billy Elliot* (2000), which take potentially serious issues such as unemployment, class warfare, economic deprivation and the miners' strike only to convert them all into light-hearted comedy, the film *Trainspotting*, too, foregrounds style over substance.

In the light of the current discussion of the trajectory of British youth- and working-class cultures away from the subcultural, it is highly pertinent to note that Morace concludes *Irvine Welsh's Trainspotting: A Reader's Guide* by talking briefly about the burgeoning creative industries in Britain. He points out that neither *Trainspotting* nor its author are even mentioned in *Creative Britain*, the manifesto by which New Labour's first Secretary of State for Culture, Media and Sport, Chris Smith, effectively launched Cool Britannia and simultaneously disarmed the radical subversive potential of Britpop. Morace is therefore obliged to conclude that the evolution away from subcultures and towards the creative industries of which *Trainspotting* is emblematic thus transforms Adorno and Horkheimer's term *cultural industry*, which had been intended as a term of radical critique, into something like 'its opposite' (85). That is, where once subcultures were sites of radical subversion of authority and power, one effect of their dissolution has been to reify those same hierarchical structures. Or as Jonathan Romney puts it, historical and cultural legitimacy have been conferred on Welsh as part of an attempt to make dangerous writing safe, at the same time that his work has been 'used to advance a "Cool Britannia" and "creative industries" ethos to which his stories and style stand in bristling opposition' (6).

THE WELSH *TRAINSPOTTING*

As William Boles and others have highlighted, the commercial success of the novel *Trainspotting*, which was itself further augmented by the status of the film, spawned for a short period of time an imitation mini genre: 'Publishers usurped Welsh's brand by designing similar covers and touting their authors as the female Irvine Welsh, the English Irvine Welsh or the Welsh Irvine Welsh' (37). Focusing on this last case and taking its cue from Moya Luckett's suggestion that Kevin Allen's 1997 film *Twin Town* was explicitly 'heralded as a "Welsh *Trainspotting*"' (93), this chapter concludes with a discussion of *Twin Town* that ultimately moves away from such surface descriptions and instead sets it in the context of the wider shift in British subcultures that has been discussed all along.

One of the things that interests Luckett about British cinema of the 1990s is the fact that it coincided with an upturn in British filmmaking. She relates this to the fact that during the decade, British national identity had become 'increasingly fraught, threatened by European federalisation and the imminent break-up of the United Kingdom' (2000, 88). In turn, that fraught condition gave rise to a desire among diverse British cinematic audiences to see new representations of their lives and identities performed on screen, resulting in 'the formation of a new British film canon that counters traditional heritage-centred ideas of British cinema' (ibid.). The films that emerged in this new, counter-heritage version of British cinema were characterised by a combination of subcultural aesthetics and realism with an 'emphasis on appearance and representation that stylises and re-imagines everyday life in ways Hollywood and European Art cinema cannot' (ibid.). It may be that writing in 2000, Luckett's words were truer than she realised when she identified both American and European cinema as significant 'others' in contrast to which British film was re-imagined, and the implications of this othering, especially with regard to Europe, will be explored further in later chapters. For the present chapter, what is significant is her identification of 'the monumental nature of constitutional changes deriving from a devolved UK' from 1997 onwards (91).

Following a discussion of *Trainspotting* and different versions of Scottishness, Luckett situates *Twin Town* within a 'series of conflicting British relationships', specifically, English and Welsh, where critical opprobrium is implicitly directed at England for the way it dominates Welsh culture; and internally back at Wales for acquiescing in British imperialism (93). The year of the film's release, 1997, was also the year of the referendums in Scotland and Wales which resulted in the establishment of the devolved national administrations. Relating the film to the growing momentum that gathered behind Welsh forms of self-expression from that year onwards, and paying attention to the auditory elements of the film such as accent and soundscape, she concludes that '*Twin Town* plays with the idea that sound might represent national specificity, with its use of the Welsh language, its reference to Dylan Thomas and the Male Voice Choir so loved by the twins' father' (93).

If male voice choirs are something of a staple of received external images of Wales, then another one is a perceived obsession with rugby. Where Luckett made sound the focus of her analysis of the film, Ben Thompson in *Sight and Sound* interprets the scene where the criminal Cartwright mollifies his pursuers Greyo and Lucy by invoking how the Welsh rugby player Phil Bennett had famously turned defeat into victory against Scotland in 1977 as an instance of 'Celtic sporting triumph as metaphor for national pride' (54). In his account the allusion to Scotland also makes possible an explicit comparison of *Twin Town* with *Trainspotting*, because he interprets the rugby club scene as a direct adaptation of the scene in *Trainspotting* where Renton watches footage of Archie Gemmill's celebrated goal for Scotland against the Netherlands in the 1978 football world cup.

In a more nuanced discussion of *Twin Town* Darryl Perrins (2000) takes a different approach, arguing that instead of uncritically celebrating these supposedly embedded aspects of Welsh culture as part of a process of apparent national revival, the film invites a critical stance with regard to them in order to reject conventional sources of Welsh cultural authority. In his account, the film cannot easily be assimilated to an emergent Welsh nationalist agenda because it is highly critical of it. In fact, Perrins makes a meaningful comparison between the film and Caradoc Evans's collection of short stories *My People* (1915), which lambasted the social hierarchy based on hypocritical chapel authority prevalent in rural West Wales in the early twentieth century. Like *My People*, Perrins argues, *Twin Town* sets out to confront and critique existing forms of cultural leadership in Wales 'against those that have the real power to construct the "artefact" of Wales' and to give the Welsh people a different image of themselves (156). As a result of this approach, where Thompson sees the rugby scene as evidence of the cohesive power of national pride, Perrins suggests that rugby in the film functions less to induce euphoria but (since Cartwright is the villain) as a warning of the dangers of blind conformity to 'national sentiment' (161). And where Luckett saw Fatty Lewis's devotion to his male voice choir as evidence of national self-expression, Perrins sees his sons' preference for karaoke over choral music as a rejection of this received idea of what constitutes Welsh culture.

Like Perrins, Geoffrey Macnab (1997) draws attention to the fact that *Twin Town* 'has no truck with stock images of Wales as a country of choirs, miners, daffodils and leeks' and quotes the director Allen as saying these things are '"an insult to youth culture"' (6). In making his review more a matter of youth culture than Welsh expression, Macnab's comments raised one of the most underdiscussed properties of the film – that is, the way it symbolically resurrects what decades earlier would have been called subcultures. In fact, structurally speaking, one of the closest parallels that exists between *Twin Town* and *Trainspotting* is the way the twins head off by boat to Morocco after defeating the villains. If we substitute Morocco for *Trainspotting*'s Amsterdam it again becomes possible to consider the later film as an adaptation of elements in the earlier because the choice of both destinations seems highly evocative of subcultural lifestyles related to drug use (especially hashish) and so signifies comparable social relationships in each film. Indeed, if the comparisons that have inevitably been made between the films *Trainspotting* and *Twin Town* have any remaining interest at all, it is less in the combination of idiosyncratic style with shock value that we find in each than it is in the way each film relates to the fate of subcultures more generally.

Renton's departure for Amsterdam with the rest of the gang's swag at the end of *Trainspotting* has been seen as representing the moment at which he finally acquiesces in the dominant ideology of competitive individualism and enters the world of consumer culture which previously he had appeared to reject. The argument above, by contrast, suggested a more dialectical approach whereby the symbolic conclusion can be read as keeping both factors in play, that is, as both rejecting and reinforcing the dominant ideology so that instability itself emerges as the primary condition portrayed. This dialectic is perhaps best expressed by the fact that Renton's choice to enter the free market (which is part of the straight culture) is also a choice to maintain a drug-based lifestyle (which is subcultural). In *Twin Town* by contrast, according to Perrins it is highly significant that the Lewis twins never use the 'exclusive' drug, cocaine (161), and prefer instead a range of social drugs, especially marijuana.

In a chapter in *Resistance Through Rituals* (1975) about the social meaning of drug use, Paul E. Willis argued that for certain drug users, the main significance of drugs was not their pharmacological effects but their inclusion in a social system of symbolic values, which is more a question of social interaction and being in the world than it is of chemical effects on the brain. John Harris (2003) has suggested that the preference of Oasis and other Britpop bands for heroin and cocaine over more social drugs was tantamount to a preference for solitary escapism over social creativity, and had the long-term effect of undermining Britpop's creative potential. With this in mind, the director Kevin Allen's association of the Lewis twins in *Twin Town* with the social drug marijuana rather than the hedonistic drug cocaine appears to posit the subcultural potential of drug use.

Another important facet of subcultures to have been identified in *Resistance Through Rituals* was that they were overwhelmingly male. In a critique of the tendency for studies of subcultures to examine only male youth culture, Angela McRobbie and Jenny Garber suggest that the issue was not about how girls are 'marginally' different, because class mediates their experience in the same way that it does for boys and men. It was rather a question of how their position was 'structurally' different (211), because subcultures mainly evolved in the interstices of work and leisure which women (at the time of writing in 1975) mainly existed outside. Similarly, Rachel Powell and John Clarke argued that women and girls tended to have been marginalised by subcultural analysis because so much of the definition of subcultures hinged on the distinction between work and not-work that was more common to working-class men. In other words, although both girls and boys of working-class backgrounds had often gone through the same kinds of institutions and relationships (schools), they also experienced them differently. For boys it was a matter of entering working-class jobs themselves; for girls (again, writing in 1975) it was more likely to have been presented as a question of how they 'transition' from one family/household to another through marriage and childbearing (225). Failure to recognise this difference, Powell and Clarke argue, is what really accounts for the analytical invisibility of women in accounts of subcultures and also why men were rarely analysed in the context of private home life.

But what of the relationship between gender and subculture by the 1990s? Claire Monk has argued that 1990s British cinema evinces a preoccupation with a series of crises in masculinity. She attributes this to the fact that it coincided in time both with the fall-out from post-industrialism and Thatcherism, and with the political, legal and cultural gains made by feminism, giving rise to a post-feminist male panic that was self-conscious, questioning, painful and therapeutic and had the effect of making men in cinema 'subjects-in-themselves' (2000, 157) as men's roles and the definition of masculinity underwent redefinition. Naturally there was no singular response to this, and the process was in fact portrayed in a range of different cinematic representations, some of which include a backlash against the gains of feminism. For this reason, the line between critique and celebration of masculinity was often blurred in the different portrayals of masculinity on film during the decade. Thus, according to Monk, 1990s British cinematic portrayals of the 'new man' who is sensitive, caring and vulnerable were ironically mostly confined to romances such as *Truly, Madly, Deeply* (1990) or historical dramas such as *Sense and Sensibility* (1995), which were mainly aimed at a female audience. She sees *Brassed Off* (1996) and *The Full Monty* (1997) as examples of films that 'transformed the problems of male unemployment and social exclusion and related psychic crises into incongruously feelgood comedy' (159) and attributes their commercial success to their being able to 'offer male audiences a symbolic, if inevitably problematic, solution' (ibid.). By contrast, Perrins says that one of the strengths of *Twin Town* is that, unlike in *Brassed Off*, the male choir is not used to extol the supposed virtues of a collective past, thereby avoiding the temptation to provide an 'easy fix' to the challenge of rapidly changing roles and identities for working men at the time, which the comedy capers inflicted on them by *The Full Monty* typifies (165).

In a discussion of *Trainspotting* and *Twin Town* that is surprisingly generous to their gender politics, Monk identifies a different strength again, which is their propensity to present the male underclass outside conventional historical or moral frames of reference. Although this may sound dangerously ahistorical, this elision of outside reference means that rather than 'attempting to arouse anger or social outrage, *Trainspotting* and especially *Twin Town* encouraged a knowing, empathetic complicity between audiences and the films' young male underclass in terms of an appealing subculture of dissent from the demands of adulthood, women and work' (160). In other words, by speaking to new male audiences in new ways, neither film made explicit attempts to invoke the male backlash against the gains of feminism that existed in other areas of British culture at the time. Although work and study are both shown as almost exclusively female pursuits in the films, the male characters do not resent this since they are not even interested in those things, which is what creates their potential subcultural status.

Monk concludes that both films 'framed the male underclass not as a "social problem" but as a subcultural "lifestyle" with certain attractions for a young, post-political male audience' (ibid.). But lest she get too enthusiastic for the anti-establishment undertones implied by the idea of subcultures, she also situates this new framing as part of a 'quantum shift' that took place in British cinema between *Four Weddings and a Funeral* (1994) and *The Full Monty* (1997), which ultimately proved to be a shift away from the creative potential of Britpop and towards the New Labour establishment aesthetic of 'Cool Britannia' (161). This shift helps to explain why, just as Irvine Welsh has had a degree of cultural legitimacy conferred on his works even though they were opposed to the concept of cultural legitimacy, the same thing happened in the end to *Twin Town*. Jane Aaron and M. Wynn Thomas have used the contemporary popular media slogan *Cool Cymru* to make connections between 'a swathe of new Welsh actors and actresses claiming the limelight in London and Hollywood' (especially the star of *Twin Town*, Rhys Ifans) and the 'sudden breakthrough to mainstream recognition' in the 1990s of Welsh bands Manic Street Preachers, Catatonia, Super Furry Animals and Stereophonics (2003, 301). But although the term *Cool Cymru* lacked precision, it was typically used to refer to the local Welsh variants of Britpop and Cool Britannia. As such it was more celebratory than critical or counter-cultural.

Moreover, it was not simply a matter of each film being divested of its latent subcultural properties through association with the mainstream practices of Creative Britain. It is also that each became part of an emergent nationalist cultural agenda in Scotland and Wales in the years leading up to – and away from – the national referendums of 1997, the same year that *Twin Town* was released. Although devolution is fundamentally a unionist political strategy aimed at forestalling the desire for full independence in the different nations, in Wales it was widely received as a moment of national reawakening. For example, in a paper about performing Welsh culture presented at the Association for Welsh Writing in English at Gregynog in 2012, Rebecca Edwards showed that 'the devolution proposal was endorsed and supported' by a number of the bands associated with *Cool Cymru*, so that *Cool Cymru* has been seen as an expression of a new cultural confidence on the part of a young nation rediscovering its voice in the wake of the 'yes' vote (n.p.). Established Welsh artists of a previous generation could also be retrospectively added to category, as when Shirley Bassey performed at the opening of the Welsh Assembly in 1999 (see Figure 4).

On the other hand, Edwards also showed that there were certain problematic aspects in the process of performing a national culture, mainly because the performers included in *Cool Cymru* were involved in producing a particular 'type of Wales' which may or may not have been typical of the Welsh population as a whole (ibid.). Similarly, it is unclear whether the connection of the film *Twin Town* to a putative national cinematic imagination was intended by its director Kevin Allen. In his interpretation of the film, which is more critical of Wales's national cultural icons, Perrins points out that it opens

FIGURE 4: Shirley Bassey, Opening of the Welsh Assembly, 1999.
Trinity Mirror/Mirrorpix/Alamy Stock Photo

with a quote from Dylan Thomas about the city of Swansea being the graveyard of ambition which 'at once distances the film from the triumphalism of the hour, and the heritage image of Thomas so meticulously nurtured by Swansea City Council' (154). What is striking about this observation is that, even though it reveals a suspicion of nationalist sentiment, the allusion to the triumphalism of the time shows that it, too, sees an unbreakable connection between the film and the positive outcome of the referendum.

The context generated by devolution also partly explains why *Twin Town* had been billed as a 'Welsh *Trainspotting*' in the first place, rather than simply being positioned as an independent film in its own right. The cultural politics of post-devolution Wales meant that Wales's own new cultural establishment was casting around for suitable cultural hooks on which to hang the trappings of nationhood, and, arising out of Scotland immediately before *Twin Town*, *Trainspotting* offered itself as an available model. In the final analysis, therefore, the relationship between the two films is a form of competition which is both capitalist and consumerist, employing pragmatic tactics to forge a distinctive place within the already crowded cultural sphere. But more than this, it is a form of competition that is implicitly nationalist in nature, positioning the emergent nations as structurally and symbolically congruent with, but at the same time distinctive and alternative from, each other. In other words, many of the contrasts that are played out between Scottishness and Britishness in the interplay between different versions of *Trainspotting* are echoed and reflected in the relationship between Welshness and Britishness in *Twin Town*.

In fact, what is really new in the latter with regard to the former is the element of comparison as such. To some extent, this is a matter of commercialisation, building a marketing campaign around a perceived success story in order to reap both cultural and economic rewards. But something else also was going on, in the fundamental assumption that Wales somehow needs its own answer to *Trainspotting* and perhaps that it needs to emulate Scotland more generally rather than simply being complete in itself. To conclude by drawing attention to this tendency is to suggest that one of the changes wrought on the relationship between the four nations of the United Kingdom since devolution is therefore this new dynamic of competition between them. It is not always manifested in explicitly competitive ways. Neither has it arisen as a result of any specific decision to compete among individuals or organisations in the nations. And yet it is as structurally operative and as tangible as the term competition suggests. This means that between the nations and cultures of the contemporary United Kingdom a distinctive form of interrelation has emerged: one that simultaneously draws on existing forms of communication and contact on the one hand; and on an openly competitive ethos on the other. This last exists not because it inheres in any one of the nations in question, but because competition itself has become the precondition for the creative industries in which so much cultural work originates. In other words, to the dialectical relationships that exist between the counter-cultural subversion of punk and the politically compromised aesthetic of Cool Britannia, and between intimations of autonomy in the nations and a reassertion of political unionism at the centre, can be added a third pair of terms: the dialectic that exists between nations as compatriots within a wider entity (the United Kingdom) in which they all participate, and nations as competitors – for resources, recognition, a place in the limelight – in a diverse field. This structuring dynamic of potential solidarity undercut by the competitive nature of cultural production is one of the key factors in understanding contemporary cultural politics in Britain, as the following chapters will demonstrate.

Endnote

[1] Compare also Marc Evans's 1997 film *House of America* and the soundtrack accompanying it.

2

THE CULTURAL CAPITAL
OF CAPITALS OF CULTURE

Following Robert Hewison's account of the emergence of the heritage industry in the previous chapter, this chapter focuses on a further aspect of the process by which the creative industries have been used as both physical and ideological drivers of social change. Beginning with the awarding to the city of Glasgow of the title European City of Culture for the year 1990, it will suggest that the bidding for – and subsequent delivery of – this year-long cultural festival should not be seen in isolation and is only comprehensible in the context of the broader regeneration of the city that was taking place through culture at the time. Though there is a vast body of research on the impact of European Cities (subsequently Capitals) of Culture, this has been carried out mainly in the domains of either tourism or urban planning. As such, it tends to evaluate the social and/or economic outcomes of the programme in this or that city, during this or that year. Surprisingly little commentary exists on the artistic quality of the programming curated by the different Capitals of Culture, and there is also little comparative analysis of them.

The chapter will point to a key irony in the European Capitals of Culture programme, which is that a programme designed to encourage European integration should take the form of an accolade that actively pits cities – and in some cases even nations – against each other in the relentless competition for attention, distinctiveness and investment. Owing to this competition, the way in which different candidate cities go about the bidding process is perhaps quite different from that intended by the founders of the programme, creating in Eleni Theodoraki's words a difference of perspective between 'event hosts' and 'event owners' (2014, 186–8). Glasgow as European City of Culture 1990 is better understood in the context of the long-term urban regeneration of the city of Glasgow more broadly than it is in the context of any number of other European Capitals of Culture. There is, in other words, a distinction to be made between what Brian Graham (2002, 1009–11) calls the cultural heritage of the 'internal city' and that of the 'external city'.

Having drawn this distinction between the external city and the internal city, and the different drivers, goals and ultimate beneficiaries of each, the chapter will go on to apply a similar set of contrasts to a number of other European Capitals of culture around the British Isles: Dublin (1991), Cork (2005) and Liverpool (2008). By the time Liverpool was announced in 2003 as the host city for 2008, hosting the festival had become so prestigious that a total of twelve cities had competed for it. When Liverpool was awarded the title, it did so ahead of five other shortlisted candidates (Birmingham, Bristol, Cardiff, Newcastle and Oxford) and six others (Belfast, Bradford, Brighton, Canterbury, Inverness and Norwich) which were rejected before shortlisting. Given that almost all research on European Capitals of Culture tends to focus on the programmes implemented by successful candidates, this section of the chapter will draw attention to the paucity of research on the dynamics of the candidature stage (although some important exceptions will be identified). In doing so, it will tacitly ask if any benefit can possibly accrue to candidate cities whether they are successful or not, simply through the fact of having participated in the competition.

This is a complex question for many reasons. Carrying out an evaluation of the impact of bidding in straightforwardly economic terms is beyond the scope of the current project. Identifying whether the experience of bidding in itself enabled any form of social or cultural activity to take place that otherwise would not have done is almost impossible to gauge in the absence of what Theodoraki calls 'counterfactual considerations of what would have changed in the cities either way' (190). So is the question of whether there was any discernible improvement in the quality of such activities. And this is before the vexed questions of how to define benefit, and who precisely might have benefited, are even raised. Since it is fairly clear that cities are not monolithic entities and cannot be said to exist in the singular but represent strata of different communities, social groups, populations and interests within relatively compressed geographic territories, it seems likely that the differences in motivation between event hosts and event owners; between the internal city and the external city; and between working-class residents and prosperous developers all came into play in bidding for European Capital of Culture 2008.

Nevertheless, the chapter will tentatively suggest that there does appear to have been some benefit accrued to the candidate cities through the fact of having been candidates. Reaching this conclusion is significant for one important reason: the fact that bidding cities can derive some kind of cultural or economic fillip from having participated in the competition alone appears to have been an important stimulus for the introduction by the New Labour Government in 2009 of the related accolade of UK City of Culture, which was first awarded to Derry/Londonderry in 2013, and then to Hull in 2017. After short discussion of each of these events, the final third of the chapter focuses on the bidding for the following instalment: UK 2021.

Just as the European Capital of Culture programme exists to promote cohesion and a sense of collective belonging in a form that (ironically) fosters competition between different participants and so arguably militates against that very harmony, so too is there an irony built into the concept of the UK City of Culture. This irony is that candidate teams in British cities appear to have learnt through the bidding process for European Capital of Culture 2008 that it is possible to receive some of the cultural goods associated with participating without necessarily securing the award. This irony, once recognised, creates a certain logic within which the establishment of UK City of Culture is best understood: accumulating the benefits in terms of the intangible, cultural capital derived from the European Capital of Culture but without having to wait for the UK's turn to host the festival, and in fact without the UK having to participate in it at the European level at all. For this reason, the chapter will conclude by suggesting that UK City of Culture can be understood as having pre-empted the UK's decision in 2016 to leave the European Union.

EUROPEAN CAPITAL OF CULTURE: HISTORY AND EVOLUTION

The European City of Culture was conceived by the Greek Minister for Culture Melina Mercouri, and was first awarded to the city of Athens in 1985. According to Susana Bernardino, J. Freitas Santos and J. Cadima Ribeiro its aims are to 'highlight the richness, diversity, and shared characteristics of European culture and to promote understanding among citizens' (2018, 151). While the concept of a shared European culture might appear nebulous and elusive, the official discourse surrounding the title in its initial phase strongly emphasised the capacity for the programme to promote unity-in-diversity – although as Clopot and Strani point out, this diversity is frequently only operative on a very 'superficial' level (2020, 159). One of the under-recognised features of the programme is the striking resemblance its objectives bear to official discourses about unity in difference in the United States of America, the economic and cultural power of which the European Community could be said to have been trying to compete with through the initiative. In Europe, the really new element was the cultural aspect, the idea that in addition to being a political union with a corporate (that is, economic) structure, the European Community could be both a bearer of culture and an entity shaped by cultural practices. Culture could be used to 'promote' shared values and hence foster greater understanding among European citizens (Lähdesmäki, 766). But wherein this culture existed, what were its principal characteristics and of what it chiefly consisted were all left very undefined.

Moreover, if the cultural element of the equation was left open-ended, so too were the understanding and citizenship elements, mainly because people in different European countries have tended to interpret the concept of citizenship differently. For instance, the concept of citizenry has a stronger emotional resonance in France than in Britain because built into the public self-imagination of French citizens is the idea that the French nation was brought into being through the revolutionary efforts and intervention of the French people, whose duty it therefore is to keep up that revolutionary ethic through participation in – and at times disruption of – civic life. This contrasts almost exactly with the situation in Britain, where the category of British people emerged out of the state apparatus during the years after the Act of Union of England and Wales with Scotland in 1707, which were also the early stages of Britain's imperial period, so that the history of the British state is above all a counter-revolutionary history. To put the contrast more precisely, in France the state was created by the people whereas in Britain the people was created by the state.

That the understanding of citizenship varies from country to country and culture to culture reveals some of the context in which the European Capital of Culture programme operates. For example,

Gabriela Popescu has drawn attention to the fact that when the Romanian city of Sibiu hosted the festival in 2007, this was not only an event of 'national pride' (2017, 6), but also one that was credited by the citizenry to their mayor, Klaus Iohannis, in a way that encouraged them to 'prove their citizenship sense every four years, during ... elections' by re-electing him (5). The point worth making here is not only that residents in other European Capitals of Cultures would not necessarily make the connection between city and nation, but also that residents of other European countries would not necessarily define themselves as citizens primarily through participation in elections. This difference is possibly attributable to the fact Romania is a young democracy in which the basic opportunity to do so had come about within living memory and could not be taken for granted, and reveals the extent to which civic understanding is not understood in the same way all over Europe. In fact, Corina Tursie has shown that when European Capital of Culture has been hosted in post-Communist societies, this has often been overtly acknowledged both as a means by which those societies insert themselves into the dominant (i.e. Western) narrative of Europe's past and in an attempt to 'make peace' with their own history (2020, 124). In a different context, Christine Hudson and Linda Sandberg have identified the Swedish city of Umeå as one in which gender-equality 'figures as an important part of its image' (2019, 31) and in which this aspect of its civic life played a key role in that city's successful bid to become European Capital of Culture in 2014.

Nicole Immler and Hans Sakkers (2014) have identified three distinct phases in the history of the European Cities and Capitals of Culture. Noting that the first five cities (1985–9) were Athens, Florence, Amsterdam, Berlin and Paris, they point out that these were cities already known for their venerable cultural histories, prominent cultural organisations and celebrated artistic artefacts. Thus, the project in its early days was characterised by a liberal humanistic outlook, in effect offering to decouple particular cultural objects from their existing national parameters and hold them up as the legacy of European civilisation more generally. The Parthenon could be presented not only as a Greek monument, but a human monument and a European one. The same could be said of the works of art in the Uffizi, Rijksmuseum or Louvre or of the Brandenburg Gate. The selection of these early European Cities of Culture therefore evinced a somewhat 'high art' aesthetic and ideological outlook.

According to Immler and Sakkers, the 'situation changed' (7) with the awarding of the title to Glasgow in 1990. Here was a city that was not known for its cultural heritage on the world stage to anything like the same degree as its predecessors. It lacked any world-renowned monument or museum like the Acropolis or the Louvre around which the festival could cluster, and in the words of Eliot Tretter 'was not even the cultural capital of Scotland' – which (he says) was Edinburgh (2009, 119). Moreover, Glasgow was a city whose large working-class population was emerging from a period of extreme economic decline throughout the 1970s and 1980s, which had in turn become manifest in the form of a highly run-down urban environment. Although chiefly owing to the foresight of earlier city councils, the city had one of the largest artistic estates in Britain, characterised by a large number of museums and galleries and a broad number of collections that were accessible to the public for free, the city was not known outside the UK – or even in other parts of the UK – as an artistic one.

Thus, the ethos of the 1990 European City of Culture was of a different order when compared to those that had come before, offering at least in potential to move away from the high art paradigm towards more inclusive forms of activity and programming. This move set the tone for capitals of culture over the next two decades (1990–2010). In Glasgow, the shift in emphasis from high art to broad participation was a necessary step in harnessing the potential for investment created by the festival to drive urban regeneration and economic development. Indeed, without a widespread participatory base it is difficult to see how the critical mass necessary to achieve any real transformation in the urban landscape could be achieved. But such transformation once achieved explains why the Capital of Culture accolade has tended to be seen as an achievement for the individual 'cities and member states involved' (Immler and Sakkers, 6) rather than as a straightforward 'success' for the European Union as a whole (Theodoraki, 183).

This realisation implies a relative underplaying of the European element of the project. When the European Union commissioned Robert Palmer (who had been Director of Glasgow in 1990) to produce a report into the effectiveness of the first twenty-five years of European Capitals of Culture in 2010, he found that 'the European dimension was not emphasized explicitly enough' (quoted in Immler and Sakkers, 4) and that 'although the concepts were of distinctly European character and quality, often the execution was not' (Immler and Sakkers, 9). This finding sparked the third phase in the history of the initiative, post-2010, in which candidate cities are much more explicitly required to 'highlight the cultural diversity of Europe', address 'European themes, history and heritage' and cultivate 'cooperation between artists and cultural operators from different European countries' (European Commission, quoted in Immler and Sakkers, 11). Thus, the question of whether to aim for a high art experience which is likely to appeal to a small specialist audience or a participatory programme that will have broader appeal has been superseded by the wider question of how (if at all) city/regional/national cultures interact in the production of a European culture. It also became European Union policy in 2006 that cities in non-Member States could no longer become European Capitals of Culture, which is probably why for Istanbul's application for 2010, 'Turkey's possible entry into the EU was a key element of the bid right from the start' (Immler and Sakkers, 13).

According to Patel, the effect of this new policy was that '"Europe" was basically reduced to the EU' in the latter's self-imagination, allotting to itself the role of sole arbiter of European culture: 'a narrowly defined, territorialized vision of Europe directly bound to an admittedly larger EU has become the yardstick for determining the scope of the programme' (2013, 549). This observation points to an instrumental view of culture in which an idea of shared European values is interpellated to the people of Europe by a congeries of political and cultural leaders via programmes such as the European Capital of Culture. Although this may seem both paternalistic and top-down, Tuuli Lähdesmäki found that such initiatives can be 'difficult to effectively implement on an intergovernmental basis due to the lack of common coordination and possibilities for operational arrangements' (770), so that when they are carried out on the ground, this is done by agents and intermediaries at a range of local, regional and national levels in what Clopot and Strani have characterised as a 'bottom-up' practice (169). Whether this is more genuinely socially inclusive than the top-down dissemination practised by the EU, or merely substitutes one political class (at European level) for another (at local level) is less clear. Patel's discussion of the role played by cultural intermediaries in an enlarged EU implies that its political apparatus was engaged in colonising the whole continent of Europe. But one of the saddest outcomes of Britain's 2016 EU referendum is the way it reduced all nuance and complexity to a simplistic for or against argument, so that it became difficult for British observers to make critical comments of this kind without appearing to endorse Brexit.

GLASGOW AS EUROPEAN CITY OF CULTURE

Glasgow in 1990 stands at the heart of several developments in European Capital of Culture. The fact that it was the first city without an *a priori* reputation for its artistic life to be awarded the title illustrates the general transition that was taking place within cultural policy at both British and European level, away from a paternalistic high art paradigm and towards increased community involvement. Indeed, although Rune Fitjar, Hilmar Rommetvedt and Christin Berg have argued that in 2008 the Norwegian city of Stavanger attempted to pursue both agendas, this only led them to the rather uninspiring conclusion that regardless of definitions of high or low art, people in Stavanger who said they were 'interested' in culture were more likely to participate in cultural events than those who said they were not (2013, 75). Overwhelmingly, bids that contained a high degree of participatory programming have been more likely to succeed than those based on an appeal to aesthetic value alone.

The practice that started with Glasgow of selecting industrial or post-industrial cities rather than inherently artistic ones as European City of Culture made it possible for the festival to contribute to a broader process of changing the image of a city. Antonietta Ivona, Antonella Rinella and Francesca Rinella have shown that when the Italian city of Matera hosted European Capital of Culture in 2019, '[f]or many decades the name Matera represented something negative' (2019, 3), and this negative perception is something that hosting the festival helped it address. The combating of negative perception is one reason why Glasgow's hosting of the event in 1990 makes more sense when understood as an achievement for the city itself than for the European Union more broadly. It is also why bidding for (and staging) the event should properly be understood in the context of urban regeneration in the city in the aftermath of the economic depression of the 1970s and 1980s, and why hosting the event makes more sense as a symptom of this wider process of urban renewal than as a terminus in its own right. But the question this urban regeneration agenda raises is: what benefits did Glasgow 1990 bring?

According to Can-Seng Ooi, Lars Håkanson and Laura LaCava, '1990 is often regarded as a turning point for Glasgow' since the city was 'rejuvenated, as it moved away from urban decay, high unemployment and its infamy for street crimes' (2014, 422). Significantly, however, their main evidence for this seems to be the European Commission's own report on the festival, which they quote at length as identifying 'many positive after-effects on the creative scene and a radical boost to its international image' and saying that 'not only do cafés fill its streets on sunny days, but it is now considered a major cultural tourism destination' (quoted in ibid.). Barring the somewhat patronising tone adopted in these official observations, the report reveals a lack of genuinely independent evaluation, and this has been a common weakness of European Capitals of Culture. Ooi, Håkanson and LaCava point out that owing to a seeming 'lack of consensus on impact measurement methodology' host cities are often 'encouraged to initiate research partnerships with local institutes and universities for the purposes of cross learning, conducting evaluations and contributing to the development of evidence based best practices' (425). Although this may sound well intentioned, they found that in many cases those same local organisations that are brought into the evaluation stage have also often been involved in the delivery of the event itself in one capacity or other, so that they are in effect evaluating themselves and 'as a result, various kinds of biases may find their way into the evaluations' (ibid.). In other words, there is a danger that the post-event reporting can become an exercise in collective backslapping rather than an objectively considered critical evaluation.

Genuinely long-term impact might take a variety of forms such as boosting tourism, renewing the urban environment, stimulating local economies, improving a city's reputation, generating new skills among its residents and creating opportunities for social inclusion. But given that the evaluation of the event tends to take place very soon after the host year, and tends to involve local consortia whose members have been involved in the delivery itself, there are very few opportunities to measure the longer-term impact of the festival in any of these terms. This may be why, despite the seeming certainty with which Ooi, Håkanson and LaCava identify hosting European City of Culture as a watershed year for Glasgow, they also go on to suggest that 'the event's specific contribution to the rejuvenation of the city remains unclear' (423). Although John Myerscough identified a net economic benefit of between £10 and £14 million and something of an improvement in the image of the city as a result of hosting European City of Culture (1990, 199), Greg Richards suggests that it was 'not possible to isolate the specific effects of the ECOC from other activities' (2015, 120).

An alternative method for evaluating the long-term benefits of hosting the event is taken by Bernardino, Santos and Ribeiro in their analysis of the legacy of the Portuguese city of Guimarães's experience as European Capital of Culture in 2012. Drawing on Giffinger's concept of 'smart' cities, they developed a matrix for measuring the smartness of a city according to six different dimensions: economy, people, governance, mobility, environment and living. These were then applied in empirical research into how Guimarães had changed five years after holding the title, thereby providing what they call 'an approach to the long-term implications of the ECOC' which had 'never been explored before' (140).

Their findings were somewhat mixed. One of the specific aims of Guimarães's original bid had been to use European Capital of Culture to 'modify the profile of the economic activities developed in the city, with a greater focus on creative and innovative activities' (155). In achieving this proposed transformation from a formerly industrial city to one characterised by the creative industries, 'results attained were less than the ones expected' leading to 'some disappointment' among the people of the city (ibid.). Overall, they conclude that the most significant benefits to be derived for the ordinary citizens of Guimarães were defined by a greater sense of pride, belonging and well-being, and to some extent by urban rehabilitation, rather than greater economic prosperity. There was therefore 'some expectations mismatch, since [the] population had expected that the economic contribution would be broader' (160).

In fact, after the difficulty of achieving genuinely independent means of evaluation, a second difficulty in analysing European Capitals of Culture is the disparity that exists between rhetoric and reality. One reason for this is that the competition to host the event has taken the form of a bidding war, whereby cities that appear to offer the most lucrative economic returns, the widest opportunities for participation and the most significant occasions for social mobility tend to be awarded the title. The award once realised is not then necessarily matched by the delivery of outcomes in either an economic or a social sense.

Moreover, the question of artistic quality seems to feature surprisingly little in either the pre-event candidature and selection or the post-event evaluation. This may be because bureaucrats are notoriously uncomfortable about making aesthetic judgements or talking about the arts as such. Without statistical measures, they do not know if the activities are any good as art and therefore tend to fall back on other indicators of social impact, primarily economic or social. This is why thirty years after Glasgow 1990 it is hard to find any discussion of the contents of the cultural programme *as art*. It might be that the artistic quality of the European Capitals of Culture – including Glasgow's – has surpassed the expectations of its audiences in aesthetic terms, but this is simply not documented.

In this way successive conceptual approaches to the European Capital of Culture have accorded with the transition from heritage industry to creative industries outlined in Chapter One. One of the best-known commentaries on Glasgow 1990, that of Beatriz Garcia and Tamsin Cox, says virtually nothing about what happened in the artistic programme or how moving / inspiring / challenging / uplifting it was, and instead falls back on socio-economic indicators of artistic impact. They conclude that it resulted in Glasgow being 'accepted as the leading creative industries hub in Scotland and one of the top ones UK-wide' as well as becoming the 'fastest growing business tourism destination in the UK' (2013, 123). Moreover, the European Commission's report into the effectiveness of the first twenty-five years of European Capitals of Culture in 2010 found that the most effective ones were those that 'embedded the event as part of a long-term culture led regeneration strategy' (12). Once again the message is clear: cultural programming is to be pursued not for the artistic goods that it delivers but for the socio-economic impact it offers to achieve.

The research literature is almost unanimous in accepting that Glasgow 1990 delivered such impacts in a way that revitalised investment in the city and stimulated the local and regional economy. This is why the narrative of Glasgow's hosting of the event is most coherent when situated in the context of the economic development and urban transformations that had in any case been taking place in the city for over a decade. In other words, and paradoxically, existing research presents an argument about the efficacy of the City of Culture event that tends to militate against identifying the City of Culture as the main driver of economic change; and an argument about the efficacy of European cultural policy that tends to undermine the specifically European dimension of it. In fact, the only thing that has really been said for certain – in the near absence of any critical commentary on the artistic programming itself – is that the (economic) success of

Glasgow 1990 was in-keeping with the economic regeneration that was already underway there. After problems of independent evaluation, and of the discrepancy that exists between rhetoric and reality, the third and final question such a tendency leaves unanswered is: who benefits, exactly?

This is the question addressed by Eliot Tretter in one of the most important published critiques of the Glasgow event. Situating it in a historical sequence that had already begun 'in the early 1980s with the property boom in Glasgow that preceded the City of Culture festival' and that continued into the year of the festival itself, Tretter succinctly identifies 'a number of political controversies that swirled around' it (113). He draws on David Harvey's discussion of how the gradual transformation of culture into an economic resource accords with the process of urban regeneration through cultural entrepreneurship more generally to argue that cultural distinctiveness created opportunities for what Harvey calls 'monopoly rents' (114). This is because when cultural facilities are treated as forms of economic resource, their cultural capital depends to a large extent on claims to special prestige and distinctiveness which are themselves always embedded in particular places or locations. In some cases particular works of art, monuments, buildings and so on are highly valued in their own right; while in others they create additional value in the surrounding geographical area more or less as a knock-on effect of this distinctiveness, through developments such as raising the value of land; increasing the number of visitors to a particular locale; training and maintaining a particular segment of the workforce in specific, highly-valued skills and so on. The outcome of all of this is that when private investors acquire properties and sites that are in close geographical proximity to special cultural resources, the landlords can claim a rental value on that land over and above its value as mere land, because of the fact of the proximity and additional prestige and opportunity this confers.

Tretter points out that there is a significant contradiction built into this process of monetising land through culture. On the one hand, the process rests on an idea that ultimate ownership of culture is implicitly held in common. According to this logic, city councils, local authorities and other organs of local government hold public cultural resources in trust for their citizens so that those resources can be accessed and enjoyed by everyone without anyone owning them outright. On the other hand, the monopoly rents derived from the private ownership of land adjacent to cultural organisations follows the opposite logic: only those with money have access. To some extent this is the nature of the contrast between public and private ownership in any sphere and is not new. But what was new was how the use of culture to leverage economic outcomes increasingly required the former to be transformed into the latter. That is, as cities have become more and more aware of the need to position themselves as attractive places for investors on a global scale, and to actively compete against other cities in other countries for such investment, they have used the symbolic capital associated with the cultural resources they hold in common as a carrot to attract multinational investors, thereby evincing a change in attitude towards those cultural resources themselves. Rather than valuing the cultural resources of the city because of the ways in which culture enriched the lives of the citizens of that city, those resources were now valued because of the opportunities they created for monopoly rents and hence private profit.

In the specific case of Glasgow 1990, Tretter points out two specific aspects that illustrate this process. The first is the process whereby Glasgow created its own brand as European City of Culture, and used it to attract private sponsorship of the arts and the festival. Sponsors were granted 'an exclusive usufruct on the European City of Culture brand' and featured 'in all brochures and other advertising materials' (123). Such exclusivity seemed to suggest that only those sponsors who had been granted use of the City of Culture brand – through purchasing it – could be considered the rightful owners of Glasgow's culture. The second, more important, aspect was the process by which the city 'began to charge people for the use of their own cultural commons' (ibid.), thereby ending the city's long-standing tradition of providing free public admission to all of its impressive number of galleries and museums. For example, the special exhibition 'Glasgow's Glasgow' that was mounted as part of the 1990 festival was located on a newly developed site under Glasgow's Central Station. Making this site suitable for the project required a £5 million development, funded jointly by public and private finance with the public purse covering most of the costs but half of the redeveloped land then being turned over to British Rail, which was subsequently privatised. Glasgow City Council proposed to recoup the money spent on the development by reversing its own previous policies with regard to free access for museums and exhibitions and charging for entry. This in turn resulted in the total number of people who visited 'Glasgow's Glasgow' being significantly smaller than had been forecast, even when the admission fee was reduced, and the council lost £4.5 million on it.

Yet economic mismanagement of public assets is not Tretter's greatest criticism of Glasgow 1990, which is directed instead towards the errors made by the city's elites 'in assuming they could monopolize the city's culture' (127). In contesting this assumption, he highlights a group known as Worker's City, which contained many of Scotland's pre-eminent cultural figures and which developed an explicit opposition to the City Council's attempts to use City of Culture to generate private profit from public resources. The representations of Glasgow, the urban transformations that were taking place, the selective version of the city's history that was put forward during the festival and the kinds of art that it was supporting were all targets of a 'low intensity campaign' kept up by Worker's City throughout the year, squarely in opposition to the City of Culture (125). To Tretter, the Worker's City movement forced the City Council to 'realize that just because they had a monopoly over the cultural resources of Glasgow did not mean they held a monopoly over the culture of Glasgow' (127). This conclusion is a world away from the self-congratulation that characterises the official evaluation of the event.

In the last instance, therefore, Tretter's discussion of Glasgow 1990 in the light of Harvey's analysis of the monopoly of culture reveals a fundamental discrepancy between the interests and agenda of an urban elite and the interests and agenda of the wider citizenry. 'The Worker's City group offered an alternative narrative about the proper use of Glasgow's history and culture that was important to questioning who owned the cultural heritage and legacy of the city' (128). In other words, the conflict between the City of Culture and Worker's City became a wider conflict over what image of the city would be displayed to the world and for whom. Far from the harmonious picture of urban regeneration through culture painted in the post-event evaluation of 1990, what emerges instead is a quite different sense of the city and its people. There was thus a disjunction between the interests of different stakeholders: European planners, local politicians, local investors and business developers and ordinary residents, which was also a disjunction between the agenda of the event 'owners' and its 'hosts' (Theodoraki, 186–8); and between external perspectives on the city and those that are internal to it (Graham, 1009–11).

FROM DUBLIN 1991 TO CORK 2005

Research by Deborah Stevenson has shown that over a period extending for approximately a decade either side of the millennium, the main tendencies in cultural policy and infrastructural development around the UK and beyond were 'significantly influenced' by their 'origins within Labour-dominated councils in the United Kingdom and the emerging Third Way schema of the British Labour Party' (2004, 125). This emergence was very much in evidence in the (Labour-run) council that hosted Glasgow 1990 and in the wider transition from heavy to cultural industries in and around the city to which its year as European City of Culture contributed. Moreover, Ron Griffiths argues that New Labour influence on cultural policy achieved 'an international purchase because of the operation of an extensive knowledge network (involving such organizations as Comedia, Demos and Partners for Livable Communities)' (2006, 428). He cites Glasgow and Dublin, both former European Cities of Culture, as examples of places frequently claimed as urban success stories by New Labour acolytes. Although such a claim is not a direct comment on the City of Culture festival in either case and is really directed at the transformation of the urban environment more generally in both cities, it is clear that the former made some contribution to the latter. When Dublin hosted European City of Culture in 1991, the year after Glasgow, even though the gains to the tourist industry were not as great as expected because the 'number of overnight stays' in tourist hotels in Dublin 'dropped' (Griffiths, 418), the involvement of the festival in more widespread strategies of urban, social and economic redevelopment nevertheless made it possible to claim it as a success.

To celebrate the enduring contribution of diverse cities to European culture, in the 1990s a total of nine Cities of Culture were selected for the millennium year 2000, including two (Prague and Krakow) from states that were due to accede to the European Union in 2004. In 1999, it became European Union policy that different member states should be allocated years in which they would host the newly re-named European Capital of Culture on a rotation basis. This meant that, with the number of EU states increasing, there was a risk that the interval between each member state's hosting of it would increase too, so it became policy that two or even three different cities could be selected every year. At that point, on the basis that the project requires lengthy lead-time, host nations were allocated for the years 2005–19 in one swoop and individual member states were free to select their host cities by whatever means they saw fit. When Ireland was allocated the year 2005 and Cork emerged as its only candidate city, Cian O'Callaghan and Denis Linehan have emphasised that this was in part motivated by a desire for urban regeneration of the city, and especially its docklands, to catch up with what had happened in Dublin: 'Long after Dublin had redeveloped significant sections of its docklands and rejuvenated the cultural quarter of Temple Bar, the city centre of Cork was rundown and the urban realm in general was in poor shape' (2007, 312).

During Cork's year as European Capital of Culture, the reach and influence of New Labour cultural policy outside Britain could still be discerned, especially in the 'increasingly central role that cultural policy has played in developmental politics of the city' and in how the city's 'new governance structures have used these policies for novel methods of place promotion' (O'Callaghan and Linehan, 320). In other words, in Cork, as had been the case in both Dublin and Glasgow, the use of European Capital of Culture to drive economic investment and contribute to a revitalisation of the urban environment was part of a wider series of developments more than a decade in the making. Among its impacts were that the city 'generated extensive national media coverage as a result of the ECoC; during the year itself, the city also received coverage in British newspapers' (Garcia and Cox, 123). A more critical summary of Cork 2005 is provided by Hudec, Remoaldo, Urbanciková and Ribeiro, who, having noted the political conflicts associated with Glasgow 1990 around public or private ownership of the cultural infrastructure, list Cork as an instance among 'other cases where controversy has been raised regarding the cultural and urban regeneration projects implemented in the aim of the hosting of an ECOC event' (2019, 4).

In Cork's host year, O'Callaghan and Linehan suggest that 'the pro-growth urban imaginary was contested, as the re-invention of the city's material and symbolic urban identities clashed with the expectations of practitioners in the local arts scene' (312). They found that among many of the residents of the city one of the causes of frustration with the 2005 programme was a perceived emphasis on high art, which, drawing on research by Kieran Keohane, they attribute to Cork's history as a provincial mercantile city in which the rapid rise in social status of merchant families involved the affirmation of that status through the appropriation of cultural capital based on models imported from abroad, which in turn set the tone for the cultural agenda of the city. Fitjar, Rommetvedt and Berg make almost the same point about the rise of an oil-rich but culturally unsophisticated class in Stavanger, Norway, and how it too resulted in a somewhat high-art cultural programme during that city's year as European Capital of Culture, 2008.

What is notable about O'Callaghan and Linehan's analysis of Cork 2005 is how closely it replicates Eliot Tretter's description of the situation in Glasgow in 1990 whereby the city council and its partners attempted to monopolise the cultural resources, thereby failing to recognise that the primary cultural resource of the city was its people, who resisted such monopolisation of the culture. (The contrast with Glasgow's strapline for its hosting of the 2014 Commonwealth Games, 'People Make Glasgow', is striking.) They identify in Cork a legal battle over planning permission for a proposed development site on Water Street, especially for a proposed iconic seventeen-storey tower to function as a 'Landmark building' (315) as an instance where the views and interests of community groups and residents did not gain much purchase with private developers, who 'promoted prosperity and growth over social inclusion and citizenship' (318). Moreover, just as Tretter identified the Worker's City group of artists and cultural figures in Glasgow as one that not only opposed the appropriation of the cultural agenda by the city planning authorities but actively maintained its own alternative cultural programme throughout the City of Culture year, so too a comparable phenomenon emerged in Cork. A popular cultural group called 'Where's Me Culture' was set up there at the end of 2004, alluding through its name to the song 'Where's me Jumper' by the local band The Sultans of Ping FC. Like Worker's City in Glasgow, it expressed gradually increasing degrees of suspicion over the city's control over the cultural agenda and eventually ran its own parallel programme of activities throughout 2005, especially its Big Party and Big Picnics.

In exploring 'how opposition to the production of Cork's image as portrayed in the Cork 2005 event was mounted' (319), O'Callaghan and Linehan make clear that they do not consider either side to represent any greater degree of authenticity with regard to cultural work than the other. What emerges from their account is the same sense of contestation over the cultural resources, definitions of culture and right to the city that Tretter found in 1990. Situating Cork 2005 in the context of the regeneration of other waterside cities in Ireland they thus conclude that 'revitalised docklands in Dublin, Cork and Limerick have become emblematic landscapes of the post-industrial Irish city' (311). Looking across the Celtic Sea they could have added two British cities that have strong historical and cultural links with Ireland: Glasgow, and another subsequent Capital of Culture, Liverpool.

LIVERPOOL AND THE CONTEST FOR 2008

The situation in 2005 whereby Cork was Ireland's only candidate to host European Capital of Culture could hardly contrast more greatly with the UK's next host year. During the allotting of host years to host countries which took place in one fell swoop in 1999, Britain was allocated the 2008 festival and, with 2008, one genuinely new element entered the field: an unprecedented degree of competition among British cities to be selected. To consider the dynamics of the bidding process for Liverpool 2008, it is necessary to go all the way back to the candidate stage.

In November 2000 the Department for Culture, Media and Sport (DCMS) announced its decision to structure the selection process in the form of an open competition split into two phases, with an unlimited number of cities able to express their interest in stage one and then a limited number of candidates being shortlisted and taken forward for serious consideration in stage two. Announcement of the winner was originally anticipated late in 2002 but, owing to the fact that twelve different cities from all four nations of the UK entered the competition entailing a lengthy assessment process, the announcement did not take place until the summer of 2003. This was the first time there had been anything like such high levels of competition for the accolade. Of the original twelve candidates (Belfast, Birmingham, Bradford, Brighton, Bristol, Canterbury, Cardiff, Inverness, Liverpool, Newcastle, Norwich and Oxford), six (Belfast, Bradford, Brighton, Canterbury, Inverness and Norwich) were rejected outright in the first phase of the selection competition, leaving a shortlist of Birmingham, Bristol, Cardiff, Liverpool, Newcastle and Oxford, from which Liverpool was ultimately successful.

As discussed above, one of the weaknesses of European Capitals of Culture has been the lack of genuinely independent evaluation of the impact made by each. Evaluation is often carried out both too soon after the event and by those too close to its activities to attain genuine clarity. According to Greg Richards:

There has been almost no evaluation work that has started in the pre-implementation phase. This is not surprising because cities do not feel it is worthwhile to conduct research on an event that may not happen. However, this runs the risk of missing an important element of the evaluation, because unless measurement starts before the event there is no baseline against which subsequent changes can be measured (2015, 123).

An evaluative baseline beginning in the pre-implementation stage, that is, before a particular city's year-long hosting of European Capital of Culture has commenced and possibly even before the city in question has been selected as host is necessary because this alone is what would make it possible to identify what (if anything) is changed in a given city by the hosting of the event. Because such a baseline was absent from the pre-implementation stage for Glasgow's host year 1990, for example, although almost all commentators agree that the impact of hosting European City of Culture was significant, almost none of them can say precisely what it was. As Theodoraki puts it, 'counterfactual considerations of what would have changed in the cities either way and baseline data for establishing event effects and causality, is missing' (190).

Richards's case study is the candidature of the Dutch city-region of BrabantStad, which was centred on Eindhoven but in fact incorporated a network of five different cities, to host the 2018 European Capital of Culture. Almost uniquely, this bid proposed starting its evaluation of the final event 'in the candidate phase of the ECOC process' (2015, 123), thereby making it possible to build the baseline from which change can be measured and the criteria by which to measure it. A potentially fertile opportunity to demonstrate the longitudinal impact of the festival in both economic and social terms was thus missed when the city lost out to Leeuwarden. Yet the approach suggested by Richards (and indeed by the BrabantStad bid) of starting the evaluation in the candidate phase is of potentially enormous value, not only because it enables successfully selected host cities to clearly demonstrate the impact achieved by their year as host, but also through the counterfactual example adumbrated by Theodoraki to identify what benefits – if any – are to be realised through the mere fact of bidding, whether successful or not. Richards's case study of BrabantStad's attempt to begin final evaluation at the pre-implementation stage therefore draws attention to the need for greater research into the candidate phase and to the potential for such research to enable a critical evaluation of the competition between cities that the bidding contest entails. Such an approach can fruitfully be applied in retrospect to a discussion of the UK's unsuccessful candidates to host European Capital of Culture in 2008, to explore what was gained through the bidding process even for candidates which were not selected.

Throughout the selection competition from late 2000 to Summer 2003, in order to create the impression of scrupulous fairness, the DCMS was at pains to point out that the selection committee contained representatives from all four nations of the United Kingdom, just as the four nations themselves were all represented among the bidding cities. Only three of these, Belfast, Cardiff, and Inverness, emphasised any sort of national dimension to their bids and the nations in question were respectively Northern Ireland, Wales and Scotland – that is, not Britain. None of the English cities took this 'national' approach or even particularly emphasised their Englishness.

In the Welsh case, the conjunction between city and nation can be glimpsed in a Cabinet Proposal dated 16 November 2000, in which Byron Davies, Chief Executive of the City and County of Cardiff, noted that 'based on the success of the Glasgow European City of Culture, a successful bid would provide a major regeneration opportunity for Cardiff and Wales' (City and County of Cardiff, 2000). This proposition is notable not only for the now-familiar rhetoric of economic regeneration through culture discussed in Chapter One, but also for the specific aspiration to emulate an existing formula that had already been tried and tested in Glasgow, and for elevating it onto a national, that is all-Wales, level (something which even Glasgow did not promise for Scotland). Building on this rhetoric, the cabinet proposal contains the summary of a report that had been commissioned for the council by its contractor, Cardiff Marketing Ltd, which made the following conclusions:

- Cardiff could lead a Welsh bid ('Cardiff, the Capital City of Wales reflecting the cultural ambitions and activity of the whole of Wales').
- There is 100% support for a bid and a willingness to share in bid [sic] within South Wales Arts organisations.
- There are serious financial implications in making a bid. Initially, in preparing the bid and in successfully managing the programme of activity.

- The funding requirements cannot be met by the County Council alone and therefore the Welsh Assembly for Wales [sic] will need to be persuaded to support a bid.
- Great opportunity to regenerate communities throughout Wales through culture (City and County of Cardiff, 2000).

Although there may have been '100% support' for the bid among those at the meeting, the idea that this could have been recreated around the whole of South Wales seems both implausible and faintly ludicrous, suggesting that even if all the arts organisations who had been canvassed were unanimously in favour, these could only have encompassed a relatively narrow selection of the total number of creative organisations in the region. The Welsh national rhetoric is equally problematic, partly because it is difficult to imagine the other subsequently shortlisted candidates, all of which were in England, treating the idea of an 'English' bid in the singular; and partly also because it is not clear what it meant to suggest that a cultural programme being proposed for Cardiff could 'reflect' the cultural ambitions of the whole of Wales.

A rhetorical gap between national imagining and city-based delivery therefore typified the Cardiff bid for European Capital of Culture. Thus, when it was shortlisted, the Lord Mayor of Cardiff, Russell Goodway, and Lynne Williams and Yvette Vaughn Jones of Cardiff's European Capital of Culture 2008 bid made a presentation to the National Assembly for Wales (now the Senedd) Culture Committee of 6 November 2002, again emphasising the twin elements of economic potential and national aspiration. They drew attention to an economic impact study showing 'the importance of the cultural sector in terms of creating and maintaining jobs in the city' (National Assembly for Wales, 5). At the same time, they also drew attention to how hosting major international events such as the Rugby World Cup and Cardiff Singer of the World had put Cardiff on the national stage, and argued that 'culture in its widest sense is now a core business in Cardiff' (ibid.). This emphasis on the embeddedness of culture in the economic life of the city led them to reflect that the bid had been shortlisted because 'the project team were able to convince the judges of Cardiff's cultural excellence and ability to deliver' (ibid.). In other words, consideration of the actual content of the proposed cultural programme, and whether it would turn out to be any good or not, was a distant third priority behind economic potential and national aspiration. The cultural programme had been branded together under the tag line: 'Take me somewhere good' but the minutes of the 6 November meeting say nothing else about its content at all. How precisely the prior events which Cardiff had successfully hosted could be said to have a national dimension was not specified. Instead, the presentation made by the bid team to the committee introduced a third element – beyond economic opportunity and national aspiration – which was the European dimension:

> The successful bid relied on emphasising the European dimension to Cardiff's bid and showed Wales as an outward-looking nation. The bid presented the distinctive culture of Wales and highlighted how Cardiff is a representative of UK culture (National Assembly for Wales, 5).

Lest it be seen to be jumping the gun, the word 'successful' here refers to the bid's success in being shortlisted rather than in securing the overall title, which it proved ultimately unable to do. While Cardiff as representative of Wales, of the UK and of Europe need not necessarily be contradictory, the earlier (and continuing) rhetoric of Wales as a distinctive nation, and of Cardiff's bid as bearer of that nationhood, does appear to undercut the vitality of the other two corners of the Wales–UK–Europe triangle and leave it in danger of collapsing. If anything, these different geographical dimensions became even more stretched when Belfast failed to proceed beyond the pre-selection stage and Welsh First Minister Rhodri Morgan played up the pan-Celtic dimension:

> Cardiff will represent the other Celtic parts and with Belfast out of the running Cardiff is definitely the only capital city in the running … We are the only city that is backed by a whole country (quoted in Butler and Parker, 2002).

A rhetoric of Celtic solidarity is emphasised alongside a separate rhetoric of Welsh nationhood and the idea that Cardiff's bid, in representing the whole of Wales, was somehow the only one with the support of a whole nation seems to undercut the idea of common culture that the festival is designed to promote. Moving in several different directions at once, in both a physical, geographical sense as well as in metaphorical and symbolic terms, may be one of the reasons why the Cardiff bid did not succeed in the end. Thus, Ron Griffiths finds that the 'city narrative underpinning the Cardiff bid is less sharply defined than Liverpool's, partly because of its status as a bid for the whole of Wales as well as for the city, and partly because Cardiff has been far less subject to the (negative) stereotyping to which Liverpool has had to respond' (425).

In fact, Griffiths's evaluation of the strengths and weaknesses of the 2008 bids is worth considering at length because it is the first time that a comparative approach had been taken to the candidate process. Griffiths finds that one of the weaknesses of the Cardiff bid was the lack of 'cultural sector expertise among the seconded staff' which 'meant that the cultural content of the bid was being given insufficiently careful attention' (421). This may account for the artistic programme itself receiving minimal prominence in the bid, although it must be said that owing to the way in which cities around Europe have used the Capital of Culture to drive social and economic outcomes, this downplaying of the cultural content of what is supposed to be a cultural programme occurs surprisingly often.

Griffiths also points out that the rationale for the Cardiff bid 'was essentially a marketing one: participating in the competition for the nomination was seen as a useful method of raising the city's profile. There was little expectation that Cardiff would be the eventual winner' (420). In making this point, it is useful to note how Cardiff's bid differed from that of another candidate, Bristol. Griffiths shows that the Bristol candidature was characterised by 'concerns among the leadership of the council about the anticipated cost of making a good quality bid, coupled with a lack of confidence about the likelihood of success' since the case for regeneration on socio-economic grounds was weaker here than Liverpool or Cardiff (421). The result of these concerns was that rather than being led by the council, the bid was driven by the independent Bristol Cultural Development Partnership, who identified 'gaps in the city's cultural infrastructure' and 'saw the ECOC bid as a means of keeping up the campaign for cultural development' in the city (ibid.).

The Cardiff and Bristol situations contrasted sharply with that of Liverpool, where the city council was enthusiastic for the bid from the very beginning, thereby creating opportunities for close interconnection between the 2008 bid and other development strategies – which had been a key feature of Glasgow's hosting of City of Culture in 1990. As Griffiths says of Liverpool:

Against that background, of an ambitious strategic vision for the city and a newly strengthened institutional capacity to bring it about, the opportunity to make an ECC bid came at exactly the right time. With the Glasgow experience very much in mind, the city's political leadership recognized that it offered an ideal way of symbolizing the city's hoped-for transformation, and instilling confidence in the city's ability to achieve it (422).

In addition to having a strong vision embedded in a long-term plan for the regeneration of the city on the part of the council, two further important factors highlighted by Griffiths are that Liverpool had been identified as an area of economic need by the European Union and so had access to European funding, which meant that its bid could be 'staffed and resourced to a substantially higher level than that of the other contenders' (ibid.); and that the city had reached an undertaking with Manchester not to oppose each other so that although none of the bids from England stressed their Englishness as such, Liverpool was left as the only contender from a geographically large and populous region, the North West of England. This Liverpool–Manchester entente is further emphasised by the fact that the Liverpool Culture Company, which oversaw both the bid and the subsequent event itself, was headed by Sir Bob Scott, who had been head of Manchester's two (unsuccessful) Olympic bids.

According to Griffiths, the only one of the other shortlisted cities to boast a local leadership network that was clearly embedded in wider strategic visions was Newcastle-Gateshead. He goes on to suggest that the amalgamation in one bid of these two cities was 'able to draw on the fierce civic loyalty of local populations that felt disregarded, disadvantaged and misunderstood by the country at large' (422). This contrasts with Bristol, which struggled to provide a distinctive identity narrative because it has not had the same adversity and so could not call on the same fierce pride. Also, Bristol's location on the edge of a mainly rural region too diverse to have a strong identity, and in which a single regional capital is not even agreed upon, militated against success – a local variant on the problem experienced by Cardiff in trying to speak for the whole of Wales. Liverpool's bid, by contrast was the 'cleverest' in terms of the way it turned 'potentially negative attributes into positive ones' and made itself able to 'speak to other, stressed, areas of Europe and the world' because of them (424). In June 2003 Liverpool was duly announced as the UK's nomination for European Capital of Culture 2008, and the unsuccessful cities 'were left with difficult decisions about how far to proceed with their intensely debated and carefully crafted plans' (419). This dilemma – what becomes of the unsuccessful bids – is a key consideration to explore further.

Having established the importance of building event-evaluation into the candidate stage (as discussed above), Greg Richards followed up his initial insight in a subsequent paper co-written with Lénia Marques, which was possibly the first detailed case study of a failed European Capital of Culture bid. As with Richards's earlier paper, Richards and Marques focused on the bid made by BrabantStad in the Netherlands to be selected for 2018, drawing attention to one of the key shifts that has taken place in the overall programme since its inception in 1985. Whereas the early cities were simply appointed, the experience of Glasgow in 1990 revealed the significant socio-economic gains to be made from hosting the event which in turn made doing so both more desirable and more competitive. One result of this is that the cost of bidding alone is now much higher than it was and can easily reach sums in excess of £2 million. In a world of tightly monitored public spending, they argue, local governments are unwilling to spend such sums if they cannot be certain of success – but, with numerous competitors, winning cannot be guaranteed. Therefore, in effect, it is necessary to structure the bid in a way that enables it to deliver a degree of success – that is, to unlock a certain number of positive benefits for the city in question – even if it doesn't actually win. Richards and Marques's first example of this is the London 2012 Olympic bid, which incorporated a plan for leveraging social benefits through the bid process itself – whether or not it was awarded the games – and therefore could be considered successful either way. To highlight the case, they note that although Madrid abandoned its efforts to host the Olympics after three unsuccessful bids, the 'whole candidacy process had generated over €9 billion in economic benefits for Madrid in spite of the successive negative outcomes' (Richards and Marques 2016, 182).

For their main example, however, Richards and Marques analyse the ultimately unsuccessful candidate of BrabantStad for European Capital of Culture 2018. One of its characteristic features was that Brabant is a province rather than a city as such, and BrabantStad (Brabant City) was a bureaucratically invented entity manufactured for the purposes of the bid and consisting of the five cities Breda,

Eindhoven, Den Bosch, Helmond and Tilburg. In this, it seemed to accord with the growing tendency both within the European Capital of Culture programme, and in worldwide city-regional development more generally, to place the emphasis on the city as an economic driver for a broader region capable of crossing administrative and even in some cases national borders. A good example among European Capitals of Culture is Lille-Métropole (2004) in which, according to Didier Paris and Thierry Baert, the whole 'territory constitutes a functional meta-system' (2011, 33) and whose hosting of the festival was presented from the beginning as a 'cross-border event' (35), emphasising ties to London and Paris as well as Belgium and the Netherlands. The bureaucratic creation of Newcastle-Gateshead for the 2008 bidding process in the UK is a comparable case: though not cross-border in a national sense, the bid encompassed more than a single city.

Drawing on Pierluigi Sacco and Giorgio Blessi's concept of a progressive cultural district, Richards and Marques identify five categories into which the different variables for judging the BrabantStad bid could be grouped. These are: Development; Attraction; Quality; Sociality; and Networking. Of the five, measures of development, the attraction of skilled workers and investment, and enhancement of the quality of life, are primarily economic metrics whereas questions of sociality and networking refer to the softer, less tangible (but no less real) indicators of cultural activity. Because economic gains tend to accrue to successful candidates to a greater degree than to unsuccessful ones, and although the London and Madrid Olympic cases show that failed bids can bring economic gain, Richards and Marques focus on these softer categories. In the process, they shift the discourse from the directly instrumental language of economic 'impact' and instead talk about broader cultural and social 'effect' (189).

Their research found that 'unsuccessful bids may also have wider-reaching effects, even if these are not as clear-cut as many policy-makers might wish' (192) and that the experience of bidding itself generates a 'halo effect' that lasts beyond the bid period, even in the case of an unsuccessful bid (ibid.). These positive effects fall into three specific areas: first, the experience of collaborating on the bid built new forms of relationship and new partnerships, which, second, enabled the development of new skills, and, third, the programming of new creative work. Cultural operators therefore indicated that they were likely to continue the collaborations formed during

BrabantStad's bidding process, even if the pace of collaborative work was likely to fall in the absence of European funding. It also appears that the new contacts formed during the bidding experience generated new projects and initiatives that are 'unrelated to the ECOC itself, simply because new links have been formed between potential networking partners' (193). In other words, through the development of new collaborations, new skills and new work the experience of having participated in the Capital of Culture selection process brought soft beneficial effects to the city-region of BrabantStad even though its bid did not win; and the examples of London and Madrid's Olympic bids suggests there may also have been direct economic impact as well, though admittedly of a lower degree than that accumulated by the eventual winner, the city of Leeuwarden. That much of the new work that had been proposed went ahead anyway downplays the impact and difference made by winning the event as opposed to merely bidding for it.

Tellingly, Richards and Marques say much the same thing about Newcastle's candidature for the UK's nomination of the 2008 instalment: 'Rather than simply licking their wounds, Newcastle-Gateshead instead invested in another cultural events programme, at least partially rationalised by the argument that the ECOC bidding process had delivered £24 million worth of economic impact for an investment of around £6.5 million' (182). Presumably, the opening of cultural facilities such as the Sage, Gateshead and the Baltic Centre are examples of what they have in mind when they suggest that merely 'bidding for events is often seen as a strategic tool for cities, allowing them to develop towards the aims stated in the bid' (188). Implicitly, the argument runs, if bidding is carried out sensitively it can contribute to promoting the region, building capacity and attracting investment, therefore enabling other positive outcomes even if it does not achieve its ostensible goal. The opening in Cardiff of the £107 million Wales Millennium Centre in 2004, the year after Cardiff failed to secure the European Capital of Culture nomination, is a comparable case.

The examples of these landmark buildings, which look and feel quite similar to each other, raise a further consideration in evaluating how culture has been used to regenerate cites: the question of local distinctiveness. Philip Boland has published a comparative analysis of the urban regeneration policies of the cities of Cardiff and Liverpool for the period 2004–14 and concluded that 'despite the aspirations to create local uniqueness, place marketing frequently results in sameness in both policy and practice' (2007, 1028). He noted, for example, that *Cardiff's Community Strategy 2004–14* 'emphasises the city-regional context and the need to promote the knowledge economy, business and cultural tourism, and events and festivals via building on its capital city status' (2007, 1029). In turn, the language and ideas of the Cardiff strategy are distinctly echoed by *The Liverpool city region: contributing to the northern way*, a strategy document produced by the Mersey Partnership in 2005 to cover approximately the same period and where there is a corresponding 'strong emphasis on retail, leisure, sport and culture... with the Capital of Culture promising significant economic and cultural transformations' (Boland, 2007, 1031). It is notable that even though Boland's analysis is about each city's urban regeneration strategy more generally and is not confined to the Capital of Culture bidding, he nevertheless alludes to it in both cases. Typically, regeneration of cities through the development of cultural industries 'is followed up by promotional campaigns and the aggressive marketing of cities through the construction of new, deliberately crafted, images that replace old and/or negative ones' (2007, 1027). But as we have seen, this 'soft' effect can be achieved with or without securing the Capital of Culture crown. Moreover, Boland draws attention to the emergence of a small number of national and international experts in areas such as urban regeneration to show that in many cases, the same external consultants, advisers and specialists are brought in to advise on city development in different places so that 'the situation is one where the same names and ideas dominate the context of local economic development policy, to the extent that local economic development policy in Cardiff and Liverpool is effectively the same' (2007, 1033).

Ron Griffiths has a different perspective on this commonly observed tendency towards uniformity among candidate cities. In his account, that the bids for 2008 were all similar is the result of the criteria laid down by the Department for Culture, Media and Sport rather than anything inherent in the character or activities of the cities themselves. Arguing that the leading contenders Bristol, Cardiff and Liverpool all eschewed a high-art definition of culture in favour of a more holistic, inclusive and participatory approach, he points out that there are numerous benefits for each city's bid team in setting the cultural agenda in this way: it makes it possible to demonstrate a base of popular support for the bid itself, especially among people not considered the typical audience for cultural events, as well as making it possible to forge connections with other policy and developmental goals.

For example, the bids in all three cities strongly argued that there was an important relationship between 'culture and social cohesion' (Griffiths, 427) and in fact Griffiths identifies this commitment to social cohesion as one of the benefits of bidding per se. One of his critiques of the 2008 selection process was the 'unhealthy' competition it fostered between cities (429) and how this required them to present themselves in an essentially homogeneous way. But in his account, although the selection criteria made them all speak the same language, what they actually did was quite different and so created opportunities for renewal in each:

> far from the cultural differences between cities being submerged by the demands of the competition, cities were in fact able to articulate substantially different cultural 'personalities' – some more successfully than others. In addition, while the vehicles created in the three cities to organize the bids seem on the surface to be remarkably similar, their relationships to wider political structures were quite different (429).

This account explicitly contests recurring accusations of homogeneity that have dogged the Capitals of Culture, and urban regeneration movements more generally. This was not simply a matter of pursuing distinctive character as an end in its own right because Griffiths argues that, although Bristol, Cardiff and Liverpool's bids all emphasised the economic benefit culture can bring to a city, 'it is the economic importance of the cultural and creative industries that is played up, rather than that of tourism and visitors' (427). That is, unlike other analyses of European Capital of Culture which measure economic impact through increased (or decreased) tourism, these bids focused on how the emerging creative industries were embedded in the life of the cities. There was thus more focus on the social effect of integration than on tourism, which Griffiths takes as evidence that the 'unrelenting economic instrumentalism of the 1980s and 1990s' had moved on to a more nuanced understanding of how 'social capital' can be 'fostered' (ibid.):

> it seems to be a matter of common agreement among them that, far from being a dry and uninspired box ticking exercise, the process was generally highly productive in provoking a wider recognition (if not a deeper questioning) of the part that culture can play in the life of cities. In each city

a range of imaginative projects were undertaken during the formulation of the bid, to encourage participation and generate ideas, that would not otherwise have occurred. Even in the losing cities there is talk about a 'momentum' around culture built up during the bid that participants are anxious to keep going (429).

Here at last is the counterfactual case that has so often been absent from analyses of the impacts, effects or effectiveness of successive Capitals of Culture. A counterfactual case is necessary to posit a baseline from which the precise difference made by the event – economically, culturally or socially – can be identified. Without such a baseline, it is more or less impossible to say what difference, if any, the festival itself has really made. This is why the official event analyses carried out on behalf of the European Union tend to be blandly self-congratulatory, without necessarily being able to measure any specifics.

However, from a European perspective, the counterfactual case provided by the examples of the failed bids of Bristol, Cardiff and Newcastle for 2008 is somewhat sobering. Since all three of them seem to have realised some economic impact and social effect through the mere fact of bidding, when compared to them the difference made to Liverpool by eventually winning the accolade appears to be downplayed. In this sense, bidding for the crown of European Capital of Culture seems to be a game which the contenders won just by entering. This realisation de-emphasises the impact of the European Capital of Culture programme and points up instead the impact of urban regeneration programmes that were happening with or without European investment.

As was the case with Glasgow, most research about Liverpool's hosting of the 2008 European Capital of Culture has focused on the capacity of the event to deliver economic and/or social outcomes rather than on the quality or content of the cultural programme. Ooi, Håkanson and LaCava see Liverpool, along with Glasgow and Lille (2004) as part of a 'trinity' of cities that have subsequently been treated as 'successes or role models' (422) in both the implementation and evaluation of the festival. However, they conclude that it was treated 'largely as an opportunity for symbolic reinvention, with little improvement to the social and economic inequality in the city' (324). Yi-De Liu suggests that the event provided the occasion to 'create a distinctive identity that captures the unique spirit of a city and to promote attractive city images' (2015, 147) in order to promote opportunities for both investment and tourism on a global stage. There is, however, a deep irony in this promotion of a distinctive identity since it is what in essence all cities of culture do. Brian Graham points out that the more this kind of policy is practised, 'the less locally distinctive identity is likely to become' (1009) because paradoxically they all become equally distinctive.

Philip Boland goes even further, arguing that Liverpool as European Capital of Culture did not involve certain sections of the city's population, especially those of lower incomes. In the process it created a new form of marginalisation which 'sidelines important dimensions of cultural life' and failed to 'incorporate *all* aspects of local life, however unpalatable some might be' (2010a, 637). Moreover, he argues, the event evinced a 'spatial bias towards the city centre' from which many residents in the poorer estates and suburbs felt 'alienated' and not only did the festival itself fail to combat this form of social exclusion but the 'regulatory mechanisms associated with culture-led regeneration negatively impacted on certain demographic groups' (2010a, 639). Overall, Boland's analysis of Liverpool 2008 thus 'challenges the hyperbole of culture-led transformation' to reveal 'different geographies of culture, different cultural experiences and different socio-economic realities' (2010a, 640). It is the dilemma of Glasgow 1990 again: what counts as success in a corporate sense does not necessarily make for an enriched cultural life among the whole population of the city and may actively distort it.

In other words, even granted that there is an economic impact to be derived from hosting the European Capital of Culture, who precisely benefits from that economic impact remains unclear and it is unlikely that members of the working-class population do so. Moreover, it appears that this impact is achieved primarily from within the host country rather than from without. The majority (83 per cent) of cultural tourists to Liverpool during 2008 came from the UK (Liu, 151), just as the majority of cultural tourists to its sister host city, the Norwegian city of Stavanger, came from Norway (Fitjar et al., 69), while 58 per cent of tourists to the Romanian city of Sibiu in 2007 came from Romania (Nicula and Chindriş, 123), and Porto experienced only a 1.5 per cent increase in foreign tourists when it hosted the festival in 2001 (Balsas, 404). These figures suggest that just as the cultural activities associated with the European Capital of Culture programme can be achieved without relying on the European element of the programme, so too the economic impact can be achieved without reference to what happens at European level, since this is not the level at which that impact is primarily generated.

In turn, these two realisations account for the fact that in the wake of the increased competition between cities for a place in the global limelight, not only has securing each country's nomination for European Capital of Culture become much more hotly contested, but a number of separate, comparable festivals in individual nations has also started to spring up. Thus, in the aftermath of the success of Lille-Métropole in 2004, Didier Paris and Thierry Baert point out that there was a proposed legacy event in the form of a regional capital of culture, 'where one of the region's major cities is awarded this title every second year' (40). Ooi, Håkanson and LaCava have likewise identified a 'proliferation of the "cultural capitals" concept around the world', with Ghazni, Afghanistan acting as Islamic Culture Capital in 2013 and Barranquilla, Colombia as American Capital of Culture in the same year (427).

One such parallel festival is the UK City of Culture launched in 2009, the year after the Liverpool European Capital of Culture. The remainder of this chapter will look at how UK City of Culture illustrates the broad process identified here by leveraging a range of the hard and soft benefits that had been unlocked first through participating in the European Capital of Culture programme, and then by bypassing it. As such, and given what subsequently happened in the relationship between Britain and the European Union, it feels in retrospect that UK City of Culture is tantamount to a breakaway movement that circumvents the European programme on which it was modelled and that has significant implications for many other aspects of contemporary British cultural life.

UK CITY OF CULTURE: AN UNLOSABLE GAME

It was argued above that paying close attention to the failed bids for European Capital of Culture is worthwhile because it reveals much about how the bids have been structured. In a scenario where hosting the event is highly prestigious, competition to secure it is fierce and city councils frequently turn to external consultants, lobby groups and bid writers at an outlay often running into millions of pounds simply on the bids themselves. Needless to say, cash-strapped city councils cannot commit to such an outlay without some guarantee of a return on their investment, but in a competitive selection process there is no guarantee of winning. In other words, a bid must be constructed in such a way as to enable the city in question to realise some of the desired benefits of hosting the event, even if that city fails to win the selection. In this regard, the candidature of Birmingham for European Capital of Culture 2008 is particularly instructive. With typically excessive rhetoric, it claimed that winning the event would result in an investment of '£100 million' into the local economy, and the creation of '10,000 new jobs' (Butler and Parker, 2002). Having failed to secure the event, the city then had to secure equivalents for these things elsewhere, a process to which the experience of having been a candidate city contributed by raising the profile of the city as a potential site for investment. Moreover, the original bid had also attempted to create a sense of urgency when its director, Stephen Hetherington, warned: 'UK cities won't get a chance at the title for at least another 30 years, so this really is the greatest chance in a generation for Birmingham's image to catch up with the amazing reality' (quoted in ibid.).

In fact, the European Union's policy since 1999 of having two or three Capitals of Culture per year meant that the UK was due to host it again in 2023, only fifteen years later rather than thirty (admittedly still a relatively long time); but the UK's subsequent withdrawal from the European Union eventually meant that Britain would never host it again. But Hetherington's sense of urgency around 2008, the feeling of not wanting to wait too long for the economic and cultural gains that hosting European Capital of Culture could bring, appears to have been more widely shared. As Clopot and Strani point out, the fact that host nations are assigned and host cities selected several years in advance 'outlines the fragility of the procedure, as cities can undergo major shifts in their political, economic and social life during that period' (157). This is the context in which the DCMS decision in 2009, the last full year of the New Labour government, to establish a UK City of Culture is best understood.

When the New Labour government launched UK City of Culture it revealed some similarities and some differences from its European forebear. Like the European version, UK City of Culture would be a year-long festival that aimed to provide social and economic outcomes through the instrumentalisation of participatory arts and cultural activity. Unlike the European version, it would take place not every year but on a four-yearly rotation, beginning in 2013. Also, unlike the European event, which 'has an associated prize of €1.5 million which is awarded at the end of the year-long celebration' (Clopot and Strani, 157), the nomination for UK City of Culture did not come with any financial provision from the DCMS, and was positioned instead as a prestige event that could make it possible to attract other sources of revenue, especially from the private sector. For obvious reasons, there was no equivalent to the requirement post-2010 for European Capital of Culture candidates to articulate their contribution to shared European culture and values. Interestingly, however, neither was there any requirement for UK cities to express a corresponding sense of common British values: the emphasis was almost solely on social and economic regeneration. The inaugural UK City of Culture was awarded to Derry/Londonderry for 2013.

To date, there has been little research into the relationship between the accolades European Capital of Culture and UK City of Culture in either a comparative or materialist way. Philip Boland, Brendan Murtagh and Peter Shirlow (2019) frame their analysis of Derry/Londonderry 2013 within a summary of the economic, social and commercial advantages that the European Capital of Culture can bring to a city and proceed to apply those findings to a discussion of Derry/Londonderry's role as UK City of Culture. However, it is done in a way that elides the two festivals, thereby ruling out the possibility of meaningful comparison between them because the latter is in effect treated purely as an interesting variant on the former with no sharply distinguished differences and therefore paradoxically no clear focus on the precise intersections and areas of overlap that exist between them. This may be owing to the fact that Derry/Londonderry was the first UK City of Culture so obtaining an appropriate conceptual vocabulary for discussion required looking elsewhere.

As is common with critical evaluation of European Capitals of Culture, Boland, Murtagh and Shirlow found that the economic impact of the 2013 UK City of Culture was not as great or as widely shared as had been anticipated, but that there were significant social outcomes derived from the festival, principally in the area of social cohesion. Derry/Londonderry had been a city divided along sectarian lines during the Troubles in Northern Ireland and the opportunity to participate in a shared cultural festival appears (after initial tensions) to have reduced suspicion between different sections of the community. In fact, Boland, Murtagh and Shirlow argue that a major context for the decision to 'award' the mantle of inaugural UK City of Culture to Derry/Londonderry was the 2010 Saville Report into the Bloody Sunday shootings of 30 January 1972. In the wake of the report, on 15 June 2010 Britain formally apologised for the shootings and a month later Derry/Londonderry was announced as the first UK City of Culture so that 'for seasoned commentators and local people securing CoC was a direct response to Saville' (250).

Philip McDermott, Máiréad Nic Craith and Katerina Strani concur with Boland, Murtagh and Shirlow in finding that the most positive outcomes from the 2013 UK City of Culture were the ways it contributed to an 'intercultural dialogue' between different sections of a divided community and different communities within a previously divided city (2016, 610). Noting that the double name of the city Derry/Londonderry was in itself contentious, with separate and distinct connotations for the mainly Irish-Catholic-Nationalist and British-Protestant-Unionist populations, they see the festival as having created an occasion to 're-rename public spaces' as well as for 'the re-framing of collective memory through performances taking places in those public spaces' (ibid.). As an example of this process they cite the Colmcille/Columba pageant, named after the patron saint of the city, in which visitors were given a picture map of the city, setting its history and geography in an international context, with almost no mention of either the seventeenth-century plantation of Ulster which historically divided the city or of the more recent Troubles, therefore creating a sense of 'political neutrality' and even of 'common ground' between different components of the community, as opposed to the deep divisions associated with those historical periods (616). This example leads McDermott, Craith and Strani to find that the 'reframing of collective memories of Colmcille and their (re)presentation as a shared narrative in a common heritage space was a central intercultural aspect of the overall programme' (617).

A further example of the festival's commitment to fostering intercultural conversation between different segments of the community was the musical section of the programme. This was a major challenge because traditional Irish Folk Music has often been seen as an expression of Irish Catholic culture, whereas the drumming and marching music of military bands is more likely to be seen as an articulation of British-Protestant identity. Both musical forms are deeply rooted in the city to the extent that they could not simply be ignored yet there was a real risk of provoking cultural conflict through their production. The Walled City Tattoo, held in August 2013, was then 'a conscious effort to balance two musical events and two musical traditions' (619). On the one hand, a Tattoo is in itself a specific kind of event, chiefly associated with British military bands and therefore potentially antagonistic to the Irish Catholic community, especially given that the Tattoo took place in Ebrington Square, on the site of a former British army barracks. On the other hand, performers were not limited to British military bands but included brass bands from throughout Ireland, dancing music that reflected elements of the Irish folk tradition and drummers and dance troupes who had been invited from across the Commonwealth. McDermott, Craith and Strani interpret this as 'an attempt to acknowledge Northern Ireland's role within this wider international group and thus de-emphasise the direct military connection with Britain' (619). In this way the Walled City Tattoo represented the 'transformation' of a military site and a militaristic musical form into a 'shared' leisure space and a multifaceted form in which everyone could participate freely and equally, and was thus 'deeply symbolic of intercultural dialogue in the city' (ibid.).

It is refreshing to read McDermott, Craith and Strani's account of 2013 because the detail they devote to evaluation of the cultural programme is somewhat unusual since, as we have seen, questions relating to the content and/or the quality of the artistic work tend to be highly marginalised in most discussions of cities of culture (whether European or British). The relatively rare prevalence afforded by them to the cultural programme is largely due to the fact that the cultural content is inseparable from what they say overall about the capacity of Derry/Londonderry as UK City of Culture to foster interculturalism in the community and hence contribute to transcending the conflicts of the past. In short it was the cultural activities, rather than any economic or commercial activity separately defined, that had this cohesive effect.

In fact, this emphasis on interculturalism in the first UK City of Culture (2013) accords with recent developments in the European Capitals of Culture programme to a greater degree than the existing research indicates. In their discussion of the specifically European dimension of European Capitals of Culture, Immler and Sakkers have highlighted the fact that the first twenty-five years' worth of festivals were not considered 'European' enough by the policy makers at the European Union who organise it, so that the selection criteria for candidate cities was therefore shifted post-2010 to require a more explicit articulation of the European dimension. This is problematic, however, because in many cases historically the relationship between different European countries or between different communities within individual countries has been characterised as much by conflict as by solidarity. To Immler and Sakkers therefore there are 'lacunae in the European memory landscape' which they think are 'responsible for shortcomings in the recent immigration policy of the European Union' (21). On the other hand, looking at how bids for European Capital of Culture status in Liverpool and Bristol recognised and addressed the historical involvement of each city with the slave trade, they suggest that the programme has the potential to create and enact a new, ethical form of memory culture which they suggest might in turn encourage other European nations to address their own colonial legacies. They then find that an acknowledgement of complicity with Nazism; of racist immigration policies; and of the marginalisation of a minority (Basque) population featured prominently in bids for European Capital of Culture from the cities of Linz, Marseille and San Sebastián respectively (17). What these bids reveal is a shift in emphasis from the instrumental discourse of urban regeneration and the economic discourse of the creative industries to a value-based discourse based on ethics and shared responsibilities:

> By translating the discourse on social responsibility, peace, human rights and interculturality into cultural programmes they show how 'culture' as a concept of city marketing and as an expression of a competitive, regional identity discourse is successively being complemented by a value paradigm linked to an interest in people, commonalities and differences between groups, addressing questions of inclusion and exclusion (Immler and Sakkers, 23).

This emphasis on interculturality as a newly emergent value in Europe in general and in the European Capitals of Culture in particular was visible in the selection process for Croatia's hosting of the festival in 2020. Desireé Campagna and Daniela Angelina Jelinčić's comparative analysis of the bids made by the three Croatian cities Rijeka, Osijek and Pula for that country's nomination applied the Intercultural Cities Index proposed by the Council of Europe to identify twelve different indicators of interculturalism and then used these as criteria for evaluating each bid. They identified Pula as the strongest bid because it 'was successful at overcoming, by means of governance arrangements, the majority-minority relationship and its implicit inequalities, promoting a reflection on the transversal themes regarding the cultural life of the city' (2018, 64). On the other hand, at the level of cultural content they found that 'none of the three cities devised a cultural programme that was completely intercultural' (ibid.) and in fact remained bounded by old-fashioned discourses of multiculturalism that failed to interrogate the division of the community into separate and non-communicating segments:

> The multiculturalist approach that was adopted from the late 1980s to the early 2000s has now been compromised because it is considered to have contributed to the cultural segregation and ghettoisation of European immigration societies. Interculturalism is seen as an alternative, and on the scheme of interaction between two cultural groups it is much closer to the extreme of fusion, while multiculturalism remains trapped in the half closer to the extreme of conflict (Campagna and Jelinčić, 51).

Although this definition of interculturality lacks complete clarity, the overall distinction between multiculturalism and interculturalism can nevertheless be discerned. It is interesting to note that in the Croatian case Campagna and Jelinčić identify 'gastronomy' as a potential activity for bringing the theory of interculturalism to fruition in practice (54), and the same point had previously been made about the potential of cuisine to bridge the historical division between European and African cultures through genuinely intercultural – as opposed to static multicultural – experience during Marseille's hosting of European Capital of Culture in 2013 (Immler and Sakkers, 15). Moreover, food also played a part in the Derry/Londonderry UK City of Culture that same year – although to the extent that cuisine was not as deeply entrenched a marker of cultural difference between Republican and Unionist communities in Northern Ireland as other activities such as music and dance, the opportunity to use it for bridging those differences may have been more limited there.

If accessing the emergent discourse of interculturalism represents a significant parallel between European Capital of Culture and UK City of Culture, the two also share a further power dynamic because, as with the former accolade, the process of bidding for and securing the latter title has become progressively more competitive over time. Following Hull's tenure as the second UK City of Culture in 2017 the competition for the third instalment in 2021 was the most fiercely contested so far. It involved a two-stage process that recalls the competition held between 2001 and 2003 for European Capital of Culture in 2008, with all the cities that had announced their candidatures being whittled down to a shortlist of five (Paisley, Sunderland, Stoke, Swansea Bay and Coventry) from which the eventual winner (Coventry) was chosen.

A short look at the official communiqués published by each candidate is quite revealing of a number of factors that might have been significant in the eventual selection of Coventry over the others. First of all, Jean Cameron (2019) has shown how once Perth was rejected at the pre-selection stage, the Paisley bid was explicitly articulated as a bid for the whole of Scotland. As with Cardiff's all-Welsh bid for the UK nomination for European Capital in 2008 this sense of national difference may actively have militated against the unionist agenda implicit in the programme overall. From within Wales, the nationalist-separatist angle was entirely played down in the bidding for UK City of Culture 2021. This may have been a result of learning from the failure of the earlier Welsh bid in 2008; and is also owing to the fact that for 2021 there were in fact two Welsh bids at the first (pre-selection) stage, those from St Davids and Swansea Bay, therefore making presenting either one of them as *the* Welsh one impossible.

In truth, there can have been little expectation that St Davids and the Hundred of Dewisland would ever have succeeded. Famously the smallest city in the UK and occupying a picturesque part of the Pembrokeshire coast, St Davids was a world away in scale, location, character and landscape from any other city of culture. Its highly creative bid extended the parameters of the tiny city into the surrounding area by using the ancient land division of the 'Hundred', which was itself based on a pre-Norman unit of land known as a Cantref. In doing so it might have enabled forms of cooperation between different organisations on a relatively modest scale while also raising the profile of a region in which tourism is a key industry.

Ironically, much the same is also true of the other bid from within Wales, that of Swansea Bay, which also raised the profile of its region through bidding (not least because the two regions are so close together). The Swansea bid was publicly supported by the director of the film *Twin Town* (discussed in Chapter One), Kevin Allen. But in terms that recall Eliot Tretter's critique of Glasgow 1990, Naomi Snelling (2017) has shown that Allen was wary of 'the disconnect between overarching cultural bodies and the impact seen on the ground in Welsh towns' and was interested in placing ordinary everyday activities, as distinct from either an imported 'high art' version of culture or a manufactured corporate one, at the centre of the city's cultural identity. These everyday activities included 'rather unorthodox ideas' such as skateboarding, surfing and a campaign to legalise cannabis, that Snelling found 'might not be part of the official bid' and were more likely to be seen as 'a celebration of counterculture' (ibid.). Here is a further instance of the mismatch that can exist between the programming of official bid teams in a city of culture and the hopes and aspirations of cultural practitioners in the same city.

In the only comprehensive analysis of failed bids for European Capital of Culture, Florin Nechita studied the bids of sixty-nine cities for the award for the years 2013–19, of which thirty-nine proceeded to the second (shortlisting) stage. Based on content analysis, and using a mixed-methods approach to identify which aspects of each bid scored positively and which negatively, he found that 'for a successful bid, the engagement of community should be considered as a top priority' (2015, 115). In fact, not only is widespread local awareness of the bid and participation in its development a common feature of successful bids for European Capital, it is also applicable to UK City of Culture. Kevin Allen's attempt to include vernacular cultural practices might have enabled a higher level of participation in the development of the Swansea Bay bid, and its failure to incorporate such activities and so involve local populations might have contributed to its ultimately being unsuccessful.

Beyond the proposed content of the programme, a further factor that may have contributed to the disconnect between the bid team and the residents of the city seems to have been its very name. The Swansea team picked up on the trend whereby successful bidding cities increasingly embody a broader network or region that is geographically greater than itself, and moved creatively to engineer into existence the amorphous entity Swansea Bay (as distinct from the mere city of Swansea) as the focus of the bid. But if the elevated focus from city to city-region has potential advantages in terms of building a network, cultivating skills and building capacity, there is also a downside – especially if the city in question takes the form of a somewhat artificially created entity, summoned into being purely for the purposes of the bid. This is what Richards found in the case of BrabantStad's bid to be the Dutch host of European Capital of Culture in 2018: as a city-region created by aggregating five different cities into a wider unit, few of its citizens thought of themselves as belonging to BrabantStad rather than to their own individual cities and so 'lack of local involvement was noted by the jury as one of the weak points of the Eindhoven/Brabant bid' (128). This contrasts with the eventual winner, Leeuwarden in the Frisian part of the Netherlands, where it was widely considered that at 'European level, the Frisian culture is less visible than other minorities of similar size, like for example Basque and Welsh' (Immler and Sakkers, 16), so that bidding for and hosting the event was seen as an opportunity to put this culture on the map and hence enjoyed widespread local support.

The failing of BrabantStad to enthuse its own population about its bid because it was not a city they recognised appears to have been replicated by the Swansea 2021 UK City bid, because while Swansea Bay is undoubtedly a beautiful coastal landscape, it is not necessarily a city with which anyone identifies: in the eyes of its residents, the city is simply Swansea. This mis-identification may have hindered awareness of and participation in the bid and hence been a factor in the city's non-selection. On the other hand, one of the other shortlisted cities for UK City of Culture 2021, Sunderland, appears to have made the opposite mistake: not making enough connections between the city and the wider region of which it was part. This neglect contrasts with Newcastle's amalgamation with Gateshead for the purposes of the 2008 Newcastle-Gateshead European bid, which was considered one of its strengths. Situated in the North East of England, Sunderland might have developed a 2021 bid based on its status as border territory, with opportunities to develop relationships and activities in both England and Scotland, which might in turn have played well in the selection process – had it happened. Failure to generate a strong sense of a regional network may then have been a factor in its eventual defeat by Coventry. Nevertheless, being shortlisted was taken in itself as an occasion for celebration in Sunderland, and some of the benefits that can accrue even to an unsuccessful city in terms of raised profile, inward investment, civic pride and social cohesion appear to have been realised there too. In fact, at the time of writing, of all the failed bids for 2021, that of Sunderland was the only one whose website, Sunderland2021.com remained operational. This may indicate that much of the new networking and cultural programming that was developed during the bid has been able to go ahead anyway, if on a reduced scale.

When looked at this way, the bidding process for the UK City of Culture comes to resemble that for European Capital of Culture. In the wake of the inaugural UK competition for 2013, a network of researchers calling themselves the *Cultural Cities Research Network 2011–12* came into being 'as a platform for discussing and debating the experience of bidding for cultural titles' using the 'UK City of Culture 2013 competition ... as the basis for this discussion' (7). Kerry Wilson and David O'Brien suggest in their very detailed and genuinely independent report for the network that the taking part was as significant as the winning. That the subsequent bidding cities for the 2021 title were able to derive various goods whether or not they won shows once again that if the bids are carefully structured and presented, entrants in the competition to host UK City of Culture can benefit through the experience of participating itself.

It appears that the final unsuccessful city on the 2021 shortlist, Stoke-on-Trent, has likewise been able to leverage a combination of economic investment, positive social outcomes and cultural goods despite not winning. The city was far-sighted enough to produce its own evaluation of the bid experience, *Together We Make the City: Stoke-on-Trent – Losing the Bid but Winning with Culture* (2019) which although not independent, and hence like many political documents open to the charge of being over-optimistic, nevertheless identifies a range of benefits derived from the selection process. For Stoke's 2021 bid, an important factor in the non-attainment of the overall title appears to have been its close proximity to a midlands rival, Coventry. Their geographical closeness contrasts, for instance, with the agreement reached with Manchester by Liverpool not to oppose the 2008 European bid. Unlike Stoke, the eventual nominee, Coventry, had three clear strengths in that its bid was highly participatory; made much of its connections around the Midlands region more generally; and was also tacitly intercultural in its conception.

Beyond the mere contest between cities to secure the event, however, a further dimension was introduced to the competition by the fact that UK City of Culture was now competing almost directly with European Capital of Culture for the same social, economic and cultural rewards. The UK was due to host the European Capital of Culture again in 2023, and the selection competition was scheduled for 2017 – the same year as the selection competition for UK City of Culture 2021 – raising concern at the DCMS that potential candidates for each award would be unable or unwilling to prepare high-quality bids for both at once. As a result, between 15 December 2014 and 23 January 2015 the DCMS held a consultation with the devolved national governments of Northern Ireland, Scotland and Wales, UK-wide local governments, arts organisations and interested individuals. These stakeholders were consulted on three key questions: Should UK City of Culture 2021 go ahead at all, given its proximity to the UK's scheduled hosting of European Capital of Culture in 2023? If so, when should the selection process take place? And what changes needed to be made to the governance structure, organisation and funding model for the competition itself?

The DCMS Consultation Response, published in March 2015, is a fascinating document insofar as it reveals much about the dynamics of bidding for the event, and even more about the new form of competition that had emerged between UK City of Culture and European Capital of Culture. For instance, seventeen out of twenty-two respondents told the consultation that the UK 2021 event should go ahead in order to maintain the momentum and reputation that had been built up during the first two festivals in 2013 and 2017. Some respondents expressed the view that postponing UK 2021 'would devalue the programme, and make the title seem to be of secondary importance when compared to the European title' (DCMS, 2015, 3). Four respondents suggested postponing UK City of Culture 2021 'because of the difficulty that funding bodies would have in supporting both the UK and European competitions' (DCMS, 2015, 4). Then again, others suggested that cities were 'unlikely to want to bid for both', and this suggestion seems to be based on the assumption that UK City of Culture and European Capital of Culture are events of an essentially comparable nature. Individuals and organisations from within Hull expressed concern that postponing 2021 would have a negative impact on the legacy of that city's hosting of the UK City of Culture in 2017 and – given that these discussions were taking place in 2014 and 2015, *before* Hull's hosting of the festival – might also undermine its potential to build relationships with potential funders, donors, sponsors and other stakeholders. Two (anonymous) individuals were enthusiastic for going ahead, suggesting that there was an opportunity to capitalise on existing momentum by having '3 cities of culture in a 5-year timeframe' (DCMS, 2015, 3). Presumably, these would be UK City of Culture in 2021, European Capital of Culture in 2023 and UK City of Culture again in 2025 – thereby implicitly revealing that each cultural festival plays a fundamentally similar role despite the rhetoric of distinctiveness and difference.

The Tory–Lib Dem coalition government's decision printed in the response to the consultation was that the DCMS would go ahead and hold a selection process for UK City of Culture 2021. Perhaps most interesting of all is the brief rationale that is appended to this decision: UK City of Culture 2021 should go ahead 'to maintain the momentum of a programme which has wide-ranging benefits for cities across the UK' (DCMS, 2015, 4). In other words, City of Culture is billed explicitly as an unlosable game, in which the benefits derived from participation – however they are reckoned – accrue to all cities simply by entering. Given that no state funding was available for the eventual winner (let alone the candidates), this positioning of UK City of Culture reveals the fundamentally neo-liberal political ethos that characterises it.

On the question of timing, too, the DCMS response to the consultation bespeaks a sense of complex interrelation between UK City of Culture and European Capital of Culture. Seven out of the twenty-two respondents felt that the competition for UK 2021 should take place in 2017, alongside the competition for Europe 2023, to give cities time to prepare their bids and also to allow for the possibility that whichever city was selected for 2021 could then take part in a hand-over event in Hull at the end of 2017. A further seven suggested that the UK City of Culture selection process should be brought forward to 2016 in order to keep it entirely separate from the European Capital of Culture process. Those who made this suggestion again expressed concern that simultaneous announcements about the European and UK competitions could detract from the impact of the UK one. From within Hull, the fear was expressed that if selection was held in 2016 the final announcement would likely take place in 2017 – that is, during Hull's own reign – and this could also detract from the impact, publicity, marketing and sponsorship potential for their city. Moreover, the Welsh Government pointed out that there were due to be elections in the devolved administrations in Northern Ireland, Scotland and Wales in 2016, meaning that cities from those nations might be 'precluded from engaging effectively with their Governments' (DCMS, 2015, 4). The DCMS conclusion in this section of the response to the consultation was therefore that the selection process would be run in 2017 rather than 2016, thereby giving candidates enough time to prepare their bids and making possible a handover ceremony in Hull at the end of the year.

It is notable that the rationale for this decision explicitly invokes the need 'to avoid the competition clashing with elections in the devolved administrations' of Northern Ireland, Scotland and Wales (ibid.), thereby elevating the UK City of Culture competition to what is in effect a multinational coalition of potential candidate nations that seems to replicate in microcosm the range of nations and potential candidates from within the EU for the European Capital of Culture title. Equally striking in the government decision section of the response document is that no mention whatsoever is made of the fact that the decision would mean that the selection competitions for UK City of Culture 2021 and European Capital of Culture 2023 (in the UK) were now scheduled to take place simultaneously. Increasingly, the feeling evinced is that the symbolic capital derived from these events could be secured by the UK from within and that UK cities of culture could go it alone.

And so it proved. Bids to become Britain's next host of European Capital of Culture in 2023 had already been submitted by Dundee, Nottingham, Leeds and Milton Keynes plus a joint application from Northern Ireland involving Belfast and Derry when, following the referendum on the UK's membership of the European Union in June 2016, the European Commission announced in November 2017 that it was cancelling the UK's hosting in 2023. This somewhat inflexible decision and the UK's protests against it are testament to the strength of feeling that existed between the UK government and the European administration during the long and protracted negotiations on Britain's withdrawal from the European Union. Not belonging to a member state had not previously prevented Bergen or Stavanger (both Norway) or Istanbul (Turkey) from hosting earlier iterations and Alexandra Oancă (2015) has shown that the Russian city of Perm was a realistic candidate, but these factors seemed not to warrant detailed consideration in the prevailing and highly antagonistic climate of the time. Such antagonism may have been particularly ironic in the case of the Northern Irish network bid jointly involving Derry and Belfast, since a commitment to interculturalism had been a key part of Derry/Londonderry's year as UK City of Culture, yet in many ways the very development of the UK City of Culture programme seems to have paved the way for Britain's secession from the European Capital of Culture programme. In Dundee, too, the 2023 bid was largely based on establishing the city's (and Scotland's) European credentials, which now appeared to have been revoked. Whether the residents of those cities could see no contradiction in thinking of themselves as citizens of both a UK City of Culture and a European Capital of Culture was then made a moot point by the rapidly shifting political currents of the time. It is a dilemma that would come up again and again – as the following chapters will explore.

3

Imaging Northern Europe: British Varieties of Nordic Noir

This chapter considers the popularity of Nordic noir television in Britain and situates the surge of interest in the genre in a wider context. It will argue that because the Nordic nations have not always been viewed from within Britain as the most enthusiastic participants in cultural and political union at a wider European level, the Nordic region is seen as somewhat separate from other parts of Europe. Norway is not in the European Union, Denmark and Sweden are not in the Euro while Finland's proximity to Russia and Iceland's remote position in the far North Atlantic mean that neither of them are likely to be the first countries that spring to mind when Europe is described from within Britain. Moreover, popular images of the Nordic countries in Britain are as much about culture and politics as they are about geography and climate. The Nordic region has been perceived to be simpler, more settled, and less fraught with the challenges of migration and globalisation than other parts of Europe such as the Mediterranean or the Alps – and Immler and Sakkers have shown that in its bid to host the European Capital of Culture festival discussed in the previous chapter, the Finnish city of Turku 'managed to put itself centre-stage by using a special map of Europe that reached no further south than Berlin' (2014, 15), thus writing those regions out of it all together.

Exploring the connection between this perception of the Nordic countries and the reception of Nordic noir television in Britain, the chapter draws attention to the fact that the popularity of the Nordic noir format in the UK developed over the same period as the UK was embarking on its slow and painful road out of the European Union to argue that the former contributes to the latter at the levels of symbolism, visual imagery and the semiotic imaginary. That is, the chapter explores how the appearance of Nordic noir in Britain might have contributed to the cultivation of a Northern European image pool which is distinct from the popular conception of the rest of Europe and so underpinned the process by which Britain has increasingly been imagined outside the European Union.

It is important to underline from the beginning that the suggestions made here are of a perceptual rather than an essentialist nature. In other words, no claim is being made that the Nordic nations fundamentally *are* any more or less European than any of the others. They have nevertheless been *seen* that way from within the United Kingdom, and this perception, once identified, might ultimately tell us more about contemporary British culture than that of any of the Nordic nations. Moreover, the situation is complicated by the fact that audiences for Nordic noir – indeed, for any subtitled television drama in the UK – are likely to be middle class, university-educated, socially mobile and global in outlook; that is, the kind of people who are most likely to have opposed Brexit. For this reason, the argument is not that Nordic noir seduced its audiences into an anti-European sentiment in any mechanical way but that beyond straightforward considerations of influence or cause-and-effect, its presence in Britain started to provide a nexus for alternative ways of envisioning Europe that were emerging during the same period.

After presenting this argument, the second part of the chapter will identify a number of Nordic noir-inspired series produced more recently in Britain. Keeping in mind the above caveat about the perceptual rather than essentialist basis of the interpretations offered here, there seem to be several reasons why some of the characteristic properties of the Nordic noir format should have particularly resonated with makers of contemporary television drama in Britain. Nordic noir series often portray the breakdown of social relationships, a critique of political assaults on the welfare state, an interrogation of global capitalism and a corresponding interest in border areas, routes of migration and other zones of contact between one nation and/or language and another. For all these reasons, it is a format that has particularly lent itself to innovative new portrayals of spaces, places and people in the different nations of Britain. Partly because of the distinctive settings of these series and partly also because of the involvement of different national and regional companies in their production, the chapter will explore ways in which British post-Nordic 'noirs' *Shetland* (Scotland), *The Fall* (Northern Ireland), *Y Gwyll/ Hinterland*, *Craith/Hidden* (both Wales), and *Wallander* and *The Tunnel* (both England) contribute to a heightened sense of cultural specificity and cultural difference between the constituent nations of the United Kingdom.

Overall, therefore, the chapter will present two related arguments: first, that owing to how the Nordic nations and cultures have been perceived in Britain, the rapid growth in popularity of Nordic noir has resulted in the dissemination of a specific visual imaginary which is distinctly Northern rather than Southern, central or Eastern European and so in often oblique, allusive and elusive ways relates to the gradual emergence of the ideological field within which Brexit also emerged. Secondly, that owing to the fact that Nordic noir reinvigorated the television crime genre, giving rise to new levels of prestige and heightened forms of cultural capital associated with it, several British television companies have invested in producing variations of post-Nordic noir series of their own, thereby contributing to a feeling of augmented difference between the four nations of the United Kingdom. In other words, just as British post-Nordic noirs contributed to the imagery of Brexit by emulating the Scandinavian genre's air of detachment from the rest of Europe, so too they should also be understood in the context of an increased level of critical questioning about the role and purpose of the United Kingdom itself, and even its future existence.

CONTEXT AND DEFINITION

As will be argued below, there are a number of significant antecedents for Nordic noir, the most immediate of which is the earlier category, Scandi noir. Although both of these have tended to be used in Britain as loosely descriptive terms rather than analytic classifications, the gradual shift in emphasis from *Scandi* to *Nordic* that has taken place comprises two key elements, one geographic and the other generic. When Scandi noir started to be popular in Britain at around the start of the century, the label was generally used without critical interrogation to refer to works of crime fiction by writers from Scandinavia or from countries that were geographically or linguistically proximate to it. Strictly speaking, the Scandinavian peninsula consisted only of Norway and Sweden; but Denmark was often shoehorned into the category, as was Finland and even Iceland. Gunhild Agger attributes the coining of the subsequent term *Nordic noir* to the Scandinavian Department at University College London, which 'launched a Nordic noir blog and a book club in March 2010' (2016, 138). The change in emphasis from *Scandi* to *Nordic* thus reflects the fact that the Nordic nations comprise all five, and had the practical advantage of referring in a more geographically accurate way to the languages and countries in which works that had previously been jumbled together under the category *Scandi noir* originated. The prior term, in other words, was a descriptive shorthand for a particular aesthetic style within crime fiction rather than a precise geographic denominator. It will be argued throughout this chapter that although its use as a term of geographic reference was frequently lazy and inaccurate, those inaccuracies contributed to a vagueness in defining the genre, and that the propagation of this feeling has had significant long-term consequences in the televisual imaginary of British audiences. This in turn is partly because at some point during the transition from *Scandi* to *Nordic* both terms gradually came to refer less exclusively to print fiction (although of course they retained this referent to some extent) and were increasingly applied to television crime drama (and film). Although this second transition is hard to pinpoint with precise historical accuracy, it is an important context for what followed because it inherited the geographical vagueness that was implicit in the loose descriptor *Scandi noir* on the one hand, while also making possible a concrete visual instantiation of what had previously seemed vague, on the other.

Again, it is necessary to point out that these transitions took place mainly within British discussion of the genre rather than in any of its 'home' countries. Sandbye suggests that when Scandinavia and the Nordic countries are falsely conflated, this is most often 'done from the outside because the Nordic countries seem to have much in common in their way of life, history, their use of Scandinavian languages, and social structure' (1). Writing of the 'alleged "mutual sympathy and loyalty" between the Nordic nations' Danbolt suggests that the 'so-called "we-feeling"' between them has prompted researchers to argue 'that the Nordic region stood out for its unique ability to resolve problems, domestically as well as internationally, by means of "peaceful change"' (Danbolt, 4). The inverted commas around 'mutual sympathy' and the repeated emphasis on any fellow-feeling between the Nordic nations being merely 'so-called' and 'alleged' rather than empirically grounded are so stagey and self-conscious as to have the opposite effect: implying that the unifying bonds of Nordic culture have only been perceived as such from elsewhere. In a similar vein, Jakob Stougaard-Nielsen has pointed out that 'Nordic noir is arguably only understood as a distinct regional genre as a consequence of its international success – otherwise, Scandinavians would happily have continued to refer to their local specimens as simply "krimi" (in Denmark), "krim" (in Norway) and "deckare" (in Sweden) without regional or national epithets. Nordic crime fiction, in other words, is perhaps only really "Nordic" when viewed or read from abroad' (2016, 4). He goes on to argue that Scandi noir crime fiction is an example of the process outlined by Franco Moretti whereby novelistic genres tend to emanate from the metropolitan centres of the literary world and 'spread to the linguistic peripheries through translations, adaptations and mimicry' before finally giving rise to 'original local variants that would add to and innovate the global form of the genre itself' (2016, 2). In other words, the export of twentieth-century Anglo-American crime fiction to Scandinavia in the form of locally specific imitators and innovators eventually resulted in the Nordic region becoming a new cultural centre from which works of fiction, film and television have been launched into the wider world.

If Nordic noir has mostly been constructed as such from the outside, however, the same is not necessarily true of the Nordic region itself. On the contrary, Danbolt has drawn attention to the fact that the cultural and linguistic ties as well as the political and geographical ones between the five Nordic nations were already strong enough in the nineteenth century to enable the imagination of a single de facto nation of *Norden* from within, to the extent that the Danish author Hans Christian Andersen 'even wrote a national anthem' for this unified nation in 1837 (7). Danbolt's suggestion that the mutual empathy and cooperation between the Nordic nations is merely perceived from the outside is therefore tempered by his simultaneous awareness that there has been a 'century-long investment in ideologies of "Scandinavianism" and "Nordism"' from within the region itself (3). He goes on to describe to those ideologies of Pan-Scandinavian and Pan-Nordic nationalism as a means of mythologising Nordic Exceptionalism with regard to the rest of the world, a myth which by the mid-twentieth century contained two key elements: the establishment of model welfare systems of equality and social care; and the self-positioning of the Nordic nations as playing a mediating role between the Cold War superpowers the USA and USSR. Owing to this intermediary role, Danish political theorist Ole Wæver suggested in 1992 that the Nordic self-imagination proposed that '"Nordic identity is about being better than Europe" – as well as "being better off than Europe"' (quoted in Danbolt, 5). Christopher Browning has made a similar point, explaining: 'On the one hand, it has been hailed as an identitarian concept that marks the Nordic difference from Europe. On the other hand, it has been promoted as a brand and model to be copied and implemented by others' (quoted in Danbolt, 6). It is this ideological sense of Nordic exceptionalism being not only different to, but in some ways superior to, other European cultures and/or political systems that Danbolt critiques. In doing so, he draws on a distinction made by Kazimierz Musiał between 'images of reality' and 'experiences of reality,' where the former have played an important constitutive role in converting the latter into a 'compelling narrative for the international public' about what Nordic culture and politics stand for: 'progressiveness, peacefulness, the egalitarian society, solidarity with the Third World and environmentalism' (Danbolt, 4). It will be argued below that this ideological construction of Nordic exceptionalism, in its guise not only as Nordic difference but more specifically as Nordic superiority, warrants closer examination in any consideration of the popularity of Nordic noir in Britain, where the 'images of reality' that it generated have provided a populist image-set somewhat different form the dominant images of either central Europe (the Alps) or Southern Europe (the Mediterranean) and has therefore cultivated and disseminated a symbolic affinity with a figurative cultural space that stands somewhat apart from them.

In Danbolt's account Olof Palme, Swedish Prime Minister (1969–76 and 1982–6) is identified as 'perhaps the most outspoken advocate' of Nordic exceptionalism (4). This is highly significant because several commentators have traced the origins of Nordic noir print fiction to the assassination of Palme in 1986, normally on the grounds that as an exceptionally safe country with a low crime rate, high levels of compassion in its social care system and little or no history of political assassination, Sweden was suddenly and dramatically shocked into a new awareness and consideration of violence, leading to a novelistic outpouring of crime writing.

Beyond the mere fact of his assassination, however, Palme's key political role both in the development of Sweden's lauded welfare state and its mediational position between superpowers during the Cold War provide two further contexts for the development of noir writing. The efficacy and humane compassion for which the welfare system was known had fallen into a certain degree of disrepute by the late twentieth century, mired in controversies related to race and immigration that raised questions about equality in Swedish society which had previously seemed unnecessary because equality itself had been treated as a given within the society's self-imagination. Likewise, if the nation had forged a global role as non-aligned and disinterested mediator during the Cold War, this role by definition 'no longer seemed to be the case' when the Cold War ended (Danbolt, 5), leaving the nation searching for a new sense of purpose and initiating a certain degree of reflexive self-questioning.

Although there was a range of crime and thriller writing from across the Nordic region during the Cold War, the book that is often cited as inaugurating the noir turn taken by the genre there is *Miss Smilla's Feeling for Snow* (*Frøken Smillas fornemmelse for sne*) by Danish writer Peter Høeg (1992), a novel that combines critique of the welfare system with a theoretical probing of the position and role of the state in the wider world in indirect ways, because its portrayal of Denmark's relationship to Greenland is also a critical portrayal of a colonial state. In general, the relationship between crime fiction and welfare structures is a complicated one, at times articulating a distrust of state organisations and at others expressing a nostalgic desire for a return to lost utopian ideals of welfare relationships. Stougaard-Nielsen has argued that although Swedish writer Stieg Larsson's *Millennium* trilogy (2005–7) is often seen as a critical representation of the failure of traditional welfare systems, the monstrosity of the post-welfare state ethically legitimates the vigilantism of the criminal heroine Lisbeth Salander, so that by underwriting a sense of individualism over collective solidarity the novel endorses 'the systemic structures which brought about the fall of the welfare state in the first place' (2017, 210) and is therefore unable to transform the neo-liberal assumptions it set out to interrogate.

Since neo-liberalism has become entrenched as the dominant ideology in the period of globalisation since the end of the Cold War both it and globalisation provide further significant contexts for developments in crime fiction in the 1990s and beyond. Although critically engaging with the neo-liberal dismantling of the welfare state, and with the complex ethical politics of globalisation, are arguably more muted in the Danish television series *The Killing* (*Forbrydelsen*, 2007–12), they are active elements in the Danish-Swedish co-production, *The*

Bridge (*Bron/Broen*, 2011–18). By this time, not only had the British popular media started to use the label *Nordic* (as opposed to the earlier *Scandi*) *noir* to refer to these and related works, but they were also much more commonly using it to refer to television drama than print fiction. This replicates Nordic noir's increasing movement from print to film and television in the Nordic countries themselves, which started with the film adaptations of Høeg (in 1997), Larsson (2009), Norwegian writer Jo Nesbø's *Headhunters* (*Hodejegerne*, 2011) and the Swedish television adaptation of Henning Mankell's *Wallander* series (2005–13). It accelerated greatly with works written specifically for television such as the later episodes of the Swedish *Wallander*, *The Killing* (2007–12), *The Bridge* (2011–18), *Trapped* (Icelandic: *Ófærð*, 2015–21) and *Bordertown* (Finnish: *Sorjonen*, 2016–20).

ON NORDIENTALISM

One of the abiding images of the BBC remake (2008–16) of the Swedish series *Wallander* is that of the eponymous detective's car, seen from directly above, gliding slowly through narrow, claustrophobic country roads. It is an image generated by a vertical camera angle which offers to flatten the vehicle and render it almost entirely two-dimensional, thereby reducing it to a part of, rather than an addition to, the rural terrain through which it moves. In other words, the human occupant of the car is terrifyingly dwarfed by the enormity of the surrounding landscape. In this, the BBC *Wallander* may be considered typical of much Nordic noir television drama. Be it inhospitable fjords, rugged mountains, fragmented coastlines, or frozen inlets the sparseness of the landscape is one of the defining features of the form. Moreover, landscape is used not as mere background or setting for the action but as an actively constituent element in it. Since the human characters are not depicted in their separation from their environment but as rooted manifestations of it, landscape is often subject to investigation and presents a number of fundamental challenges to the investigation underway so that landscape is not merely traversed but consciously experienced and dialogically expressed. That is, landscape has something important to say about the police procedural aspects of the plots. This is as true of the de-industrialised cityscapes and industrial zones where danger seems to lurk as it is of the distant country retreats and ramshackle dwellings that the narratives compellingly move towards.

At the same time, there is a second kind of landscape in play: the psyche, or inner psychological landscape of the detective. One of the other recurring features of Nordic noir is how often the detectives are subject to the recurrence of past traumas, troubling memories, social anxieties and insecurities of all kinds so that in many cases investigating whatever criminal case is before them also presents an opportunity for achieving troubling forms of self-reflection and self-knowledge. Moving through the outer landscape as part of a criminal investigation is therefore inextricable from working through the inner landscape of memory and the emotions, wherever they might lead. Related to this process is a tendency to represent 'a reversal of traditional gender stereotypes', which is something that Agger finds typical of Nordic noir (2016, 137). In conventional crime fiction, women are often presented as vulnerable and indexically linked to the degree of threat being faced, and overcome, by assertive men. In Nordic noir, the male detectives are often rendered weak and vulnerable by one or more past experiences that have physically and emotionally scarred them. Their female colleagues, rather than occupying conventionally feminine roles such as caregivers, then tend to take the lead in the criminal investigation which is simultaneously an investigation into the damaged psychological profile of the detectives.

These features are summarised only briefly here because they have all been discussed in much more detail elsewhere. They all point to the importance of landscape and the social construction of space as defining features in Nordic noir as a whole. What has less frequently been remarked upon is the importance of considering how Nordic space more generally has been constructed, especially from the outside, along with the context this construction generates for the reception of the Nordic noir format and the implications it has for the reception and discussion of Nordic noir, again from the outside.

In an innovative article entitled 'Nordic noir in the UK: the allure of accessible difference' (2016), Jakob Stougaard-Nielsen draws on the work of the translation scholar Lawrence Venuti to argue, with a nod to Edward Said, that the upturn of interest in Nordic cultures in the UK in the early decades of the twenty-first century is tantamount to a form of 'Nordientalism'. That is, through diverse means from food to fiction, from sociology to sport, and from journalism to politics, the relative rise in interest in the Nordic nations when taken together adds up to the cultivation of a particular image, or set of related images, of those nations. But just as Said used the term

Orientalism to explore how the tendency of Western cultures to depict and construct images of the East during the period of empire ultimately revealed more about the former's frenzied appropriation of the latter than it bespoke any fundamental truths about them, so too this gradual development of a dominant imaginary with regard to the Nordic nations 'has come to function as a medium for intercultural communication wherein the perceived Nordicness of the genre plays a central role in negotiating social and cultural desires and challenges pertaining mostly to the receiving culture' (2016, 2). The examples he gives of particular social challenges and causes of cultural anxiety in Britain, which Nordic noir then presents an opportunity to critically explore and negotiate, are growing economic inequality, the unequal experience of globalisation (especially in the aftermath of the financial crisis of 2007–8), and the politics of austerity (which in turn have an impact on the availability of welfare provision and the structure of state services from education to healthcare).

So far, so Nordiental, but the question raised by identifying this dynamic is why Nordic noir should provide such a powerful vehicle for the exploration of contemporary concerns in Britain, when German documentary, Italian sitcom or Spanish soap opera apparently do not. To use terms discussed in Chapter One in relation to Hebdige's concept of subcultures, Nordic noir seems to have offered British audiences a degree of specificity and conjuncture in the alignment of particular contemporary anxieties that is not provided to the same degree by other genres, from other regions of the world or in other languages. Mapping out why this should be the case is necessary in understanding the broader context in which the form has been received.

One possible answer lies in the earlier tendency in the UK to conflate the different Nordic nations together and flatten out precise cultural and political differentials between them. Citing the celebrity chef Hugh Fearnley-Whittingstall's cookery series *Scandimania*, Stougaard-Nielsen goes on to discuss the 'flood of journalistic and popular ethnographic explorations of the Nordic region in the UK' over the past two decades (2016, 6). According to Sandbye, the different areas of social life that such pop cultural analyses have addressed include food, fiction, television drama, as well as 'liveable Nordic architecture and sustainable Nordic design' and the oft-cited claim that 'Scandinavian countries now also take the lead in world-wide happiness surveys' (Sandbye, 2). To Stougaard-Nielsen the cumulative effect of these portrayals is that 'Nordic social realities are treated as alluring, homogeneous, exotic tourist destinations, where their difference to a proximate yet imagined more complex British, globalised reality are managed to conform to an essentialising view of culture one would be more cautious of applying to the United Kingdom' (6).

In a discussion of how the international promotion of *The Bridge* was coordinated with the tourist agency Visit Sweden, Kim Toft Hansen and Anne Marit Waade have suggested: 'Generally speaking, the new and emerging collaborations between screen content producers, tourism operators and local authorities can form part of a long tail strategy aiming to maintain the interest around the television series and to fill the gap between seasons' (2017, 282). Although there has been an upturn in British tourism to the Nordic region, it remains likely that more people in Britain have taken an interest in the new trends in Nordic culture, design and lifestyles discussed by Sandbye and Stougaard-Nielsen than typically travel there. This means that more is at stake than mere choice of an ephemeral holiday destination, so that Stougaard-Nielsen's proximate imagined other should be seen less as a real place that people empirically visit than a symbolic hinterland in which they invest their own interests and concerns and to which they are by the same token culturally attuned at the figurative level. In a period marked by the gradual eclipse of British popular culture by its American equivalents, anxieties over migration that have brought the concept of multiculturalism into dispute on the grounds of ghettoisation and cultural fragmentation, plus the fact that increased calls for independence in the devolved nations of Britain have placed the unity of the United Kingdom in question, the 'allure of these strange lands across the pond' is that in lifestyle, in architecture, in food and in fiction the Nordic nations 'are un-problematically imagined as expressions of a homogeneous national identity' (Stougaard-Nielsen, 2016, 6). Quoting Stephen Greenblatt, he suggests that this allure is related to the attraction of the 'firmly rooted', which seems to offer comfort and solidity in a world where much else has rapidly changed and which 'we should not ignore when considering the mobility of cultures even if the geographical and cultural distance, as the one between Britain and the Nordic countries, appears insignificant' (3). That the firmly rootedness of Nordic society and the homogeneity implicitly assigned to its culture are both illusory does not in any way undermine the affective nature of this symbolic appeal and may positively enhance it.

In this account, the actively imagined cultural unity of the Nordic region is recoded as a vehicle for the expression of an atavistic desire to recuperate a putative lost national unity in Britain itself, with one mirroring the other in idealised form. Overall, the Nordientalist discourse in Britain therefore:

> provides less in terms of real insights into the complex and changing Danish or Nordic social realities, of what it actually means to be Danish in a post-welfare, multicultural, globalised world, than it does about trends in the receiving culture: the desires and dreams of a segment of the UK population, who find their own values challenged by the socio-political climate of an imagined more complex, wayward nation. The flood of journalistic and popular ethnographic explorations of the Nordic region in the UK is an expression, perhaps, of a search for a lost sense of identity, a nostalgic longing for an imagined past society more in tune with pre-Thatcherite welfarist values, by way of consuming, appropriating and exoticising proximate cultural identities such as the now much hyped Danish or Nordic utopias (Stougaard-Nielsen, 2016, 6).

This sense of the Nordiental provides an important context in which the circulation of Nordic noir in the UK can be situated and discussed. The cultural proximity Stougaard-Nielsen emphasises is temporally defined, because in effect the collective Nordic discourse posits the region as existing at some point in a lost and idealised past that it then offers to symbolically recover and perpetuate. But in addition to this temporal component, it also has a significant spatial aspect, one which can be glimpsed through contradistinction with Raymond Williams's famous remark that the difference between British and French culture must be one of the greatest cultural differences in the world relative to the short geographical distance between them (1989, 78). If Williams's France was tantalisingly close in a physical sense but remote culturally, then the Nordic region as an object constructed by the discourse of Nordientalism is almost exactly the opposite: a little further away (though still not too far) geographically, yet symbolically adjacent and culturally available. It thus provides what Stougaard-Nielsen terms an 'accessibly different' locus for a whole series of values, desires and anxieties 'that a segment of British consumers may feel have been lost sometime in the 1990s' (2016, 7). Maribel Blasco makes a related point, underlining the transnational dynamic of multinational capitalism which provides a wider structure within which the consumption of Nordic noir in the UK takes place and which mobilises a dialectical interplay between global products and local consumers, which in turn is only possible because 'even cultures that appear very un-exotic to us – say the Swedish, the German, the Dutch – must have their differences, however slight, exposed, managed and exploited' (2004, 33). It may even be possible that the allure of various Nordic series, like the appeal of Danish design, Swedish furniture and other elements of the imagined Nordic lifestyle, appeals not only in spite of their relatively slight differences from Britain but positively because of them – or rather, because they are only relatively slight. In this sense, the accessibly different might turn out to be a variation on the almost familiar. If so, it would be important to consider how Nordic space has been constructed in a way that makes it amenable to such an interpretation.

THE CONSTRUCTION OF SPACE

Although 'setting is an important, yet often undervalued component of crime fiction and fiction in general' (Waade, 2011, 48), according to García Avis the 'element of place tends to take a backseat in mainstream writing for film and television, where characters, plot structure, and dialogues drive the screenwriting process' (2015, 128). For Les Roberts, one of the characteristic features of Nordic noir television drama, in addition to its critique of welfare capitalism, tortured souls, transformed gender roles and bleak landscapes is the fact that it mobilises new spatial practices converting location from mere background setting into galvanic presence and agency. This means that in his consideration of post-Nordic noir drama in Britain such as *Broadchurch*, *Y Gwyll/Hinterland* and *Southcliffe*, 'it is necessary and instructive to approach the case of British procedural dramas by considering in what ways (and to what extent) their geographical imaginaries bear the imprint of their Nordic procedural counterparts' (2016, 366).

Neil Archer has argued, however, that it would be misleading to take a binary approach to different audiences for Nordic noir in its home countries and in Britain. In a study of the adaptation of Jo Nesbø's 2008 novel *Hodejegerne* (*Headhunters*), he argues that it makes little sense to disaggregate audiences in this way, given that within the global economy productions are increasingly made with multinational audiences in mind and are therefore constructed in ways that appeal to such audiences simultaneously rather than separately. Arguing that it is 'from this perspective that we can read both *Headhunters* and also some of the wider strain of Nordic films (and television series), especially those produced by Yellow Bird, who seem to have grasped particularly well how to produce and market regional specificity in trans-national terms' (2013, 67), he explores the techniques by which the film 'already organized most of its strategic representation prior to its publicity' (60). These include: a reduction in the novel's 'numerous allusions to its Oslo location and historical contexts' (59); a similar lessening of 'cultural or political' referents (ibid.); its 'resistance to naming place' (60); and its use of 'non-culturally specific names' for its Norwegian protagonist, Roger Brown (ibid.). Taken together these strategies for transculturation cause Archer to conclude that 'the way the film feels no need to mark itself geographically makes *Headhunters*' approach much closer to Hollywood's non-differentiation of American space, its "planetizing [of] entertainment"' (60).

This chapter argues that the simultaneous destruction and reconstruction of place, the capacity offered by Nordic noir to look, feel and crucially act like somewhere else, are of central importance in understanding its dissemination in Britain. Thus, according to Gemzøe, the remaking of series like *Bron/Broen* (*The Bridge*) is part of 'a remake trend that, on the one hand, is inspired by all things Nordic, but on the other hand, actively engages in removing the Nordic feel from the remade productions' (2013, 283). García Avis says the same thing about *The Killing*: that it 'does seem to highlight a paradigmatic pattern, where the "*Nordic-ness*" of the format becomes a global trait that coexists with local re-interpretations of place' (132). Marklund's discussion of three recent Nordic noir television series *Bordertown* (*Sorjonen*) from Finland, *Trapped* (*Ófærð*) from Iceland and the Danish- Swedish *The Bridge* (*Bron/Broen*) emphasises the fact that border regions figure prominently in all three because border regions are places where visual signifiers pertaining to several different cultures openly interact with each other, so that analysing the portrayal of that interaction makes it possible to explore the way 'foreign influences are represented and used in these stories' as well as showing how 'a borderland trope serves the purpose of relativizing the national and thus facilitating international viewing, otherwise possibly hindered by too many national references' (2019, 179).

The capacity of its discursive space to foster a sense of connection to rather than alienation from its cultural content is one of the hallmarks of the accessible difference which Stougaard-Nielsen associates with Nordic noir. But if space can be dismantled and reassembled in the mind of the viewer in this way, the question still remains: why should this be particularly true of Scandinavia rather than Southern European space? To try and answer this, an empirical study carried out by Ushma Chauhan Jacobsen into Japanese audiences' responses to Nordic noir can usefully be applied to British audiences for a number of reasons. First of all, Jacobsen identifies the same reciprocal principle at work in Japanese television that Archer finds with Yellow Bird in Sweden and Denmark. That is, Japan simultaneously has a successful track record of exporting television drama to other parts of Asia and Europe, while also having a number of television networks interested in importing non-Japanese drama to Japan so that, again, production increasingly takes place with the potential for transculturation in mind. Jacobsen quotes Koichi Iwabuchi as suggesting that Japan's long and successful history in the production and transnational export of television dramas in East and Southeast Asia has 'influenced Japan's self-imagination as being "in but above" or "similar but superior" to the rest of Asia' (quoted in Jacobsen, 2018, 619). This feeling of being 'in but above' directly recalls the self-construction of the Nordic region during the mid to late twentieth century, which Danbolt characterised as the myth of Nordic exceptionalism with regard to the rest of Europe and indeed the rest of the world. This paradoxically shared feeling of exceptionalism may account for the fact that although audience figures for Scandinavian drama are relatively low in Japan, the emotional investment made in it by those audiences is relatively high.

The Japanese sense of being connected to the continent but also detached and distinct from it (not to mention superior to it) also appears to characterise an increasing feeling in Britain with regard to Europe over the period in which Nordic noir has been successful. Although many Nordic noir productions are inherently transnational (Swedish-Danish; Danish-American; British-Danish and so on), Jacobsen's study found that Japanese audience members nevertheless tended to associate the dramas with specific 'nations, territories or regions' (618). In other words, although transnational collaboration plays a crucial role in getting programmes commissioned, exported, scheduled and promoted it is not necessarily something audiences think of when they view the final content. This is why, in a separate paper written with Pia Majbritt Jensen, Jacobsen proposes a 'three-leaf clover' consisting of (1) buyers and distributors; (2) journalists, critics and other cultural intermediaries, who act as arbiters of taste and agenda setters; and (3) regular viewers (Jensen and Jacobsen, 2017, 435), where each of these agents acts in different ways in making a particular series visible internationally, yet without 'erasing the importance of national contexts' altogether (438).

One of the recurring themes discussed by Jacobsen's Japanese audience members was that they considered Nordic drama to have constructed Nordic space in a way that distinguishes it from the rest of Europe. One of his interviewees told him:

> I really like Northern European dramas and when I turn them on and see them I know immediately if it is from Northern Europe because it is very grey – like the background, the nature – it is very grey (Japanese interviewee cited by Jacobsen, 2018, 621).

Drawing on Jacobsen's approach, the tentative suggestion made here is that in the identification of specifically Northern European visual traits, his Japanese interviewee expresses something that is potentially transferrable to the discussion of Nordic noir in Britain, the proliferation of which has put into circulation a recurring set of imagery which is distinctly Northern European. Through the downplaying of cultural differences discussed above, this imagery has the effect of situating Britain within a loosely conceptualised Nordic world, on the one hand; and in an alternative geographic imaginary to that of the rest of the continent, on the other.

For the present study, the most important question is then how far these alternative geographies can be considered to have contributed to Britain's decision in 2016 to leave the European Union. To interpret the popularity of Nordic noir in Britain as a direct cause of the British people's decision to leave the European Union is a project that seems doomed to fail – most notably because the typical audience for subtitled drama in Britain is well educated and middle class, the same demographic that was most opposed to Britain leaving Europe, so that there can be no direct cause and effect correlation between the viewing of Nordic drama and the adoption of a 'Leave' mentality.

In a survey of British audiences for the Danish series *The Killing* (2007–12, first aired in Britain 2011), Andrea Esser has rejected exactly this mechanical relationship of cause and effect. Having asked her sample group what motivated them to watch the series in the first place, she notes that out of twenty-eight interviewees only 'three people actively remembered seeing the trailer before *The Killing* started. No one mentioned having watched foreign films on BBC Four' (2017, 423). Instead, Esser found a number of other factors that contributed to the success of *The Killing* in Britain: a dramatic cut in the BBC's budget following the election of the coalition government in 2010 and its politics of austerity, which resulted in the need to find dramas that could be imported relatively inexpensively from sources that at that point had no particular reputation for producing them; the need to compete with high-budget American drama in the transnational field; and the fact that streaming and digital services had not yet taken off so that the overwhelming majority of the UK audience still accessed drama on a traditional platform such as the channel, BBC4, where *The Killing* was first shown in Britain.

Thus, the effect of media coverage in promoting the series is actively disavowed among Esser's audience members: 'when asked whether they remembered media coverage and/or had started watching because of favourable media coverage (after no unprompted references had been forthcoming), most could not remember. Some even repudiated having been influenced by media coverage' (424). On the other hand, the fact that *The Killing* aired in Britain in 2011, relatively soon after both the Swedish *Wallander* and its BBC remake (both in 2008) created some degree of precedent and so opened a doorway to British audiences for Scandinavian drama, causing Esser to suggest that '*The Killing* thus may not have been as unfamiliar as it first appeared' (423).

The question of 'effects' is therefore a tricky one and, as we have seen, British audiences are unlikely to have been persuaded by their viewing of Nordic noir into adopting a political attitude in favour of leaving the European Union any more than the advertising and promotion were key factors in their decision to watch the series. But the key suggestion made by Esser is that although a direct causal relationship is inoperative, *The Killing* was amenable to circulation in Britain because its cultural differences were relatively low, and in the process of being aired it had the effect of acting as a trailblazer for subsequent Nordic noir and therefore again of downplaying cultural differences between Britain and the Nordic countries. In this way, the genre as a whole has created a number of human and geographical landscapes in which the North of Europe is constructed as simultaneously culturally proximate with Britain and culturally remote from the rest of Europe. The dialectical interplay between proximity and remoteness that characterises the positioning of Nordic noir in Britain can therefore be said in hindsight to have laid in indirect ways some of the symbolic and visual terrain on which the path towards Brexit would be constructed. This is why in a study of social space in the British post-Nordic noir television dramas *Broadchurch*, *Y Gwyll/ Hinterland* and *Southcliffe*, Roberts argues that the extent to which Nordic noir drama ushered in new spatial practices in British television 'can perhaps be partly approached by paying attention to ideas of "North" and "Northernness" in a broader sense than that tied specifically to discussions of landscape and location in post-*Wallander* or post-*The Killing* television crime drama' (365–6).

As we have seen from Archer's discussion of Yellow Bird, Nordic production companies have been strategically adept at devising formats that downplay regional specificity in order to be amenable for consumption by a multinational audience. But even so, it is not a simple case of Scandinavia pretending to *be* Britain; because even if alienating difference is minimised, the locations still present themselves as themselves. Rather than straightforwardly trying to dupe a gullible viewer into mistaking one place for another, a much more subtle process is at work. For example, although crime drama series from other European countries have been imported to Britain, such as the Italian *Inspector Montalbano* and the French *Killer by the Lake*, the landscapes they depict are respectively Mediterranean and Alpine and therefore propagate a visual imaginary quite different from the bleaker, flatter, colder landscapes of Nordic noir. But the much greater impact enjoyed by this latter on British television suggests that audiences are not only not alienated from its landscapes and urban spaces, but also form active degrees of accommodation and symbolic connection within them. It is this accommodation which makes it possible for Neil Salt on behalf of BBC Acquisitions to say with reference to Nordic noir that the BBC feels 'immensely proud that BBC Four is home to such great international series' since 'in recent years BBC Four has enjoyed huge success with international series and Scandinavian programmes particularly' (quoted in Hughes, 2014, 30–1). If British producers are able to declare themselves at home in Northern Europe presumably the same is true of their viewers, and the accommodation of both to the Northern European imaginary contrasts with the lesser headway made by series like *Inspector Montalbano* or *Killer by the Lake* and their corresponding landscapes, in which British audiences appear to feel proportionately less 'at home'. In other words, the presence of Nordic noir television drama in Britain has tacitly cultivated a discursive and mental space that is somewhat apart from the spaces associated with other European cultures; and this cultivation has coincided with a steadily increasing feeling of British detachment from Europe over the approximate two-decade period in which Nordic noir has come to prominence in Britain; so that it is possible to argue that the former process both informs and is informed by the latter.

One reason for this relates to how the Nordic region as a whole is perceived in Britain. For example, in Scottish writer Iain Banks's novel *Espedair Street* (1987) about a fictional rock band in the 1970s, Banks sends his musicians first on a tour of 'the UK, Europe and Scandinavia, and the US' (123) and then, when they are more successful, of 'South America, Japan, Australia ... India and Nigeria before heading back through Europe (East and West) and Scandinavia' (198). That is, although Banks was a thoroughgoing Europhile, and one of the songs composed by his fictitious band in the novel is an anti-capitalist ode to 'Europe' (98), he nevertheless treats Scandinavia as not just distinct within, but distinct from, the rest of Europe. In fact, the character McCann, a working-class pub philosopher, mocks the idea of Glasgow as European City of Culture for representing the gentrification of the city: 'God, this place is goin tae the dogs all right' (36). Five years later, when Denmark's national football team achieved a shock win over world champions Germany in the final of the 1992 European Championship, the BBC television commentator John Motson compared it to the way the Danish people had refused to follow the expected script earlier that year by voting not to ratify the Maastricht Treaty (which effectively converted the European Economic Community into the European Union).

These two instances from popular culture, one in music (albeit fictional) and the other in sport do not by themselves prove anything, but they do indicate the general way in which the Nordic countries have been viewed from within Britain. In a more strictly analytical sense, it is true that Denmark and Sweden have, like Britain, remained outside the Eurozone while Norway and Iceland are not in the European Union at all. In fact, in *The Break-Up of Britain* in 1977 Tom Nairn warned that 'the very expansion of the EEC will generate counterwaves, of which the first was the Norwegian referendum in 1972 – the first important rebuff suffered by the European

Community' (298). Although the expansion he was referring to was that of the mid-1970s when Britain joined, his identification of the counterwaves provoked in Norway by expansion seems to concisely anticipate the second great expansion of the European Union in 2004, and the anti-European backlash it provoked in Britain.

A second reason why a certain affinity has been cultivated between the Nordic North of Europe and the United Kingdom relates to their languages having a shared origin. Jacobsen's study of Japanese audiences for Danish drama is further instructive here, because he found among his interviewees that although Danish is thought of as 'a "strong language" ... and one that plays a critical role in texturing and layering the "Danish-ness" of Denmark's citizens' it nevertheless fails to elicit strong visual images of Denmark when heard in another country (625). Linguistically speaking this tendency of the Danish language to evoke few if any connections or images in the minds of the Japanese audience therefore functions in a manner analogous to the downplaying of visual difference that Archer found typical of the Norwegian film *Headhunters* as a process of dis-alienation. Applying Jacobsen's findings to the British context (with a caveat that this has not been tested empirically), it might also be the case therefore that the languages of Danish, Swedish, Norwegian, Icelandic or Finnish drama are similarly un-marked and comparably fail to evoke a strong set of images for British audience members, so that rather than being overwhelmed by a sense of otherness generated in and through language, the languages themselves function as a verbal blank space which the audience members can catch hold of and latch on to, even if they don't understand.

In other words, at the level of language too it is possible to discern Stougaard-Nielsen's accessible difference in the British reception of Nordic drama. Although in the twenty-first century English contains words that can be traced in origin to just about every other language in the world, the historic emergence of English from the period of the Saxons to that of the Vikings was inflected by Scandinavian speech in formative ways, leaving certain traces of that evolution even today. In syntax, structure, rhythm, word order, occasionally in vocabulary and perhaps above all in pronunciation Scandinavian languages sound and feel very distinct from their Latin, Romantic or Slavic counterparts. English then sounds and feels comparably distinct from them, in a way that tacitly re-establishes it as a Scandinavian language. It may then be that part of the pleasure of viewing Scandinavian drama for British viewers is following the words in the order in which they are spoken, and at times being able to discern the meanings of some words and phrases before their English translation appears in the subtitles.

Perhaps surprisingly, however, little attention has been paid in critical discussions of Nordic noir to the cultural context generated over the *longue durée* by either the shared history between Scandinavia and Britain in the medieval period or by the linguistic connections forged as a result of that shared history – let alone to any consideration of what implications that shared history and common linguistic origin have on contemporary cultural production. An important exception to this is the Master's thesis completed by Welsh postgraduate student Daniel Hughes at Stockholm University between 2012 and 2014. Pointing out that '[p]revious criticism has centred on the exoticism of the Nordic landscapes and Nordic languages' (2014, 51–2), he provided an alternative reading, based on pragmatic testing in the form of interviews with six British viewers of Nordic noir, which in effect suggested that both the landscapes and languages of the Nordic region might be relatively less exotic than had previously seemed the case.

Hughes then went on to discuss the relationship between the languages of the Danish-Swedish production *Bron/Broen* and its English-language remake, *The Tunnel* (2013). Having suggested that the biggest aesthetic difference for British audiences was the language, he also explained: 'In the original Danish/Swedish production this was also a factor, but in a British context neither of the languages are spoken widely in the UK, and [neither] Danish nor Swedish are mutually intelligible with English to the same extent that they are with each other' (48). Perhaps the most interesting point to emerge from this comparison is then contained within the words 'to the same extent'. Although ostensibly written to suggest that neither Swedish nor Danish can be mutually understood by English speakers, this qualifying clause has the opposite effect – that is, hinting that to some extent, they can be. And this is what makes possible the linguistic pleasure for British viewers mentioned above, of being able to understand linguistic snatches and fragments of a language which they do not overtly 'speak'.

Lastly, Hughes also relates the linguistic overlap between these languages to the shared history of the countries over the course of a thousand years or more:

> Historically and culturally there are links between Denmark and Sweden, and the UK's national history, due to the period of time known as 'Dane Law' (865 until 1012 A.C. [sic]) where the Vikings ruled the north and the east of England, and parts of Scotland. English, Danish and Swedish also all belong to the Germanic language family. The countries as of 2014 were all members of EU, however none are part of the Eurozone. In the lead up to the 2014 European Union elections, focus on populist right-wing parties stance against multi-nationalism in all countries was covered widely by the media in all countries. (32–3)

To emphasise Britain's connection with Scandinavia is not necessarily contradictory to a wider European imaginary, but does perhaps hint at a specific way of being European that differs from other regions. Although there is much that is in need of further unpacking and clarification in Hughes's slippage from the Danelaw to the European Union, the overall suggestions are, first, that the points of contact between Scandinavian history and British during the Viking period gave rise to a language – English – that was part of the same family of languages as Swedish and Danish themselves and that this creates a particular form of commonality between them that implicitly sets them apart from other nations and the languages spoken in them. Secondly, that the common resistance shared by the Scandinavian countries and Britain in the twenty-first century to entering a full political union with Europe via the Euro also sets them apart in an economic sense (although it might also be an expression of the fact emphasised by Robert Tombs that in these countries citizens have actually been asked about Europe in elections, while Euro scepticism is at least as high in other countries whose citizens have not). Finally, that these degrees of separation are an important context in which the reception of Nordic noir in Britain should be understood.

SONIC GEOGRAPHY IN *SHETLAND* (2013–)

As the crow flies, the UK's closest region to Scandinavia is the Shetland Islands, which Anna Leask and Ivana Rihova describe as occupying an 'extreme geographical position in between the Atlantic Ocean and the North Sea' at the 'same latitude as Anchorage in Alaska, Bergen in Norway or Siberia' (2010, 118). Owing to both its position and its nature as an archipelago of sparsely populated islands they then suggest that Shetland has a 'very distinctive culture, which comes from its location at the crossroads between Scotland and Norway' (123).

Archaeological traces of that distinct culture can be discerned in the remains of neolithic stonework, Viking settlements, early-modern longhouses and nineteenth-century crofts. Anthropological aspects of the culture include certain forms of song and dance, wool working and other traditional crafts and certain forms of folklore, especially the distinctly Shetland folklore of trows, selkies and other supernatural beings. But although Leask and Rihova note that there has been a significant growth in small island tourism in recent years, they also find that most cultural tourism focuses 'on the islands of the Mediterranean, Pacific or Caribbean regions' which are 'traditionally associated with the three S's of tourism – sun, sea, and sand' (120). This means that Shetland is positioned in the popular imagination as somewhat apart from those sunny, sandy, southern places – which is one reason why it is an appropriate setting for a Nordic-noir style drama. So far, despite Creeber's view that the BBC television drama *Shetland* has a 'geographical and psychological terrain that is strangely Nordic in tone' (27), little analysis has considered it, or the novels by Ann Cleeves on which it is based, as instances of post-Nordic noir. However, Gunhild Agger suggests that the 'cultural heritage Shetland derives from and shares with Norway' (2020, 25) makes Shetland the place a 'highly suitable' setting for *Shetland* the series as an 'appropriation of Nordic noir' in which 'Nordic realism prevails in theme and style, and the relationship to the Nordic sphere is emphasized in references to common history, culture, and language' (2020, 33).

In a comparative work that pre-dates the arrival of Nordic noir drama in Britain by several years, Bjarne Thorup had already started to explore '[r]esponses, in body, landscape and discourse terms, to questions of peripherality in Norwegian, Danish and Scottish literature' (2007, 10). But for the most part the essays in his collection focus on aspects of shared or intertwined histories between these places in the historic past, through the middle ages and early modern period into the nineteenth and early twentieth centuries. Stougaard-Nielsen brings the argument more up to date in a paper about translating Nordic noir, in which he argues that the global success of Scandinavian crime fiction, itself the outcome of various mechanisms of consecration and canonisation, has had the effect of enhancing the 'cultural prestige and literary value, or canonization, of "peripheral literatures"' (where a peripheral literature is one written in a language that has far fewer native speakers than the languages that dominate the publishing world: English and French) (2020, 192).

Although there is a simultaneous risk that the 'marketization of these new, peripheral "indigenous crime fiction cultures" also threatens to confirm their peripheral position in the literary system by condemning them to their own quirky foreignness, distinct only by their national or regional colour' (185), it is possible that Nordic noir has provided an example of how relatively minor literatures can perpetuate, develop and articulate a sense of their own distinctiveness. This in turn might have been what made emulating it in Scotland attractive for the producers of *Shetland*. In this sense, an attraction of the Nordic has been that it has provided legitimacy and a form within which to resituate peripheral locations and languages with regard to both the UK and perhaps also to Europe: in the run-up to Scotland's 2014 independence referendum the concept of a Nordic Scotland was explicitly used by pro-independence leaders to countermand the argument that Scotland was too small to be an independent country. But another feature of the 2014 referendum debate was the moment when the Scottish people were told by European leaders that an independent Scotland would not automatically be in the European Union, and would have to apply to (re)join. The concept of a Nordic Scotland is not incompatible with the idea of a European one, and the decision of some Scottish people to remain in the United Kingdom might have been partly motivated by a desire to remain in Europe. That they have subsequently been taken out anyway might produce a new galvanising effect on calls for independence, in which case the concept of a Nordic Scotland (i.e. an autonomous one with a relatively small population in the extreme North of the continent) would be alive and well.

It was suggested above that the dissertation submitted by MA student Daniel Hughes at Stockholm University was one of the first critical studies to draw attention to the significance of the shared history of the British Isles and the Scandinavian peninsula since the late middle ages in laying the ground for twenty-first century British variants of Nordic noir. Hughes's early death prevented him from being able to follow up these ideas in the depth they warrant, and in fact it is another postgraduate researcher, Adam Grydehøj at the University of Aberdeen, who has carried out a more detailed evaluation of how the shared historiography of Picts, Vikings, Scots and Shetlanders have influenced the evolution of Shetland culture today. He showed that although people in the islands in the immediately post-Medieval period spoke a Scandinavian language as well as Scots, 'there is little to suggest that Shetlanders at that time considered themselves particularly Scandinavian' (2009, 228). This changed during the romantic period when, according to Grydehøj, exponents of Shetland folklore started to 'make a point of emphasising the essentially Scandinavian character of Shetland belief', especially in the characterisation of the supernatural beings of its imagination (ibid.). But it was not until as late as 1932, in Jessie Saxby's *Shetland Traditional Lore*, that the Scandinavian element was established as a 'permanent feature of Shetland writing about folk belief' (229). Grydehøj then shows how Saxby adapted this feature to fit both 'a Shetland nationalist' and a 'Norse romantic historical narrative', which he argues is 'the same narrative in which the most prevalent form of present-day Shetland identity is rooted' (229).

In the last part of his thesis, Grydehøj explores how this fused narrative and island mythology has retained its efficacy in Shetland in the twenty-first century. With particular emphasis on the role of heritage in economic development, he identifies a dichotomy between place branding (which is external facing) and lived experience of space and identity (which is internal) to conclude that 'whereas most Shetlanders are dedicated to promoting tradition', the Shetland Islands Council has an 'integrated branding policy' which looks forwards and outwards (230). Although he does not say it, it is precisely this tension between the global and the local that Nordic noir drama frequently explores. This – along with its geographical and historical proximity to Scandinavia – is the reason why the Nordic noir format appears to lend itself to a series in Shetland.

Sam Wollaston has identified all of these factors as potentially rich sources of alignment between *Shetland* (2013–) and Nordic noir. For example, in his review of the second series of *Shetland* in 2016, he asked rhetorically:

> If you were to swim due west from the top of Shetland, where would you make landfall? Maine? Nope. Canada? Not even. Greenland; that's how far north Shetland is. And if you swam east? Well, Scandinavia: the coast of Norway, round about Bergen. Which is way further north than Borgen, The Bridge, The Killing, all that. Shetland totally has latitude attitude, every right to have its own brooding dark cop drama – Celtic noir, which is what you might call Shetland (n.p.)

Accepting Wollaston's invitation to refer to *Shetland* as Celtic noir, this section argues that such a category usefully distinguishes it from its Nordic forebears on the one hand, while also implying a form of connection to them on the other. That is not to say that Wollaston himself uncritically adumbrates treating the series as a direct manifestation of Nordic noir, having warned in an earlier review of the first two series that 'Shetland doesn't have the scale and ambition of The Killing or The Bridge (though imagine how good we'd think it was if there were subtitles)' (2014, n.p.). His main reservation seems to be that rather than following a single story-arc throughout a whole series as per *The Killing* or *The Bridge*, the first two series of *Shetland* are divided into several discrete two-part procedural narratives in a way that militates against the slowed-down time scale and contemplative atmosphere that characterise those series. On the other hand, his joke about subtitles masks a deeper point about linguistic richness that is worth exploring. Although *Shetland* is filmed in English, owing to the distinctive culture and geography of the place there is nevertheless a rich degree of linguistic variation at work in the series. This variation both contributes to the pattern of perception by which *Shetland* constructs Shetland, and in turn strengthens the argument for situating the series within the post-Nordic tradition.

In a study of the politics of place and identity, Philip Boland argues that in 'addition to our understanding of existing spatial and social factors' it is necessary to take account of 'the importance of linguistic characteristics in local identity' formation (2010b, 2). Attaching his research to a recent specialism within human geography based on soundscapes and auditory experiences of place (his example was Liverpool), he goes on to suggest:

> moving beyond the visual to engage with the sonoric landscape and aural geography of place, for example sounds and local identity ..., music and identity ..., music and the politics of sound ..., geographies of music ... and sounds in/of the city (2010b, 4).

The sonoric landscape, or more succinctly the sonic geography, of a place is then differently nuanced to a purely spatial or visual geography, notably because spatial identities are bound up with accents and these extend beyond existing political, administrative or geographic boundaries of place to intersect with social class, profession, age, gender and ethnicity in complicated ways so that 'the influence of local and non-local forces' are equally important 'in shaping local people's identities' and hence in the production of particular soundscapes (2010b, 2).

This concept of sonic geography can usefully be applied to an extrapolation of *Shetland* as a manifestation of Celtic noir for a number of reasons. First of all, what the place sounds like is an influential factor in the construction of the series's distinctive atmosphere, capable of switching between the quaintly domestic and the deeply foreboding. For example, a review of the series for the *Drama* channel quotes these lines from the first *Shetland* novel by Ann Cleeves on which the television series is based: 'In Shetland, when there was no wind it was shocking. People strained their ears and wondered what was missing' (Drama, n.d.), before going on to suggest that this 'haunting quality of the novels is exactly captured in the way the TV series is filmed, making it a true adaptation in the most meaningful and important sense' (ibid.). For the purposes of dramatic clarity the series could not be filmed in high wind, but there is nevertheless a firm evocation of the difference between the tamed domestic spaces of human habitation and the wild interior and coastline of the island. This evocation is reinforced by the different sounds associated with each: the hustle and bustle of the police station contrasts sharply with the near silence of the outdoors. The sonic geography of the place thus illustrates the process García Avis finds in the Danish series *The Killing* whereby space and sound interact with each other in the advancement of character and theme:

> landscapes and settings ... are not only used to establish the geographical context of the story. They also have social and cultural dimensions, and they interact with other tools of audiovisual storytelling in order to reinforce and enhance the genre, themes, and plots of the series. Beyond that, they can be used to reflect the characters' emotions and identities, as well as their inner conflicts and struggles (136).

In *Shetland*, a good example of how the nexus of outer landscape with inner exploration is portrayed both using both auditory and visual means is in the characterisation of Michael McGuire played by Ciaran Hinds in the third series. Unlike the previous two series, which had been based on two-part adaptations of the first four Ann Cleeves novels, the third series took a different approach, not only in creating an original storyline, but also in devoting all six episodes to that single story, thereby more closely resembling Nordic noir where the slow burn is the norm. When the character McGuire arrives on Shetland he is taciturn and morose almost to the point of silence. This marks him out as someone to be suspected, especially given that he arrives on the same ferry as a young man who has disappeared, and is thus an instance of the discrepancy between what Matless refers to as a place's 'particular voice' (in which he does not speak) and sounds and accents that are deemed by the community to be 'out of place' (2005, 750), a discrepancy that adds up to a form of 'sonic exclusion' (758). This suspicion of the outsider is turned on its head when it is revealed both that McGuire is not an outsider (he comes from the islands originally) and that he is in the process of giving evidence against a criminal gang who have a vested interest in trying to eliminate him, so that he is in far more danger than he poses to the community. Shortly before he is killed, he is shown desperately fleeing along the open fields and coastal hills of the island, as if place itself is converted into an active character because although it is somewhere where he could hide it is also somewhere into whose yawning silence he could disappear unnoticed forever. As Broster says: 'there is just something about that wild terrain, and the way in which the characters are all so interlinked adds greater depth to the mysterious plot lines' (2019, n.p.). Through these sonic inversions of McGuire's insider/outsider status and of the degree to which he is perceived either as *a* danger or someone *in* danger, the series raises and complicates the assumption held in small, geographically isolated and rural communities that outsiders are inherently threatening (as well, perhaps, as problematising the metropolitan assumption that such communities think this in the first place).

If McGuire's accent is used to complicate the sonoric landscape of Shetland both by originating from but also interrupting its local voice, this leaves the question of what the 'particular voice' of the place sounds like before the interruption. The auditory soundscape can be described as the combination of accents and intonation of the regular cast members acting in concert to add up to a whole performance. Thus, for example, Jimmy Perez (played by Douglas Henshall) speaks in a relatively mild and somewhat generic Scots accent that endows him with a quiet authority but also the occasional linguistic deviation from the norm that reflects how he pursues his investigations. The Spanish heritage that Cleeves had imagined for him in her novels is not apparent at all either in speech or appearance, but retains a tantalising trace presence in his name, which is unexplained, and which hints through its very existence that straightforward distinctions of the insider/outsider variety are unlikely to hold water for very long. His superior in Glasgow, Rhona Kelly (Julie Graham) speaks in an accent that is stronger, more urban and less idiomatic. Alison McIntosh (played by Alison O'Donnell) speaks more quickly and often using sentences that are left hanging or words that trail off. This is perhaps used to reflect the fact that she is more likely to be involved in physical action than Perez himself. It also creates an occasional impression of inarticulacy which is quite at odds with both her bravery and efficiency so in this case the sonic effects are used to create a misleading impression that viewers are later obliged to retract or correct – as they do with McGuire – so that, as often happens in Nordic noir, the investigation turns out partly to reveal something about the investigators themselves.

But it is the accent of DC Sandy Wilson (Steven Robertson) who most contributes to the elusive, ethereal atmosphere of the series as a whole. His accent is soft like Jimmy's but idiomatically colourless like Rhona's; his speech is very unlikely to give way to the rapid pace of Tosh's but he is able to use non-verbal sounds as succinct expressions of both insight and intelligence as well as warmth and concern. His speech has the uncanny quality of sounding like someone speaking in a second language but without having a prior first language. In this, it is the closest of any of the characters to a traditional Shetland accent, which sounds much like the accent of a Norwegian person speaking in English. The world of Shetland is not England, but in sonoric terms this accent implies that it is not, or not typically, Scotland either.

This sense of equal connection to and simultaneous distance from both Scandinavia and Scotland is cemented by the fact that Tosh's flight in Series Three to Glasgow where she is kidnapped during the course of her investigation into the racketeer Arthur McCall prefigures her flight in Series Four to Bergen in Norway to investigate the death of journalist Sally McColl while looking into the murder of teenager Lizzie Kilmuir twenty-three years earlier. By virtue of being a roughly equal length flight away from both Scotland and Norway, Shetland is symbolically positioned within the orbit of both. Each is the location of political, economic and legal authority with which the Shetland police have intersecting interests. Each is also the source of various cultural activities that are again somewhat aligned with those of Shetland, but also somewhat distinct from them. These nodes of intersection imply a fundamental connectedness between Glasgow, Shetland and Bergen even though it is not always obvious on the surface.

At the sonoric level, this connectivity is conveyed through Sandy's Norwegian-sounding accent in all of the first three series, a symbolic harmony made manifest in speech and accent that finally comes to full realisation when the action moves to Norway in Series Four. Not only is Jimmy and Tosh's investigation there an extension of their investigation and hence interests back in Shetland, but they also find their accents are oddly non-discordant with those of Bergen. In an auditory sense, their speech does not stand out particularly from the English of their Norwegian counterparts so that linguistically they are quite at home. To some extent this device is a dramatic one to facilitate access by the largest possible Anglophone audience without resorting to the use of Norwegian with English subtitles. But it also has the effect of reinforcing the auditory impression of connectedness between the two places.

In his analysis of the significance of border politics and identities in the Nordic noir series *Trapped* (Iceland) and *Bordertown* (Finland), Marklund finds that the 'moral and ideological centre of the series lies with the investigators and they are ... significantly, not at the centre of the nation, but living in a borderland at some distance from the capital and in contact with others' (192). In other words, the border region itself is a particular kind of place with particular properties not the least of which is its geographical distance from metropolitan centres of power and the dialectical relationship this sets up between distant authority, local practice and increasing experiences of mobility. By setting *Shetland* at a crossroads between Glasgow and Bergen, the series taps into exactly this dialectic so that although it appears to be a small, remote and unchanging community it cannot avoid being transformed through contact with other parts of the country and the world. This helps account for the fact that the characters in *Shetland*, like those of the series discussed by Marklund, 'embody a slight nostalgia, not for the national in an excluding sense, but for values belonging to an era less influenced by both outside forces and, more generally, modernity, centralization and globalization' (ibid.).

This nostalgia in the face of the complicating forces of globalisation is made manifest during Jimmy and Tosh's visit to Norway and subsequent return, when they discover that the earlier murder of Lizzie Kilmuir twenty-three years ago had been a response to a love affair between her and Duncan Hunter, who in the present is the biological father of Jimmy's adopted daughter, Cassie. The journalist Sally had discovered this affair prior to her own death, so that Jimmy has reasonable grounds for treating Duncan as a suspect in both murders: the scene where he confronts Duncan – his dead-wife's ex-husband – with the evidence against him is intensely powerful human drama. The accent of Mark Bonnar playing Duncan is somewhat more astringent than Jimmy's and as with the 'stranger' McGuire in Series Three, this is used to augment the feeling of outsider-ness and thus suspicion associated with him. As with McGuire this feeling is later confounded in a way that undermines simplistic distinctions between being a part of the community and being an alien, and as with Tosh's flight to Glasgow the investigation explores the inner dramas and conflicts of the characters as well as the crimes in question. Lizzie is found to have been killed by a local woman, Donna Killick, because she and Lizzie were both having affairs with Duncan. Sally had discovered that her father, the retired police officer Drew McColl, had allowed the innocent Thomas Malone to go to prison so that Donna could escape justice because he loved her, but when she had confronted him about this he had killed her too. Although this seems like slim motive for killing his own daughter, it is portrayed with such high intensity and depth of feeling that it feels plausible both as an exploration of human relationships and the means by which they break down. Paul Hirons goes as far as to see its capacity to explore the nature of fatherhood in different contexts as one of the most original aspects of *Shetland* Series Four, so that 'Jimmy and Duncan and Drew McColl all represented different elements of this status and responsibility' (2018, n.p.).

In many ways, therefore, the journey to Bergen that dominates the middle part of the series is a diversion. Jimmy and Tosh's investigation into potential malpractice and corruption at an oil firm planning to operate in Shetland leads them to Mathias Søderland, a member of an extreme right-wing splinter group whom they only identify as an undercover police officer after his cover is blown and he is killed, placing them too in extreme danger. But if it is a diversion at the level of plot, the journey to Norway is absolutely integral at the level of theme. The rise of extreme right-wing groups, anxieties over the role of global corporations, and concerns about the fragility of Earth's natural resources as represented by the oil company are all subjects that have received widespread attention in Nordic noir. Although in the series they are distanced and attributed to Norway, in contrast to the nostalgically less troubled portrayal of home that Marklund describes, they are nevertheless raised as legitimate domestic concerns.

Marklund's conclusion about *Bordertown* and *Trapped* – that 'the national should indeed be cautious about foreign influence, but also assume a significant share of responsibility for its society's problems' (192) – also therefore holds true for Shetland. Thus, at the levels of thematic development, visual landscape and sonic geography, *Shetland* the series is aligned with the Nordic noir format in ways that make Shetland the place feel in but not wholly of the United Kingdom, and in but not wholly of the rest of Europe.

MAPPING THE POST-CONFLICT CITY IN *THE FALL* (2013–16)

Grydehøj's discussion of the position of Pictish and Viking elements in Shetland historiography makes two observations: the fusion of historically different components into the active construction of a singular distinctive culture for the islands in the late nineteenth and early twentieth centuries; and a more recent process that converts identity politics into regional 'branding' primarily for the purposes of cultural tourism and economic investment in the twenty-first. This branding process coincides with the growth of heritage tourism and of the cultural industries more generally, a growth which this section of the chapter discusses in the separate case of Northern Ireland.

In an innovative article about the role of film and television production in changing external perceptions of Northern Ireland, Ipek A. Rappas identifies the rise of the creative industries as a key factor in developing forms of post-conflict civil society in Ulster. Beginning with a comparison of two visits made by Queen Elizabeth II to Belfast, she points out that the first was to launch a passenger liner in Harland and Wolff shipyard in 1954, while the second in 2014 was to the Titanic Studios in the docks area where much of HBO's critically and commercially successful fantasy television series *Game of Thrones* was filmed. To Rappas, the 'two visits, 60 years apart from each other, symbolize the official support for then the shipbuilding industry and now screen industries' (2019, 540). They thus illustrate the general replacement of manufacturing by creative industries discussed in Chapter One, while also revealing Belfast's attempts to join the ranks of 'creative capitals' discussed in Chapter Two (ibid.). This transition is further highlighted by the name of the Studios themselves: named both after the best-known liner to have been built in the history of Belfast, the Titanic, and after a hugely commercially successful film, James Cameron's *Titanic*, that told its story. Although *Titanic* was 'neither produced in nor represents Belfast' (Rappas, 541), the city has nevertheless been able to make use of the film in establishing a place for Belfast in the imaginations of international film audiences, especially after the opening in Belfast in 2012 of the maritime heritage museum, Titanic Belfast, at the opening of which Cameron promoted the new 3D version of the film. Ever since then, the museum holds film-related events and promotions, so that the film can be said to have been used to tell the story of the city, even though in fact it does not portray it. According to Rappas, one of the most popular rooms in Titanic Belfast is the one dedicated to the launch of the Titanic – which also happens to be one that has windows giving an open view of the privately owned Titanic Studios, where parts of *Game of Thrones* were filmed. She quotes a museum tour guide saying that 'many visitors go up to this hall to take pictures of the studios that are closed to [the] public' (542), thus allowing her to suggest that the museum hall is 'experienced in parallel with the view of Titanic Studios in the distance' (ibid.).

In fact, in Rappas's account, one of the biggest factors in attracting HBO to shoot *Game of Thrones* in Northern Ireland was the narrative it established 'of turning Titanic Studios, defined as a post-industrial garbage space, into a creative haven' (550). But there is also a second factor in play, not merely about the shift from heavy industries to creative enterprise, but about defining a city through its heritage in the aftermath of conflict. Belfast, she points out, had been 'synonymous with strife' (540) from the start of the Troubles until the Good Friday Agreement of 1998, so that it would have been no more likely to attract either a major American television network or a film company to film there than it would have been to attract other forms of outside investment or cultural development more generally. The creative industries have then played a key role in transforming the image of the city from one of inherent sectarian violence to one that is upwardly mobile and committed to peace and creativity. Thus, the emergence of Northern Ireland as a major site for film and television production can be used to suggest a level of continuity with the industrial past, a narrative according to which the modern-day creators of film are the industrial inheritors of the early-to-mid twentieth century creators of ships. On the other hand, this creative narrative conveniently skips the intervening history of the Troubles, which would be a much more divisive history and so militate against establishing the city as a peaceful player on the world stage. Or as Rappas says more fully:

> While cities are increasingly valued as images to attract tourists and investors, image production and exhibition activities not only are used to promote a brand image but also erase troubled histories and create new stories of value for cities. This value or a new global visibility may be generated through association with screen industries as much as through images of locations. Neither *Titanic* nor *GoT* show or take place in Belfast, but they add a 'creative' value to its image as a global media capital (542).

As in other parts of the UK where the transition to a post-industrial society has taken place, the process raises significant ethical concerns about new forms of inequality among members of the traditional working-class who are best equipped for jobs and roles that might not exist in the new creative economy, even while the process offers the double promise of peace and prosperity. Rappas's description of Belfast's 'association with screen industries' even in films that are not set or filmed there thus identifies an important tool in changing the image of Northern Ireland. It directly parallels the situation described by My Nguyen Diem Tran in Wellington, New Zealand, whereby the city established itself as the centre of the Tolkien cultural industry even though 'no filming' of either the *Lord of the Rings* or *Hobbit* trilogies took place there (2015, 26).

The relationship between Tolkien's *Lord of the Rings* and Martin's *Game of Thrones* (2011–19) is worth dwelling on for a moment both because the resurgent fantasy genre has been one of the most popular of the twenty-first century so far and more importantly because Martin was significantly influenced by Tolkien, who in turn drew extensively on elements he found in Norse and Scandinavian mythology. Just as the positioning of Nordic noir in Britain has been a particularly visible element of the Nordientalist discourse outlined by Stougaard-Nielsen, works in the fantasy genre such as *Game of Thrones* and *Lord of the Rings* (as well as other examples such as the *Thor* and *How to Train Your Dragon* film series) can be traced to comparable historical, cultural and linguistic roots. Although none of the series are straightforward adaptations of those myths, the fact that they employ a range of signifiers such as people and place names, linguistic syntax, imaginary languages, plot structures, mythical characters and fantastic creatures implicitly belies the unspoken trace of a Scandinavian presence within some of the most popular cinematic works in Britain of the past two decades. To draw attention to the fact that these works have come to prominence at the same time both that Nordic noir was becoming established as a major paradigm for crime drama and the United Kingdom was starting to move towards Brexit is to emphasise the tripartite relationship between these things which relate to each other in a complex, interlocking and mutually constitutive process. Although no research has yet been carried out into the simultaneous and parallel growth in these two genres, both rooted in the Nordic region, Rappas's analysis of Northern Ireland's transition to a post-industrial and post-conflict creative economy comes closer than anyone else to making a connection between the two. This is because alongside her discussion of *Titanic* and *Game of Thrones* she also situates the BBC Northern Ireland post-Nordic noir drama *The Fall* within these twin processes – thereby bringing together for the first time in critical analysis the two traditions of post-Norse fantasy and post-Nordic noir drama.

In a detailed discussion of *The Fall* as a portrayal of post-conflict society in Belfast, John Lynch further emphasises the growth of a creative sector there. He notes, for example, that the second and third series of the BBC One police drama *The Line of Duty* were filmed in Northern Ireland, but without including any visual identificatory markers of the city or explicitly referencing the location so that the action takes place in generic, undefined urban space – unlike *The Fall*, which identifies itself as Belfast. Following Rappas's logic, which showed in the case of *Titanic* that work need not represent a specific city in order to contribute to raising its profile within the international creative industries, it is arguable that even *The Line of Duty* was able to feed into Belfast's establishment of itself as such a city. The Belfast of *The Fall* too is an international city constructed through an international collaboration off-screen between its British writer Allan Cubitt, Belgian director Jakob Verbruggen and various local crews, extras and operatives. But by being explicitly identified as itself rather than standing in for somewhere else, it was able to mobilise aspects of cultural heritage and the legacy of conflict, which relate to each other in uneasy ways in the post-conflict phase of Northern Ireland's history. Lynch therefore finds that the 'film and television industries have played an important part in this process and, through the state-funded agency of Northern Ireland Screen, have sought to boost the region's economy and celebrate what they describe in inclusive language as "our culture"' (2017, 62).

In *The Break-Up of Britain* (1977), Tom Nairn suggested two distinct possible avenues for Northern Ireland's future: either as a 'relic' of the colonial period that has not been fully accommodated into either Britain or Ireland's postcolonial transition and therefore liable to pose a number of challenges for the transition itself; or as a 'portent' for how a transition to a fully postcolonial civic society, based on peace and legal equality, might be achieved (205). However, this was in many ways a problematic distinction, partly in its consigning of Northern Ireland to the remote past and thus denying it present validity and future growth, and partly in its reinscription of binary either/or-type thinking – which has been an obstacle to, rather than a component of, the peace process.

Lynch's approach to Troubles and post-Troubles drama mobilises a more complex temporality, looking both backwards and forwards rather than only looking one way. He suggests post-conflict drama can be divided into three distinct phases, where the first two phases 'were produced, respectively, during the conflict and in the immediate aftermath of the 1998 peace agreement' (66). The third phase comes almost two decades later, and, unlike the portrayal of conflict in the first phase and its consequences in the second, third-wave Troubles drama explores possibilities for transcending the divisive and confrontational experiences of the past in the service of a new identity politics and indeed a new politics of place based on reconciliation and civic participation. It is in this third phase that Lynch situates *The Fall*. Its characteristic feature is its dynamic interplay between past and present rather than the straightforward replacing of one by the other. Thus, situating *The Fall* in the related transition from an industrial economy to a creative one, Lynch says that in the series:

> it is possible to identify that the newly enabled professional class is, in many ways, aligned with these processes of globalization but that this process has, problematically, not succeeded in resolving suppressed issues of identity, class resentment and a culture of past abuse. Indeed, in what can be considered an almost forced articulation of this, the serial killer's name, Paul Spector, suggests a haunting that personifies the return of a repressed and unresolved violence that the force of law is no longer able to keep in place, and which, in this context, can be seen as pointing to the fear of a collapse of the consensus for peace in the province (62).

Street murals, the defunct courthouse and a memorial to 'Our Murdered Colleagues' are all visual testaments to the continued presence of the past in the uneasy present of post-conflict Northern Ireland and to the relative fragility of peace itself. In an earlier study of Northern Irish fiction since the Good Friday agreement, Neal Alexander identified a general trend within the writing, which he calls its 'retrospective' tendency, in which 'there is an explicit or implicit preoccupation with the ways in which the unresolved events of the past threaten to disrupt or jeopardise those of the present' (2009, 281). This retrospective tendency is evident in *The Fall* where the serial killer is investigated by the Police Service of Northern Ireland (PSNI) which historically had replaced the Royal Ulster Constabulary (RUC) in 2001, largely owing to the unionist and hence sectarian connotations of the latter. But just as the newly emerging PSNI was rooted in the RUC, addressing the same cultural and historical challenges and staffed by many of the same people, so too their fictional equivalents in *The Fall* are portrayed as compromised through historical failings.

The subplot about a political leader using his connections to bury the crimes committed by his grown-up son makes a striking contrast to the main serial killer plot in this respect: whereas the subplot involves various vested interests, including those of senior police officers, and therefore creates the sense of a community still divided along sectarian lines, the Paul Spector plot is surprisingly free of such associations. To Lynch, this way of constructing the character and his relationships has the effect of switching emphasis away from the portrayals of political violence and its consequences that typified the first two waves of Troubles drama, and portraying instead the different social relationships involved in the criminal justice system within civil society. In other words, the fact that Spector is not portrayed as a representative of any party, cause, community or paramilitary organisation means that his violence takes on the qualities of a rogue individual to be punished within the system, rather than the behaviour of those committed to wrecking the system. In this way, the system itself is upheld and the concept of civil society is ratified.

When compared to the violence portrayed in the earlier stages of Northern Ireland's history, this portrayal makes a significant contribution to the establishment of the structures and functions of a post-conflict society which depend on the efficient operation of such systems. Lynch refers to this as a 'paradoxical' strategy of 'normalisation' (62), according to which setting a serial killer narrative in

Belfast during the Troubles might have been too uncomfortable to countenance, too close to home, given the large numbers of families living in the aftermath of violence and the degree of anxiety likely to be provoked. By contrast, the fact of assigning a fictional serial killer to Belfast for what Lynch calls 'the first time' in *The Fall* (ibid.) emphasises that murder can now be dealt with as a fictional genre without provoking quite the same degree of uneasiness. The logic of paradoxical normalisation then tells us that having a fictional murderer of its own – just like noir series set in Oslo, Copenhagen or Malmo – offers to liberate Belfast from its troubled past and take its place among them as a world city.

As part of a study of cityscapes in television crime drama, Charlotte Brunsdon has drawn attention to a different component of the paradoxical normalisation that Lynch outlines. Seeing in *The Fall* a discursive strategy by which Belfast attempts to catch up with the post-industrial social structures of other Western cities, she also sees in it an uncritical acceptance of gender inequality: 'Belfast appears on the television screen in a way that is fresh for Belfast but generically familiar for the television city: a place where women get murdered' (2018, 14). She is forced to conclude that this is at best 'a complicated benefit of the peace process' (ibid.), and possibly a somewhat limited and compromised one when gender equality is considered.

In a critical article about how *The Fall* draws on the high-cultural capital of the noir genre, Lindsay Steenberg draws attention to the unsettling and ambiguous qualities of the noir format, qualities which have 'provided for feminist film scholarship' rich ground to 'imply or insist on readings that consider complex gender politics' (2017, 62). It is arguable, for example, that one of the clearest debts owed by *The Fall* to Nordic noir is in its portrayal of Stella Gibson, a strong female lead detective compared to whom her male colleagues are physically and emotionally more vulnerable and compromised by their proximity to the people and events being investigated. This aspect of the series causes Steenberg to conclude that 'television noir can function to map the shift in the way crime television texts are shot, told, marketed, and received' and also 'as a critical resource in questioning the gendered ways in which violence is narrativized and mythologized' (71).

Much popular discussion of *The Fall* in the mainstream press at the time of its first broadcast centred around the extent to which its representation of women as victims of a sexual predator was misogynistic, and the extent to which this was offset by the presence of a powerful female officer dedicated to achieving justice for them. However, Deborah Jermyn has convincingly argued that it makes no sense to consider one without the other in reaching a holistic evaluation of the series: 'to talk about Stella Gibson without simultaneously talking about the tortured and murdered women that serve as the prompt for her work and the premise whereby she may showcase her place as a "powerful" woman in the 21st century police service, I argue, would be to persist with a major critical omission' (2017, 262). Like Jermyn, Lisa Coulthard has argued that a better understanding of *The Fall* – as well as a number of other Nordic noir and post-Nordic dramas – is achieved when the relationship between criminal, victims and investigator is considered holistically, and that to try and evaluate its gender politics through discrete consideration of either the female detective or the female victims it to miss the point of the whole. In a highly original approach based on analysis of the sonic effects, musical scoring and other muted elements of non-verbal communication through sound she argues that the '"feeling-thinking music" of female detectives gives expression to the inner turmoil of those who are presented as too traumatized to verbalize their own experience' (2018, 565). Critically, this is then as true of the victims of violence as it is of the female detective. In a comparative discussion of the 'soundscapes' of *The Fall*, the Danish series *Forbrydelsen* (The Killing), and the New Zealand drama *Top of the Lake*, Coulthard shows that '[p]resenting the detective's relation to the victim/corpse as one of emotional rather than investigatory attachment, this music is less significant for what it purportedly represents (the mechanics of crime solving) than for what it stands for (affective engagement, impenetrability, and inaccessibility)' (ibid.). In other words, sonic effects are used to slow down the time of narration and substitute inner reflection for external speech and action, thereby contributing to the pervasive atmosphere of contemplation that characterises Nordic noir. Maybe this temporal aspect, rather than its frontier setting or the emotional strength of its female lead, is what really positions *The Fall* in the aftermath of that genre.

In a study of how the heritage industries have been employed in Northern Ireland to create new forms of collective memory as the province undergoes these transitions, Crooke and McGuire divide the political history of the region as a whole into three phases, which they suggest were accompanied by three corresponding 'moments' of heritage construction: 'first, the consolidation of unionist identity through monumental buildings [1920–68]; second, the growing confidence of nationalist and republican communities expressed through remembrance and murals [1968–98]; and later [1998+] the dual uses of heritage to, on the one hand, continue a legacy of the Troubles and, on the other, as a medium through which to explore conflict transformation, reconciliation and resolution' (2018, 4). This way of classifying periods in Northern Irish history, which perhaps owes a debt to the Hegelian dialect of thesis–antithesis–resolution, gives them a somewhat longer perspective than Lynch's correspondingly tighter focus on the three stages of Troubles drama since 1970. Yet in both cases the third stage – that is, the present – is characterised by a high degree of temporal ambiguity: the very means that are made available for forgetting the past also turn out to be means of summoning it forth in the present so that there is a danger of the fragile consensus that has been created since 1998 being overwhelmed. Indeed, Laura McAtackney sees in the power struggle between the two main parties, the Democratic Unionist Party and Sinn Féin, which resulted in the suspension of the Stormont Assembly in January 2017, an 'internal low in relationships within Northern Ireland' (2018, 155), while also warning that the stand-off has been exacerbated by 'the instability caused by external pressures, especially the moves towards Brexit and its previously underconsidered impact on Northern Ireland' (ibid.). This political situation emphasises not only what is at stake in the creation of new forms of collective cultural memory and public heritage in Northern Ireland but also how incomplete and vulnerable to disruption the process remains.

With a different focus again, Robert Moore has analysed the means by which the city of Belfast undertook an exercise in corporate rebranding as part of the gradual movement beyond sectarian division. Drawing attention to the colour schemes used in the new city brand, he points out that the newly embraced colour schemes used in official publications, advertisements and signage were careful to avoid too close an association with either the traditional colours of the Loyalist or the Nationalist communities, and instead deployed colour combinations that were relatively free of such associations: 'the best description of the colors composing the new official color palette of the rebranding of Belfast would probably be business casual: it's precisely the color palette of the workday uniform of knowledge workers and the "creative classes" – the very type of postsectarian citizens that the new branding hopes to conjure into existence' (2016, 159). However, noting that scrupulously avoiding this or that colour combination can in its own way end up drawing attention to their absence, he also concludes that 'by gesturing away from the sectarian colors, the rebranding cannot help but gesture toward them – a perfect example of the surfeit of social meaning' (ibid.). In other words, the corporate rebranding he analyses has the same effect as the heritage practices identified by Crooke and McGuire: one of looking backwards into the future.

Situating *The Fall* within these corporate and heritage practices, and within the transformations wrought on Northern Irish society by the advent of the creative industries more generally, Lynch concludes that what it 'articulates through its Belfast location, therefore – amongst all its other elements of genre and cliché – is the difficulty of establishing a new people, a people not defined by the old hatreds, which can help enable a stable future of economic prosperity' (67). This is perhaps why images not only of death but also of birth pervade the series: Spector's profession as a grief counsellor and that of his wife Sally Ann, a midwife, symbolically drawing attention to the simultaneous need to remember the traumas of the past while also trying to forget them.

THE ROLE OF SPACE IN *Y GWYLL / HINTERLAND* (2013–16) AND *CRAITH / HIDDEN* (2018–22)

In an article expanding on Danish scholar Anne Marit Waade's suggestion that the distinctive note of melancholy which characterises Nordic noir television can be traced back to Nordic romanticism in the nineteenth century, Berit Glanz has compared the presentation of nature in the work of Icelandic romantic poet Bjarni Thórarensen to that in Baltasar Kormákur's Icelandic television series *Ófærð* (*Trapped*, 2015). The paper contains Glanz's provisional translation of these arresting lines from a hymn to *Iceland* by Thórarensen:

> You land of renown, which gave us life,
> a land that never harmed its children,
> all your inaccessibility has until now been of use,
> it is your future protection against iniquities.
>
> Even if temptation in the shiploads of welsh [*sic*] men

drifts onto the shore, no harm I can see;
for if away from Iceland's trading-places
into the weather she dares, to death she will freeze.

(*Ísland*, verses 1 and 4, 1825,
quoted translated in Glanz, 2019, 132).

Who are these shiploads of Welshmen who personify temptation and haunt the imagination of nineteenth-century Iceland? Discovering these lines during the coronavirus lockdown of 2020 I contacted Glanz, who helpfully replied with a threefold explanation: firstly, the 'W' sound of 'Welsh', in the Icelandic, appeared to fit a complex alliterative pattern that is not present in translation; secondly, that the same word was used to refer to people from Wales and France in that period, so that it is tantamount to a synonym for foreignness in general (which ironically is also the root meaning of the Anglo-Saxon word *Welsh*); and, thirdly, that it is most often used as an adjective to describe specific kinds of sword and therefore implicitly hints at the potential for danger posed by foreigners. His argument is then that in Icelandic romantic poetry, nature is constructed as a benign presence protecting the island from malign outside influence; whereas in contemporary Icelandic noir, the threat is concealed within and nature has a much more ambiguous position, concealing secrets and lies at the heart of the society's internal structure.

There might turn out to be no Welshmen as such in these portrayals of Iceland, but the metaphorical use of Welsh to explore the tension between fear of the outsider and fear of the threat that lurks within suggests a starting point for discussing the joint BBC Wales/ S4C drama *Y Gwyll / Hinterland* (2013–16) as an instance of post-Nordic Celtic noir. Les Roberts makes precisely this suggestion, arguing that the connection between the series and Nordic noir more generally lies less in this or that specific plot structure or checklist of features than in 'the extent to which an idea of the Nordic landscape may connate a sense of "otherness" in ways that are not intrinsically tied to the actual geography of the Nordic countries themselves' (374). This section will identify some of the signifiers utilised in *Y Gwyll / Hinterland* and the later series *Craith / Hidden* to convey this feeling of otherness, before analysing the ways in which they are deployed and finally evaluating the effects of doing so.

One of the unusual features of *Y Gwyll / Hinterland* is that it was filmed in two different forms: one almost entirely in Welsh, and another mainly in English, using Welsh with English subtitles in certain scenes. But although the Welsh version aired first, it would be misleading to treat the latter as a mere adaptation of the former since to do so would be to assign it a temporal priority unwarranted by their simultaneous creation: both are originals. Existing in these different incarnations endows the series with a state of radical linguistic instability in which just as no single version dominates the other, neither does one language. Language itself then takes on an interstitial property as a medium in which the boundaries between people and places are at times distinct, at times porous, at times overlapping and at times obscure. Acknowledging this to be an effect of the coexistence of each, this section will mainly discuss the bilingual version, where the properties of linguistic boundary-crossing are most evident. It also situates the series in the tradition of Nordic noir, where García Avis has argued that 'the bilingualism present' in series such as *Bron / Broen*, its American remake *The Bridge* and its British equivalent *The Tunnel* 'merits further consideration' because the 'linguistic tensions' between different speakers 'play a rather relevant role in each series' (137).

As we have seen in the Icelandic and Anglo-Saxon examples, Welsh has long been stigmatised within Britain as an innately strange and estranging language, perceived to use harsh guttural sounds and an illogical syntax. That these common stereotypes are quite at odds with another popular stereotype of Wales as a land of poetry and song has not rendered either any the less tenacious. For this reason, Welsh-language drama has rarely acceded to anything like a large audience share around the UK. Nordic noir offers a possible means for addressing this obstacle, because not only are many of its series fundamentally bilingual, but also because the success of the genre has cultivated a potential transnational audience numerically larger than Welsh drama has previously attracted. As Jessica Walford says in reviewing another Welsh-language noir, *Bang*: 'Bilingualism and subtitles have become a distinctive style within the Scandinavian noir genre, born from the success of crime dramas like *The Bridge* and *The Killing*. Like the Scandi-noir hits, Bang follows a similar model' (2017, 16).

In fact, Walford suggests that *Bang* was the 'first major bilingual Welsh show of its kind with characters speaking in both Welsh and English, reflecting how language is used by many people in Wales in 2017' (ibid.). This claim can only really be made if one assumes that the most 'authentic' version of *Y Gwyll / Hinterland*, which pre-dates

Bang by four years, is exclusively the Welsh one. If we assume that the bilingual presentation is as authentic (and arguably more so because of its dynamic linguistic interplay) then it got there before *Bang*.

Yet although Welsh has long been seen as alien in other parts of Britain, and although Roberts argues that the patterns of Nordic noir are used in *Y Gwyll / Hinterland* to connote a sense of otherness, the language of *Y Gwyll / Hinterland* is paradoxically normal and ordinary. It is not at all the case that Welsh = strange any more than it is the case that English = standard. Rather, all of the characters speak some degree of Welsh, from the fully fluent to the merely incidental, just as they all speak some degree of English. Switching between one and the other is then a strategic choice, variously used to connote familiarity or mystery; inclusion or exclusion; trust or paranoia.

So, if Welsh is used in an ironically normative way in *Y Gwyll / Hinterland*, it cannot contribute directly to the construction of otherness that Roberts describes and which is an important component of the Nordic noir genre on which the series draws. Everyone lives within and between the two languages of Wales and this is presented as the daily empirical reality of the society. Moreover, although the linguistic border between Welsh and English is frequently crossed, the area around Aberystwyth in which the action takes place is not constructed as a borderland in itself. This contrasts with the BBC Wales series *Keeping Faith* (2017), where illicit activity in Carmarthen is rooted in the actions of Irish gangsters across the Celtic Sea to the West, and London detectives at the end of the M4 to the East, so that the town emerges as one of a number of different intersecting nodes of communication and contact elsewhere. *Keeping Faith* was also shot in both English and Welsh, but unlike *Y Gwyll / Hinterland* no bilingual version exists so that the border crossing *Keeping Faith* portrays through plot and action is not recreated symbolically at the level of crossing between languages. By contrast, the strength of *Y Gwyll / Hinterland* is to dispense with border crossing (except in language), thereby jettisoning the idea that outsiders (the London cops or Irish criminals of *Keeping Faith*) are inherently less trustworthy, and instead directing attention to the inner dynamics of its own society. The 'outsider' is not the danger – which almost always comes from within – and DCI Mathias, returning to Wales, is as 'foreign' as anyone.

The result of Mathias's arrival in Aberystwyth is that although it is not a borderland in the sense of revealing hidden connections to activity in other countries on the globe, the construction of different kinds of space in the sprawling hinterland around the town is a formative part of the drama. If, as we have seen, bilingualism is used to create a sense of normality rather than inherent difference, then the feeling of otherness that gives rise to the atmosphere of both mystery and contemplation is more likely to arise from the portrayal of landscape and place. This rather than the mere fact of bilingualism is where Roberts finds *Y Gwyll / Hinterland*'s clearest debt to Nordic noir:

> the Nordic influence 'at home' may in part be read as a kind of 'importation of otherness': landscape viewed, or re-imagined, through a de-familiarising lens. The sheer scale of the landscape (juxtaposed to that of the human presence within it or moving through it) and the sense of openness and peripherality serve as a mechanism by which the affects of place conducive to the procedural genre – an air of mystery, the unknown (or unknowable), fear and uncertainty, a sense of existential disquiet or dread, the disturbingly irrational – can be more palpably felt. Landscape steps into the frame as a character or provocateur not merely as a setting provider (374).

An example he gives of landscape as character is the episode entitled (in English) 'Night Watch', where the body of an elderly man is found in a remote farmhouse, along with a large collection of photographs taken by the man. One of these, depicting a ruined cottage, catches Mathias's eye and although a colleague warns him, 'that could be anywhere', the key to the murder turns out to be contained in the history of ownership of this cottage and the land around it so that finding it is tantamount to solving the crime. When Mathias finally does so, he stands outside the cottage in vast hilly terrain and holds up the photograph for visual confirmation in what Roberts calls the 'consummatory' moment (378).

Towards the end of his discussion, Roberts points out that there is now a booklet published by Ceredigion County Council featuring locations used for filming *Y Gwyll / Hinterland* for the purposes of promoting tourism in the area. This replicates the reception of Nordic noir, where Stougaard-Nielsen shows that there is a Millennium Tour of Stieg Larsson's Stockholm, Nordic noir tours to locations used in *The Killing* and *The Bridge*, and a digital tourist guide, *In the Footsteps of Wallander*, published by Ystad municipality in Southern Sweden (2016, 10). Moreover, the touristic feeling of knowing a place from its use on television was to some extent built into the series themselves. Daniel Hughes argued that the opening montage of the series *The*

Bridge featured a number of 'internationally recognisable landmarks and tourist attractions from Copenhagen and Malmö' (35), which include the Øresund bridge, Hans-Christian Andersens Boulevard, The Carlsberg Brewery, Slottsmöllan, The Little Mermaid statue and Tivoli Gardens, and which are used as part of a strategy of familiarisation and immersion for a global audience, rendering the place less strange than they might otherwise think and therefore creating a feeling of a world they can enter. Redvall makes a comparable point about the use of 'well-known crime locations, such as the remarkable pentagonal building of the Copenhagen police (known from *The Killing* and *The Bridge*) and tourist locations such as Nyhavn' (2016, 354).

In the case of *Y Gwyll / Hinterland*, Roberts describes using the tourist guide as a '"follow-through" process of discovery, as if, performatively, the tourist is continuing the work of Mathias and his team (to the extent that such work is about unlocking the stories and histories inscribed in space)' (379). But to the extent that this is the case, it depends on the assumption that locations familiar to viewers from the series were once unfamiliar to the detective during the investigation, and thus points to a complex interplay between recognition and estrangement. Although the first storyline is about historical sexual abuse at a children's home near Devil's Bridge, which Roberts describes as 'a picturesque location and well-known tourist attraction not far from Aberystwyth' (378), the effect of the visual portrayal of the landmark is not to heighten viewer familiarity with the region, but rather to negate it. That is, the effectiveness of the bridge as this kind of locative signifier depends on the undoing of its recognisability as a landmark: it does not feel like a tourist attraction that we recognise in either a specific or generic sense. Its new positioning in a narrative about sexual violence presents it as disquieting and eminently menacing so although bilingualism in *Y Gwyll / Hinterland* feels paradoxically ordinary, through its construction of space the place itself feels very distinctive and unusual.

This may be part of a production strategy whereby too strong an insistence on the local can exclude potential audiences who do not recognise them – a strategy deployed, for example, by the Norwegian film *Headhunters* which according to Archer is 'much less clearly marked in terms of place than its association with "Nordic noir" might suggest' and contains surprisingly few 'allusions to its Oslo location and historical contexts' (59). Even viewers who do recognise the Devil's

Bridge are likely to see it in a different way when it figures as a metonym for the past mysteries under investigation. It thus forms part of the series's wider strategy of estrangement, which as we have seen is marked in spatial ways to a greater degree than it is marked linguistically, and in which seemingly ordinary everyday places, objects and locations can turn out to be the site of hidden meaning, repressed memory and suppressed transgression.

Two further examples illustrate this process. During the Devil's Bridge investigation, Mathias's team come across a copy of the 1908 painting 'Salem' by Sydney Curnow Vosper, depicting the seventy-one-year-old widow Siân Owen arriving for a chapel service at Capel Salem in Gwynedd in traditional dress. Ordinarily, the long shawl and tall hat, familiar in the iconography of Wales, are limited either to cultural celebrations like St David's Day or to the gift shops of tourist attractions across Wales, from Caernarfon Castle to Wales Millennium Centre. Here, however, it has a different effect when Mared Rhys (played by Mali Harries) draws attention to the well-known fact that, looked at in a certain light, it appears as though a figure of the devil can be glimpsed within the folds of the shawl. This means that the costume, as a visual signifier of Welshness most commonly associated with stock tourist activities, takes on an uncanny and unsettling aspect. This, combined with the eerie music playing while the picture is introduced, plus its presence in a deserted cottage whose occupant has disappeared, contribute to the atmosphere of uncertainty which thus sets the tone for the drama that follows. To some extent it can be considered an example of what Pierre Nora terms *lieux de memoire* or sites of memory (1989, 7) because to Nora the particular sites in which memory is embedded need not be geographical places but can simply be objects *in* places, which because of their association with events that occurred in those places then emerge as bearers of particular kinds of memory. On the other hand, in this case collective cultural memory is repressed; the costume's prior connotations of picture postcard Wales have to be negated in order for a new set of implications – those of mystery and even menace – to take their place. The costume as a site of memory operates in the series because it has been detached from one set of cultural coordinates and inserted into another. Whether the devil was really depicted in the shawl by the artist or whether this is a mere incidental *trompe l'oeil* or line-of-sight effect is impossible to answer and thus symbolises Mathias's quest to solve an apparently unsolvable problem.

Having moved to Aberystwyth from Cardiff, Mathias lives in a caravan on the outskirts of the town, a location which is highly significant within the spatial economy of the series for a number of reasons. First of all, the caravan itself has long been associated with traditionally respectable working- and middle-class holidays in Wales. As early as Raymond Williams's novel *Second Generation* in 1964, the character Kate complains that her husband's family have been going to the same caravan park on holiday for so long that it has become tedious and thus symbolises her entrapment: 'All my life I've wanted a holiday in France' but 'every year, without fail, we go to a couple of caravans by Myra's father-in-law's garage, in Wales' (54). Mathias's caravan too feels like a place of entrapment and suffocation and is therefore a world away from the cultural, social and leisure associations that the idea of caravanning would otherwise suggest. It conveys a sense of the fragile and vulnerable existence to which Mathias becomes subject during the investigation, which will bring him into opposition with a number of influential adversaries. It also depicts a degree of spartan living which thus becomes an aspect of his character: unconcerned with owning much in the way of goods or property and interested in the pursuit of truth and justice above all else. It contrasts with the spacious house and gardens of his superior, Chief Superintendent Brian Prosser, so that when Mathias confronts Prosser in his own home over his potential complicity in covering up historic sexual abuse, the differing scales and dimensions of their houses underlines the relative difference in power and stature between the two men, and therefore amplifies the enormity of the challenge confronting Mathias in his quest for justice.

Perhaps most notably of all, the caravan is a liminal place, simultaneously connecting Mathias to the town and distancing him from it. Failing to live in an ordinary respectable bourgeois home seems to have the effect of stacking local opinion up against him and this in turn complicates his investigations even when he appears to be in the right. Thus, although the West Walian hinterland in which the series unfolds is not constructed as a border region, Mathias's fragile caravan on the edge of Aberystwyth creates a feeling of transition between inside and outside, or between transient and resident, which the series renders highly ironic precisely because the outsider Mathias is treated with the hostility that should be reserved for those whom he investigates, but whose position as highly privileged insiders insulates them against such suspicion.

The construction of space as active character in *Y Gwyll / Hinterland* can usefully be compared to that in the later S4C/BBC Wales series *Craith / Hidden* (2018–22). It was suggested above that a breakthrough moment for the drama *Shetland* occurred with the launch of the third series, when its producers stopped adapting from pre-existing literary texts, created an original storyline of their own and allowed that story to occupy the whole six episodes of the series. *Craith / Hidden*, which was initially broadcast in Welsh but then followed-up with a bilingual version like that of *Y Gwyll / Hinterland*, takes this process of embracing long-form drama even further. As a police procedural, each of its two series is dedicated to a separate case but the aftermath of the first case reverberates into the second series, notably because at the end of the first DI Cadi John (Sian Reese-Williams) had been obliged to uncover the failings of her own father, the retired Detective Superintendent Huw John, in a prior investigation. Although the second series is concerned with an ostensibly different crime, its portrayal of the disintegration of the John family as a result of this discovery is directly related to the first series, creating the impression of a single, gradually unfolding narrative trajectory. This means that many of the features we recognise from Nordic noir – such as the slow-paced storyline, contemplative atmosphere, inner self-discovery paralleling external investigation, and, above all, the sense of a social structure rotten to the core and guilty of betraying the people it should protect – are all present. It also has the effect that the second series of *Craith / Hidden* is even more powerful than the first.

Beyond the ongoing collapsing domestic relationship in the John family, Series Two also reveals a number of visual and spatial signifiers which form part of its semiotic system, cultivating a series of continuity with Series One. For example, Huw John's home occupies a liminal space comparable to that of DCI Mathias's caravan in *Y Gwyll / Hinterland*: he lives 'in a unique house that is cut off from the Welsh mainland' (Craig, 2019) on a tiny island connected by a ford to Anglesey, across the Menai Strait from Gwynedd. Ellie Harrison has shown that the location used for John's fictional house was Ynys Castell, 'a private holiday home on its very own tiny island off the coast of Anglesey' which is separated 'from the main land for about four hours twice each day' (2018). But like Devil's Bridge in *Y Gwyll / Hinterland*, the potency of the place as an active agent in the drama depends on its misrecognition as mere tourist destination and corresponding re-presentation as a site of claustrophobia and menace. Throughout Series One and Series Two, Cadi is shown driving out over the ford at the start of each investigation, and returning across it at the end, thereby creating a feeling of her domestic space as somewhat apart from the city of Bangor, the police station where she works and the wider region into which she is drawn. Traversing that region then turns out to be an exercise in psychogeography, which she must map and navigate effectively in order to uncover the truth.

An even stronger spatial evocation of the continuity between Series One and Series Two is the home of the serial kidnapper and murderer Dylan Harris. By Series Two, this has become shut up and abandoned, remaining as a haunting presence in the woods around the small unnamed town where the action takes place. The moment when the sociopathic teenager Mia Owen leads Connor and Lee through the woods so they can see the house, now boarded up, feels like the crossing of a symbolic boundary so that when Mia takes Connor into the house and seduces him, apparently in order to secure his loyalty and silence, this feels like a transgression as great as anything that happened in the house in Series One.

In other words, the woods and wilderness have a part to play. Several times, scenes are intercut with static shots of the housing estate where Connor lives, and where the retired teacher Geraint Ellis is found dead in Episode One. Trees and mountains loom dramatically over the houses as if to convey a sense of their innate vulnerability and the mystery that lurks within. The road containing the petrol station where Hefin Mathews works with his daughter Beca and the house of his tenant, the former convict Siôn Wells, is very isolated, with few other amenities close by, as if to separate and isolate these three people and thus prepare the ground for the gratuitous killing of Siôn by Lee, apparently to impress Mia. The cabin home of the former social worker James Rhys lies in the interstices between town and country, and the key to connecting Mia to the murder of the old man is a photograph Cadi John discovers in Rhys's collection which shows her in the background, so that as in the 'Night Watch' episode of *Y Gwyll / Hinterland* using the photograph to find Rhys's physical location ultimately leads to the truth of the murders and space itself is not just a background but an organising principle of the drama. The wild spaces around the woods, hills and lake are where Mia, Lee and Connor meet when they should be in school, and also where Mia is finally caught.

And yet the feeling at the end of the investigation is one of tragedy. Cadi catches Mia but is given no pleasure by doing so, and only a very limited sense of justice arises. The much stronger feeling that emerges is of a wider social malaise that has brought a talented teenaged girl to this point. That Mia is apparently the most intelligent girl in her class, capable of participating in a complex intellectual discussion about the poetry of death and remembrance with her English teacher, in no way alleviates this feeling and actually intensifies it: her father is long gone; her alcoholic mother is barely aware of her existence and her mother's boyfriend is lecherous and potentially abusive towards her at every opportunity. Since Mia's school days are anything but golden, this outcome refuses the temptation towards nostalgia that characterises many of the British variations on Nordic noir, so that the series focuses its critical attention on contemporary society and makes a widespread critique of it.

VARIETIES OF ENGLISH IN *WALLANDER* (2008–16), *THE TUNNEL* (2013) AND *BROADCHURCH* (2013–17)

Craith / *Hidden*'s refusal of the nostalgic atmosphere that Stougaard-Nielsen associates with the discourse of Nordientalism in Britain stands in stark contrast to the series that started the proliferation of post-Nordic noirs in Britain, the BBC's adaptation of *Wallander* (2008–16). In a semiotic reading of the set and costumes in this series, Stougaard-Nielsen has shown how they:

> are consciously styled in the fashion of 1950s Scandinavian modern design giving them an air of functionalist welfare aesthetics, the mono-ethnic, coolly rational, socially engineered society, which is presumably disintegrating in the Sweden of Mankell's 1990s and has become a desirable nostalgic fantasy with contemporary 'white' British viewers (2016, 8).

Drawing on the work of the sociologist Ben Pitcher in *Consuming Race* (2014), he suggests that the idea of the Nordic has been constructed through recourse to features such as gender equality, social justice, a functioning welfare state, and a blend of the functional with the aesthetically pleasing in art, design and architecture, which add up to a perceived high standard of living and low crime rate. These things may or may not turn out to be intrinsic features of different Nordic countries; but their perception in Britain provides a 'corporate model of Nordic ethnicity' that 'has given Nordic style such a strong purchase in a contemporary British context' (Pitcher,

66). More specifically, noting that the audience for Nordic noir crime fiction is predominantly white and middle-class, Pitcher suggests that it provides such viewers with an 'ethnically appropriate form' of consuming whiteness (63), which Stougaard-Nielsen contrasts with 'inappropriate or excessive cosmopolitan consumption' that such an audience would find unsettling (8). In this way, Nordic noir has come to function as a 'proxy' for 'white cosmopolitan desire to imagine rooted identities in an age of globalisation steeped in complex identity politics' (ibid.).

The desires that Stougaard-Nielsen discusses have not been tested empirically, and it would be instructive to know what difference (if any) is made by vectors of class and race to precise viewers' impressions of particular Nordic noir drama series. Nevertheless, his suggestion is usefully indicative of the general mood of *Wallander*, which seems expressive of an imagined simpler time before the encroachment of globalisation and the changes in Britain's social structure which it wrought. At another level, however, *Wallander* cannot help revealing the same complexities of globalisation and transnationalism that its stylistic features appear to downplay. This is above all because although it is a British remake, it was nevertheless filmed on location in Sweden. To some extent this parallels the one hundredth episode of the less noirish crime series *Midsomer Murders*, which owing to its popularity in Denmark was filmed in Copenhagen, and in which Redvall approvingly notes that 'Denmark was shot as Denmark – unlike when for instance Vancouver is regularly used as a stand-in for big American cities' (359). Similarly, the use of Welsh locations in the Welsh noirs discussed above depended on their being presented as themselves because although they were accompanied by various forms of estrangement and uncanny alienation effects causing viewers to see them in new ways, they were not pretending to be other places – as had previously happened, for example, when Welsh locations were used for various episodes of *Holby City* or *Doctor Who*.

Although to some extent the same applies to the BBC *Wallander*, where Sweden is presented as Sweden, it is a Sweden that is almost entirely de-estranged and that hardly feels like another country at all. The biggest single reason for this is of course the language: the fact that Wallander and his colleagues all speak English all the time so that there is no cultural discount effect as there would be if subtitles were used. This means that although ostensibly taking place in the country where it was filmed (Sweden), linguistically and culturally it feels much closer to Britain. The true setting of the BBC *Wallander* is thus Sweden-imagined-as-England and the complexities of ethnic, cultural and linguistic diversity which its stylistic features offer to repress return at the point of perception.

Going on from *Wallander*, this section concludes with the suggestion that analysing the particular use of language holds an important key for situating the specifically English dramas *The Tunnel* (2013) and *Broadchurch* (2013–17) in the tradition of post-Nordic noir. This is because a certain degree of linguistic acclimatisation is needed when the characteristic properties of a series from one culture are transplanted into another and the use of a familiar language invites the viewer into a place that is otherwise constructed as Other (which is exactly what happens in the English *Wallander*). In an article discussing transnational remakes of several Nordic noir series, Richard Berger identifies this process at work in the US remake *The Killing* of the Danish series *Forbrydelsen*:

> The name of the central character was changed from Sarah Lund to Sarah Linden, and the name of the murdered teenager from Nanna Birk Larsen to Rosie Larson. These anglicizations aside, *The Killing* also expanded the narrative, so that the first season covered the first half of *Forbrydelsen*'s initial run (2016, 152–3).

The key point to be made here is that these 'anglicizations' are actually 'Americanisations': not so much in the names Linden or Larson, which could as easily be seen as English as American, but in the language deployed by the series overall. The conflation of English with American implied by the term *anglicization* hints at a feature of television drama that has so far been under-studied: the distinction between British and American Englishes in the use of subtitles. When one or other is selected consciously, it can create particular effects, contributing to the construction of character, relationship and plot just as accent and argot do through spoken language. But when applied unthinkingly, it contributes to an unspoken and uninterrogated hierarchy of languages.

In the study of the distribution of Danish noir in Japan discussed above, Jacobsen comes close to addressing this point. Building on the work of Philip Seargeant, he draws a distinction between languages like English which have come to seem as though they are 'universally available' and therefore sound as if they come 'from nowhere', and languages such as Danish which cannot be considered 'socially neutral' in the same way because they very clearly come from a particular place, 'from somewhere' (Seargeant, 2012, 5). Of course, this apparent neutrality of English is both profoundly ideological and deeply related to the past imperial and present economic dominance of Britain and America on the global stage. Being able to pass as a socially neutral language then confers on English a degree of social, cultural and commercial advantage compared to Danish, so that although Danish is important in the content of the programmes, English was used as the language of commercial negotiation in securing the broadcasting rights in Japan. As a result, Danish mainly existed as a means of generating local colour, with Japanese audiences able to hear what the characters sounded like while reading the subtitles directly into their own language, and hence contributed to the staging of authenticity that is always to some degree in play when drama from one country is received in another.

Jacobsen found that among Japanese audiences, although Danish played a role in mediating the portrayal of Denmark's citizens, it does not create a strong impression of what Denmark is like. This is 'unlike other European languages' (625), which he says very powerfully evoke connections to particular places and cultures. These presumably are the more widely spoken languages of the Mediterranean (French, Spanish and Italian), because although Ash Amin describes the Mediterranean as a region that has for centuries 'existed as a mutable space of adjacent and overlapping cultural and historical currents, defying neat cartographic or civilisational delineations of national identity' (2), it is perhaps better understood as visually overdetermined, conjuring up powerful images and strong connotations.

The inability of Japanese audiences to form distinct visual images of Denmark triggered by hearing its language might also be shared by British audiences. It has been argued throughout this chapter that one of the reasons Nordic noir gained a broad foothold in the UK was that it enabled British audiences to imagine one kind of European landscape without being overwhelmed by its dominant imagery. The contrast noted above between languages that offer themselves as coming 'from nowhere' and those that are clearly rooted and come 'from somewhere' might then provide a further level of understanding for how British audiences for Nordic noir have imagined themselves apart from the rest of Europe. In such an interpretation, the capacity of Nordic noir to disseminate a pool of images that are distinctly

Northern European rather than Alpine or Mediterranean is backed up by a corresponding collision between English as a language from 'nowhere' and the other languages of Europe which all come from 'somewhere', precisely because their capacity to evoke powerful visual signifiers in the imagination affords a sense of otherness which the ideology of the socially universal then overrides.

There is, however, one point that Jacobsen does not make, which is the need to distinguish between kinds of English. The universally available English that he refers to, like the 'Anglicizations' found by Berger in the adaptation of *The Killing*, turn out to be Americanisations and this difference warrants brief attention. Ordinarily, it is understood as the distinction between American and British English. But consider the English crime series *The Tunnel* (2013) and *Broadchurch* (2013–17): both are better understood as specifically English in a tangible concrete way rather than generically British (which is a valid minimal description, but also a weak descriptor that tells us less about them). Since it makes little sense to suggest that their characters speak 'English English', the overall distinction between American English and British English needs to be overhauled and re-expressed as that between American and English – where the former is the language described by Jacobsen as appearing to come 'from nowhere' and therefore associated with the ideology of neutrality; while the latter clearly insists on the particular places it comes from. English is not then the language of global advantage to quite the same degree as American and in fact one of the challenges for the creators of new television drama specifically in England has been to overcome the conflation of American with English that for some time has left the latter with nowhere to go.

This sense of English and American as in some ways competing with each other at the linguistic level is touched upon by Berger, when he notes that neither the American remake of *The Bridge* nor its British equivalent *The Tunnel* were aired or released on DVD in each other's countries. He attributes this to the fact that the same production company, Shine, had made both and did not want to compete with itself so that 'the two remakes thus have an "open" relationship with their source, but a "closed" one with their (non-identical) twin' (156). He then likens the UK and US remakes to Boolean logic gates, which allow access and comparison to the original Danish-Swedish series while simultaneously 'denying access to each other' (ibid.).

After his discussion of the remakes *The Bridge* (US) and *The Tunnel* (UK), Berger suggests: 'Given the success of English-language versions of Nordic crime television dramas, it was inevitable perhaps that an original UK drama would attempt to appropriate the model for its own ends' (156). He then sees such an attempt being made in the ITV series *Broadchurch* (2013–17). Since, as we have seen, most of the 'English-language' success was in fact American language success, the argument can be extended slightly to suggest that a further feature motivating producers in England to attempt a version of Nordic noir was the opportunity it afforded to re-insert English (that is, the language of England) into the format.

Creeber found that *Broadchurch*'s Dorset coastal setting lends it a 'profound sense of place' (28), which is one of the recurring features of Nordic noir. However, other commentators have suggested that *Broadchurch* does not really fit into the category of Nordic noir at all, most notably Roberts who finds that space is used as background setting rather than active agent so that the series fails to explore the question of 'agency ... with regard to place' (376). Perhaps, then, the concept of sonic geography, or soundscape, would be a more fertile place to look than visual landscape for instances of close alignment with Nordic noir. What Matless describes as the 'particular voice' of a place is then in this case very distinctively West country, Southern English and semi-rural. The Australian accent of the hotelier Becca Fisher (played by Simone McAullay) and the Scottish accent of the detective Alec Hardy (David Tennant) are palpable instances of 'sonic exclusion'. By contrast, local detective Ellie Miller (Olivia Colman)'s accent identifies her as fundamentally belonging to the place so that when the killer turns out to be within her own family this is all the more shocking. This means that although the physical contours of the place do not contribute to the twists and turns of the plot as they do in *Y Gwyll / Hinterland* or *Shetland* at its best, the sonic landscape nevertheless has discernible contours of its own. In other words, it would make no sense to consider the language of *Broadchurch* through recourse to the ideologies of the universality of English or its coming from 'nowhere' which typify the transnational reception of Nordic noir, since in the series the opposite of this is revealed and English is re-situated in a smaller, more localised and particular 'somewhere'.

As was suggested in the Introduction to this volume, one unforeseen effect of political devolution in Northern Ireland, Scotland and Wales in the 1990s that has become visible more recently is how it has elicited reactive moves within England to re-articulate representations of Englishness, in contradistinction to those other nations. This is a process which has only started to unfold in the recent past, and which has both political and cultural implications. In making this connection we might say that the avowed Englishness of series such as *The Tunnel* and *Broadchurch* provides a form of cultural and artistic representation that corresponds to the more directly political form of representation that gave rise, for example, to the introduction in the British Parliament of the provision for English votes for English laws.

At the same time, this chapter has argued that the transmission of Nordic noir in the UK put into circulation a new set of imagery which through association visually positioned Britain in the far North of Europe and symbolically distinguished it from the rest of the continent so that productions that have sought to emulate it within the UK also have this differentiating tendency. It is an argument not so much based on effect as on presence. Although there is no straightforward relationship of cause and effect, we can say that the presence of such drama in Britain forms a background of imagery which is semiotically – that is, both linguistically and visually – alternative to the dominant images of other parts of Europe. In doing so, it laid out (perhaps unwittingly) some of the groundwork on which the Brexiteers would build in suggesting a different kind of European future in which Britain, like Denmark and Sweden, would not be part of the Euro and like Norway and Iceland would not be part of the European Union at all.

Subsequent history has shown that Brexit has done more to polarise political differences between the nations of the UK than any other single event, except perhaps the responses of the devolved governments to the coronavirus pandemic of 2019–22. That is, if Nordic noir indirectly contributed to the evolution of a mental perception of Britain as in Europe but not of the EU, and if Brexit exacerbated structural differences between the British nations, then the British varieties of post-Nordic noir discussed here also participate in the self-imagining of all four nations as increasingly distinct from each other. How writers from each of those nations have responded to Brexit and participated in those different self-imaginings are then questions to be explored in the final two chapters.

4

Aspiration by Proxy: National Book Awards in International Markets

The previous chapters argued that during Britain's de-industrialisation from the 1970s to the 1990s the cultural economy took on a greater degree of importance than ever before. The transition from manufacturing to creative industries via cultural ones was accompanied by a new series of mechanisms by which the creative industries vied for space in the crowded cultural sphere, including festivals and industry prizes. As the example of the Brit Awards demonstrated, it was not only the individual winners of each award that profited from the experience, but the cultural industries as a whole, because the logic of such ceremonies is that attention is raised for everyone who participates in them so that they function like a game that everybody wins.

This chapter will explore the implications for bringing a competitive ethos into the domain of culture in another area: that of national book awards. It will argue that the free-market context generated by the European Economic Community historically created many of the conditions in which different national book awards participate, so that the histories and structures of the awards in question reveal a complex dialectical interplay between national self-assertion and international participation in what Pascale Casanova (2004) has referred to as the world republic of letters. This is because national book awards offer to assert distinctive local or national voices on the one hand; but are also involved in transnational networks of production and reception in which the nation is not the most important unit, on the other. In Britain this tension is very evident in the case of the Booker Prize, about which there is already a significant body of critical research.

But although most histories rightly set the Booker in the context of the decolonisation of the British empire; the expanding of publishing markets after the end of post-war austerity; and the more permissive culture of Britain in the 1960s, the chapter will argue that these accounts are geographically short-sighted, looking neither at historical developments in other countries that anticipated the establishment of the Booker, nor at subsequent book prizes in the UK that have sought to emulate it, especially in Wales and Scotland.

Although the Booker is not limited to writers from England, the chapter will explore how journalists, authors and scholarly researchers have been guilty of conflating *England* with *Britain* in their discussion of it, with the effect that the Booker has been positioned as a de facto prize for literature from England. Frustration with this situation might partly have motivated the Saltire Society to create the accolade Scottish Book of the year in 1982; and the Arts Council of Wales to establish a Wales Book of the Year in 1992. Although Stevie Marsden (2021) plays down the relationship between the Booker and the Saltire Society Scottish Book of the Year, arguing that the tendency for critical discussion of literary prizes to focus on one or two major awards and then extrapolate from them into a discussion of other literary prizes more generally perpetuates existing cultural hierarchies and fails to address the precise motivations applicable to each, discussion of these prizes will show that the emergence of national books awards in these nations is related to the growing momentum of their nationalist movements. Yet this process is not unproblematic, since the writers who garner the acclaim are often assimilated to a national tradition and/or canon of Scottish or Welsh works regardless of whether they have conceived of their work as contributing to a national corpus or not.

In fact, one of the ways that nationalist movements in Scotland and Wales have constructed their cultures as national is through the articulation of values such as diversity, transnational solidarity, interculturalism and cosmopolitanism as fundamental components of Scottish and Welsh culture. This has been both to combat earlier perceptions of parochialism and insularity, and as a means of articulating the distinctiveness of each nation from Britain as a whole. But recently the cultural politics of Brexit has presented various challenges to these forms of nationalism, with the effect that a renewed commitment to them emerged partly as a means of contesting Britain's withdrawal from the European Union and partly as a means of Scotland and Wales reaffirming their solidarity with other European nations. Through close discussion of the national book prizes awarded in each nation in the years surrounding the European referendum (2016), the chapter will argue that the awards themselves reveal how the values of diversity, interculturalism and global solidarity have been re-articulated as integral aspects of the nascent national cultures.

Although there is no national book award in Northern Ireland, there has been one winner each from Northern Ireland for the Nobel Prize for Literature (Seamus Heaney) and the Booker Prize (Anna Burns). Close examination of these writers, and more importantly, of the prize discourse that laid claim to them, will demonstrate how both awards accord with the post-conflict logic that characterises Northern Irish society by downplaying potentially divisive elements and emphasising instead opportunities for common participation in a shared culture. This characteristic has been an important hallmark of Northern Irish society since the Good Friday Agreement of 1998, which created the open border arrangement on the island of Ireland as a basis for the peace process. Since Brexit threatens to reverse that arrangement it is likely to create new challenges for the development of peace and reconciliation. For this reason, the chapter will suggest that the tactical avoidance of controversial elements has resulted in the awarding of cultural prizes in Northern Ireland being somewhat more muted than in other parts of the UK.

PRELUDES TO THE BOOKER

In her study of the genealogy of book prizes in France, Gisèle Sapiro (2016) identifies four phases which are worth summarising here to explore if they can be applied to the British case. First she finds the mechanics of state building in the seventeenth century, the standardisation of the French language and the rise of print culture coalescing in the founding of the *Académie française* in 1635. Arguing that the *Académie* played a key role in the creation of the state and the construction of a national identity while also being delegated power over linguistic and literary consecration, Sapiro suggests that its establishment of prizes for elocution (1671) and poetry (1701) represent France's first literary awards. However, rather than promoting later virtues such as freedom of expression and artistic creativity, they had the role of determining what could and could not be published and hence of deploying literary consecration as an armature of the monarchic state and its ideological legitimation.

In contrast to this situation, the second broad phase Sapiro discusses in the history of book prizes is the economic liberalisation of the nineteenth century, when the publishing industry expanded rapidly in the aftermath of the Industrial Revolution and when market growth had the effect of taking literary activity somewhat outside the purview of state control. Although the *Académie française* retained its authority, this period was typified by societies of authors taking the lead in advancing the professional interests and ethics of their members in order to distinguish the professional writer from both the 'amateurism of aristocratic elites' on the one hand and from the 'figure of the "mercenary writer" whose only objective is to make money' (Sapiro, 8) on the other. The single group which she says embodied this new form of cultural authority in France was the *Académie Goncourt*, which permitted only professional writers (as opposed to politicians or aristocrats) to become members and which 'explicitly aimed to challenge the consecrating power of its older sibling, the *Académie française*' (10). The *Prix Goncourt* (Goncourt Prize), first awarded in 1902, was then the public expression of the new professionalisation of the literary field.

Although the *Académie Goncourt* has never held an official state position, its reputation for disinterested judgement and preference for creativity over moral policing had the effect of turning it into what Sapiro terms, following Bourdieu, a 'consecrating authority' (11). This means that like many practices that emerge in opposition to some real or perceived set of reactionary circumstances, it ended up taking the place of the body whose authority it had set out to contest. During the third stage in France's book prize history in the mid-twentieth-century, this resulted in the dominance of the prize – and, through the increased market profile created by the prize, of the French literary market – by three main publishers: Gallimard, Grasset and Seuil.

Following the end of the Second World War, not only was there an increase in the availability of paper and an increased access to mechanisms for distribution of printed materials, there was also a change in attitude towards other cultures and societies, approaching a greater degree of cooperation and interrelationship than the mutual suspicion that had characterised the 1930s and 1940s, even among allies. This attitudinal shift was enshrined in international relations, in Europe at least, with the founding of the European Economic

Community and the establishment of a common European market, in which the publishing industry was an active player. The fourth phase in the growth of book prizes discussed by Sapiro is therefore one in which the industry engaged in more avowed practices of internationalisation: the market for literary translation grew rapidly, specific prizes for translated fiction such as the *Médicis* Prize (1958) and the *Prix Femina étranger* (1985) were established and a more recent form of literary recognition started to supplement the awarding of book prizes: literary festivals. These too have an intrinsically international outlook.

Sapiro's work makes connections between forms of literary authority and practices of consecration at different stages over the long-term evolution of French history. Although precise historical and cultural developments vary significantly from one place to another, if applied to the Anglophone sphere it has the potential to offer a model for how we think about book prizes and material culture. Before evaluating how far her four phases can be mapped onto the history of book prizes in Britain it is worth briefly considering comparable developments in Germany and Spain, where the historic inculcation of publishing and book prizes with national integration and subsequent economic liberalisation is especially prominent.

* * *

According to Rebecca Braun, the single European country that awards the highest number of literary prizes is Germany, which has had prizes for literature longer than it has been a nation. Like Sapiro, Braun situates her analysis of German book prizes within a much longer historical timeframe, beginning with the period surrounding the unification of the country, the contribution made by literary society to that unification, and accompanying forms of state authority and control. For example, she shows that:

> the first major German literary prize, the *Schillerpreis*, was founded in 1859 in response to attempts made by the rising middle classes to assert themselves against an autocratic government. The dead author [Schiller] had become a rallying point for the bourgeoisie ... The Prussian *Schillerpreis*, while also nominally recognising and supporting literary achievement, represented a counter-attempt by the monarchy to assert cultural authority, as the Prussian king formally had the last word in conferring the prize (Braun, 2014, 40).

This example suggests that as with the *Académie française*'s elocution prize in 1671, the first significant literary prize in Germany was associated with the ideological legitimation of a reactionary and autocratic state rather than with emergent discourses of creativity, far less democracy. But if the *Académie française*'s role was partly to police what could and could not be printed and disseminated, it was also partly to oversee for the first time the formal documentation and definition of the French language. To a certain extent the same can be said of German and the role played by its standardisation in the unification of the country. With the economic liberalisation that followed unification, not only was there a rapid growth in the German publishing industry and rapid expansion of the book market there, but these also contributed to the shaping and imagining of the German nation as such. Accompanied by a myriad of literary awards such as the *Kleist-Preis* (1912), the *Fontane-Preis* (1913), and the *Gerhart-Hauptmann-Preis* (1922), Braun finds that this development 'shows a consistent attempt on the part of private individuals and learned bodies publicly to curate German culture as a set of shared values throughout the German-speaking areas' (41).

That is not to say, however, that German literature or the rapidly reproduced number of awards available within it fostered the growth of German national self-imagining in either a straightforward or an unproblematic way. This is partly because, as Braun shows, such a construction 'when backed by influential political and literary personages and institutions, is inevitably a hegemonic act that imposes racial and gender norms' (ibid.). Moreover, in the specific case of Germany, owing to its recent experience of unification, there remained strong residual feelings of attachment to local entities such as cities, regions, and above all the German *Länder* (States), which pre-dated the nation as such and commitment to which militated against an easy feeling of unity. Braun shows, for example, that beginning with the *Goethepreis der Stadt Frankfurt am Main* (the City of Frankfurt Goethe Prize) in 1926–7, 'regional government began to profile successful authors whose creative output was judged worthy of comparison to the memory of Goethe – whose cult as the ultimate white, male, genial German author was at this time very much in the ascendancy' (41). Similarly, noting how many different prizes are named after Schiller, she notes that these are conferred 'as each region seeks to realize the cultural capital to which they stake a claim by engaging with the author's legacy on a local level' (43). This practice, which continued until long after the Second World War, not only entailed a provincialisation of the culture, but also had the effect that for all the diffusion of literary prizes in Germany, these did not succeed in raising the profile of German literature as a whole, or of individual German authors, internationally.

With reference to the four stages of book prize history extrapolated from Sapiro, it is clear that the first stage (national unification) and the second stage (economic liberalisation of the market) are both highly visible in Germany, but that the third and fourth stages leading to internationalisation of the market are less operative. For this to change, Braun argues, what was needed 'was a more consciously international outlook and global market awareness within the array of promotional mechanisms' (46) such as transnational literary awards. She sees this altered outlook in the establishment in 2005 of the *Deutscher Buchpreis* (German Book Prize), in which:

> unlike the many named regional and national prizes that seek to tie an author to a geographical place and/or a cultural tradition, the award deliberately does not reward authors for fitting in with a pre-existing, normative understanding of German culture. Instead, it aims to construct both authors and their work as cultural ambassadors, who, in their anticipated international success, will help shape an understanding of German culture as inherently embedded in wider global discourses (47).

In other words, the goal of the *Deutscher Buchpreis* is specifically to free contemporary German literature from its national parameters and so position its authors outside and beyond the German frame of literary valuation so that they can serve the dual function of representing German culture beyond Germany; while also being consumed by readers from the wider world who might otherwise be alienated by too strong an emphasis on the national character. This is why the prize is not named after a historical person or place, but merely invokes 'Germanness as its lead criterion' (47). However, it does so in a highly paradoxical way since the most archetypal German seems to be the one least in danger of being confined to the cultural context of contemporary German society. In doing so it instantiates a form of dialectic that is in fact quite typical of contemporary book prizes.

* * *

Unlike France's *Prix Goncourt* or Germany's *Deutscher Buchpreis*, Spain's National Award in Narrative Literature (*El Premio Nacional de Literatura, Modalidad Narrativa*) is awarded neither by a private academy nor by the publishing industry, but by the Spanish government. In a discussion relating the establishment of the prize to the democratisation of Spain following the death of Franco in 1975, Sally Perret (2015) argues that as the country became more open to the world, and less repressive to its people, successive governments used the *Premio Nacional* as a means of cultivating relationships with other countries through participation in increasingly open and transnational markets in general, and through membership of the European Economic Community in particular. Her main findings are that through its ostensible openness to fiction published in Spain's three largest 'minority' languages (Basque, Catalan and Galician) alongside those written in the dominant language (Castilian), the *Premio Nacional* has been used to create an impression of linguistic equality which in turn promulgates a feeling of democratic inclusivity for each of Spain's autonomous self-governing regions within the national culture; and that this image of an egalitarian post-dictatorship Spain played a key role in normalising its relations with the outside world. At the same time, Perret finds, the ostensible commitment to equality obscures the hierarchical relationship that continues to exist between Castilian and the other languages, a hierarchy which reinforces the domination of centre over periphery that characterises the central Spanish state's relationship to those regions. In other words, the *Premio Nacional* modulates between Spain's regions on the one hand and the transnational economy on the other and hence participates in processes of ideological legitimisation vis-à-vis the construction of the national culture that are highly neo-liberal in nature.

For example, because the National Awards appear benign indicators of humanistic worth, they have often been perceived as apolitical, as if the recognition and conferment of literary value was somehow separable from ideological content. Perret draws attention to the fact that the first non-Castilian text to win the award, the Catalan poet Joan Vinyoli's *Passeig d'aniversari* ('Birthday Stroll', 1984; National Award 1985) was awarded posthumously, with Vinyoli's widow's public acceptance of the prize money enabling the Spanish state to interpellate his work as part of a national culture. This in turn reveals 'the power the state has to use the prize to extend the cultural boundaries of citizenship in democratic Spain to include works by authors who might define themselves otherwise' (82). That is, through promotion of the National Awards the Spanish state converted ideological judgements into aesthetic criteria, as if to suggest that writers and artists were all equally free to write, and that the very best would be promoted on merit alone. This aestheticisation downplayed ideological considerations in the governance and conferral of the awards, and enabled the state to construct itself as a promoter of democracy and a guarantor of freedom in a period when that state was severing links with its Fascist past to embrace a greater number of external relationships. Or as Perret puts it: 'at a time when Spain was becoming an important member of the European Union, the existence of many National Award-winning works from diverse authors helped to portray the country as a modern and free democratic nation where literature is valued and respected' (82).

Although Spain had been a united country for centuries by the time of Franco's death, the relationships between each of the languages eligible for entry in the *Premio Nacional* and between the regions and people they represent reveals that there is nevertheless an imbrication of the prize with processes of both national unification and state control, as per the first of Sapiro's phases in the genealogy of national book awards. It was a process of modernisation and ostensible democratisation from the 1970s onwards, in which entering the European community was both the goal and the guarantor of conditions appropriate for obtaining the goal. Spain's relative rush towards Sapiro's fourth (international) stage therefore reveals the extent of its ideological commitment to the conditions of the open market.

In fact, research carried out by Frank de Glas (2013) has shown that Europe's first international prize for literature originated in Spain in 1960 when Victor Seix and Carlos Barral of the Barcelona-based publisher Seix-Barral met with representatives from Gallimard (Paris), Einaudi (Turin), Grove Press (New York), Weidenfeld & Nicolson (London) and Rowohlt (Hamburg) at the Formentor Hotel in Mallorca to discuss the establishment of what would become the *Prix Formentor*, a prize for the best novel by a first-time novelist, along with another award recognising an established writer, the *Prix International des Éditeurs*. These were joined at the Frankfurt Book Fair later that year by seven further publishers from Canada, Sweden, Denmark, Norway, Finland, Portugal and the Netherlands and an agreement was made not only to put up the $10,000 prize money, but also by each publisher to translate the winning work into their own language for publication within a year of the award. The immediate occasion for the establishment of the *Prix Formentor* was the context generated by a desire for post-war cultural reconciliation and economic reconstruction in the years after 1945. In reality, however, it was awarded only five times, from 1961 to 1965, after which the British publisher George Weidenfeld withdrew citing political intrigue among the jury members as the cause, and the consortium fell apart.

In an effort to track how far the *Prix Formentor* achieved its aims of transnational cultural cooperation and economic integration through publishing, de Glas mapped out how many of the thirteen publishers fulfilled their undertaking to publish the five winning novels in their own languages within a year of each award; how many subsequent editions of each novel were issued in their 'home' country; how many reprint editions of the translations were published in each of the other countries (and languages); and finally how many later novels by the winning authors were published both with their 'home' countries' and (in translation) in the other countries represented in the consortium. The tables he uses to track the translations and reprints show that very few of the winning novels ever went into more than one reprint outside their home country, and that the only English-language winner, American Stephen Schneck's *The Nightclerk* in 1965, all-but disappeared within a few years. This is unfortunate because de Glas sees in the *Prix Formentor* not only a 'model of international cooperation' (148) but also a forerunner of a much later initiative which 'took shape in 1993 when publishers from five different European countries selected and published a collection of non-fiction history books in "*Faire l'Europe*"' ('Making Europe', 149).

Neither the Formentor prize nor in truth many of its winning books are much remembered today, but de Glas's research implicitly shows that its significance in the history of book prizes is greater than any of the individual works awarded. As with the *Premio Nacional de Literatura* discussed by Perret, the *Prix Formentor* and the *Prix International des Éditeurs* were both 'instrumental in counterbalancing Spain's cultural isolation in the first decades of the Franco regime' (de Glas, 171) so that combating political isolation went arm-in-arm with performing a cultural and economic *rapprochement* with the rest of Europe. Literary prizes, the literary industries which the prizes publicised, and the literary products thereby disseminated all contributed to this process of European integration through cultural and economic means: de Glas goes as far as quoting an anonymous participant in the original Formentor discussions who said that 'the Formentor meetings were the heralds of a "Literary Common Market"' (ibid.). Finally, what de Glas terms the 'Formentor Principle' of 'a (pre) selection of authors ready for national and international promotion, either chosen by the publishers themselves or by a jury arranged by them' (174) would become an influential model for literary prizes across the Western world, and was to be echoed in Britain at the end of the decade with the establishment of the Booker.

FROM SEPARATE SPHERES TO COMMON MARKET

The sequence of events leading to the establishment of the Booker Prize in 1968 are now quite familiar. Steven Levin has shown that the 'idea for a British novel of the year prize originated with Tom Maschler, a young publisher at Jonathan Cape who sought a British equivalent to America's Pulitzer (1917) and France's Goncourt' (2014, 479). A desire in the publishing industry to market books more aggressively was a key factor and Maschler also had a key position inside the main trade body, the Publishers Association, which collaborated with Booker McConnell to develop the prize. Claire Squires has shown that although the latter's main business activities – rum, food distribution, engineering, shipping – seemed to have 'little to do with the business of books and publishing' (2013, 294), it nevertheless had developed an Authors Division, investing in authors such as Ian Fleming and Agatha Christie for tax purposes, and saw sponsoring a literary prize as a way of expanding this interest. The prize was initially open to works in English from Britain, Ireland and the Commonwealth (with the USA added in 2014).

One of the most enthusiastic early critical commentators, Richard Todd, heralded the Booker Prize's capacity to extend the literary canon outside Europe and North America, arguing in his book-length study *Consuming Fictions* (1996) that 'the catchment area comprises one quarter of the world's population' (8) so that the Booker Prize was able to disseminate a literary perspective on colonial history that was 'not that of the colonizer but of the colonized' (82). Graham Huggan (1994) takes a different view, drawing attention to the 'constitutive paradox' whereby through its marketisation of African and Indian writing, the Booker Prize contributes to a cultural exoticism that lavishes 'praise without knowledge' on other cultures and hence is more effective at rejuvenating the literary market place in Britain than it is in allowing diverse global voices to be heard equally (22).

The tendency of the prize to repeat the cultural and political hierarchies of the imperial period, which it ostensibly offered to challenge, was noted as early as 1972 by that year's winner John Berger, who used his acceptance speech to denounce the Booker company as a colonialist enterprise based on slave labour in plantations in Guyana, and announced that he would be donating a share of his prize money to the Black Panther movement. In a critique of the prize on grounds of its racial exclusion, the New Zealand researcher Paula Morris (2020) points out that the leading Maori novelists Witi Ihimaera and Patricia Grace have never been shortlisted; neither has any indigenous Australian or Canadian writer or any black South African novelist.

One reason Morris identifies for this racial exclusivity is the dominance of a small number of British and American publishing companies over the Anglophone book market worldwide. These publishers' 'insistence on British and Commonwealth rights when buying books, and American publishers' insistence on North American rights' has the effect of 'cutting out local publishers who help develop and support local writers' (Morris, 265). In fact, the division of English-language publishing into American and British and Commonwealth areas of control was itself reflected in the Booker Prize from its inception. Writing before American books became eligible, Claire Squires showed that the prize's entry requirements of British, Commonwealth or the Republic of Ireland citizenship 'refers to the imperial history of Great Britain and the concomitant colonial structure of its publishing industry' (2004, 45). She went on to quote Giles Clark on highlighting that 'UK and US publishers ... have divided the world English book market between them' before concluding that the 'link between Empire and business is clear in both actual and metaphorical terms' (ibid.).

The origin of the Booker Prize as a prize for British, Irish and Commonwealth writers therefore bespeaks a tacit agreement between British and American publishers not to compete on each other's turf. This is a significant characteristic of the period in which it was first awarded, at a time when the publishing industry was starting to expand after years of wartime restriction and post-war austerity. Moreover, this market orientation is further inflected by the dominant ideology of the mid Cold War period. It is notable, for example, that only three years before the launch of the Booker, the 1965 Nobel Prize for Literature was awarded to the Soviet writer Mikhail Sholokov for 'the artistic power and integrity with which, in his epic of the

[River] Don, he has given expression to a historic phase in the life of the Russian people' (Nobel Foundation, 1965). Sholokov had been involved in a number of confrontations with Stalin over artistic freedom, and had in fact been bugged by the Soviet authorities, so it is difficult not to see these lines as an endorsement of an outspoken dissenting perspective with regard to those authorities. Mustapha Marrouchi sees this award as not only 'politically motivated' but also 'one of the academy's worst acts' since he considers Sholokov 'not worthy in any way' (1999, 51). In giving the lie to the repeated insistence by Nobel academy members that political considerations do not influence their judgement, Marrouchi goes on to note that the Finnish writer Frans Emil Sillanpää won the Nobel in 1939, 'just as the Soviet Union was attempting to make his country disappear', and that Czeslaw Milosz's selection, in 1980, came 'in the year that Solidarity was born in Gdansk shipyard' (ibid.).

Three years after the politically motivated awarding of Sholokov's Nobel, the Booker Prize was launched in Britain with a nod to the same political ideology. Sharon Norris's archival research has shown that the press release of 4 October 1968 announcing the launch of the prize expressed the hope that writers would 'not need to be censored, imprisoned or labelled outrageous and controversial before hitting the headlines' (Norris, 2006, 143). She sees in this an oblique reference to the Prague Spring of August 1968, when Warsaw Pact troops had marched into Prague to crush Dubcek's government and 'one outcome had been a crackdown on writers' (ibid.). The allusion to it shows that although the binary distinction between total censorship and total freedom is in most cases illusory, the ideological construction of Soviet otherness in this period tended to enforce it, with the Booker positioned as a cultural contribution to the existential quest of an enlightened, emancipated West fighting for freedom against a repressive, censorious police-state, the Soviet Union. The allusion to Cold War ideology is heightened all the more when Norris points out that in the UK, 1968 had also seen 'the official end to censorship in the theatre' (ibid.).

As the discussion of both the *Premio Nacional de Literatura* and the *Prix Formentor* indicated above, these book awards were material means by which the Spanish state and the Spanish publishing industry sought to normalise their relations with the rest of Europe as Spain moved towards a post-Francoist stage in its history, through participation in the emerging European Common Market. Although the primary market for Booker-shortlisted work was not European, it is nevertheless true to say that the Booker too contributed to the overall expansion in the publishing industry in that period through its commitment to the principles of opening new markets. In *Consuming Fictions* Todd draws attention to the fact that the prominence of the prize became closely related, in the public consciousness, to the spirit of 'entrepreneurship' that characterised the dominant ideology of the 1980s (61), so that people are sometimes surprised to learn that the prize dates from somewhat earlier. It is then necessary to emphasise not so much historical rupture as historical continuity between the capitalist ideology of the 1960s and the free market ethos of the 1980s, and the position of the Booker Prize within both. This ideology became even more entrenched in the latter decade, when:

> the increase in the number of literary awards at this time was not confined to Britain, and the fact that a similar 'proliferation of prizes' occurred in the United States suggests that the trend in both countries may have been linked to the wave of free marketism that was sweeping the West and which was actively promoted by Margaret Thatcher and Ronald Reagan (Norris, 153–4).

All of this suggests that the three primary contexts in which the origins of the Booker Prize should be understood are: (a) the end of empire and the opportunities for new markets in English-language publishing; (b) the Cold War with its existentialist ideology of 'freedom'; and (c) the development of the European Common Market between 1957 and its transformation into the European Union in 1993. With regard to transnational book markets the Booker Prize thus has the dialectical position of participating in extended networks for the exchange of cultural capital in a way that surpasses national parameters, while also converting that cultural capital into political and economic capital in the metropolis.

This role became even more explicit in 1991, the year of the demise of the Soviet Union and the end of the Cold War, with the establishment of the Russian Booker Prize, which sought to further expand the frontiers of the publishing industry in a period when the world was no longer divided into the dominant competing factions of Capitalism and Communism. Noting that the Russian Booker was one of many new cultural awards in Russia at this time, Marina Abasheva says 'the hope was that they would be instrumental in bringing about ideological and aesthetic decentralization' (2012, 64). The extent to which this parallels and repeats the situation in Spain, where book awards in the 1960s and 1970s ostensibly offered to contribute to a new openness to European markets, and to nascent forms of capitalist democracy, is striking. Norris makes a similar point, seeing in the subsequent establishment of the Man Booker International Prize in 2004 'echoes' of 'the original sponsor's founding of the Russian Booker Prize in 1991' and 'an attempt, one assumes, to gain entrance to the recently-opened Russian market' (153). Its first winner was Ismail Kadare, an Albanian intellectual who grew up during the Cold War and whose reputation for outspokenness against totalitarianism thus made him a perfect embodiment of the prize's signifying commitment to the principles not only of freedom in the abstract but to a free market more specifically.

Writing that same year, 2004, Claire Squires drew attention to the then-embryonic field of international book-prize scholarship, calling for more research into 'how it links to the study of book history and the contemporary publishing industry' and 'what it might reveal about the European context' (2004, 38). Drawing attention to the need for comparative analysis with a European dimension, Squires goes on:

> Although the practices of literary prizes and cultural industries throughout Europe can vary widely (as well as display similarities) it is perhaps in the creation of communities of articulate voices – and hopefully the ears to listen – that literary prizes achieve the common ground of European culture, thus making their study a highly relevant act (2004, 45).

Given the context in which this common ground of European culture was developed, the most salient feature of this insight is that 2004 was the year of accession of ten new member states to the European Union. When looked at with this in mind, Squires's contemporary rallying call for greater cross-European discussion reads like a cultural manifesto for what was no longer simply the European Common Market but also by now the European Union.

Two years earlier, when *The Europa Directory of Literary Awards and Prizes* (Leckey, 2002) had indexed such awards by country, three of the states that eventually joined the European Union in 2004 (Latvia, Lithuania and Cyprus) had no entries at all. This does not mean that they did not have such awards but should rather be taken as an indicator that the awarding institutions in those states had not yet succeeded in establishing the same degree of international visibility as France's *Prix Goncourt*, America's Pulitzer or Britain's Booker. In Lithuania, for example, the Lithuanian Writers Union Award has been conferred annually since 1992 'for a high value literary work which has been published within the last 2 years' (Lithuanian Writers Union, 2020). This situation is replicated in Latvia, where since 1993 there has been an award for 'The Best Designed Book of a Year', which has 'become [an] important event rising the prestige of books, stimulating professional achievements of publishers and getting high acclaim within the society' (Latvian Publishers' Association, 2011). Along with Estonia, Lithuania and Latvia were two of the first three Soviet republics to declare their independence in 1991, thereby precipitating the break-up of the Soviet Union and the end of the Cold War. That their book prizes coincide in time almost exactly with both this historical development, and with the parallel establishment of the Russian Booker Prize, underlines the fundamental imbrication of book prizes with an open international market in general, and with the European Common Market in particular. It may well be the case that their degree of visibility has seen a relative increase in the years since entry into the European Union in 2004 gave them access to transnational circuits of capital and culture, in which case the publishing industries in those countries have moved from Sapiro's first stage in the evolution of book prizes (national unification) to the fourth stage (transnational participation) within less than thirty years – a remarkable pace.

The third 2004 accession state to have been absent from the 2002 *Europa Directory of Literary Awards and Prizes*, Cyprus, also has a history of book prizes that pre-dates its entry in the *Directory*: Lawrence Durrell was awarded the 1957 Duff Cooper Award (one of Britain's oldest) for his novel *Bitter Lemons*, which drew on his time living there. More recently, the 2019 Commonwealth Short Story Prize was won by the Cypriot author Constantia Soteriou for 'Death Customs', an English translation from a Greek original, which portrays the plight of women during the 1974 war with Turkey, when mothers and wives often did not know if their sons and husbands had been killed and which arguably places the question of both Cyprus's and therefore the European Union's border with Turkey in active question.

Most notably of all, Antonis Georgiou, who had received the 2014 Cyprus State Prize for a Novel for *An Album of Stories*, was one of the thirteen authors to receive the European Union Prize for Literature in 2016. This award operates on a rotation basis whereby winning authors are nominated by national juries in a third of the European Union's member states every year, 'making it possible for all countries and language areas to be represented over a three-year cycle' (European Union Prize for Literature, 2018). It was established in 2009 and aims to 'put the spotlight on the creativity and diverse wealth of Europe's contemporary literature in the field of fiction, to promote the circulation of literature within Europe and to encourage greater interest in non-national literary works' (ibid.). It is striking that despite the declared intention to position literary works in a pan-European framework decoupled from national traditions, the rotations through which it operates are nevertheless organised along national lines.

Overall, there is a long but traceable path connecting the *Prix Goncourt* (1902), the *Prix Formentor* (1961), the Booker (1968), Spain's *Premio Nacional de Literatura* (1978) and the Russian Booker (1991) with the profusion of national awards that came into existence with the independence of former Soviet Republics at the end of the Cold War in the 1990s and the Man Booker International in 2004. Coming after this profusion, the European Union Prize for Literature (2009) more than any other reveals the deep tension that national book prizes express, looking inwards at the nation at the same time that they look outwards to the global market. The implications of that tension for the emerging national prizes in the four nations of the United Kingdom are discussed in detail below.

THE BOOKER AS DE FACTO 'ENGLISH' PRIZE

Although the Booker Prize was originally open to novels in English from Britain, Ireland and the Commonwealth (with American fiction being made eligible in 2014), both its role in the field of cultural production in Britain and the way in which various journalists, scholars and authors refer to it have the effect of positioning it as a 'relatively' English prize. Sometimes this is done through simple conflation and error; at other times it is done in the interests of generating provocative commentary and argument. For example, in an article drawing attention to the fact that major literary awards such as the Nobel Prize, Pulitzer Prize and Booker Prize have historically been dominated by white, male authors, Tom O'Brien wrote in 2003 that 'the

Nobel list still echoes the old wisdom, "England has an empire on which the sun never sets"' (29). Through the allusion to empire this not only conflates England with Britain as a whole, but also conflates the Nobel Prize with the Booker. In fact, although the two prizes have both frequently figured in critical discussion of literary prizes, only five people have won both: J. M. Coetzee, William Golding, Nadine Gordimer, Kazuo Ishiguro and V. S. Naipaul. O'Brien's comment is therefore less notable for its analytic precision than for its symptomatic confusion, which reveals much about how the Booker has sometimes been treated.

In an article critiquing the tendency of the Booker Prize to reinforce the cultural and economic hierarchies that exist between one or two metropolitan centres and the extended periphery, Mustapha Marrouchi makes the same mistake:

> A prize for fiction in English, England's Booker is not the only literary award in England; it is not even the most lucrative. Yet it is a cultural institution of incomparable influence ... The prize does not sell books, it canonizes authors ... A glance down the list of winners since the Booker began, in 1969 – V. S. Naipaul, Nadine Gordimer, Iris Murdoch, Kingsley Amis – confirms that the judges mostly have got it right (30).

This summary of early and prominent winners of the prize makes no reference at all to the second winner, Bernice Rubens, who as a Welsh writer does not in any case accord with the category, 'England's Booker'. To make this point is not to dismiss the importance of Marrouchi's critique, but to draw attention to how it has unwittingly positioned the Booker in effect as a prize for English writing *from England*.

Paula Morris makes more extensive criticism of the Booker, drawing attention to the fact that for 'most Commonwealth writers, their books – however feted and awarded and critically acclaimed at home – will not be eligible' to receive it (265). This is because there is a requirement for them to have been published in the UK, whereas books by new writers from Australia and New Zealand are seen as a gamble by London publishers, so that many such authors find it hard to get published in Britain. To illustrate the extent of the difficulty, Morris quotes a personal communication from Harriet Allan, fiction publisher at Penguin Random House New Zealand, telling her: 'I reckon it's easier to get a New Zealand novel published in a

European translation than in an edition in the UK. Certainly, most of our fiction rights sales in recent years have been for French or German editions' (264).

Not being published in Britain makes a book ineligible for the Booker, so that, for example, the Australian novelist Melissa Lucashenko's novel *Too Much Lip*, which won Australia's most prestigious literary award, the Miles Franklin Award, in 2019 was not eligible for the Booker Prize because it did not meet this requirement. Pip Adam won the 2018 Acorn Foundation Fiction Prize at the Ockham New Zealand Book Awards, valued at NZ$53,000, for her novel *The New Animals* (2017), but at the time Morris was writing, rights had 'yet to be sold to a UK publisher' so that it remained 'ineligible for the Booker Prize' (Morris, 264). Moreover, this requirement has affected 'indigenous writers from anglophone countries' disproportionately because Booker-winning books from those countries 'are largely historical novels centred on white experience' (Morris, 266), while Maori or Aboriginal writers are marginalised. Thomas Keneally's *Schindler's Ark* (1982), Peter Carey's *Oscar and Lucinda* (1988) and *The True History of the Kelly Gang* (2002), and Richard Flanagan's *Narrow Road to the Deep North* (2014) all bear this out.

This privileging of white European experience over indigenous lives is one reason why, as Nick Sidwell finds, the most frequently used setting for a Booker shortlisted novel is London – which in turn helps explain why the Booker has often been treated as an English prize. To Morris's credit she does not conflate England with Britain but nevertheless she stops short of interrogating that same conflation when she quotes the novelist Philip Hensher's response to the opening up of the award to American authors:

> Hensher predicted the US novel could not 'fail to dominate' the Booker shortlists: not 'through excellence, necessarily, but simply through an economic super-power exerting its own literary tastes': the 'sort of English novelists who speak to an English readership about English matters, however refined or profound their technique and subject' would no longer be able to compete in the Booker Prize if 'they do not speak to a global readership' (Morris, 268).

Neither is Hensher the only author to associate the Booker with Englishness. Salman Rushdie, winner of the so-called Booker of Bookers for *Midnight's Children*, which was judged to be the best of the first twenty-five winners in the prize's history, writes in the introduction to the *Vintage Book of Indian Writing* (1997) that '[i]n England, at least, British writers are often chastised by reviewers for their lack of Indian-style ambition and verve. It feels as though the East were imposing itself on the West, rather than the other way around' (quoted in Marrouchi, 43). In the slippage between *England* and *Britain* Rushdie anticipates Krishan Kumar's subsequent argument that English nationalism did not emerge until very late because it had been obstructed by the tendency to use the terms *English* and *British* interchangeably, a tendency with which Kumar ludicrously claims 'many non-English members of the United Kingdom' were historically 'content' (2003, 186).

More accurate is the researcher Jaya Parveen whose statistical analysis found that '[o]f the 49 authors who have won the Man Booker Prize since its inception in 1969, 28 have been British and 75% of those, English' (2019, 186). Picking up on the elision of Scottish writers in the canon of Booker winners, Sharon Norris has drawn attention to the irony that although Scottish fiction underwent an extensive and widely recognised period of creativity and innovation in the 1980s, this was never reflected in either the short- or longlist for the prize. She describes Alasdair Gray's *Lanark* (1983), which is credited by many as having marked the beginning of the resurgence of Scottish fiction, as 'conspicuous in its absence' (151), so that although 'the Booker Prize from the 1980s was characterised by an openness to postcolonial fiction, it remained relatively closed to a significant body of writing from within the UK' (ibid.).

In fact, Norris's research in 2006 revealed that no Scottish author had ever been shortlisted for the prize in a year when there was not either a Scot or an American on the judging panel. In a way this observation serves as a corrective to Hensher's fears, quoted above, that including American authors in the Booker would result in British authors in general and English authors in particular being swamped. To Norris, it shows that 'despite fears of a potential sidelining of UK fiction were the Booker to be opened to US authors, it seems that Americans, or those who judge the Booker at least, may have a more inclusive view of British fiction than the usual (south east English) judges, among whom "British" fiction appears, for the most part, to have been understood as "English" fiction' (151).

Again, this comment is borne out by the facts, since as Norris observes (writing before Douglas Stuart's 2020 win): 'Only one

Scottish writer, James Kelman in 1994, has ever won; only one Welsh writer, Bernice Rubens in 1970, has ever won. When Anna Burns won the Booker in 2018 for *Milkman*, she was the first writer from Northern Ireland to win' (264). Likewise, in Nick Sidwell's discussion of the most common settings for shortlisted books, he found that three shortlisted books had been set 'at sea', which was the 'exact same number' as in Wales (2013). Moreover, the number set in the Indian city of Mumbai (seven) totalled the 'whole' number set in Scotland. This relative neglect of writing from the other nations of the UK might have provided some of the impetus for separate book awards in them.

SCOTTISH BOOKS OF THE YEAR

Like the Booker Prize, there are a number of important precursors to the Scottish Book of the Year, especially in the field of children's literature. In an article arguing that transnational book prizes can serve as a guide for teachers selecting curriculum content from other countries and cultures, Ruth E. Cox Clark, Maureen White and Nancy Bluemel cite the example of the Hans Christian Andersen Award, 'often referred to as the "Little Nobel Prize"' (2004, 12). This prize, which has Queen Margrethe II of Denmark as its patron, has been awarded biennially since 1956 by the Swiss organisation the International Board on Books for Young People to a living author (and, since 1966, an illustrator) who has made a lasting contribution to children's literature. Its first winner was the English writer Eleanor Farjeon, whose contribution today may not seem to have stood the test of time but whose best-known work, the hymn 'Morning has Broken' (1931) is significant in the current discussion because it is set to an old Gaelic tune inspired by the Scottish village of Bunessan on the Isle of Mull. Her use of the traditional tune is the only real example of a lasting work in her oeuvre (her books and plays being long out of print), so that although Farjeon was ostensibly inspired to write it by the English village of Alfriston in East Sussex, it represents a trace presence of Scottish writing in the then-nascent field of international book prizes.

A year before her receipt of the Hans Christian Andersen Award, Eleanor Farjeon had already received the 1955 Carnegie Medal, awarded by the UK's Library Association for the year's best children's books, for the collection of stories *The Little Bookroom*.

Andrew Carnegie was a Scottish-born American industrialist and philanthropist who supported the extensive building of public libraries in Britain in the early twentieth century. According to Jennifer Horan, the medal that bears his name 'was introduced by the Library Association in 1935' and given his Scottish origins it is perhaps fitting that the first two Scottish winners of any book prize should receive it: Eric Linklater for *The Wind on the Moon* (1944) and Mollie Hunter for *The Stronghold* (1974) – with fellow Scot Theresa Breslin joining them in 1994 for *Whispers in the Graveyard*. In a moving blog about her own trajectory from library user to regional judge for the Carnegie Medal and finally chair of the judging panel, Alison Brumwell sees a connection between the centenary of Carnegie's death and the thirtieth anniversary of the UN Convention on the Rights of the Child in 2019, with the 'right to an education, to be able to read, to see one's own experience and community reflected and to soar into imaginary lands' fostered both by the libraries Carnegie supported and by the UN Convention (Brumwell, 2019).

Stevie Marsden places the starting point for Scottish book awards one year after the establishment of the Carnegie Medal, with the founding of the Saltire Society in 1936, in the context of the wider renaissance taking part in Scottish culture during the 1920s and 1930s. The Society aimed – and aims – 'to improve the quality of life in Scotland and restore the country to its proper place as a creative force in Europe' (quoted in Squires, 2013, 294). Although it has been making awards to Scottish books off-and-on since then, Marsden notes that the 'earliest awards were referred to as "commendations" and came with little, or no, monetary reward' (2019, 46). Its more formalised Book of the Year Award was instituted in 1982, contemporary with the revival in Scottish fiction writing that was taking place in the 1980s.

The Saltire Society awards are structured into different categories for Fiction, Non-Fiction, Research, History, Poetry and First Book. The overall prize is selected from the category winners and since 1982 it has gone to two different biographies of Robert Burns, those by James A. Mackay in 1993 and Robert Crawford in 2009. That more than one book might address the same subject is not unusual in itself, but the award of the overall prize to two books within sixteen years for biographies of the same poet appears to be an instance of what Jonathan Arac refers to as hypercanonisation, that process which links 'a book to a nation at a key moment in history' (Arac, 1997, 7).

The hypercanonisation of Robert Burns through the award of Scottish Book of the Year to two different biographies of him in such a short time indicates one of the functions of literary prize-giving overall: to draw attention to and legitimise a small corner of the wider literary field. Through conferring the prize on Mackay and Crawford for biographies of the best-known Scottish poet, the Saltire Society recognises not only them but also the field of Scottish writing more broadly. In other words, individual writers win the prize but the field of Scottish writing also increases its cultural capital through giving it. It is a situation that can be compared in Wales to the international Dylan Thomas Prize for young writers, sponsored by Swansea University, because, although it is not restricted to Welsh writers, conferral on an international writer by a Welsh institution of a prize bearing the name of Wales's best-known anglophone poet strengthens the cultural legitimacy of the institution and of the field of Welsh writing to confer it.

This tendency to venerate a whole field over and above the individual winners of a prize is especially common in prizes named after figures from the historical and literary canon. An equivalent case is the Walter Scott Prize for historical fiction (first awarded in 2010), which has the tacit effect of recognising not only its annual winners, but also the genre of historical fiction itself – a genre which was for a long time associated with a low level of prestige. Although it is named after a Scottish writer, there are no Scottish national parameters on the eligibility for the Walter Scott Prize, and this creates a key difference from how Robert Burns has been positioned in the history of recipients of Scottish Book of the Year. It is worth exploring this difference in detail because it reveals much about the different valences in play in the field of Scottish literary award culture today.

In *Devolving English Literature* (1992) Robert Crawford argued that the field referred to as English Literature can be understood as a product of the material processes through which the 1707 Act of Union between England and Scotland effectively became operationalised. To some extent this was a matter of elaborating an aspirational feeling of what it might mean to belong to the new union in a straightforwardly ideological way. But Crawford emphasises pragmatic factors to at least the same extent as ideological ones, and possibly more so: most notably, in the growth of mechanisms for the gradual standardisation of the English language, so that bourgeois and upwardly mobile Scots could participate in the machinery of government created by the new Union and take advantage of the material opportunities it afforded. It is largely owing to its status as the outcome of this combination of ideological with pragmatic factors in the century and a half after 1707 that Michael Gardiner (2012) has argued that English Literature should better be understood as a pan-British discipline which eclipsed both England and Scotland in the service of the Union. It is therefore ironic that according to Murray Pittock, although the Scottish people became enthusiastic participants in the Union during that period, Scottish writers more specifically were often 'ambivalent' about it (2003, 249). In his later study *Bannockburns: Scottish Independence and Literary Imagination, 1314–2014* Crawford identifies Robert Burns as the true progenitor of a distinctly Scottish – as distinct from British – literary tradition.

The forms of prestige associated by the Walter Scott Prize with Scott and by the Scottish Book of the Year with Burns exemplify the difference between Gardiner's *British* English literature and Crawford and Pittock's distinct Scottish literature (in English) in a number of ways. This difference is reflected in the use of Scott's name for a prize open to British writers in general whereas Burns has been associated (through the fact that two books about him have won Scottish Book of the Year) with a specifically delineated Scottish literature. The eligibility rules for the Walter Scott Prize define a historical novel as one set at least sixty years in the past – thereby ruling out any work that addresses the lead-up to and aftermath of key referendums in 1979, 1997, 2014 and 2016 and rendering work that engages with contemporary culture ineligible. It is thus the case that this particular prize, named for a Scottish writer, not only fails to recognise but actively disqualifies from consideration any writing that deals with contemporary questions of culture, politics and identity in Scotland today. In this sense it forms an interesting contrast with the Scottish Crime Book of the Year, which was 'renamed' the McIlvanney Prize in 2016 to honour the Scottish crime writer William McIlvanney (1936–2015) (Hamilton, 2016, 26). This award could as readily have been named after a writer such as Arthur Conan Doyle, who was an archetypal crime writer but also arguably an example of a Scottish writer prominent in the British canon. In other words, whereas the Walter Scott Prize has a broadly British (and Commonwealth) remit and rules out the contemporary, the McIlvanney Prize focuses specifically on both the contemporary and Scotland. This is unsurprising since the question of Scottish nationhood, whatever one's view on it, is a predominant political and cultural issue in Scotland today so that in some senses an award like the Walter Scott Prize that rules out an interest in the contemporary also has the effect of forestalling the question of nationhood and disavowing it in advance.

Although Aileen Christianson and Alison Lumsden have rightly shown in the introduction to their study of contemporary Scottish women writers that categories such as 'Scottish' and 'writer' are mutable (2–3), a total of five authors who could be considered 'Scottish' have been shortlisted for the Walter Scott Prize: C. J. Sansom (2011), Kate Atkinson (2014), William Boyd (2016), Allan Massie (2016) and Robin Robertson (2019). This list is further instructive of the general unionist emphasis of the prize, since Atkinson is an English-born writer living and working in Edinburgh while Sansom was born in Scotland but works in the South of England and was a vociferous opponent of Scottish independence. Sansom donated money to the 'no' campaign in the 2014 independence referendum, as did another English-born writer of a certain Scottish affiliation, J. K. Rowling, whose *Harry Potter* novels are cited by the Scottish children's writer Pamela Butchart as her 'favourite' Scottish children's books (n.p.) – thereby reclaiming them for Scotland.

Of course, the national parameters erected around the Scottish Book of the Year are as ideological in their own way as the unionist tendencies of the Walter Scott Prize. In outlining the need to distinguish between the British field of English literature and the literature of England, Michael Gardiner has argued that one means of doing so is to make a further distinction between the literatures of Scotland and England, both of which he considers to be 'minority' literatures in Deleuze's sense (2006, 5). But although the categories of 'Scottish literature' and 'English literature' are both numerically smaller than that of British literature, this alone does not constitute a minor literature as Deleuze defined it. In Deleuze's account, a minor literature is one which has an inherently oppositional political stance with regard to the dominant ideology of the society in which it arises. To make this claim of the overwhelming majority of either Scottish or English writers would be to claim a degree of activism, or even authority, that they probably would not claim for themselves. Politically speaking, however, it probably does explain why works in popular genres such as history or romance have tended not to win Scottish Book of the Year, with its ideological commitment to Scottish nationhood. Since books addressing themes of a political or national dimension tend to have been written by male authors whereas genres such as history and romance are commonly associated with women writers, it also accounts for the fact that, as Stevie Marsden observes, women writers tend to be 'ostracised' from Scottish Book of the Year, which has far more often been awarded to men than women (2019, 49). For this reason, Douglas Gifford and Dorothy McMillan argue that Scottish women writers are in a double bind, treated as 'unequal to their male Scottish counterparts' on the one hand but also 'as junior literary sisters of English women writers' on the other (1997, xix).

Even more problematic in wresting either Scottish or English literature into Deleuze's category of minority literature is Deleuze's emphasis on the de-territorialisation of minor literature. Deleuze's examples of major and minor literatures are German literature, which he posits as major; and German-language Jewish literature which is not defined by the German nation and so is minor. It is difficult to see how this de-territoriality could be applied to either English or Scottish writing since in the former case it is largely the territory that defines the Englishness; while although in the latter there are plenty of Scottish authors resident in England, which makes for a potential basis in de-territorialisation, in practice many of them have been neglected by theorists and commentators seeking to establish a canon of Scottish literature along national lines. Of those, Sansom is not alone in opposing Scottish independence: shortly before the 2014 referendum, the *Guardian* carried out a detailed survey of Scottish writers' voting intentions, with the dividing line between 'yes' and 'no' falling approximately between those who continued to live in Scotland (Val McDermid, Kathleen Jamie, Alan Warner, John Burnside, Janice Galloway) and those who did not (James Meek, plus A. L. Kennedy who lives in England and did not clearly state yes or no) – with only Irvine Welsh supporting independence from outside Scotland, and only Allan Massie opposing it from within (Kidd, 2–3). Neither is Sansom alone among Scottish writers in having been shortlisted for a wider British award (the Walter Scott Prize) without having been shortlisted for Scottish Book of the Year. This is also true of Robin Robertson, a Scot resident in London who has been shortlisted for both the Walter Scott Prize and the Booker Prize but has not received a national award in Scotland; and William Boyd who also resides outside Scotland and has also received a plethora of British prizes but not Scottish Book of the Year. This apparent preference for works by Scots in Scotland somewhat contradicts the entry criteria of the

Saltire Society, which 'invites entries from the publishers of authors of Scottish descent *or* living in Scotland' (quoted in Marsden, 2019, 48 emphasis added).

Although individual judges of course have different views, the relative neglect of Scottish writers living in England and opposed to independence reveals some of the ideology of the Scottish Book of the Year, not merely in its attempts to publicise the field of Scottish literature but also to declare the nation's literary independence from the rest of the United Kingdom. In a discussion of the different lists of the best/most popular/most loved Scottish books to have proliferated since the 1980s, of which the annual shortlists for each category in the Saltire Society Scottish Book of the Year awards are an example, Stephanie Preuss has argued that such lists result from 'institutionally driven processes that had the intention to strengthen a sense of national identity after the failed devolution referendum in 1979' (2011, 2). Rather than conveying to readers a definitive set of representative works, they play an active role in constructing what constitutes a Scottish book, while at the same time omitting others that do not or cannot be made to conform to the implicit definition of Scottish literature. It is notable, for example, that James Kelman won the 1994 Booker Prize for *How late it was, how late* – which did not win Scottish Book of the Year, so that the book was positioned as that year's best in the English-speaking world, but not apparently in Scotland. This might be related to the fact that Kelman himself has made clear his reticence about being shoehorned into a national canon of works, indicating that his political affiliations (such as they are) lie more with the urban working class than with Scottish nationalists per se, thereby sidestepping the question of nationalism altogether. Robert Morace has suggested that a year earlier, in 1993, another work of Scottish urban noir, Irvine Welsh's *Trainspotting*, was 'undervalued and underestimated by the literary prize committees' but did receive 'good, even enthusiastic notices in the popular press and the literary reviews' and attracted a prominent cult following 'among British youth' (2001, 11). He thus finds that, through Welsh, interest in Scottish fiction was 'just accelerating', so that *Trainspotting* can be said to have prepared some of the ground for Kelman's Booker win, just as arguably Alasdair Gray's *Lanark* (1981), which won the inaugural Saltire Society Scottish Book of the Year Award in 1982, helped pave the way for both. On the other hand, including Welsh into a national canon of Scottish literature is as problematic as Kelman since, as was argued in Chapter One, to do so risks assimilating him to the institutionalisation of the creative industries which he resists.

In fact, Preuss argues that it is partly in contradistinction to the literature of England that the Scottish canon has been constructed. Drawing attention to the fact that one list of the *100 Best Scottish Books of All Time* included works by Virginia Woolf, George Orwell and Joseph Conrad, whose links to Scotland were considered by many to be 'tenuous', she goes on to argue that 'appropriating these works was, in fact, not an absurd presumption, but a deliberate strategy to present Scottish national identity as multi-cultural, pluralistic and inclusive' (3). These things are then presented as 'inherent characteristics that define Scottish literature', the cathecting of which *as* Scottish then follows 'trends that are currently valued highly within the international literary field' (ibid.) and promises a high level of cultural capital.

The construction of diversity and inclusivity as innate properties of Scottish culture, through contrast with the real or perceived cultures of England, became particularly prominent in the years after the 2016 EU referendum, when a majority of Scottish voters had voted to remain in the EU, creating a feeling that they were being dragged out of it by a large number of their English counterparts who were hostile to and suspicious of other cultures. This difference then prompted a re-affirmed commitment to diversity and plurality in Scotland in the years after 2016, which can be seen by considering the first three winners of Scottish Book of the Year to be awarded after the EU referendum: Kathleen Jamie (2016), Kapka Kassabova (2017) and Leila Aboulela (2018).

According to Magnus Linklater, Kathleen Jamie's volume of poetry *The Bonniest Companie*, which won the 2016 award ahead of books by Kelman and Welsh as well as fellow Booker shortlistee Graeme Macrae Burnet, is 'gentle in tone, and reflects a passion for nature and the countryside' (19). Linklater goes on to quote from Jamie's acceptance speech at the awards ceremony in the Central Halls of Edinburgh, in which she explained that she does not consider herself a political person in party terms; but in which she also explained: 'This country is undergoing a profound change ... and I feel enormously energised by that' (quoted by Linklater, 2016, 19). More specifically, she acknowledges that she had detected a change in mood across the country in the build-up to the referendum on independence in 2014, and sensing that this altered mood would likely only last for the year of that referendum campaign, felt galvanised 'to act now, and write a poem a week, to tap into the energy, as a poet who is alert to conversations' (ibid.).

These poems became *The Bonniest Companie*. Its main themes are the Scottish landscape and its wildlife, memories of childhood, and of course the Scots language. To Linklater, this combination endows the volume with both a 'sense of tradition' and 'the need to break away from it' (ibid.), so that a critical interrogation of themes and forms that might seem familiar has the effect of reinvigorating the tradition itself. This is a highly significant feature of the poetry because in retrospect the suggestion of 2014 as some kind of terminus seems misjudged. In her speech, Jamie acknowledged that the shift in mood that had inspired her to write prior to 2014 had in fact gained further momentum since: 'There's been a change of confidence, a change of mood, even since the referendum. Things are moving very quickly. I can't tell the difference between a political change and a change in confidence and a change of heart, they're all intermingled, it's a sense of doing our own thing' (quoted in Linklater, 19). Despite the tactical downplaying of the political components of her work by both the poet and the judges, this interest in a changing Scotland appears to underpin their decision to confer the national award on her.

To some extent, Kapka Kassabova's 2017 Saltire Society Scottish Book of the Year winner *Border: A Journey to the Edge of Europe* picks up the challenge implied by Jamie's discussion of the relationship between political change and a change in heart. Kassabova was born in Bulgaria in 1973 and after leaving with her parents in her late teens studied in New Zealand before settling in Scotland. *Border: A Journey to the Edge of Europe* is a work that combines travelogue, memoir, ethnography and imaginative reconstruction in its narration of Kassabova's journey to the place where Bulgaria, Greece and Turkey intersect and which during her childhood was the heavily militarised frontier not only between Europe and its others, but also between the Communist world and the West.

Petya Ivanova has shown that two of Kassabova's motivations in the project were dissatisfaction with 'the growing corporate ownership and deforestation of Britain's fringe lands, in particular, rural Scotland', and a desire to undertake a journey in which she would find out more about her 'native Balkan peripheries' (2019, 81). This journey of discovery then became an exploration into the forbidden spaces of her childhood in that tightly controlled and rigidly policed frontier territory, which was often the dividing line between life and death for those seeking to escape persecution at the hands of Bulgaria's totalitarian state, so that painful memories and the long, slow aftermath of traumatic experience forms much of the fabric of the text. As Ivanova puts it, '[t]he local stories she weaves into her narrative belong to witnesses, sufferers, survivors, family members of victims, most of whom themselves migrants, more or less comfortably settled on one or the other side of the border after ethnic persecution, ungrounded police arrests, false incrimination on accusations of spying, or as a sequence of the sorrowful expulsion of ethnic minorities' (ibid.). In other words, this account of a journey to Europe's borderland becomes a moving exploration of modern European values, based on the very things that had been denied in the past: human rights, freedom of movement and the rule of law within a democratic framework.

Given that the Saltire Society was established to improve the visibility of Scottish culture in Europe and to make the nation conscious of its heritage, and given also Stephanie Preuss's comments quoted above about the assumption of plurality and inclusivity as fundamentally Scottish attributes, the Society can be said to have demonstrated a logic consistent with these aims in awarding Scottish Book of the year to Kassabova, since doing so affirms her Scottish heritage on the one hand while also associating her with an openness to multiculturalism and other European cultures on the other. Although they are not specific judging criteria for the prize, awarding it to Kassabova therefore tacitly upholds these broader tendencies of the Society. Since *Border: A Journey to the Edge of Europe* was published in the twelve months following the decision of the United Kingdom to leave the European Union even though a clear majority of Scottish people had voted in favour of remaining in it, the selection of a writer exploring these values must have seemed all the more appropriate for Scottish Book of the Year.

Kassabova's writing has not always been as enthusiastically received in the country of her birth, or in Eastern Europe more generally. Ivanova has shown that there is 'something in her writing that imbues her genuine experience with a more distanced spirit of condescension and a patronising attitude which may even take the dimensions of stereotyped representation – particularly in her comments on certain external markers of difference such as ethnic dress and appearance, economic or intellectual status' so that 'Bulgarian readers tend to be more critical of her fleeting returns and attempts to "relocate" both herself and her origins' (80). The Romanian critic Ludmilla Kostova goes further, sensing in Kassabova's earlier book *Street Without a Name* an element of voyeurism that is akin to cultural 'colonialism' (2009, 35), functioning in the manner of a tourist guide book or marketing pamphlet that makes Bulgaria 'visible' to visitors from the West without fundamentally challenging its status of relative economic dependency (68). That these critical interpretations of Kassabova's work do not figure in the discourse of the 2017 Scottish Book of the Year is perhaps unsurprising in the light of the urgency created by the 2016 European Referendum, when Scotland sought to reassert its commitment to Europe in contradistinction to the position of England, but it does reveal the ideological undercurrents in which the giving of the prize is involved.

A year later again, in 2018, the overall winner of Scottish Book of the Year was the Non-fiction category winner, Sue Black's account of thirty years working as a forensic scientist, *All That Remains*. At the same time, Leila Aboulela won the Fiction category for her short story collection *Elsewhere, Home* and became the first person to receive both a Saltire Society literary prize and the Caine Prize for African Writing, of which she had been the inaugural winner in 2000 for her story 'The Museum'. In fact, Aboulela can lay claim to a unique treble, having also received in 2011 the Scottish Arts Council Fiction Book of the Year for *Lyrics Alley*. These latter awards were given annually from 1972, and were known for sponsorship reasons as the Scottish Mortgage Investment Trust Book Awards from 2009 until being discontinued in 2013. Confusingly, both in title and scope they were very similar to the Saltire Society literary awards, with £5,000 each awarded to winners in the categories of Fiction, Non-Fiction, Poetry and First Book, from which the overall Book of the Year emerged (with a prize of £30,000). This is a good example of what James English (2002) refers to as the 'intraconversion' of different forms of capital – symbolic, cultural, economic and political – in the field of cultural prizes, because although the Scottish Mortgage Investment Trust Book Awards came with considerably more prize money than the Saltire Society Award (which give £2,000 to each category winner, and £5,000 to the overall Book of the Year), the relatively high prestige of the Saltire Society seems to have been the occasion for the winding up of the Scottish Arts Council (now Creative Scotland) awards once their sponsorship by the Scottish

Mortgage Investment Trust had come to an end and Creative Scotland decided to allocate its own funding elsewhere.

In the year that Aboulela received the Scottish Mortgage Investment Trust Book Awards prize for best work of Fiction (2011), the overall prize was awarded to Jackie Kay for *Red Dust Road*, an account of her journey in adulthood to the Nigerian village of the biological father whom she had never known, having been given up for adoption by her Scottish mother. *Red Dust Road* in turn revisits the thematic material of Kay's earlier verse narrative *The Adoption Papers*, for which she had received the 1992 Saltire Society First Book of the Year, jointly with Christopher Whyte's volume of Gaelic poetry, *Uirsgeul* ('Myth'), and this joint award is notable for a number of reasons. On the surface, the mere fact of dividing the award (and its already modest prize money) between one work in Scotland's ancient language, Gaelic, and another that hints via Kay's exploration of her adoption at Scotland's openness to the wider world is indicative of the tensions inherent in all book prizes that announce themselves as 'national'. That is, the tension between looking inwards at the nation and outwards at the world, or between renewal of existing traditions and their expansion or transformation.

More to the point, the fact that Kay only won the 1992 Saltire Award for 'First Book' for *The Adoption Papers* and had to wait another nineteen years to win the Scottish Mortgage Investment Trust overall Book of the Year Award for *Red Dust Road*, a book on an ostensibly similar theme and with a comparable degree of innovation, is indicative of the plight of many of Scotland's female writers. In her analysis of past winners and shortlisted entrants for the Saltire Society Awards between 1988 and 2014, Marsden (2019) finds that women are more likely to be both shortlisted and to win the First Book Award than the overall Book of the Year Award (although they are still less likely than male writers to be shortlisted for or win even the First Book Award). Since the proportion of female winners (in any category) is also 10 per cent lower than the proportion of shortlisted women, she senses that between the progression from shortlisting to final award certain mechanisms are activated that lead to the regular and consistent exclusion of women writers. Britta Zangen has argued that 'although women have been trained to value men's novels more than women's, they still prefer the writings of their own sex, just as much as men do theirs' (2003, 293). The outcome of this situation is that women writers are more likely to win prizes when there is a significant number of female members on the judging panel than when there is not.

In the case of the Saltire Society Awards, Marsden shows that between 1987 and 1993, 'the academic and writer Isobel Murray was the only woman on a panel of up to seven people' (2019, 57). This situation only very gradually started to change thereafter. Drawing on Zangen's insight into the relationship between the gender of jury members and those of eventual prize winners, this very low representation of women on the judging panels for the Saltire Society Awards at the time might help to explain – if not condone – why Jackie Kay received only a prize for best 'first' book in 1992, and not one for best 'overall' book until 2011 even though the later book was fundamentally related to the earlier. Marsden shows that the fact that women writers are far more likely to win an award for best first book than for overall best book of the year has significant cultural and social ramifications because although it could be argued that it has made the awards more accessible for women writers in general, 'the First Book of the Year Award has repeatedly been presented and viewed as a "minor" award by the Society and Literary Award judges, both in terms of economic and cultural value' (2019, 59). Indeed, she notes that on numerous occasions, 'internal reports and minutes from judging panel meetings have referred to the Book of the Year award as the "main" award' (ibid.). In other words, women have been positioned by the Saltire Society Awards as relative beginners in a field where they accede to the high status conferred by winning the overall prizes only infrequently. This delay in recognising women writers until somewhat later into their careers than men is further reinforced by those cases where women receive prizes only jointly: Kay's joint award with Christopher Whyte in 1992 is not the only case of this; on the contrary, Marsden shows that of the twelve female winners of the Saltire Society First Book of the Year in the period she studied, four were awarded jointly (2019, 54). This delayed recognition means that an extended period of apprenticeship is created for women writers relative to male ones.

If this is the case for Scotland's women writers, it is also more particularly so for women of ethnic minorities. In this sense, Kay's joint reception of the 1992 First Book prize seems to pre-empt and even anticipate the 2019 Booker Prize, in which Bernadine Evaristo became the first black woman winner (for *Girl, Woman, Other*) but was only admitted to this status by sharing it jointly with an established prior winner, Margaret Atwood (for *The Testaments*) so that the effect of conferring the prize on Evaristo was lessened in both a symbolic and also a straightforwardly economic way. One of the ironies of the tendency for book prizes to inflict this protracted period of apprenticeship on women writers is that when Kay received the Scottish Mortgage Investment Trust overall Book of the Year for *Red Dust Road* in 2011, she did so ahead of Leila Aboulela, whose *Lyric Alley* was a category winner for Fiction, but not the overall winner that year.

The prolonged apprenticeship implied by Kay's progression from winning a prize for First Book in 1992 and Scottish Book of the Year in 2011 is replicated by the trajectory of Aboulela, whose life experiences having moved from Sudan to the UK and settling in Aberdeen are nevertheless quite different. Aboulela won the Caine Prize in 2000 for 'The Museum', the 2011 Scottish Mortgage Investment Trust Best Fiction category for *Lyric Alley* and the 2018 Saltire Society award for the fiction category for *Elsewhere, Home* – but is yet to win the overall Saltire Society award for Book of the Year in Scotland. Of course, writers do not write with the specific objective of entering competitions and winning prizes. But since these prizes are related to the construction of a national literary canon and the implicit valorisation of certain areas of experience and outlook over others, the under-representation of both female writers and those of ethnic minorities has the effect of undervaluing their work both economically and culturally.

In Aboulela's case, the idea that women writers should wait a certain amount of time before being deemed worthy of a national award is flatly rejected by Sally Bland, whose review of *Elsewhere, Home* points out that it is a collection of stories which shows that Aboulela 'has had this talent from the beginning of her writing, for it includes her very first stories as well as recent ones' (2018, 216). Susan Butterworth makes a similar point, showing that the collection makes available Aboulela's prize-winning story 'The Museum' among 'nine previously published stories and four new ones' (2019, 169). Nathan Suhr-Sytsma points out that the Caine Prize itself has a tendency to 'assign the winner to a single country, from "Sudan's Leila Aboulela" in 2000 to "Bushra al-Fadil (Sudan)" in 2017, neither of whom lives in Sudan' (2018, 1102). Thus, Aboulela has been variously positioned as a Scottish writer, a British writer, a Commonwealth writer, an African writer, a Sudanese writer, an Arab writer and a woman writer.

The Caine Prize itself is a further instance of the intraconversion of symbolic for economic forms of capital facilitated by cultural prizes. It was established in Britain in 2000 and named after Sir Michael Harris Caine, former chairman of the Booker Group, causing some commentators to see it as tantamount to an 'African Booker' prize (Flood, 2012, n.p.). Drawing attention to the importance for new cultural prizes to gain the level of prestige necessary to compete with other awards in an already crowded cultural sphere, Doseline Kiguru has shown that 'economic capital' alone cannot provide this degree of cultural legitimisation (2016a, 164–5). She then suggests that part of the prestige of the Caine Prize comes from the fact that 'its patrons are sourced from the Nobel Prize in Literature's African winners': Wole Soyinka, J. M. Coetzee and the late Nadine Gordimer (164). Beyond the role and prestige of the patrons, Kiguru also draws attention to the importance of the judges. But whereas Zangen highlights an approximate correlation between the gender of prize jury members and that of the eventual winners, Kiguru draws attention to the fact that for the Caine Prize, the judges are usually selected in regard to the symbolic capital that they would bring to the prize. In this regard it is quite notable that Jackie Kay was asked to serve as chair of the judges in 2014, three years after she had been awarded the Scottish Mortgage Investment Trust Scottish Book of the Year, thereby completing the apprenticeship implied by her receipt of the Saltire Society Award for Best First Book nineteen years earlier, so that she became positioned as a figure of high cultural capital and international visibility as key attributes that she could contribute. In other words, there is a reciprocal relationship between the prize and its judges, whereby being invited to chair the judging panel extended Kay's already significant prestige while at the same time her presence on the panel enabled the transfer through association of some of that prestige to the prize itself, and thence to the field of African writing.

Aboulela's career also illustrates the bridging effect the Caine Prize can have on writers by bringing them to global attention, since 'The Museum', the story that won her the 2000 Caine Prize features in *Elsewhere, Home*, the collection for which she subsequently won the Fiction prize in the 2018 Saltire Society Scottish Book of the Year awards. Drawing attention to the fact that writers who enter the Caine Prize are often 'first published in Western-based literary magazines such as *Wasafiri, Transition, Guernica, St Petersburg Review*,

The Paris Review, Open Wide, African American Review and *Granta*', Kiguru shows that this practice 'emphasizes the significant role the diaspora continues to play in African literary cultural production' (2016a, 167).

The stories in *Elsewhere, Home* are set in Cairo, Khartoum, London and Scotland. According to Susan Butterworth the themes of the collection are those of 'cultural encounter, exile from home, contrast between secular and faithful life, tradition and modernity' which are 'particular to her Sudanese/Scottish/British characters and settings' (170) on the one hand, but which are also likely to resonate with the increasing number of people who are obliged by the vicissitudes of globalisation to 'move back and forth between worlds' and for whom '[c]ultural contrast is everywhere' (169) on the other. There are of course many different factors in play that might influence a judging panel's decision to a greater or lesser degree, so although it would be reductive to suggest that Aboulela won the fiction category in the 2018 Saltire Society awards because of this interest in the experience of cross-cultural mobility and exile, it is nevertheless possible to identify high degrees of synergy and cultural continuity between the experiences that her collection explores and the values that had been recognised by the Saltire Society in the preceding years. Moreover, Bland has drawn attention to the fact that although Aboulela is interested in portraying experiences of cultural dislocation and even conflict, she nevertheless tends to eschew violent rupture: 'In her rendition, addressing cultural differences does not seem intended to pull people apart, but to help them genuinely understand each other' (216). For this reason, just as the 2016 EU referendum in Britain renders the award of the 2017 Scottish Book of the Year to Kapka Kassabova intelligible as an instance of counter-hegemonic affirmation of transnational solidarity re-codified as a typical component of Scottish culture, so too the politics of enmity and division that have typified the period provide a context in which Aboulela's portrayals of cultural reconciliation in miniature received recognition in 2018 as an extension of the same gradually unfolding narrative of Scottishness and Scottish values on the part of its canon makers. Such tensions between the domestic, the international and the transnational provide a further context in which Leila Aboulela's positioning as both a leading African writer, and a specifically Sudanese one – and as both an eminent British writer, and a more particularly Scottish one – can be understood.

WALES BOOK OF THE YEAR AS INDICATOR AND DRIVER

In the Chairing of the Bard for the winner of the poetry competition at the National Eisteddfod, which has been running since 1861 and has genuine precursors in the middle ages, Wales can legitimately claim the oldest and longest continually running literary prize in Britain. As a cultural festival, the National Eisteddfod initially focused on music and poetry more than other art forms, and did not hold a competition for prose writing until 1937, almost eighty years after its establishment. These dates alone do not prove anything, but they are general indicators of two highly salient properties of Wales's literary culture: first, that it was primarily a poetic culture prior to the twentieth century, with prose writing making only a belated entry to the field (the novel prize in the Eisteddfod is named after Daniel Owen, the most eminent Welsh novelist of the nineteenth century); and, secondly, that because this belated recognition of prose as a literary practice coincides with the period when English overtook Welsh as the majority language of Wales, Welsh prose in English, and especially the Welsh novel in English, dates almost exclusively from the end of the nineteenth century onwards. This is the argument presented by Stephen Knight's *One Hundred Years of Fiction* (2004), although Belinda Humfrey (2003) has identified a number of antecedents for Welsh writing in English prior to the twentieth century. Moreover, even when Welsh writing in English became established as a distinct branch of Wales's literary culture, and as a field of analysis and research, early critical works emphasised the Anglophone poetic tradition in Wales: *The Dragon Has Two Tongues* (1968) by Glyn Jones discussed poetry alongside fiction and *The Cost of Strangeness* (1982) by Tony Conran focused solely on poetry. Separate discussion of prose fiction came later.

The established prior existence of the National Eisteddfod and the relative belatedness of prose writing (in both languages) and of the Welsh novel in English into the literary firmament of Wales might help account for the fact that Wales Book of the Year, established by the Welsh Arts Council in 1992 and organised by the promotional agency Literature Wales since 2004, post-dates many other book prizes in Britain by a considerable degree. On the other hand, it would be misleading to create the impression of a clear break between the National Eisteddfod and the later awards for several reasons. In

Corresponding Cultures: The Two Literatures of Wales M. Wynn Thomas explores the relationship between literary production in the two (main) languages of Wales, primarily by exploring how Welsh and English have inflected and transformed each other, and when applied to the sphere of literary prizes this implies a degree of interaction between the language of the poems written for competition in the National Eisteddfod (exclusively in Welsh) and that of books considered in the Wales Book of the Year awards (which give separate prizes for works in English and Welsh in each of the categories of poetry, fiction, creative non-fiction and children's literature).

There is also a more direct form of continuity between the former and the latter since past winners of either the Chair or the Crown in the two main poetry competitions at the National Eisteddfod have frequently served as judges for Wales Book of the Year, especially in the Welsh language categories. Emyr Lewis, a judge for Wales Book of the Year in 2020, had won the Chair at the National Eisteddfod in 1994 and the Crown in 1998. Idris Reynolds, a judge in 2019, had won the Chair in 1989 and 1992. Although in these cases there was quite a long interval between winning at the National Eisteddfod and judging Book of the Year, that interval can be significantly smaller: Aneirin Karadog, a judge in 2018, had won the Chair in 2016; and Lleucu Roberts, winner of both prose medals at the 2014 Eisteddfod in Carmarthenshire, was a Book of the Year judge in 2017. In some cases, there are examples of past winners presenting awards to family members: at the National Eisteddfod of 1995, as a member of the *Gorsedd* of Bards former Chair John Gwilym Jones was responsible for chairing his son Tudur Dylan Jones and crowning his brother Aled Gwyn Jones.

If former chaired or crowned bards often go on to judge Wales Book of the Year, this can also happen the other way around: former judges of Book of the Year have gone on subsequently to win one of the competitions at the National Eisteddfod. Eurig Salisbury, a Welsh-language judge for Book of the Year in 2014 won a prose medal at the 2016 Eisteddfod. Lyn Ebeneser, a Welsh-language judge for Book of the Year in 2004, went on to win the Crown at the 2007 Eisteddfod. As with the former Eisteddfod bards who have judged Book of the Year, the number of former judges who have become successful bards too can reveal a certain dynastic element: Gwion Hallam was a Welsh Book of the Year judge in 2007 and won the Crown at the 2017 Eisteddfod, while his brother Tudur won the chair at the 2010 event.

There is thus evidence of an open correlation between recognition at the National Eisteddfod and the kind of prestige that comes with being asked to serve as a judge for Book of the Year. It is also the case that former winners or nominees for Book of the Year have subsequently been asked to judge it: in the Welsh categories, this happened when Caryl Lewis was a judge in 2018, having won in 2005 for *Martha, Jac a Sianco*. In English it occurred when Tessa Hadley became a judge in 2015, having been longlisted in 2008 for *The Master Bedroom*; and in 2012 when Trezza Azzopardi was a judge, having already been shortlisted for *Remember Me* in 2005 and longlisted for *Winterton Blue* in 2008. When Jason Walford Davies became a Welsh language judge for the 2012 award he completed an unusual treble, having been shortlisted for Book of the Year and won the crown at the National Eisteddfod, both in 2004. This replicated the triple-recognition conferred on Grahame Davies, a judge for 2004 Book of the Year, winner of the 2002 Welsh Arts Council Book of the Year (the forerunner of Wales Book of the Year) for the poetry collection *Cadwyni Rhyddid*, and winner of the 1994 Crown at the National Eisteddfod. Davies is without question one of several Welsh writers whose work merits a broader readership outside Wales than it has often enjoyed. Overall, there is an observable tendency for former chaired or crowned bards at the National Eisteddfod to judge Wales Book of the Year, and vice versa; and for former shortlistees or winners of Book of the Year to later judge it. This also happens in reverse: the 2007 English-language judge Patrick McGuinness subsequently won Wales Book of the Year twice, for *The Last Hundred Days* in 2012 and *Other People's Countries* in 2015.

All of this points to Wales Book of the Year as an active mechanism for a complex three-way consecration: it increases the personal prestige of the judges who are selected, the writers who win in each of the categories as well as those who win the overall prize, and perhaps above all it augments the position and status of Welsh literature itself. It also does this in a slightly differential way between the two languages of Wales and between the forms of prose and poetry since in Welsh poetry winning the Chair at the Eisteddfod remains arguably more prestigious than winning the poetry category in Wales Book of the Year. Not only is membership of the top level of the *Gorsedd* a form of recognition in itself, but the judges at the National Eisteddfod can and do withhold the prizes if they feel the overall standard of the competition does not merit awarding them. Also, competitors for the

Bardic Chair are given specific themes to base their entries on. The first woman to win it, Mererid Hopwood (2001), has spoken movingly of what winning it meant to her (see Price, 2009), and although winning Wales Book of the Year brings more financial gain, it is unlikely that any writer would write a book with the specific intention of winning such an award in quite the same way that she actively wrote for the Chair. She thus illustrates the general argument made by Claire Squires (whose example is the IMPAC Dublin Literary Award, the annual value of which is €100,000) that the richest prize fund does not necessarily equate to the highest symbolic 'capital', and may be an attempt to compensate for the lack of it (2004, 44). In Wales, the Artes Mundi prize open to visual artists from all over the world might be considered a comparable case. Since its launch in 2003 it has been one of the most valuable art prizes in the world, but it is debatable whether it has increased the prestige of Wales as a major home of the visual arts when compared either to metropolitan centres such as London, Paris, Berlin, New York or Tokyo or to the National Eisteddfod's visual arts competition.

The profile-enhancing effect of Wales Book of the Year is therefore not as great for poetry as it is for prose fiction and this is especially true of poetry in Welsh, since the Eisteddfod remains the most important single mechanism of literary consecration for Welsh poetry, with its high symbolic capital offsetting its lower economic value. To some extent, the poetry categories in Wales Book of the Year have therefore had more of an impact on attracting greater prominence for English poetry in Wales, which has no direct equivalent of the National Eisteddfod and therefore prior to 1992 had no leading mechanism of consecration except perhaps the publication *Poetry Wales*.[1] The biggest difference made by Wales Book of the Year, however, has been to works in the prose categories of Fiction and Non-Fiction; and of these the biggest difference has been made to English fiction. Not only has English prose fiction become more prominent, but there is also an imbalance between how much English language fiction gets translated into Welsh than the other way around. This imbalance replicates the situation in other countries whose literary cultures exist within and between two or more different languages in complex ways: in Agnes Whitfield's study of the recent shortlists for the Governor General's Literary Awards for translation in Canada, she has shown that 'five times' more works get translated from the dominant language, English, into the official minority language, French, than vice versa (2016, 268). By contrast Mario Santana's study of Spain's *Premio Nacional de Literatura* finds that whereas translation from texts written in one of the minority languages Basque, Catalan or Galician into Castilian Spanish are relatively common, not 'a single Spanish-language book winner of the Critics Prize in these three decades has been translated' into any of them (216) – a situation which arguably reinforces the dominance of the majority language in a complementary way to that practised in Canada. In Wales both trends are operative. Alys Conran's debut novel *Pigeon* won the English-language fiction prize and overall Wales Book of the Year in 2017, and was published simultaneously in Welsh translation by Sian Northey. An English translation of Manon Steffan Ros's 2019 Welsh-language fiction book of the year *Llyfr Glas Nebo* (*The Blue Book of Nebo*) was published in 2022.

As we have seen, the Welsh novel in English is a mainly twentieth- and twenty-first-century phenomenon. But although there were many fine prose writers from Wales throughout this period, the empirical existence of individual authors alone – however talented – does not guarantee the establishment of a specific field. Certain material tools, of which Wales Book of the Year is one, are necessary to help construct the field as one of both artistic endeavour and critical research in its own right. In other words, the history of Welsh writing in English is the history of a field that had to be materially created in order to exist and the veneration and increased visibility that come with the prize are among the material forms that this history has taken.

One of the effects of this material history is that Welsh writers in English have started to become relatively more successful in other British literary prizes than was the case prior to that time, possibly because they have a slightly greater profile than they would have done earlier on. For example, although the second winner of the Booker Prize, Bernice Rubens (1970) was Welsh, the novel for which she won, *The Elected Member*, deals with incest and the memory of traumatic experience among Jewish immigrant communities in London and in subsequent critical discussion Rubens has tended to figure as a Jewish writer rather than a Welsh one. Thereafter, no Welsh writer was shortlisted for the Booker until Rubens again in 1978, Jan Morris in 1985 and none again until 2000. This paucity of Welsh nominations in the first three decades of the Booker's history contrasts with the situation in the twenty-first century, where several writers to have either been shortlisted for or won the English Fiction section of Wales

Book of the Year have subsequently been recognised by the Booker: Trezza Azzopardi was shortlisted in 2000 for *The Hiding Place*; Stevie Davies was longlisted in 2001 (the first year in which the longlist was published) for *The Element of Water*; Sarah Waters in 2002, 2006 and 2009 for *Fingersmith, The Night Watch* and *The Little Stranger*; Peter Ho Davies was longlisted in 2007 for *The Welsh Girl* as was Nikita Lalwani for *Gifted*; and Patrick McGuinness was longlisted in 2011 for *The Last Hundred Days*. In some of these cases of course being nominated for Wales Book of the Year has been a way of claiming the writers *as* Welsh.

Over the same period, Waters has been shortlisted three times for the Women's Prize for Fiction (formerly the Orange Prize) for *Fingersmith, The Night Watch* and *The Paying Guests* (2015); and Tessa Hadley, a past winner and past judge of Wales Book of the Year, has been longlisted for it twice – for *The Master Bedroom* (2008) and *The London Train* (2011). Cynan Jones, who had earlier won the 2015 Wales Book of the Year English Fiction category, was winner of the 2017 BBC National Short Story Award for 'The Edge of the Shoal'; and this award was also won by Sarah Hall in 2013 for 'Mrs Fox'. Hall is not a Welsh writer, but went to university in Aberystwyth and some influence of the culture and history of Wales can perhaps be glimpsed in the fact that her first novel *Haweswater* (2002) is about the destruction of a rural Cumbrian community to make way for a new reservoir, thus melding an English story with that of the flooding of the Welsh-speaking village of Capel Celyn in 1960 to create a reservoir to supply water to Liverpool, an act of cultural trauma that Iwan Bala notes has provoked numerous cultural and political 'responses' in Wales (2005, 245).

Like Hall, Wales's culture has a personal significance for Alan Kent, a writer from Cornwall who is the leading researcher on the history and literary traditions of writing in the Cornish language, as well as being a practising novelist and poet in both English and Cornish. Kent also went to university in Wales, which frequently gets fleeting references in his fiction, and it seems likely that he sees in Welsh culture an example of a successful recuperation of an ancient language and literature which he might hope to replicate in the Cornish case, so that Wales symbolises a certain aspiration by proxy. In fact, since 1996 there has been a series of Cornish Book Awards, the *Holyer An Gof*, run by the *Gorsedh Kernow* or Cornish Gorsedd, to promote books about Cornwall or in Cornish, and Kent is a past winner.

All this suggests that, although still not widespread, the increased number of nominations for Welsh writers in the leading British book prizes indicates a certain increase in momentum for the field of Welsh literature in general, and for Welsh writing in English in particular. Although to suggest that these writers have received Booker/Orange/BBC nominations *because* they have won Wales Book of the Year would be to assign a false causality, it does seem as though the improved status of Welsh writing of which Wales Book of the Year is both an indicator and a driver has contributed to this upturn.

The cases of Trezza Azzopardi and Rachel Trezise are especially instructive. Azzopardi studied creative writing at the University of East Anglia, where she now lectures in the department that has produced frequent Booker nominees such as Ian McEwan, Rose Tremain and Kazuo Ishiguro and the founder of which, Malcolm Bradbury, was also a Booker judge. This institutional background provides a certain context for Azzopardi's comparatively rare achievement of having her first novel *The Hiding Place* (set in Cardiff Docks) shortlisted for the Booker Prize in 2000. The following year, twenty-three year-old Trezise was given a prestigious Orange Futures award for *In and Out of the Goldfish Bowl*. Comparing these two writers, one shortlisted for a prize normally dominated by established writers and the other a recipient of an award that recognises new talent, therefore make it possible to evaluate the impact of winning these different kinds of award on authorial careers.

In a highly distinctive piece of research, Shusaki Sasaki, Hirofumi Kurokawa and Fumio Ohtake (2019) have explored the different impact on an author's career between winning a prize for established writers and winning one for a newcomer. Building on research into other kinds of professional recognition including winning Olympic medals for athletics; becoming head of a state; and receiving a Nobel Prize for Physics they come to the sobering conclusion that the high status that comes with receiving public accolades sometimes leads to the individuals in question being asked to participate in various specialist working groups, thereby increasing the amount of time spent working, which in turn increases the likelihood of work-related stress which is bad for the health and can therefore hinder performance and even lower life expectancy.

Focusing their research on two book prizes in Japan, the Akutagawa Prize and the Naoki Prize, Sasaki, Kurokawa and Ohtake then seek to see if a similar outcome can be observed in the literary sphere. These two awards were both founded simultaneously by the same person, Kan Kikuchi, and have the same sponsors, similar selection procedures and identical prize money. The key difference is that the Akutagawa Prize 'is awarded to yet unknown or emerging novelists' while candidates for the Naoki Prize 'include a larger number of already established novelists' so that 'at the time of final nominations (or winning), the winner and unsuccessful nominees of the Akutagawa Prize are less experienced and in the lower strata of the literary community than those of the Naoki Prize' (3). Since recipients of either award go on to publish more books (averaged per year) after winning than before, this shows that they have a higher annual workload. But the impact of this increase is different for each award: in the case of the Akutagawa, it significantly raises the profile, income and material standard of living of the author and hence contributes to both health and prosperity. In the case of the Naoki, because it is awarded to established authors (who are presumably already prosperous and well-known) these benefits are negated: 'If we consider workload to be positively correlated with working hours, and that a considerable increase in working hours generates stress …, the recipients, particularly for the Naoki Prize, feel greater stress' (9). They found:

> that the recipients of the Akutagawa Prize for yet unknown or emerging novelists live 1.7 years *longer* than fellow nominees, while those of the Naoki Prize, which mainly targets already established novelists, live 5.3 *shorter* years than their fellow nominees. Our additional analysis indicates the possibility that receiving a prize has a life-prolonging effect when candidates belong to a lower social stratum (10).

If the same findings can be applied from Japan to Britain this would demonstrate in the case of Trezise that winning her Orange Futures award has a significant potential impact both on her status and material standard of living, and also more significantly on both the quantity and quality of her future output. Admittedly, this question of how far results from one country can be generalised and applied to another is a big one, but although Sasaki, Kurokawa and Ohtake suggest that to 'the best of our knowledge, there are no other two literary prizes [than the Akutagawa and the Naoki] in the world that share most characteristics but whose candidates are in different strata of the literary community' (4) it appears they have not looked very hard, because it is a relation that almost exactly describes that between the Orange

Futures and the Orange Prize. More specific comparison between Azzopardi and Trezise would therefore have been possible had Azzopardi been nominated for the Orange rather than the Booker, but nevertheless there is still a viable contrast between the impact of an early-career award like Orange Futures and one for established authors like the Booker. In another context, this comparison would also be possible in the cases of both the Saltire Society literary awards in Scotland and Wales Book of the Year, where separate awards are made for best first book and best overall book, where the latter generally goes to a more established writer (though this is not part of the criteria). If it is true that Trezise has received a greater boost to her career for winning an Orange Futures award than Azzopardi did for being shortlisted for the Booker, this may reinforce the idea discussed with regard to Jackie Kay and Leila Aboulela above, that the conferment of an early career stage award assigns women writers a lengthy period of literary apprenticeship.

In a now well-plumbed metaphor, Sasaki, Kurokawa and Ohtake contrast the positive difference made to the career of recipients of the Akutagawa Prize with that of the recipients of prizes for emerging talent in the field of professional sport, specifically, the Major League Baseball Rookie of the Year award in the USA. They find that whereas as a debut author 'might not be known in the society before winning' the Akutagawa Prize, and therefore is more likely to receive a greater boost through winning it, the standing of the 'most dominating rookie baseball player' follows on from a whole year's effective performance in the public eye, and is therefore 'settled even before the award' (4) so that receiving it, though no doubt welcome, makes less of a difference to the recipient's already established career prospects. In Wales, a comparable example is that of the football player Chris Gunter, who received the English Football League Apprentice of the Year award in 2007 when he emerged into Cardiff City's first team, and who by the time he played for Wales in the semi-final of the 2016 European Championships had become Wales's most-capped outfield player of all time. In fact, the metaphoric comparison between sporting prizes and literary ones was rendered peculiarly literal when the Welsh team once again qualified for the European Championships in 2020: the Football Association of Wales held a young people's poetry competition to celebrate the achievement.

It is tempting to suggest that for Wales, whose team in 2016 had never previously qualified for the European Championships, the sheer fact of participation could have symbolised Welsh connectedness to Europe. But this feeling was brought savagely crashing down when, concurrent with the tournament in France that June, not only did the UK as a whole vote to leave the European Union but a majority of voters in Wales specifically also did so – thereby creating a particular difficulty for Welsh intellectuals, who have historically been interested in Europe. To some extent an alibi is provided by Danny Dorling's suggestion that 'Wales was made to look like a Brexit-supporting nation by its English settlers' (quoted in Perraudin, 2019). However, more precise analysis by Moya Jones has given the lie to the simplistic assumption that pro-European Welsh citizens were outweighed in Wales by their incomer English counterparts, pointing out that 'many leading Welsh politicians were on a different side to the voters in their areas' and these included the leader of Welsh Labour, Carwyn Jones, in Bridgend; the leader of Plaid Cymru, Leanne Wood, in Rhondda; and the Conservative Secretary of State for Wales, Stephen Crabb, in Pembrokeshire (2017, 6). In other words, the leaders of all the main Remain parties in Wales represented areas where voters chose to leave the European Union, so that this decision cannot be attributed solely to a middle English mentality in Wales and the role of the Welsh people in voting to leave has to be addressed.

The particular challenge involved in doing so for Welsh intellectuals can be glimpsed through a critical reading of Jeanette Winterson's recent novel, *Frank**iss**stein* (2019). Whereas Salman Rushdie in his latest book *Quichotte* presents the outcome of the referendum as an exclusively English decision – a 'wild nostalgic decision about their future' (2019, 53) in which 'England-for-the-English white populism' had 'risen from its grave in the dead imperial past to haunt the fractured, second-class nation present' (278) – Winterson in *Frank**iss**stein* associates it uniquely with Wales. The novel is a re-working of both the *Frankenstein* narrative and of the legendary circumstances in which Mary Shelley wrote it, updated for the age of artificial intelligence and transgender identities. In it, Lord Byron is re-presented as Ron Lord, an oleaginous manufacturer of sex robots who affirms repeatedly that there will be good opportunities for opening factories based on cheap labour in Wales after the withdrawal from the European Union because public sector investment from Europe will be gone so unemployment will rise, and that this is the Welsh people's own fault for supporting the referendum and voting 'Wales for the Welsh' (50).

But although Winterson is to be congratulated for creating in Lord a character who departs from stock images of Welshness, this slogan never existed or featured in the discourse surrounding the referendum, mainly because Welsh nationalists have tended to articulate their identity as European, not against it. Ned Thomas, the author of *The Welsh Extremist* (1971) and one of the leading figures of Welsh cultural nationalism in the second half of the twentieth century, had founded *Planet: the Welsh Internationalist* magazine (first published in Aberystwyth in 1970) specifically as a means of articulating the relationship between global affairs and Welsh experience. If (as suggested) Wales has been aspirational to the Cornish writer Alan Kent because it is an example of a small nation succeeding in keeping its minority language alive and vibrant against the odds, then for the editors of *Planet* comparable models have been suggested by several different autonomous self-governing regions across Europe. Twelve of these are discussed comparatively in Roger Scully and Richard Wyn Jones's 2010 collection *Europe, Regions and European Regionalism*, but *Planet* itself had featured so many of these in one form or another, especially those from within Spain, that by February 1997 the author Alun Richards was able to mock it for doing so, writing to his friend and fellow author Ron Berry that he had decided to cancel his subscription: 'fuck Basque Nationalism!' (quoted by Dai Smith, 2010, 268). When Raymond Williams, possibly the best-known public intellectual from Wales (and certainly the most influential outside it) declared that he considered himself a 'Welsh European' (1979a, 296), he did so not only to distinguish his outlook from a more old-fashioned suspicion of European affairs that had existed in left-wing politics in Britain prior to that time, but also as an affirmation of his role in a more avowedly pro-European tradition specific to Wales. John Osmond consciously alluded to Williams in the title of his 1996 book *Welsh Europeans*, which argued that European citizenship offered the Welsh people a way out of what Osmond took to be the contradiction between Welshness and Britishness; and M. Wynn Thomas has explored that tradition in more detail in *Eutopia: Studies in Cultural Euro-Welshness, 1850–1980* (2021).

The broad outlook towards Europe and the world that is common among Welsh intellectuals inflects the literary culture of Wales and the work that is especially prized there in a variety of ways. Andrew Whitehead has recently shown that the Bardic Chair at University College Wales's 1914 eisteddfod in Aberystwyth was awarded to

Dorothy Bonarjee, making her both the first woman and the first non-European to win a bardic prize. Grahame Davies argues in *The Dragon and the Crescent: Nine Centuries of Welsh Contact with Islam* (2011) that in order to understand recent anxieties over the relationship between Islam and Western cultures it is necessary to trace their historical origins. The book then proposes to carry out this work 'for one small European nation' (synopsis blurb), and thus forms a conjunction between images of Wales as intercultural and open to the world on the one hand, while also being specifically European on the other.

Davies was presented with his 2002 Book of the Year award at that year's Hay Festival of Literature in the Welsh borders, and in fact the Hay Festival has become another medium through which the increasing internationalisation of Welsh writing has been steered. Although the Hay Festival is not a state-run event, agencies such as Visit Wales and Literature Wales are both frequent exhibitors there. Moreover, as the Hay Festival has taken on an increasingly prominent role as a site for the brokerage of international literary production its physical horizons have rapidly expanded to incorporate events in South America, Africa and Asia. Kiguru points out that in Kenya a series of events known as the Storymoja writers' workshops 'are usually held during the annual Hay Festival, which is a literary event that brings to Nairobi different acclaimed writers and literary enthusiasts from all over the world' (2016b, 210). The connection between Wales and the world is pointed up if we realise that Tiffany Murray, a judge for Wales Book of the Year judge in 2020, is also a Hay Festival Fellow. Likewise, John Barnie, a former editor of *Planet*, was a Wales Book of the Year judge in 2009. Mererid Hopwood, winner of the Eisteddfod Chair in 2001, studied French and German at university and Cynan Jones, winner of the 2017 BBC National Short Story Award, wrote and published his second novel in Italian, *Le Cose Che Non Vogliamo Più* ('Things We Don't Want Anymore', 2010). Presumably, the fact of having studied modern European languages presupposes a certain transnational outlook and world-view.

As was the case in Scotland, the assertion of Wales as a nation characterised by a series of outward-reaching relationships, horizontal solidarities and interests that transcend the nation in political, ethnic and linguistic ways has thus been articulated in part through the mechanics of its book prize culture. This particular construction of global solidarity as an inherent component of the national identity by conferring cultural value on specific works that display it was visible in awards on either side of the 2016 European referendum. Patrick McGuinness won the overall prize in the 2015 Wales Book of the Year for *Other People's Countries*, a book of sixty-two prose portraits of Bouillon, the 'small town in Walloon Belgium where he spent part of his childhood, and which he still visits several times a year with his own wife and children' (Hofmann, 2014, n.p.). Though the book is mainly about the perplexing aspects of memory as such, it may well have appealed to the Book of the Year judges because this portrayal of a national minority within Belgium echoes and enforces the feelings of aspiration by proxy that has led Welsh intellectuals to pursue a comparable interest in other small European nations, autonomous regions and minor languages for decades.

Even more poignant was the winner of the 2016 Chair at the National Eisteddfod, which was awarded to Aneirin Karadog for 'Ffiniau' ('Borders'), a sequence of poems in the strict metrical form of *cynghanedd*. According to Eryl Crump, the background for the poem is the 'turbulent year across the world, with wars and terrorism, and seeing the politicians' rhetoric becoming more extreme' (2016, n.p.). It opens with a father driving his son to the barracks where he has enlisted to become a soldier, but Karadog told an interviewer that it is really about the 'big picture' in which 'war creates most of the world's problems like famine and refugees who have to cross seas to seek asylum' (quoted in ibid.). The farm at Hendre in the poem is juxtaposed with the airport at Aberporth which borders it, and where pilots are trained in flying military drones. The narrative of the poem therefore speaks of the father's fear not only for the safety of his son, but also that his son will become a danger to other people in other places, and thus that a cycle of misunderstanding, hatred and violence will be perpetuated. Delivering the adjudication Tudur Dylan Jones said: 'They are poems which make us think. They encourage us not be [*sic*] helpless' (quoted in ibid.).

The Chairing of the Bard ceremony took place at the beginning of August 2016, less than two months after the result of the European referendum and although Karadog was presumably thinking about these things even before the vote, his poem must have been made to seem all the more topical in the light of its result. Given the commitment to international solidarity discussed above, the fears of political extremism, hostility, mutual misunderstanding and violence expressed in the poem are thus likely to have resonated with participants at the 2016 Eisteddfod to a particularly strong degree. As was the case with the winners of Scottish Book of the Year in 2016, 2017 and 2018, this resonance must have created a sense of urgency and topicality, an urgency which perhaps explains the relatively short time delay between Karadog winning the Chair (2016) and being asked to serve as one of the judges for Wales Book of the Year (2018). Interestingly, Crump has drawn attention to the fact that Karadog 'became interested in languages at a young age, as he was brought up in a trilingual household, where he and his brother spoke Welsh, Breton and English' (n.p.). In the figure of this poet who speaks Breton as well as both Welsh and English there is a further instance of the commonly expressed interest among Welsh intellectuals in the minority languages and cultures of Europe.

The emerging political rhetoric of extremism that led to the 2016 referendum was thus something which Welsh intellectuals, like their Scottish counterparts, reacted against and as was the case in Scotland this reaction renders intelligible the process that resulted in the award of Wales Book of the Year to Patrick McGuinness in 2015 and of the Bardic Chair to Aneirin Karadog in 2016. If there are these similarities between the literary circles in both nations, however, there is also one key difference. In Scotland, the majority of voters had voted to remain in the European Union so that the intellectuals who expressed this preference accorded with the outlook of the population more generally and could be considered examples of organic intellectuals in Gramsci's sense. In Wales, although nationalists, writers, and intellectuals were in favour of remaining in the European Union, their mood was not replicated by the majority of the population, which in fact voted against remaining in the EU. Thus, in the aftermath of the referendum it has been difficult for intellectuals in Wales to lay claim to the same degree of organic connection to the people as those in Scotland, which is why the process of Britain withdrawing from the European Union has created a different feeling of crisis in Wales from that in Scotland. The only way to square these positions appears to be to consider the possibility that the Scottish people voted remain as a protest against Westminster politics, whereas those in Wales voted the opposite – for the same reason.

PRIZING RECONCILIATION IN NORTHERN IRELAND

In 2004, the year that administration of Wales Book of the Year was transferred from the Arts Council of Wales to Literature Wales, one of the longlisted entries was Mike Jenkins's poetry collection *The Language of Flight*. Jenkins, a native of industrial South Wales, had lived for several years in Northern Ireland where he met his wife Marie and his experiences in Ulster provided material for some of the poems in his earlier collections *Invisible Times* (1986) and *A Dissident Voice* (1990), so that it is an under-recognised aspect of his work that he can be considered a poet of Northern Ireland, if not a Northern Irish poet. In several poems in *The Language of Flight* the culture and politics of Northern Ireland provide metaphorical means of conceptualising both experience and memory during a period when the poet no longer lived there, having returned to South Wales. In the poem 'Gulag Gurnos, Stalag Merthyr', for instance, he writes:

> At the top of a pillar
> are the red spikes
> of a Medieval weapon.
> Regeneration schemes happen
> behind steel meshing
> seen before on pubs, barracks
> along the Falls.
>
> Ranks of green lances
> around schools and hospital.
> Cameras spy with General's eyes
> planning the next manoeuvre.
>
> Like Saracens on past Belfast streets
> the police wear metallic suits,
> reflections of those rows
> soon to be demolished:
> Acacia, Cypress, Willow
> wither with rust, will not grow (2004, 31).

In comparing the Gurnos housing estate in Merthyr Tydfil first to the gulags and stalags of Stalinist Russia and then to the Falls Road of Belfast, a city divided by religious and sectarian violence until the recent past, the poem creates the impression that Merthyr too will emerge as a town riven by political hatred and violent confrontation. In the case of the Gurnos estate, an area of significant economic deprivation, the particular form of political violence is that of capitalist society so that the people of the estate, rather than being divided into different political factions as in Belfast or Siberia, share a common experience of inequality. The artefacts of religious intolerance associated with the crusades and the Saracens of the poem are projected back into the medieval period; seeds of new life struggle to grow in their place; and various urban regeneration projects are planned. In other words, Northern Ireland in the poem is a catachresis not merely for a society divided by political animosity but for one struggling to build new forms of memory culture to transcend and supersede the politics and animosity of the past.

In this general approach to portraying Ireland in his poetry, Jenkins shows himself to be a highly prescient writer because over the past two decades various forms of cultural production in Northern Ireland have contributed to the building of a shared, cross-community post-conflict culture. In diverse ways those attempts have subtly directed the cultural memory of the people of Northern Ireland away from contentious, controversial or conflicted episodes in their past and emphasised instead common elements that can be presented in a less contentious light and so enable the evolution of a new cultural sphere in which all can participate without the sense of divided loyalties or painful political confrontation that characterised the past.

Northern Ireland has no national book award at the time of writing, perhaps because Northern Ireland itself has rarely been conceptualised as a nation: for people there of a unionist conviction it is an integral part of the United Kingdom, so that the term *nationalist* itself, when applied in the context of Northern Ireland, is generally used to refer to the aspiration for a single united Ireland. Arguably, establishing a national book award for Northern Ireland would risk provoking forms of sectarian animosity beyond the merely aesthetic controversies that have long accompanied book prizes because, as Claire Squires has argued, literary prizes 'are established with certain eligibility requirements which reflect past and present – and sometimes, aspirationally, future – concepts of communities of writers' (2004, 44–5). Since the question of how to define the nation has been (to put it mildly) a vexatious one in Northern Ireland, not having a national book prize might be a form of negative capability, a way of avoiding unnecessarily difficult questions during the period while Northern Ireland continues to undergo its transition towards peace.

Not having a *national* book award, however, does not necessarily mean that Northern Ireland does not have book prizes at all. In fact, the Northern Ireland Book Award, which was awarded annually to a children's author between 2010 and 2015 and resumed in 2020, was partly created to enable Northern Irish reading habits to catch up with those of the rest of the United Kingdom:

> Local book award schemes to encourage and develop a love of reading had been springing up in England and Scotland but no such award existed in Northern Ireland. In an attempt to rectify this, two school librarians, Ann Cowdrey and Kathy Lindsay, decided to introduce such a scheme to the Province in 2009 (Northern Ireland Book Award, 2015, n.p.).

In other words, like the Carnegie medal discussed above in regard to Scotland, the objective of the Northern Ireland Book Award is to cultivate a new generation of readers by fostering an enjoyment of reading among children and young people. Funding for the award came from an application to the Wendy Drewett bequest at the Chartered Institute for Information and Library Professionals (CILIP; confusingly, the equivalent CILIP awards for children's books in Wales are named the *Tir na n-Og* awards after the Land of the Young in Irish mythology). No Alibis, the last independent bookstore in Belfast, was supportive of the venture in Northern Ireland, and workshops were held at the city's Lyric Theatre. Year Eight and Nine students from schools in Northern Ireland were invited to submit their recommendations based on preference and booksellers were invited to do so based on sales figures, in order to give a clear understanding of what young people were popularly reading. It was from these that the eventual winners were chosen. Unlike other awards such as the Saltire Society Scottish Book of the Year or Wales Book of the Year, the Northern Ireland Book Prize had neither a national agenda nor a requirement for entries to be from Northern Ireland, by Northern Irish writers, or even about the place. On the contrary, the 'whole emphasis is on books that are exciting and encourage children to read more books and the over-riding aim is to see book-centred social interaction and debate amongst young people from all community sectors' (ibid.).

This emphasis on appealing to readers from all sections of the community perhaps explains why there was no requirement for the entered books to reflect on contemporary Northern Irish life since to do so might be to solicit the kinds of controversy that building a post-conflict society in Northern Ireland has generally avoided. Thus, although the first winner in 2010 was the Irish writer Derek Landy for *The Faceless Ones*, the runner-up was the internationally recognised English writer Neil Gaiman for *The Graveyard Book* and other subsequent winners have been equally well-known outside Ulster – especially David Walliams in 2012 for *Gangsta Granny*, and Anthony Horowitz in 2014 for *Russian Roulette*. Moreover, in 2011 and 2012 first, second and third prizes all went to English writers: respectively, Chris Bradford, *The Ring of Earth*; Alex Scarrow, *Time Raiders* and Tim Collins, *Diary of a Wimpy Vampire* in 2011; and Walliams, *Gangsta Granny*, Chris Westwood, *Ministry of Pandemonium* and Barbara Mitchelhill, *Run Rabbit Run* in 2012. The 2013 winner, *Wonder* by R. J. Palacio, was written by an American author whose parents had emigrated to the United States from Colombia; and the top three in 2015 were two Americans and a Canadian: Carter Roy, *The Blood Guard*, Kenneth Oppel, *The Boundless* and Holly Goldberg Sloan, *Counting by 7s*.

Clearly it would be a mistake to try and yoke all these books together at the level of content. Some are works of fantasy, escapism and adventure, others of science fiction and others again of critical realism, addressing difficult life experiences that particularly resonate with children and young people growing up in the twenty-first century. What this means, nevertheless, is that two general tendencies can be observed. One is for an overall cosmopolitanism, that is, a world outlook that is not limited by national boundaries and which by transcending the individual nation neatly avoids having to engage with questions and criteria of eligibility in defining the nation itself. The other is to value and reward work which can be presented as dealing with universal themes of relevance to young people, rather than engaging in the specifics of recent Northern Irish culture and politics, so that again the need to evaluate and judge different portrayals and interpretations of that culture is scrupulously avoided.

As it happens, this latter tendency can be observed in the discourse and public positioning associated with two prominent Northern Irish literary prize winners: Seamus Heaney, winner of the 1995 Nobel Prize for Literature, and Anna Burns, winner of the 2018 Booker Prize for the novel *Milkman*. For instance, Heaney's Nobel citation explains that he received the award 'for works of lyrical beauty and ethical depth, which exalt everyday miracles and the living past' (Nobel Prize in Literature, 1995). In the process, it employs language that reveals a certain vagueness and generality, perhaps even an interchangeability with that of other citations for Nobel laureates in literature before and since. After all, which really great writer has not shown beauty or depth? Which author is not interested in either the reality of everyday experience or the ongoing presence of the past? But in the case of Heaney, these generalities appear all the more pointed because they so consciously avoid reference to the political context in Ireland in which, for a long time, Heaney was writing. And where Irish history is invoked, it is not so much in the interests of reviving past conflicts as it is in asserting the possibility of a living past: that is, a culture and society that have evolved by consigning troubling elements to the distant past and carrying through less threatening aspects into an unbounded present where they can take root and live.

The purpose of this chapter is not to explore the interests or preoccupations of Heaney's oeuvre at the level of precise textual analysis (which would be a large-scale undertaking on its own). It is rather to draw attention to how Heaney's relationship to Irish history has been positioned by the discourses of literary prize culture, which even presents him at times as a figurehead or leader of a certain approach to cultural production in Ireland. Thus, in his article about literary prizes Tom O'Brien suggests that contemporary culture is characterised by a:

> split between a sensation-seeking public and the rarefied world of many fine arts practitioners and theorists ... At such a time, any artist who expands the audience for the arts in an intelligent way deserves special recognition. Many Nobel winners have done this; my favourite recent Nobel winner (bias admitted) would be Seamus Heaney but too many have ... confused cerebral style with intelligent art (2003, 31).

In presenting Heaney as a figure who managed to avoid confounding rarefied art with mere sensation, O'Brien's praise detaches Heaney's life and work from the political and historical context of Ireland during the Troubles, so that the binary categories of Irish nationalists and unionists, or Catholics and Protestants, are transcended. In their place, a different binary distinction, that between sensationalism and intelligent art, is activated as the primary indicator of Heaney's achievement as an artist.

This positioning of Heaney as a figure capable of transcending the politics of division in the interest of a poetics of reconciliation can fruitfully be compared to the representation of Ireland in Anna Burns's 2018 Booker Prize-winning novel, *Milkman*, which, although 'set in an unnamed town in an unnamed country' (Morris, 264), re-inscribes the Irish Troubles in a highly abstract and metaphorical way. Its location feels very much like the Northern Ireland of the 1970s, although Burns scrupulously avoids using proper nouns, so that everyone is identified by their role or relationship to the narrating character, middle sister: ma, older sister, third brother-in-law, maybe-boyfriend, oldest friend. Through this means, Burns creates a series of monologues and free associative shifts in which the conventional categories into which different members of the community have tended to be placed are removed and navigating either the community or the people in it according to those categories is rendered meaningless.

The tragi-comic irony of this novel which scrupulously eschews personal nouns is that Milkman is the name of the man who pursues middle sister, but there is also a separate milkman, identified like everyone else only by his role. This other milkman is the lover of middle sister's ma, and he is hospitalised as a result of being shot by state enforcers mistaking him for Milkman (whom they also later shoot and kill). Ma's lover is a renouncer of violence who years earlier had been tarred and feathered for refusing to allow paramilitaries to hide guns in his house, and for actually throwing the guns out on the street (where they could have been found by security forces). On the other hand, the people who tarred him had not gone as far as to actually kill him because they were not sure whose side he was on. His refusal to pick sides seems to be what blindsided them and made them most suspicious. To them: 'It had to be political ... Had to be about the border. Meaning comprehensible' (Burns, 2018, 146). When he does something that is not political or about the border and so not comprehensible within the taxonomy of different political loyalties, they feel threatened and so he suffers for it. This means that the social structure in *Milkman* is one where everyone recognises the oppositional distribution of state and paramilitary power but nobody discusses it; and everyone knows where their own loyalties lie but never examines them so that from the outside – that is, from the position of the reader – these things cannot be understood and cease to make sense.

A question that then emerges is how far the success of *Milkman* in becoming Northern Ireland's first novel to win the Booker Prize can be attributed to its deconstruction of the mechanics of political violence. In an article exploring what kinds of work tend to appeal to Booker judges, Ronit Frenkel focuses on the Indian novel *The

Inheritance of Loss (Kieran Desai, 2006) and the South African one *Bitter Fruit* (Achmat Dangor, 2001) to argue that the discourses within which the texts are positioned by the prize are 'mediated by a politics of loss in terms of assessing post-colonial fiction from India and South Africa, where texts must fulfil western stereotypes of post-colonial pathos in order to contend seriously for this award' (2008, 78). In Desai's novel, for example, 'India is represented in terms of constant suffering where people are connected across barriers through "an inheritance of loss"' where everybody 'may expect betrayal and hardship in a world where the weight of history crushes possibilities and resigns post-colonial India to perpetual victimhood' (83). In the case of *Bitter Fruit*, about a woman who was raped in apartheid-era South Africa and comes face to face with her rapist during the sessions of the Truth and Reconciliation Commission (TRC) through which the post-apartheid nation attempted to heal the wounds of the past, Frenkel says:

> The inconclusive nature of such archaeological endeavours therefore becomes paramount to understanding the TRC and the construction of histories in South Africa, where the consequences of either recalling or suppressing the past are severe, because ultimately post-colonial pathos shapes all response and history cannot be redeemed (84–5).

The most notable point about this conclusion is that if we substituted Northern Ireland for South Africa and the Good Friday Agreement for the Truth and Reconciliation Commission, it would still work almost exactly as an accurate interpretation of *Milkman*. In the Northern Ireland portrayed by Burns, too, the consequences of either recalling or suppressing the past have significant implications for human relations and for the society as a whole in the present, and the struggle to redeem a violent and conflicted history emerges as its own theme.

This struggle appears to accord with what Levin refers to as the Booker 'aesthetic' (2014, 477). Such a model, expressing the simultaneous necessity and impossibility of addressing the conflicts of the past, might then be symptomatic of how building new forms of collective culture operates in post-conflict societies such as India, South Africa and Northern Ireland. It is very much akin to the politics of naming and the distribution of political authority that we find in *Milkman*, where many of the most important things cannot be said or explored out loud because to do so, even on the most seemingly trivial or innocent of subjects, is to risk breaching the fragile consensus on which a possible peace depends. A comparable Irish novel is Sebastian Barry's *Secret Scripture*, about a one-hundred-year-old woman in an asylum in Roscommon in the early years of the twenty-first century, who has blotted out virtually all memory of her Presbyterian father's involvement in the civil war that followed the establishment of the Irish Free State in 1922 and who finds that the few memories she does retain of those events contrast with the facts about them found in the archives dug out by her consultant. Then again, this is not surprising since the archive itself is incomplete: the people who fought in the civil war had destroyed most records themselves, 'wiping out the records of the very nation they were trying to give life to, actually burning memory in its boxes' (Barry, 2008, 262). In other words, *The Secret Scripture* is about the merging of individual and collective forms of memory in post-conflict Ireland. It thus taps into the same aesthetic of pathos and melancholia that Frenkel suggests is valued by prize judges: it received both the 2008 Costa Book of the Year and the James Tait Black Memorial Prize.

A further example of the high premium that has been placed on work that accords with the process of forging new forms of collective culture in the service of peace and reconciliation in Northern Ireland is the folk musician Ríoghnach Connolly. During the COVID-19 lockdown of 2020 she participated in the *Folk on Foot* podcast's *Front Room Festival 2*, an online music festival organised to provide financial support for musicians whose incomes had all-but evaporated during the lockdown. Her set culminated with a traditional song about Roddy McCorley, an Irish Nationalist who might have participated in the Irish rebellion of 1798 and who was hanged in Duneane, County Antrim, in 1800. Connolly prefaced the song by describing it as:

> The oldest version of this song my family can possibly find ... from the Parish of Duneane, where Roddy McCorley was from. But no one in Duneane can really sing it because the families it sings about still live in that parish so it's a bit controversial. Anyway, what I like about this one is it's from the 1798 sort of perspective when United Irishmen were Presbyterians and they were Irish speakers – and that's something you don't really hear of in the sort of discourse of today when you hear about the North of Ireland (*Folk on Foot*, 4.12.00–4.20.35).

The folksy charm with which the song was presented belies a number of interlocking issues. First of all, there is the appeal to authenticity evinced through describing the song as the oldest version that Connolly could find. But the sense of mining back into the historical past is accompanied by a complementary awareness that the song itself is potentially uncomfortable because of the way that political conflict and political violence continue to resonate in existing communities and among living people in Antrim today. Most strikingly of all, her framing of the song decouples a number of elements that have typically featured in the polarised structures of Northern Irish culture, which often associate the Irish language with Catholicism and Irish nationalism, and Presbyterianism with the English language and the British state. To present Roddy McCorley as someone who is both an Irish speaker but also a Presbyterian is to challenge that neat compartmentalisation of cultures and thus to question the rigid binary categorisations of this kind that characterised the Irish Troubles. In this way, like *Milkman* in fiction, Connolly interrogates the logic and assumptions on which the stark polarisation of the community was based and seeks to replace the historical narrative of how those polarities arose with a different historical narrative that is more complex, less categorical, and emphasises connections between different sections of the community rather than division between them. As with *Milkman*, high forms of cultural capital are associated with work that contributes to altering the narrative of violence and this high level of capital was made manifest in the form of a national prize: Ríoghnach Connolly was named BBC Radio 2's Folk Singer of the Year for 2019.

Unlike the Scottish and Welsh Book of the Year Awards, it is too soon to tell what difference will be made to Northern Ireland's already less advanced culture of awarding book prizes by Britain's withdrawal from the European Union, an uncertainty that is perhaps symbolised by the fact that the Northern Ireland Book Prize was dormant between 2015 and 2020. It is certainly the case that the British Conservative Government's Internal Markets Act of 2020 has not only damaged the reputation of British politics by violating international law but also placed Ireland's open border in question. At a time when Britain was at least ostensibly attempting to negotiate a post-Brexit trade deal with the European Union, the Irish government repeatedly threatened to veto any deal unless or until the Act was revoked. At the same time, the election in November 2020 of Joe

Biden, a pro-Irish president of the USA (with whom the UK was also attempting a trade deal) might have the effect of putting further pressure on the British government to alter the legislation or risk becoming entirely isolated in global trade terms. To the extent that this complex web of relationships between Britain, Ireland, Europe and the United States represents a danger of a hardening of positions on all sides, maintaining such forms of cultural production in Northern Ireland that emphasise shared participation by downplaying contentious elements might take on even greater importance.

That practice is discernible in the Irish writer Eimear McBride's first novel to be published after Britain's exit from the EU, *Strange Hotel* (2020). McBride had won the 2014 Kerry Group Irish Fiction Award for *A Girl is a Half-formed thing*, and *Strange Hotel* can be said to apply the same strategic depoliticisation that characterises Northern Ireland's book prize culture to its allusive (and elusive) engagement with Brexit politics. It takes the form of a short, stream-of-consciousness novel about a thirty-five-year-old woman meeting men in hotel rooms in various different cities around the world and gradually reveals itself to be a book about loss, mourning and their aftermath.

After sexual encounters in Avignon and Prague, the third takes place in Oslo where the woman wakes up before the young man next to her and feels unable to leave briskly as intended because she realises that he looks like a lover she had lost years before. Looking out of her windows at the city she imagines people's conversations in the surrounding buildings, which might discuss 'sport. Some local outrage or international disgrace. Politics. Europe. TV. The United States' (McBride, 70). Although the relationship between Britain, Ireland and Europe is present in the background, it is reduced to the status of an imagined topic of conversation on a par with entertainment or sport, and therefore not the primary means by which the Brexit process provides meaningful context for the novel.

During the fourth encounter, in Auckland, the woman is now forty-nine and the next day, her birthday, she will become older than the lost lover was when he died. She feels a strange sensation of the floor being uncertain under her feet and thinks that the hotel is a 'place built for people living in a time out of time – out of their own time anyway' (87). This sense of temporal disjointedness is reflected by the structure of the novel, in which the passages of time between each section are very uneven and get gradually longer, and which creates an impression of time running out, but without having any specific deadline for it to run out on. It thus feels tempting to interpret the novel as a psychological manifestation of the Brexit process, where deadlines for settling Britain and Europe's relationship with each other came and went repeatedly throughout the years 2016–20 without anything being settled.

But it is only after the fifth meeting, with a man in Texas, that the novel makes a more powerful allusion to Irish politics beyond the mere surface. Having made the unusual decision to let the man take her to breakfast, she thinks of her son, born shortly after her former lover had died, for whose sake she has never formed a lasting relationship. Now that he is on the cusp of adulthood he has hinted he would be happy for her to do so and she imagines how her life could have been different – how all the hotel-room assignations could have been avoided – if her relationship with that first lover had endured. More specifically, she recalls a time early in the relationship when the lover was just starting to trust her and had made a terrible confession about himself in order to promote mutual openness, before offering her the chance to end the relationship because of his shameful confession and leave his house for a hotel. Despite the revelation of his guilty secret, she had chosen to remain in the relationship and only imagines years later what this hypothetical hotel would have been like, and how her life would have been different if she had gone to it.

Yet what awful secret her dead lover had told her is never revealed: 'I learned how the body I had loved and touched had lived another life. Pitilessly, physically. In its recounting, guiltily. Even, when younger, brokenly, in ways similar to mine' (142). There is a lack of specificity which enables the dead lover's guilty secret to function as a catch-all for anything that readers might imagine to be shameful. In the context of Northern Ireland in the years following the Troubles, the two most likely subjects for such a confession are participation in sectarian violence or sexual abuse within the Catholic church (which, given the association of Catholicism with Irish nationalism also has a sectarian element). But by refusing to spell out the specific content of the confession, the painful experiences of the Troubles are filtered out and readers from all communities in Northern Ireland can equally relate to it precisely because differentials are not there. This, more than the reduction of Europe to a subject of tittle tattle or the endlessly deferred temporal structure in which imaginary deadlines never arrive, makes it possible to read *Strange Hotel* as a response to

Brexit. On the one hand, the Irish peace process has been potentially imperilled by Brexit; while, on the other, the affirmation of peace has been most effective in Northern Ireland by sidestepping the question of taking sides altogether. This means that just as readers from different sections of the community can imagine *Strange Hotel* representing their own communities, so too it can speak to readers on either side of the European Leave/Remain divide, precisely by hinting at this social and political context and then by shying away from it.

Endnote

[1] The Roland Mathias Prize for Poetry was integrated into Wales Book of the Year in 2012.

5

BREXIT AND BEYOND

> Brexit Note: I apologise in advance if this issue reaches you later than normal. We have printed *Granta* in Italy for many years now, transporting it across open borders – good luck with that, someone said. Good luck indeed.
> We all know that our mother is mortal, none of us knows that our home is mortal.
> (Sigrid Rausing, *Granta*, Autumn 2019)

In a sense, all literature after Brexit is Brexit literature, since (as the *Granta* editorial shows) Brexit will affect our economy, transport, print, finance, shipping, pay, jobs, food, leisure, salaries, pensions – in short, our lives as a whole. Following Robert Eaglestone's suggestion that 'Brexit is not only political, economic and administrative: perhaps most significantly it is an event in culture, too' (2018, 1), this concluding chapter focuses on the emerging literary sub-genre of Brexit literature. Petra Rau has argued that the 'conflation of the referendum as a democratic iteration with its – then still debated – consequence (exit from the European Union) was not uncommon' and that this conflation gave rise to a 'time lapse particularly favoured by those who felt the referendum result licensed them to freely express racism and xenophobia' (2018, 35). One implication of the time lapse is that many fictional portrayals of the Brexit process were written in the period between 2015 and 2020, before Britain had left the European Union, so that they are provisional in nature, referring forward to a time when it was imagined the UK would have left. In other words, what Kristian Shaw (2018; 2021) calls 'BrexLit' is anticipatory in nature, constituted by what it is looking towards, rather than what it comes after. In this way, it bucks many recent definitions of contemporary culture: thinkers as diverse as Gilles Deleuze, Giorgio Agamben and Jean-Luc Nancy define the contemporary more through reference to a feeling of afterwardsness than of anticipation. They are echoed in contemporary literature by Roger Luckhurst (2012), who has argued that our feeling of familiarity with the Iraq War stems in part from our prior encounters with so many representations of other wars, which have the effect of mediating and framing in advance how we receive depictions of the latest. A temporal belatedness is thus the most common way in which the idea of contemporaneity has been conceptualised.

By moving away from these definitions of the contemporary and looking forward rather than back, Brexit fiction unwittingly chimes in with the feeling of a symbolic new start which was actively propagated by the Brexiteers. Even though many of the writers of Brexit fiction are actively critical of the politics, the tendency of the oppositional novel is therefore to uphold some of the dominant assumptions on which the ideology of Brexit was based. This is true not only of the anticipation of a new start, but also in the recurring portrayals of a whole series of dichotomies between urban and rural populations, between those with university educations and those without, and between those committed to socially progressive forms of politics and those who oppose them. Many writers of BrexLit fail to interrogate these binary dichotomies, thereby creating a sense of entrapment and revealing the extent to which the dominant ideology had set and determined the terms of debate in advance. Raymond Williams once warned about the Cold War: 'If I say, estimating, for example, whether we'll avoid a nuclear war "I see it as 50-50", I instantly make it 51-49, or 60-40, the wrong way' (1989, 322). Following Williams's logic, we might say that as soon as the term *Brexit* was coined, it became both more real and more likely. Unable to transform the dominant assumptions on which Brexit was predicated, Brexit fiction ends up repeating the simplistic dichotomies on which it is based. This, the chapter will argue, is evident in the various ways it constructs and depicts diverse settings – which it again polarises, exacerbating 'national' and 'regional' differences as opposed to merely reflecting them.

THE PRE-EMERGENT

In an article arguing that the crisis in Britain's external relationships engendered by the 2016 referendum occluded another internal crisis (of social inequality), Birte Heidemann has drawn extensively on Raymond Williams's critique in *The Country and the City* (1973) of nostalgic myths of a national golden age. Applying this critique to analysis of recent fictional portrayals of those crises by Ali Smith and Amanda Craig, she concludes that the 'literary readings that followed are testament to how recent British fiction continues along the same lines (of division) that have long been in the making' (2020, 686).

Among the many useful contributions made by Raymond Williams to our critical cultural vocabulary, the distinction he made in *Marxism and Literature* (1977) between dominant, residual and emergent ideologies was one of the most important. Following Gramsci's notion of hegemony, this distinction replaces a static notion of ideology with a dynamic sense of contestation and conflict between different ideological currents in a society at any given time. However, a genuine limitation in Williams's thought is that he applied the concept of emergent ideologies in an exclusively positive way, as an indicator of a radical progressive politics. The possibility of an emergent ideology that is neither radical nor progressive, that on the contrary is conservative and reactionary, is not discussed in his work. Yet in the period 2010–20 Brexit has been just such an ideology. Thus, in Williams's work, the concept that most appropriately refers to this ideology is therefore not dominant, residual or emergent but the highly retrospective category of the *pre-emergent*.

Williams used this term both to refer to elements that would gradually coalesce into a discernible ideological current but have not yet done so, and to enable a critical reading of them. The pre-emergent, in other words, can only be identified as such in hindsight and in hindsight it can be applied to the years before Brexit to identify not only instances of the pre-emergent ideology, but also instances of emerging critique and opposition to it. This is the case with Sarah Hall's *The Wolf Border* (2015) and A. L. Kennedy's *Serious Sweet* (2016), both published before the 2016 European referendum and retrospectively able to be situated in the pre-emergence of what has subsequently become the Brexit novel genre.

Hall's *The Wolf Border* (2015) is about a woman in Cumbria working for a wealthy aristocrat on a seemingly whimsical project to reintroduce wolves into the wild in Britain. She presents the Cumbria wilderness and the wolves' wild nature as symbols of the potential darkness at the heart of human civilisation itself. This offers to elevate Rachel's role in the Earl's project onto an existentialist plain where she is pitted against the forces of the cosmos in a transcendental, metaphysical way: the lurking incipient darkness at the heart of the civilised world is mainly signified by the breakdown in human relationships the novel portrays.

Yet the release of the wolves does not quite succeed in living up to the burden of symbolising the capacity for human savagery, for two main reasons. First of all, the wolves themselves are not in fact wild, even when released. Although they are released into an area that is quite large compared to the garden of an individual household, it is miniscule compared to the reserve in Idaho Rachel had left behind to work there. Neither is it a wilderness: the land on which they are released is in effect a large enclosure, created when the Earl made a large financial contribution to the central government and in return successfully lobbied Prime Minister Sebastian Mellor (a thinly disguised David Cameron) to allow the sale of parts of the Lakeland National Park by private Act of Parliament. When the wolves escape from their enclosure two of the cubs are immediately killed but the remaining two, plus their parents, head North into Scotland.

Secondly, although there is opposition to it, the release of the wolves does not in itself seem like a major existentialist theme. In a novel like Mark Twain's *Huckleberry Finn* (1884), crossing a boundary between one American state and another could be the difference between being enslaved and living in freedom. In Hall's own earlier novel, *The Electric Michelangelo* (2004), crossing the boundaries between different generations expressed the difference between female disenfranchisement and emancipation. Compared to ending slavery or votes for women, Rachel's struggle with the wolves seems somehow smaller in importance.

What saves the novel is then something unexpectedly different: not the plot about releasing wolves, but Hall's distinctive way of imagining the politics of national devolution in Britain. This factor is significant because in the world she imagines Scotland had voted for independence in the 2014 referendum, and it is notable that according to the Earl in the novel the last time there had been wild wolves in Britain was the 1680s, which was also the last time that Scotland and England had been formally separate nations. The wolves' flight over the border therefore symbolises Scottish difference more effectively than it does human savagery. Hall's post-2014 Scottish government is presented as more progressive than the English one, and when the Earl flies up to meet the new Scottish Prime Minister Caleb Douglas (possibly modelled on Alex Salmond) they agree that the wolves can simply be left in the highlands to roam free.

In hindsight it is tempting to see this quest for freedom as a harbinger of that second referendum the year after the novel was published, not over Scottish independence but over Britain's membership of the European Union, since during that referendum campaign rhetorical notions of freedom were passionately (not to mention inaccurately) invoked at every turn. Although the image put about by the leave campaign of a vote to leave the European Union as a vote in favour of freedom from some phantom oppressive power is somewhat at odds with the symbolism of *The Wolf Border* a year earlier, where the idea of freedom is bound up with Scottish destiny rather than withdrawal from Europe, it is nevertheless true that the use of the same metaphor in both cases is more than merely coincidental. The people of Scotland were explicitly warned during their own independence referendum campaign that an independent Scotland would begin life outside the European Union and could not be certain of achieving membership of it. This in turn means that although there is no way of knowing how much difference this made in terms of how many voters based their decision on it, the desire to remain part of the European Union clearly played some part in the Scottish 'no' vote of 2014, even though, following the 2016 'leave' vote, they subsequently found themselves being taken out of the European Union anyway. In other words, they were presented with two incompatible electoral decisions. *The Wolf Border*, published between these two moments of historic decision, hints at the instabilities and inconsistencies which would come out into the open in the months and years after its appearance.

* * *

Published in 2015 between two referendums, *The Wolf Border* anticipates how the 2016 European referendum in Britain would retrospectively complicate the 2014 Scottish referendum on independence. Though presumably written even earlier than 2015 and therefore unable to literally predict events of 2016 and beyond, this anticipatory mode would in fact come to characterise the output of Brexit-related fiction over the years that followed. If, for example, *The Wolf Border* anticipated the way the European referendum result would newly galvanise the Scottish independence movement following its defeat in 2014, then A. L. Kennedy's ninth novel *Serious Sweet*, published the following year, anticipates the European referendum itself.

Serious Sweet (2016) is a Bloomsday style narrative about a middle-ranking civil servant, Jon Sigurdsson, who has become profoundly disillusioned about the inequality and social injustice unleashed by the coalition government's policy of austerity during the years 2010–15 and has started to have panic attacks. It takes place over the course of a single day during which the Civil Service has gone into 'purdah' (41) in the run-up to the 2015 general election which eventually returned the first majority Conservative government to power in the UK since 1997, and in which the promise of an In/Out Referendum on Europe was a central battleground. Apparently without any work, Jon has arranged to see Meg Williams, a recovering alcoholic for whom he had been writing *billets doux*, and with whom he tentatively considers starting a relationship. But their date is almost endlessly deferred when Jon is sent on a mission by his superior to talk an investigative journalist, Milner, out of publishing some dirt on a government minister who had caused public offence by making a comment about 'the Hun in the Sun' during a recent trip to Leipzig (38).

Kennedy's portrayal of a minister travelling overseas and apparently going out of his way to provoke and offend Britain's European partners is almost certainly modelled on Boris Johnson, the then-Foreign Secretary who would eventually become Prime Minister. 'God save us from a sly buffoon' (38) reflects Jon, allowing Kennedy to allude ironically to the common media presentation of Johnson as a boyish buffoon who though spoilt was unlikely to cause any real harm. Jon then tells a minor colleague that the whole Civil Service is treated like 'an anachronistic smug elite' by professional politicians, until they need them to disentangle the chaos they cause (43). In this nexus of relationships between the buffoonish government minister, the supposedly elitist civil servant and the hackneyed reporter, much of the language that would subsequently crystallise into the lexicon of Brexit was already starting to coalesce. The great irony of the novel is that although Jon's side line in writing love letters for single women is deemed to pose no security threat, the extent of his disillusion means that he actually is one: accusing the government of failing to protect vulnerable children and of illegally bugging private telephones in an effort to bring it down. Although he knows he might be arrested for these information leaks, he refuses to run away because as he tells Milner:

> I can't bolt off to Morocco, or somewhere, because – not the only reason – but because this is my home, my complicated home, and I want to

be at home in my home and I want my country to be the country that I have believed could exist ... Not the nation as a blade ... The nation as love (398–9).

From here, the political plot (which remains unresolved) deflects into the resolution of the Jon–Meg romance plot. To readers after the 2016 referendum, it is almost impossible to read these words without thinking of the specific tagline of the Leave campaign: I want my country back. Yet here it is presented in opposition to it – which is especially notable since the novel pre-dates the referendum. Having kept her ear very close to the shifting ground of British politics during the years 2010–15, Kennedy was able to assemble many of the elements that would feature prominently in the Brexit campaign, without yet being able to name it as such. That is, written in 2015–16 the political story told by the novel inevitably feels unfinished because there was no way of knowing how it would end.

BREXIT AND FICTION FROM SCOTLAND

One of the most notable features of the two pre-emergent Brexit novels discussed above is how important the Scottish context is in both of them. Hall uses the wolves' flight into Scotland to symbolise an existential quest for freedom in which the evocation of Scottish political and cultural difference from England ends up playing a more important role than the flight narrative itself, and Kennedy's disillusioned civil servant Jon Sigurdsson was born in Scotland. As a Scottish writer living in England, such cross-border implicatures can hardly have failed to interest Kennedy, or her compatriot Ali Smith. In fact Smith's *Autumn* (2016) was among the first novels to explicitly address the aftermath of the EU referendum, and it is highly significant that, together with *Serious Sweet* written just before, two of the first novelists to do so should both be Scots working in England, just as two of the four poets discussed in Anne Varty's (2018) commentary on 'Brexit and Poetry' are Scots (Carol Ann Duffy and Jackie Kay), while a third, Imtiaz Dharker, is sometimes resident in Scotland (and the fourth, Gillian Clarke, is Welsh).

Yet the Scottish context is barely present in *Autumn* beyond the fact that when Elisabeth receives a new passport she dislikes the 'Scottish pipers' and 'ethnic stereotype dancers' (196) that illustrate its pages. The only other reference to Scotland in the novel comes when, after the European referendum, Elisabeth's mother watches the opening of the Scottish Parliament on television with her partner Zoe and is so inspired by the words on the mace: 'Wisdom. Justice. Compassion. Integrity' (197) that she tells her daughter: 'I'm still looking at properties up there ... I'm not leaving the EU' (ibid.). In other words, Smith (or at least, her character) shares Hall's assumption in *The Wolf Border* that the referendum result was likely to hasten Scottish separatism and independence, but without pursuing this thought further.

Instead, through the friendship of a one-hundred-and-one-year-old former light entertainer and a thirty-two-year-old university lecturer in the years up to and after the referendum, *Autumn* juxtaposes the hostile feelings unleashed during the 2016 campaign with those of Nazi Germany. Having managed to escape the Nazis with his father, Daniel Gluck has gone on to have a moderately successful career in London as a composer and music hall performer, becoming friends with pop artist Pauline Boty, prior to her death from cancer. Through his subsequent friendship from the 1990s onwards with his young neighbour Elisabeth, Elisabeth rediscovers the lost talent of this neglected artist and dedicates her academic research to Boty. In other words, although the contemporary political situation is clearly juxtaposed with the authoritarianism of 1930s Germany, it is also contrasted with Elisabeth's rediscovery of Boty and hence with a commitment to art, ideas, hope and renewal. Even when Smith portrays the aged Daniel of 2016 as now unable to remember the name of his sister who died in the Holocaust, he is nevertheless able to remember a letter she sent him at the time:

> It's a question of how we regard our situations, dearest Dani, how we look and see where we are, and how we choose, if we can, when we are seeing undeceivedly, not to despair, and, at the same time, how best to act. Hope is exactly that, that's all it is, a matter of how we deal with the negative acts towards human beings by other human beings in the world, remembering that they and we are all human, that nothing human is alien to us, the foul and the fair, and that most of all we're here for a mere blink of the eyes, that's all (190).

Smith depicts Daniel's sister speaking (in his memory) across the years, from the time of the Holocaust to the intolerance and hostilities of Brexit. Indeed, Petra Rau finds that: 'Time is at the heart of *Autumn*: its perception, its pace, its peculiar loops and cycles, its relativizing quality, its ideological uses as "the past", its waste as an abuse of power' (36). But those abuses are contested when, in an act of improbably generous imagination and empathy, Daniel's sister speaks not in favour of one or other of the opposing forces of the Second World War, or even in the typical dichotomy of good and evil that might be expected, but in a way that transcends these categories and attempts to speak for a common humanity. This capacity to transcend categorical imperatives is then an important feature of the novel, and its engagement with the politics of contemporary Britain.

In the novel, Daniel first meets Elisabeth as an eleven-year-old who has to interview her neighbour for a homework assignment, and he introduces her to art, books and critical thinking. This provokes the disapproval of her bourgeois mother who dismisses him as an 'old queen' (43), but Elisabeth later retorts that even if Daniel is gay, 'he's not *just* gay. He's not *just* one thing or another. Nobody is' (77). In this mild corrective, there is an implicit deconstruction of the language associated with hegemonic heterosexuality in favour of the non-binary sexual identities that had become both better articulated and more widely and openly recognised in the years leading up to the novel's publication. The point is not that the character Daniel is either gay or not gay, bisexual or not bisexual, binary or non-binary, but that none of these things alone would be sufficient to define who he is. By a similar logic, Elisabeth has a sexual relationship with a French student, Marielle, and her mother enters a relationship with the woman, Zoe, whom she meets on the television show 'The Golden Gavel' without these things defining either woman.

These small textual features contribute to an overall pattern of signification and meaning. Elisabeth's student fling, for example, could as easily have taken place with another British woman, but by including the tiny detail that Marielle is French, Smith has the effect of associating a non-binary sexual orientation with a personal outlook to life that also includes an implicitly European solidarity. And the same is true the other way around: when Elisabeth's mother and Zoe take part in 'The Golden Gavel', the antiques they hunt for in flea markets and salesrooms symbolise an attempt to preserve the nation's heritage but mostly turn out to be meaningless junk: 'All across the country all the things from the past stacked on the shelves in the shops and the barns and the warehouses' (219), making Elisabeth's mother think of 'entering what you think is going to be history and finding endless sad fragility' (218). This rejection of the baubles and trinkets of an imagined past seems to parallel Elisabeth's mother's (and Smith's) rejection of the myth voters in 2016 were asked to buy into, of a heroic past that had been somehow taken over by malignant foreign forces, from which control somehow needed to be wrested back.

Elisabeth's mother's non-heterosexual relationship is explicitly associated with her rejection of the idea of a national culture in need of salvation; and Elisabeth's brief non-binary relationship is associated with a positively European attitude and identity politics. Through these relationships, the achievement of Smith in *Autumn* is to bring the non-binary thinking associated with recent gender politics to bear on her critique of Brexit itself. The EU referendum had reduced a vast and interrelated set of complex questions to the banal antinomy of In/Out which is insufficient to articulate the real range of issues and responses that it conflated into a single stark choice. Throughout the novel, Smith uses a series of seemingly straightforward and mutually exclusive categories of this kind. But by continually erecting stark binary categories, what the novel ultimately dramatises is their own incompatibility and hence the untenability of such simplistic, categorical thinking. Thus, when Daniel takes the teenaged Elisabeth for a walk and introduces her to his game of Bagatelle, a game of storytelling that challenges what she considers to be her ordinary, everyday common-sense experience of the world, she asks if her story can be about anything she chooses, 'Like truth or lies? That kind of choice?' and he replies: 'A bit oppositional, but yes' (118). Although this conversation takes place in the 1990s, it is difficult not to read it as Smith's response to the hate-making ideologies of the 2016 campaign. In this way, the language of non-binary affiliation, which had gained currency in the specific area of sexual identity during the previous decade, is used to deconstruct the simplistic binary presented by the referendum, and the novel performs an act of queering Brexit in this specific sense: breaking down barriers – between people, genders, races – and enacting a sense of their mutual interrelation.

* * *

The second instalment of Smith's *Seasonal* quartet of novels *Winter* (2017) again takes the politics of Brexit as its starting point, but then subsumes it into the background where it becomes an aspect of individual characterisation rather than broader theme or plot. To some extent this is Smith's way of underlining the new urgency given by political developments since 2016 to the old maxim, the personal is political. It is also undeniably true that with all the politicking and counter-politicking that took place throughout 2017, eighteen months after the referendum the process of leaving the European Union had not only not concluded, but had barely even begun. This means that the options for a novelist seeking to use it as the backdrop for a work of contemporary critical realism are either to project an ending into a somewhat imagined future based on the likely direction of travel at the time of writing, or retain the minimum of what was already known and develop a wider – but separate – plot around it. In *Winter* Smith opted for the latter approach and Scotland is again surprisingly absent.

Winter opens with Art, a man in his thirties, travelling from London to the home of his mother Sophie in Cornwall for Christmas. His girlfriend Charlotte has deserted him after an argument about his nature blog in which she accused him of not being critical enough of damaging human behaviours. So instead he is paying a young woman called Lux to come to Cornwall for three days posing as Charlotte. Once there, however, Lux soon admits to not being Charlotte and in fact relates to Art's difficult mother much better than he does himself. Lux is of Croatian-Canadian origin and, although she has had to drop out of university due to the cost, she tells Sophie that one of the things that inspired her to come to Britain was reading Shakespeare's *Cymbeline* (1611). A country that can handle so much complication, animosity, chaos and confusion and set all right in the end, she explains, must be worth living in.

She does not, however, make the obvious point: that the play was written before the United Kingdom had formally been created and is set in a time – the Roman period – before there was any such geo-political entity as Britain. It also depicts a land in which transition between the British Isles and continental Europe appears almost unfeasibly easy and unobstructed. It might be this, in the end, that Lux really admires. Moreover, her reading of *Cymbeline* forms an intertext with Virginia Woolf's modernist experimental work *Mrs Dalloway* (1925), which frequently alludes to the same play to bolster its own thematic material. There is then a further hint of how Woolf throughout her oeuvre repeatedly critiques patriarchal notions of Englishness based on imperialism and masculine identity (Beer, 1992). By layering these different allusions on top of each other, Smith endows *Winter* with a palimpsestic quality, drawing attention to how much literary and cultural history has already preceded her. This sense of coming after a long before is at odds with the novel's sense of time deferred in its specific handling of Britain's withdrawal from the European Union and this interplay between afterwardsness and anticipation gives the novel, and the quartet as a whole, its temporal dynamism and sense of a world in transition.

At the real heart of *Winter* are Art's ageing mother Sophie and aunt Iris. Sophie has been in her time a successful designer of interior furnishings and other *objets d'art*. Iris, by contrast, was a professional protestor – notably at Greenham common in 1981, but more recently in parts of Greece affected by the currency crisis and migration controversy. In fact, as a young woman Iris had scandalised their bourgeois father by leaving education and home to go on protests. Memories of Christmases throughout the intervening years permeate the novel but rather than providing the family with a reliable structure or sense of solidity they in fact do the opposite: indicating the process by which the sisters grew apart and the family itself became dissipated, especially after the deaths of their grandfather (who had been shell shocked in the war) and their mother. In other words, Sophie and Iris have ostensibly different values, in a perhaps too neat division. They have led such separate lives that they have not spoken for decades when the novel starts, and the fact that Sophie voted leave in the EU vote whereas Iris voted remain is presented as an aspect of the fundamental differences in their world-views and lifestyles.

Having established this opposition, Smith then uses it to open a critical perspective on the referendum outcome, which she does through the introduction of magical realism. *Winter* includes a spectral presence in the form of a disembodied head, an incarnation of a smooth, round stone removed from a Barbara Hepworth sculpture entitled 'Mother and Child' that Art's father had given Sophie during their passionate affair, that supernaturally hovers over Sophie, with the quality of a haunting manifestation. When the memory of that affair comes back to haunt her, she therefore implicitly is placed in the position of wondering how things could have been different in her relationship with her sister, her husband, her son and his father. Given that the novel is about the relationship between the personal and the political, and that the sisters had differed over myriad political issues, especially Brexit, thinking about how Sophie's relationships might have been different also implicitly makes it possible to wonder what would have happened if the outcome of the vote had been different.

Heidemann suggests that this method was already used in Smith's earlier novel *Autumn*, where a supernatural element 'reinforces the provisional nature of the political context in which it was written' (2020, 682). In other words, when deployed in a novel portraying the changes in Britain after the 2016 referendum, magical realism has the capacity to unsettle the common-sense logic of the Brexit ideology and draw attention to Brexit as a (then) unsettled question rather than a given fact. Using a related technique, *Ghost Wall* (2018) by Sarah Moss depicts the hauntedness of the present by the past in its juxtaposition of ritual human sacrifice in ancient Britain with the frustrations of a contemporary disempowered, Northern working-class man who uses amateur archaeology to seek a time in the past when the country was entirely free from foreign influence – a moment which turns out never to have existed. It thus brings the literary method of 'hauntology' (Katy Shaw, 2018) to bear directly on the discourses of race and immigration that were prominent in the years surrounding the 2016 referendum.

In *Winter*, Smith reinforces this point by making Art subject to strange visions and hallucinations when he has nightmares of the Cornish cliffs falling in and burying him. The crumbling of the physical landscape creates a sense of foreboding that seems to warn against imminent national collapse in the wake of the outcome of the referendum. This contrasts with the symbolism at the climax of the novel, where Iris is summoned to Cornwall by Art at Lux's behest and she and Sophie cuddle beneath their blankets. The fact that no bed is present metaphorically implies that their embrace is entirely non-sexual therefore unthreatening and hence a symbol of potential reconciliation. In the context in which the novel was written, where instances of hate crime against Eastern Europeans living in Britain, and members of other persecuted minorities such as Muslims, transsexuals and rough sleepers had all increased, this must have felt like an important outcome to Smith. Just as she uses Art's dream to reinforce the symbolism of his mother's visions, so too she uses the end of the crisis in his personal relationship to bolster this sense of possible reconciliation across the political divisions of the period.

* * *

Unlike *Winter*, the next novel in Smith's Seasonal quartet, *Spring* (2019) explicitly engages both with the political landscape of Brexit Britain and with the implications those politics have for the relationship between Scotland and England. For this reason, it is her most overtly Scottish novel since *Girl Meets Boy* (2007), which was set entirely in Edinburgh but which, through a plot about the politics of water supply, posited significant connections between Scotland and the rest of the world so that the kind of Scotland evoked was one where its protagonists are most Scottish when they are also most globally aware. This feeling is recreated in *Spring*.

The first part is about how television director Richard Lease is brought to a moment of crisis: his wife and daughter have left him, and his oldest friend and sometime screenwriter Paddy has died, leaving him alone and bereft of their accustomed conversations about the nature of artistic inspiration (which is a frequent theme for Smith). They had both been interested in the modernist writers Katherine Mansfield and Rainer Maria Rilke, but since Paddy's death Richard has only been able to discuss them with the new media mogul Martin Terp, who commissions him to write a sensationalist screenplay imagining a passionate love affair between Mansfield and Rilke in the Swiss Alps – for which Richard feels little enthusiasm. The first time he met Terp was at a conference entitled *Adjust Your Set: The Future is Spectacular* where Terp had presented a new technological platform that can stimulate feelings of mourning and sympathy among people who have not empirically experienced them, thus rendering Richard highly suspicious of Terp's integrity. On the other hand, at an earlier suggestion made by Paddy, Richard has started to have imaginary conversations in his head with the daughter who has left him, even taking her to museums and galleries so that he can maintain the feeling of a genuine father–daughter relationship in her absence, so Smith is clearly aware that emotions can be both stimulated and to a certain extent simulated in this way.

Richard feels the loss of Paddy particularly acutely because she was a person who had no truck with the chauvinistic politics of the day. One of the films they had made together was called *Andy Hoffnung*, after the German *An die Hoffnung* ('To Hope') and he seems to feel more proud of this than another earlier documentary, *Panharmonicon*, in which he had used a machine designed by Beethoven for playing all the instruments in an orchestra simultaneously to enact in music the Battle of Trafalgar. In the film, different instruments stood for different sides and the battle was transposed into the setting of an English village at war with itself over who has the right to park in the central reservation. The symbolism of this imagined film, offering to portray a conflict between Britain and mainland Europe while also reimagining it as an internecine struggle within English society, has clear resonance with the post-2016 context in which the novel was written. John Masterson interprets *Spring* as an intervention which 'examines the dialectic between displacement, conceived both physically and psychically, and Brexit-era populism' (2020, 356). The fact that, among his own works, Smith's fictional director feels closer to a work entitled 'To Hope' than to this work about civil war perhaps recreates the note of desired reconciliation with which she had finished *Winter*.

But reconciliation is harder this time precisely because the politics of Brexit are more explicitly foregrounded. Just as Part One is about how Richard misses the way Paddy would have scorned the feelings of chauvinism Brexit appears to have unleashed, so Part Two portrays those feelings in a much more concrete way. It focuses on a woman symbolically named Brittany Hall who works in an immigration detention centre for a company called for SA4A, a fictional avatar of the notoriously heavy-handed security company G4S. Though Brittany's self-image is basically decent, honest and hard-working she has been worn down over time into treating the detainees ('deets') like objects and nuisances and thus blaming them for her own feelings of fatigue. The centre had only ever been built to house people for three days at a time and many of them have been there for three years so that the cruel system of incarceration rather than its victims is really the cause of Brittany's emotional exhaustion, but acknowledging this is an aspect of her own humanity that she must repress because if she allows herself to feel any empathy at all it will become impossible for her to go on working in that system.

As with *Winter*, Smith's critical realism in the portrayal of the centre and its operatives is combined at different stages in the novel with a magical element that elevates both the writing and its content onto a higher perceptual plain. When a detained child gets in to see the centre's director and as a result the toilets in all the migrants' rooms are cleaned for the first time in months, Brittany considers it a minor miracle. Although this might not feel very magical, it is the point from which Smith begins to introduce more and more details that cannot easily be explained and which have the effect of disturbing and unsettling the statistical logic on which the centre's functioning depends. Soon afterwards, Brittany meets a mysterious girl on a train who asks her how she would get to a place called Kingussie.

Somehow, the girl – Florence – seems to have a mysterious hold over her and others around her, so that Brittany ends up travelling with her to Scotland, while Florence manages to charm the ticket inspector and hotel receptionist to waive payment. She appears to have this power simply by talking in a polite, courteous and respectful way, but it is also hinted that as a young, black female child Florence is culturally invisible and therefore passes often unnoticed between one setting and another. Through this device Smith is able to transgress a number of physical and conceptual boundaries. In other words, realism is associated in the novel with narrative closure and the logic of the ideology which has made possible the long-term imprisonment of human beings who have not committed any offence beyond the desire to come to Britain. Magical elements, by contrast, creep in as a means of counter-balancing and contesting those same ideologies.

For example, a highly poetic section narrates the fate of an unnamed girl in an unnamed time and place who is apparently sacrificed to propitiate one or more pagan gods of Spring and fertility. The narrative style at this point is both poetic and mystical on the one hand, but also pragmatic and vernacular on the other. This means that the unspecified location feels simultaneously like an extension of our own world but also more ancient and more archetypal. The girl in the myth ends up refusing to be sacrificed and therefore being turned into a story to be owned by others. She may therefore represent Florence who, because she stands up to the politics of hate-making ideologies, suffers a significant emotional backlash. The section entitled '140 seconds of cutting edge realism' (223–4) is made up of a series of online tweets in which she is subjected to trolling, animosity and hatred of all kinds, simply because she has tried to resist those very things. Smith's point is not simply that people are inherently spiteful, malicious or envious but that the feelings directed towards Florence in the novel can only exist if they have been cultivated and fostered. This is why the juxtaposition with Martin Terp's platform for s(t)imulating emotions is so prescient because it identifies the material basis on which such cultivation occurs. The particular platform in *Spring* happens to be fictional and invented, but there is a strong parallel between it and the algorithm-based fostering of anti-European and anti-immigration sentiment via Facebook and other social media in the real world during the referendum campaign.

Brittany and Florence arrive in Kingussie in time for Florence to save Richard from throwing himself under a train. They then all meet up with Alda Lyons, an ex-librarian who drives them out to the nearby site of the Battle of Culloden, which was both the last battle on British soil and also the last major battle between Scotland and England. In other words, like Hall in *The Wolf Border* Smith associates stepping across national borders with the transition between different periods in history and so the physical, geographic landscape is also an indicator of the temporal, sidereal one. Although Alda corrects Brittany's description of the battlefield by saying that the Jacobean rebellion was a conflict between dynasties (Hanoverians and Jacobites) rather than discrete nations (England and Scotland), the latter seems more apposite, given that the novel cultivates a strong sense of Scottish difference. In her correction, there may also be an ironic comment by Smith on the tendency for the politics of the Brexit era to throw up hardened battle lines and heighten relatively minor differences between nations, when really things are both less distinct and more complex.

It gradually becomes clear that Alda is part of a network of people dedicated to helping migrants and other detainees escape the inhuman system so presumably Florence's meeting with her was pre-arranged. Brit's response is to call the SA4A helpline and, as a result, Alda is arrested on the battlefield while bemused tourists look on and Richard tries to get hold of the footage they record of it on their phones so he can make a film out of it. In other words, Brit is not transformed by her encounter with Florence and goes back to being the organ of state power she was at the start. This polarised ending is very unlike that of *Winter*, which gestured towards reconciliation rather than a continuation of the stand-off, and this may reflect the fact that, as the third novel in the quartet, it was written during the years 2016 and 2017 when just such a stand-off was the primary characteristic of the Brexit process and where endless confrontation with neither resolution nor reconciliation were the main feelings.

If there is one note of hope, it is that the final passage of the novel is about Spring itself – just as one of the opening passages appeared to be actually spoken by 'Spring'. It is a time of rebirth and renewal and possibly therefore of optimism. But the metaphor is complex and ambivalent: the detention centre is euphemistically called Spring, so it could be that the novel *Spring* is about how the public myth/fiction is always a simplification or even untruth when compared to complicated reality. Thus, the box hedge that grows outside the Spring detention centre where Brittany works could symbolise many different plants coming together as one, *or* a form of boundary and barrier that delineates the centre and so imprisons the detainees. The metaphors collapse into each other and a feeling of closure is postponed.

THE METROPOLIS VERSUS THE PROVINCES

Like Smith's quartet, Jonathan Coe's 2018 novel *Middle England* is a satire on British public life in the years leading up to and away from the European referendum. But whereas Scottish devolutionary politics are important to Hall, Kennedy and Smith, Coe situates his political satire in a specifically English context. *Middle England* picks up the characters from Coe's earlier books: *The Rotters' Club* (2001) where they were studying for their A-Levels in the 1970s and *The Closed Circle* (2004) which follows them into the early years of professional life. As was the case with the earlier texts, the fiction in *Middle England* is interspersed with anchoring references to contemporary events and current affairs: Prime Minister Gordon Brown referring to a traditional Labour voter as a bigoted woman before the 2010 general election; the swimmer who disrupted the Oxford and Cambridge boat race as a protest against privilege and inequality; the 2011 London riots; the 2012 London Olympics; the introduction of gay marriage; the celebrity deaths of Victoria Wood, Prince, Alan Rickman, and David Bowie; the murder of MP Jo Cox; American President Obama's warning that a Britain outside the European Union would have to join the back of the queue for any trade deal with the USA. One of the most innovative aspects of Coe's fiction is that these allusions make it possible for readers to map occasions in their private lives onto the timeframe of the novel because these public affairs take on the character of epoch-making events so that we remember, or imagine that we remember, what was happening in our own lives at the time they happened and therefore understand them chiefly through reference to our own life trajectory. In this way, Coe's work facilitates a peculiar form of life reading whereby, simultaneous with encountering the plot, we are also to some extent filling in its gaps with images from our own stories and therefore reading our own lives. This is how Petra Rau interprets Ali Smith's *Autumn*, in a context where '[m]y own "now" – and quite a few plans for the future – fell through the floor in the wake of the referendum's outcome' (31–2).

Middle England opens with the funeral of Benjamin and Lois Trotter's mother Sheila and this catalysing death of a parent seems to function as a herald for imminent generational change just as it does in Hall's *Wolf Border*. Benjamin, now in his fifties, has moved to a large old mill in Shropshire on the banks of the River Severn and, having already lost the love of his life Cicely and with a daughter in the States he never sees or talks to, is resigned to living alone – although he feels obliged to take a more active role in the care of his ageing father, Colin. His sister Lois is less involved because, although she is married to Christopher, she works in York and stays there half the week, so she is distanced.

The sense of colliding values between different generations is best illustrated in the novel by the conflict between Lois and Christopher's daughter Sophie and her mother-in-law Helena, who is suspicious both of Sophie's intellect and her apparent preference for pursuing an academic career in art history over having children. Sophie and Ian settle into a routine of regular visits to Helena in the Midlands village of Kernel Magna, a name by which Coe signifies Helena's desire to retreat into a shell insulated against the outside world, in contrast to the work Sophie gets delivering art lectures on a Baltic cruise ship. Here, the spoilt guests seem to bring out the worst in Ian, making snide comments about the female couple who share their dining table and encouraging him to think that the only reason he recently missed out on a promotion at work was because his colleague Naheed was prioritised because she was an Asian woman. In other words, though white, middle-class and male and therefore among the most privileged sections of the population, he is portrayed as believing himself to be unjustly disempowered and his mother encourages him in this belief. Sophie cannot really bear this, a feeling which is enhanced when she goes with him on one of his regular golf outings back home and one of his friends, a farmer who sells milk to China, tells her it is much easier to do so than to sell to customers in Europe because of Brussels red tape, a world-view with which she is out of sympathy and that causes her to begin re-evaluating her relationship with Ian. On the other hand, a female Dutch colleague with whom she is making a television programme about art tells her it does not matter if your partner does not share your politics: she had a socialist boyfriend who beat her up. Sophie thus wonders if she can put politics aside in her personal relationships and in this way the novel foregrounds the question of how far the personal can be detached from the political.

This question is given further poignancy when the Lithuanian woman Grete, who out of simple kindness does far more to care for

Helena than the mere cleaning for which she is ostensibly employed, is threatened and attacked by thugs shouting: Poles go home. Rather than provide a witness statement to the police, Helena says she thinks Grete and her husband should leave, thus betraying the people who have looked after her. Likewise, when Sophie is suspended from her lectureship in London because a comment she makes about students not being able to make up their mind is interpreted as an insult against a Welsh transgender student, Emily Shamma, Helena and Ian see this as an instance of metropolitan political correctness (negatively defined). Far from supporting Sophie, Helena and Ian encourage her to think this would be a good opportunity to give up the regular commute to London and settle down in the Midlands to start a family. It is only when her television programme becomes a success and increases her cultural capital that she is allowed to go back and teach, but by then she has left Ian to live in London. Emily had never wanted to make the complaint against her, which was lodged by one of the other students looking for a fashionable cause to support, and came to see Sophie during her suspension just as Sophie visited her in hospital at the time of her gender reassignment surgery.

One of the problematic features of the novel is that Emily is described as half Welsh and half Muslim, as if it were impossible for her to be wholly Welsh and Muslim – an assumption that was squarely rejected by plans to 'include the terms "Asian Welsh" and "Black Welsh", as well as Asian British and Black British' on the 2021 census (BBC, 2020). The same assumption is made in the subplot involving the rivalry between the professional clowns Charlie Chappell and Doctor Daredevil: Charlie offers himself as a surrogate father figure for his girlfriend Yasmin's Muslim daughter, Aneeqa, but not only does Yasmin resent their closeness and break up with Charlie, he also finds himself taunted by his professional rival Doctor Daredevil who accuses him of having an improper relationship with the girl. Daredevil then rubs salt in the wound by gloating that after Brexit it will be much harder for Aneeqa to follow her dream of living and studying in Spain, whereas the same opportunity will still be available to his own daughter Krystal because he has made sure to apply for Irish passports for all his family, thereby guaranteeing they retain the right to live and work in the European Union even though he had voted for Brexit. This hypocrisy so maddens Charlie that he gets into a fight with him and is imprisoned for assault.

Through these relatively minor characters, the portrayal of Emily and Aneeqa provides a focus for a number of themes: the intersectional politics of gender, race and sexuality, the different ways in which these things are predominantly expressed between members of different generations, and apparently different attitudes to them between the metropolis and the provinces. To some extent their inclusion fosters a conjunction between the European referendum campaign on the one hand and incipient islamophobia on the other. Much of the campaign itself was focused on an emotive but only vaguely defined concept of immigration, with an implicit promise on the part of the Leave campaign that leaving the European Union would somehow result in a reduction in immigration from parts of the world outside Europe and therefore ostensibly not affected by the referendum. When Coe depicts both Emily and Aneeqa as half Muslim and therefore by implication also only half British, he replicates this populist assumption that the Britishness of British Muslims was only partial, provisional and incomplete, an assumption that became expressed in the actions of Theresa May's government when it rescinded the British citizenship of Shamima Begum even though she had no other citizenship and was rendered state-less by the action. Although this conjunction between British state policy and the growth of islamophobia is not necessarily endorsed by the novel, it is also not really interrogated by it, either.

Overall, Coe is somewhat too schematic in his presentation of the differences in social outlook between young, upwardly mobile, metropolitan adults and their older, provincial, working-class forebears, which comes over as something of a stark and unbreakable binary in the novel. For instance, when Sophie quits academia she takes a job running a skills academy for undereducated young adults, which is established by her gay Sri Lankan Londoner friend Sohan (who, we note, is doing a PhD on Englishness) and his hedge fund millionaire husband, Mike. A socially progressive outlook on class and education is automatically associated with a socially progressive outlook on the politics of both race and gay rights; and all three are clearly associated with the metropolis as opposed to the provinces.

In fact, this rigid schematisation has become one of the dominant tropes of fictional portrayals of Brexit Britain. Chloé Ashbridge has argued that Anthony Cartwright's Brexit novel *The Cut* (2017) portrays the limits of such 'binaristic discourse' without being able to envision alternatives (4). In a discussion of Adam Thorpe's 2017 novel

Missing Fay, which is set in the area of Britain that had the highest Brexit vote (Lincolnshire), Vedrana Veličković made a connection between English nationalism and anti-immigration rhetoric before observing: 'Recent literary representations often tend to reinforce stereotypes about Eastern Europeans, even when they try to deconstruct them' (651).

In the case of *Middle England*, the entrenched binary thinking is most apparent in the portrayal of Sophie's uncle Benjamin, now living in semi-retirement on the banks of the Severn between the Welsh borders and the English Midlands. Towards the end of his father Colin's life, Benjamin takes him on a visit to the site of the old car works at Longbridge where Colin once worked. But, rather than providing him with a comforting feeling of nostalgia, the visit makes Colin feel profoundly anxious and displaced. All the factories have been replaced by department stores and boutiques, so the place is unrecognisable to him and he is left with a troubling uncertainty that recalls Robert Hewison's critique of the transition from heavy industry to the cultural industries discussed in Chapter One. Unable to understand where all the work, jobs and lives have gone he exclaims: 'If we don't make anything then we've got nothing to sell, so how… how are we going to survive?' (261). The allusion to the cultural politics of Brexit is pointed up when Coe has him go on: 'No wonder the rest of the world's laughing at us' (262). Soon after this, Colin arranges for a postal vote in the European referendum and, although weakened by a stroke, he walks out to the post box to post it – and collapses and dies. The symbolism here is hard to miss, as though voting for Brexit has killed Colin just as it killed Ian and Sophie's relationship. Meanwhile, Benjamin has spent forty years working on the manuscript of a novel, *A Rose Without A Thorn*, based on his doomed relationship with Cicely. But when it is shortlisted for the Booker Prize and a female journalist comes to his riverside home to interview him, her article 'Outsider on the Inside' (222) is a stinging character assassination based solely on the detail that Benjamin had briefly shared a corridor with Boris Johnson at Oxford in 1983 and on the assumption that Benjamin is tainted with the same radical Conservatism as him simply by association. In other words, Brexit is portrayed as an extended pathological disease from which Britain cannot apparently cure itself. This portrayal precisely reverses one of the dominant metaphors by which British entry in 1973 into the European Economic Community had been conceptualised: 'as an external answer to the British disease' of failing industry and social disaffection (Nairn, 1977, 54).

The other aspect of Brexit as an unending saga, a nightmare from which there is no waking up, comes about when Doug discovers papers produced by the Imperium Foundation, a right-wing think tank founded by another ex-schoolmate of the protagonists, Ronald Culpepper, a character who appears to be modelled both on the extreme Conservative Jacob Rees-Mogg and the Leave campaign's communications strategist (and subsequent special adviser to Boris Johnson), Dominic Cummings. In the papers, Culpepper warns his fellow radical Conservatives that, if Brexit itself is achieved, the fervour that had been whipped up during the campaign might dissipate during the two-year implementation period and cause the party's extremists to lose their electoral appeal. Therefore, his documents suggest, the country's sense of betrayal 'must be sustained' beyond Brexit (358), and they set out various ways of using the mass media to manipulate public information and maintain this feeling in order to continually re-galvanise populist support for extreme authoritarian assaults on the public sphere. However, Coe cannot really imagine a way to defeat this nexus of populist politics and media spin, so all he can do is have Benjamin, Doug and the others walk out in protest from a speech given by the millionaire Culpepper at a school reunion.

Metaphorically speaking, Benjamin continues his walk all the way to France where he and Lois open a Bed and Breakfast, as if to abandon Britain altogether. In a set piece ending to the novel, Coe brings many of its characters together for the opening of this business, at which Sophie tells the others that she has reconciled with Ian and is expecting a baby, due on 29 March 2019, which when Coe was writing was the date on which Britain was due to leave the European Union. In the wake of Theresa May's repeated failure in January 2019 to gain a parliamentary majority for her European Withdrawal Agreement, and the subsequent deferral of this deadline, Sophie's child cannot strictly be referred to as a Brexit baby, in the concise way forecast by the novel. In another sense, however, she is absolutely typical. This is not just because – like the UK's departure from the EU – she will be born at the wrong time, but more fundamentally because she is a child who will inherit an uncertain world. When Coe was writing the novel, it was impossible to foresee precisely when the final departure would take place. In other words, by trying to insist on an absolute finality to the Brexit process which was in the future at the time of its writing,

Middle England ends up having the opposite effect and rebounds on a present whose cultural contradictions have no clear end in sight.

BREXIT AND WRITING ABOUT NORTHERN IRELAND

When Lois eventually separates from Christopher in *Middle England*, she admits it was unfair to marry him because she has never got over losing her first boyfriend in the Birmingham pub bombing of 1974, as portrayed in Coe's earlier novel *The Rotters' Club* (2001). Through this means Coe provides a muted allusion to the Irish Troubles which had been halted by the peace process of the 1990s – which in turn is one of the things most at stake in the Brexit process.

It was argued in the discussion of Derry/Londonderry's hosting of UK City of Culture in Chapter Two and of Northern Ireland's conspicuous lack of a national book prize in Chapter Four that two of the characteristic features of Northern Ireland's development of a post-conflict society are the downplaying of cultural work that could be considered politically divisive and the production of work that can be commonly experienced and enjoyed. It is largely in keeping with these features that, given the enormity of its significance, Northern Irish fiction writers have had very little to say about Brexit. Nevertheless, they have briefly alluded to it in perhaps unexpected places. For example, it was argued in Chapter Four that Eimear McBride's *Strange Hotel* (2020) engages with Brexit politics in a highly subjective and impressionistic way. McBride's unnamed narrator has a lifestyle that involves frequent global travel and each section of the text is punctuated by a list of towns and cities around the world, each time ending up with the name of the place the next section takes place in. Some of the places are marked with an x on the lists to indicate the locations of her sexual encounters with men. Thus, the whole emotional process portrayed in *Strange Hotel* is one of remembering and accepting: the female narrator had once chosen to stay in her relationship to a now-dead lover even after he had revealed to her a shameful and disturbing secret from his past and she has spent most of her adult life in mourning for his subsequent death. But because the precise contents of his shameful confession are never revealed, the possibility that he might have been involved in one way or another in communal hostilities during the Troubles is both raised and simultaneously distanced and displaced. In this way, the novel avoids aligning either the narrator or her lost lover with any specific position within the community as a whole, and as a result it also avoids alienating readers from different positions and is able to speak equally to all of them via the universality of themes such as love and grief. The novel performs a coming to terms at last with the ineluctability of loss and the narrator gives herself permission finally to move on. Potentially troubling political emotions that might be raised if the novel specified what exactly the dead lover had confessed to are forestalled and the deflection into romantic resolution does the same for the Brexit context that is alluded to several times in the text without ever being portrayed explicitly.

A similar trajectory is conveyed by Nick Laird's earlier novel *Modern Gods* (2017), a novelistic juxtaposition of the tendency for sectarianism to give rise to violence in two very different communities: post-Good Friday Agreement Ulster, and the remote Pacific island of New Ulster in Papua New Guinea. It concerns Liz Donnelly, a professor of anthropology, who is commissioned by the BBC to make a documentary about an emerging religion on the island, and travels there from her New York home via Ballyglass in Ireland for her sister Alison's wedding. Alison has already left her first husband, a policeman who turned to alcoholism after being caught up in violence and became abusive. Her new fiancé, Stephen, seems to be blandness personified, and this feels very desirable by comparison. When they go and see their priest to plan the wedding, Stephen tries to tell Alison that he has done bad things in the past – but she simply tells him she doesn't need to know. So it is only the day after the wedding that Alison finds out from a newspaper that he and a partner had murdered five people in a pub shooting, having been recruited into a paramilitary organisation during the Troubles when his own father, a policeman, was murdered; and that he had been released from prison after only two years under the terms of the Good Friday agreement.

Alison is repulsed by this. During the honeymoon in Greece, she gets an email from someone purporting to be an academic researcher in history, wanting to contact them to record his testimony of what happened for posterity. But when she sets up this meeting after the honeymoon, the 'academic' turns out to be the husband of one of Stephen's victims, wanting to confront him. Alison leaves the house while they talk, but returns in time to hear this revelation, as well as a good part of Stephen's own account of what happened. But though her presence implicitly saves Stephen from any kind of retributive violence on the part of the widower, she finds she cannot live with Stephen either, and the marriage is over before it has begun.

While all of this is being played out, Liz is in Papua New Guinea researching the new religion and its founder, Belef, whose name clearly hints at the concept of religious and spiritual faith ('belief'). She meets two American missionaries who do not take Belef's new cult seriously as either religion or political insurrection. Instead, they think it is merely a traumatised reaction to the death of her own daughter, Kaykay/Kasingen, and worry she is undermining all the Christian proselytising they boast of having achieved. Kaykay died when a branch fell on her outside their church, which seems to be one reason why Belef has turned against it and set up her own Cargo Cult. It is a cult in which the evil visited on people in the past sets a price to be redeemed in the present, but it also fuses modern elements: Belef refers to the trees as telephones, and clears a runway for air travel although she has no plane.

Faith in the power of symbolic gods is a linking theme of the text. But if the different societies share a common impulse towards belief, they also share the capacity to be riven apart by the politics of factionalism. The missionary Josh tells Liz that before the New Truth mission, the local tribes were lost in darkness and fought each other all the time. This is borne out by Belef's deputy Leftie, and by her own son Usai, who is still a member of Josh's Christian church. At the ritual of drinking and dancing at the climax of Liz's visit to New Ulster, Belef announces that the goddess Amulmul will return to atone for all the women who have been murdered by men down the ages, and her followers will get their 'cargo' (or material reward). Therefore, they do not need money – and she makes her followers burn their banknotes. At this point Usai is watching from the forest, and Belef and Leftie think he is a spy, and even though he is her own son they appear ready to kill him until Liz intervenes. The next day, Josh is furious with Liz and Margo not only for taking part in a pagan ritual he has been trying to stamp out, but also for allowing the crowd to burn their money – when they have so little. So he calls the head of his mission in Texas, who threatens the local Deputy Administrator Raula that all funding for schools, clinics and development will be stopped unless Belef's cult is stopped immediately. When Belef surrenders to the policemen who come to arrest her, they push her to the ground and kneel on her back. Usai is angered by seeing his mother treated like this and, when he tries to free her, he is shot dead by the police. Liz flies back to Ulster reflecting on what she has seen, how Usai was killed supporting the mother from whom the politics of religion had estranged him, and thinking:

> What divides us is as nothing to what joins us ... She would journey out beyond the reef of her body and into open sea. The period of watching was over; she knew that as a fact within her. A change had come. But what? And what came next? She would be kind. She would learn to love the world. She would try. As if for the first time, she felt the grief inherent in all things, in all relations, in all love (299).

In other words, although the novel is about how sects and beliefs are divisive, like *Strange Hotel* it ends with this commitment to reconciliation in the abstract. Liz and her cameraman Paolo appear to be falling in love with each other and may start a life together in London. Her parents have always thought her brother Spencer was gay, but he too is giving his relationship with Trisha a go. Even the estranged sisters Liz and Alison are somewhat reconciled to each other. Sectarian difference is displaced by personal relationship in the interests of a symbolic set of final accommodations from which any troubling difference is filtered out; and the fact that peace was only achieved in New Ulster through violent erasure is allowed to lapse out of collective memory. In this way, the novel accords with the dominant mode of cultural production in post-conflict Northern Ireland.

Although *Modern Gods* does not explicitly mention the politics of Brexit at all, the date of its publication one year after the European referendum is very striking, the more so if we consider that the open border, a fundamental component of the peace process and one which was guaranteed by the European Union's commitment to the free movement of people, goods and services, is potentially jeopardised by Brexit. As we have seen, the primary mechanism through which cultural producers in Northern Ireland have contributed to the peace process has been through playing up shared heritage and mutual relationship while playing down dissonant elements and avoiding political controversy. Like McBride's *Strange Hotel*, *Modern Gods* follows this logic and alludes to Brexit by not alluding to it: creating a hollow core into which the components of reconciliation can be poured.

Describing Eimear McBride as an Irish writer is not strictly accurate since she in fact comes from Liverpool. On the other hand, she is of dual Irish parentage and clearly feels a strong affinity with Ireland, a feeling that is enhanced by the strong history of migration and interconnection between Ireland and Liverpool. This interconnection informs the choice of another Liverpudlian writer, Linda Grant, to place an Irish woman, Chrissie, at the heart of her Brexit novel, *A Stranger City* (2019), which differs from Grant's earlier work in that, rather than tracing a single family across several generations, it depicts the intersecting lives of different people in London and is therefore a montage novel which explicitly engages with the atmosphere and mood of Britain in 2016 and beyond. It starts with the odd coincidence of two young women both apparently going missing off London bridge on the same night, although the young Irish nurse Chrissie has not really gone missing at all: merely moved in with a man – Yusuf – after meeting him on the night bus. From here, the novel's focus shifts to the second woman to go missing that night, an unnamed woman whose body is subsequently found in the Thames, and the film-maker and policeman who both investigate her death. Pete retires from the police to care for his sick wife, but when they retire to the Lake District the locals are presented as parochial, small minded and sometimes even outright prejudiced against incomers, a narrow-mindedness which contrasts with the portrayal of a fifty-year friendship between a wealthy Jewish woman and her working-class Asian neighbour back in London.

In this juxtaposition of the insularity Pete discovers in the rural Lake District with the openness of the cosmopolitan city, the novel creates an impression of an unbridgeable gulf in lifestyles and social outlooks. The implication is that when London's rich cosmopolitanism starts to fragment, this change is associated with a hardening and polarising of attitudes towards race, immigration and multiculturalism in the country as a whole: Chrissie's former flatmate Marco is permanently disfigured in an apparently racist acid attack by thugs unable to discern whether he is Arab or not; her second flatmate Yusuf is subsequently deported; and many of his Romanian roommates choose to go home, so that Chrissie then moves in with some Jamaican girls – who also end up leaving the country. The strangeness of the title thus refers to how the vibrant intercultural make-up of the city is turned into something like a travesty of itself by these recent developments. When there is an upturn in casual violence against ethnic minorities, Francesca's ageing Iranian grandmother Amira simply stops going out – but within two months of adopting this inactive lifestyle she is dead. The owners of a Greek delicatessen on the street where Francesca works decide to sell up and return to Greece and a German family make a similar decision when their daughter Gaby is bullied by classmates who ask her: 'aren't you all going home now?' (116). Like Coe, therefore, Grant posits the national mood in the wake of the 2016 referendum as toxic and potentially fatal.

The resolution to the mystery of the dead woman comes when Chrissie moves in with one of her patients, Rob, and his Romanian decorator recognises her not only from a YouTube video but also from Alan's documentary in which her 'disappearance' had been contrasted with the dead woman found in the Thames whom, he now reveals, he knew. The woman is finally identified as a human being, Valentina Popov, rather than simply as case number DB27. She had been working as a cleaner in London to save money for her daughter at home, but had been blackmailed by a people-smuggling gang who discovered that as a Moldovan, rather than a Romanian, she had no official status in the UK and was highly vulnerable to their demands. Unable to pay them and too frightened to go to the police she had killed herself because she could not see any other alternative.

The detail of Valentina coming from Moldova is highly significant, because Moldova is lodged between Romania (and hence the European Union) on one side and the Russian Federation on the other. Its physical distance from both entities is small, but because it is also the distance between different geo-political entities and hence different legal jurisdictions it is a difference that has absolute power over her life. Through this means Grant is able to create a critical portrayal of such arbitrary constructs as borders and frontiers. Similarly, the novel ends with Chrissie boarding a plane for Australia because her father back in Ireland has advised her to get out of England. But when the plane turns back to London because someone onboard is ill, she is tempted to get back out and stay in London after all – and this is not resolved. The idea of going 'home' is thus rendered highly relative and provisional by this closing passage, as if to ask what the concept of home even means.

By making Chrissie resolve the missing person plot, Grant also portrays the interrelationship between a number of different elements in contemporary culture. It is notable, for example, that Grant automatically associates Chrissie's presumably pro-European stance (as an Irish woman living in London) with an egalitarian sexual politics concerning gay lifestyles – where both things are implicitly contrasted with the assumed reactionary tendencies of people in Pete's Lake

District. This conflation is not necessarily problematic in itself, but it does make it necessary to wonder whether things might in reality be more complex. Might there not, for example, be some people who were in favour of Britain leaving the European Union while also supporting gay rights; and others who were pro-European but resistant to them? Failing to consider these complexities makes more entrenched the assumption that a progressive outlook in one area necessarily implies a progressive outlook in all others and that the enlightened metropolis can straightforwardly be contrasted with the benighted hinterland, thereby passing on uninterrogated the simplistic compartmentalisation of thinking that was a feature of the original referendum campaign, and that failed to accommodate any degree of nuance or critical complexity at all.

The result is that, although it seems clear Grant intended the novel to be a critical portrayal of the forms of chauvinism, racism and violence that have become more prominent in British public life since 2016, the premise on which it is based unwittingly reinforces the binary thinking on which that chauvinism drew and is not really able to displace it. When Pete decides to leave London and re-join his wife in the Lake District, it is not because he is portrayed as believing that its cultural politics are any more inclusive than London's, but because he is giving up altogether on a long and exhausting fight. This means that Pete's despair at the emerging politics of Brexit Britain is also ironically bound up with a sense of decline, a feeling that the nation is not able to live up to the greatness of its former values. By couching his lament for the downturn in mutual respect for other human beings in the language of a wider English decline narrative, the novel perhaps unwittingly passes on the sense of a loss needing to be stemmed which was at the heart of the Brexit process and with which it is therefore more closely accommodated than its characters seem to wish.

INTERIM NATION

The representations of the English Midlands in *Middle England* and the Lake District in *A Stranger City* reinforce rather than interrogate the metropolis/province divide and reify the feeling of a prosperous, cosmopolitan, city-dwelling elite at odds with the lifestyle of working-class people in regional towns and rural areas. The single English region to have most commonly attracted this kind of negative representation in the aftermath of the 2016 referendum is Cornwall, which has been used by a number of different novelists as a metonym for the state of the nation overall in this period. This is no doubt in part because from Daphne Du Maurier and Agatha Christie onwards, there is already a significant history of using Cornwall in literature to symbolise an uncultivated hinterland on the periphery of British civilisation. Moreover, with its connotations of occupying the extremist limit of mainland Britain, and a number of high-profile complaints about European fisheries and agricultural policy, it might have seemed like a natural setting for writers seeking to pen a fictional work about Brexit Britain. But the result is that in many cases the portrayals become self-fulfilling prophecies and the writers find in Cornwall exactly what they had expected to find, rather than challenging the hypotheses and assumptions with which they set out.

One of the earliest novels to explicitly engage with the culture and politics of Brexit was Amanda Craig's *The Lie of the Land* (2017) which uses the juxtaposition of London and Cornwall as a metaphorical way of depicting the breakdown in a marriage of two middle-class Londoners, Quentin and Lottie Bredin, who have lost their jobs as journalist and architect and can't afford to divorce because if they sell their house they can't afford one each. They thus plan to rent out their London home for a year and rent a much less expensive cottage in the rural South West in the hope that at the end of the year the value of the London house will have increased enough to meet their needs. There is also a mystery subplot concerning why the cottage is so cheap: specifically, because in it, the previous tenant Oliver Randall (who was also the son of the landlord, the rock star Gore Tore) had been violently murdered by Tore's ex-partner Janet, out of jealousy that he had started to get close to their daughter, Dawn. In this portrayal of strange goings on in the rural countryside, Craig's portrayal of the region therefore very much follows those earlier representations of otherness that we find in *Jamaica Inn* (1936) or *Evil Under the Sun* (1941). In fact, the sense of dislocation is heightened by the fact that it is unclear to Quentin and Lottie whether the village they have moved to, Trelorn, is even in Devon or Cornwall: it has a 'Cornish name and postal code, but counts as part of Devon' (67).

Naturally, they hate it: all 'one bungalow deep in village idiots, and old people waiting to die' (26). Their experience is one of poverty on a scale they have never encountered before, cultural backwardness and a stereotypical suspicion of outsiders. Their daughters Stella and Rosie are not thriving, especially Stella who had been a high-achiever at her prep school and therefore comes over as a snob to her new classmates. When Lottie's teenage bi-racial son Xan fails to get into Cambridge University and takes a job at Humbles pie factory, looking up from the factory floor at the top storey where the foremen work makes him think of the balcony at the 'Royal Opera House' (69), as if to emphasise how culturally remote his new surroundings are from the metropolis. The casual racism he encounters when he gets his 'buttocks fondled' by his bullying co-worker Rod and 'feels the man's erection grind into his back' (73) is a further part of the assumed inferiority of the place and its people: 'The locals don't even know how racist they are' (65). Even when he starts a relationship with a Polish co-worker Kayta she too compares his skin to smooth wood which he tells her is 'not polite' (213). The physical gesture of being groped by Rod also has an implication of homophobia, which contrasts with the fact that Lottie's gay cousin Justin is getting married back in a presumably more enlightened London. This combination of racism and homophobia solidifies a feeling of South Western underadvancement in both a cultural and a political sense and hence constructs its people as adherents to a set of cringing values and outdated beliefs.

The hostility towards the European Union that Quentin and Lottie encounter is presented as a logical extension of this combination. The health visitor Sally and her farmer husband Pete are exhausted by 'mountains of paperwork for the hated EU' (94). Another factory worker, Maddy, explains to Lottie that when the Polish workers go home for Christmas, local workers get fifty pence an hour more because the pie factory is desperate for staff – but this is cut when they return: 'No wonder Maddy and the other Devonians say that next election, they'll vote UKIP' (160). When Lottie gets a job with a local architectural firm working on a project that might revitalise the town, Maddy explains that at the moment it's hard to get school places or doctor's appointments: 'You want to know why we want to leave Europe? That's why' (216). Even when Sally, the health visitor who is heartbroken by the experience of spending her days caring for other people's children while having none of her own, considers absconding with the baby she rescues from Janet and Dawn, it 'isn't virtue that stops her; it's the regulations. Everybody in modern Europe lives for better or worse in an inescapable web of Health and Safety. An unregistered child will not have access to health care, education, a passport and an identity' (410).

This anti-European sentiment is constructed by Craig in a way that could hardly be more contrasting with Quentin and Lottie, a contrast that is pointed up by the fact that neither of them is 'entirely English' (18) since his mother is South African and hers German. In fact, Lottie's mother Marta, a 'popular figure in the cosmopolitan circles she moves in' (271) seems to symbolise all that is bright and shining about life in London. By contrast, Quentin's father the irascible poet Hugh is slowly dying of cancer on the edge of Dartmoor and laments that the London of his memory 'doesn't exist now' (206). Thus, although Birte Heidemann suggests of the novel that with 'the socio-economic crisis at its peak, Quentin seeks refuge in a rhetoric that reminds one of the new round of imperial nostalgia forged by Brexit' (681), it seems truer to say that his association of open-mindedness with the metropolis is contrasted to the lives and attitudes of the people he and Lottie meet during their rural sojourn. When Quentin starts asking people in the Trelorn pub about the murder in the house he now rents, the locals all think either 'gypsies', 'hell's angels' or 'Islamic Fundamentalists' are to blame – thus conveying a suite of different hostilities at once (202). When we are told that Lottie was 'once so close' to her gay cousin Justin's sister that she had been mistaken for her own, we are also told that she was a 'Brexit voter' – and this seems to be why they are no longer close (272). The lifestyle of the city dwellers and their values is validated over that of the rural and the provincial, where the former are cosmopolitan, comfortable with the new politics of gender and sexuality, and avowedly European; while the latter are without exception none of these things.

To some extent, of course, this extreme juxtaposition of different ways of life is Craig's way of satirising the spoilt lifestyles of the metropolitan Quentin and Lottie just as much as it is a way of demonising the people of Devon and Cornwall. When Quentin thinks to be a Londoner 'is to be in a Britain that is more confident, more tolerant, more civilised, more enterprising and more beautiful than the rest of the country' (80) this feeling is not necessarily endorsed uncritically by the novelist, any more than his dismissal of the locals in Devon: 'People here are so rooted in one place, through generations, that they might as well be trees. They hate London, the EU, politicians, newspapers – effectively, everything he's interested in' (283). It is also important to point out that the association of the South West with a nexus of negative feelings that came together in the European referendum is to some extent justified by the electoral geography of the place, where a majority of voters did favour leaving the European Union (Watson, 2016).

However, after a certain point neither of these arguments will really stand up. First of all: although there may be some statistical basis for associating the place with a 'leave' mentality, this could never be the whole story for the simple fact that there were thousands of people from Devon and Cornwall who voted remain, and who presumably are not ignorant, racist, or homophobic. Yet the presentation of Devon and Cornwall in *The Lie of the Land* presents no degree of nuance, no refracted range of positions, attitudes or identities at all. Thus, Craig appears to violate the principle that rather than passing on a series of *a priori* assumptions about a place and its people, the job of the novelist should more properly be to interrogate those assumptions and at least challenge them if not transform them. Moreover, even though Craig satirises the outlook of Quentin, Lottie and Xan it is difficult to escape the feeling that their world-view is also strongly redolent of her own. Thus, we are expected to believe that Xan had 'never, until he left London, experienced racism' (213) – a belief which would be unlikely to stand up to much serious analysis of everyday life in the capital itself and which therefore makes little sense as a comment on either London or the South West. Similarly, although Lottie gradually starts to feel some attachment to the place and ends up buying Home Farm at the end of the year so that she can stay there, this is very clearly not a part of any major shift in perception or cultural conversion. Her ability to remain is dependent on the fact that she has got a skilled professional job of a comparable standing to what she had in London, which gives her both financial control in the relationship with Quentin and the capacity to maintain the middle-class lifestyle of her previous life. Quentin only stays because her willingness to forget his adulteries depends on it.

All of this means that, throughout the novel, Craig uses Brexit like Alison Lurie uses the Vietnam War in *The War Between the Tates* (1974): as a way of allegorising the tensions in a marriage. This connection is strengthened when Craig says in the acknowledgements that many of the characters had already featured in her earlier novels, and then goes on to confess: 'Some novelists, from Balzac to Alison Lurie, can't bear to let go of their invented world, and I am unabashed to be one of them' (443). Judie Newman has pointed out that in *The War Between the Tates*, a clash of values over Vietnam had provided 'an analogy' for a narrative about the dissolution of a marriage, which ended up being more about gender politics than about Vietnam as such (1990, 104). A similar feeling of internecine war appears in the hostility between Quentin and Lottie for almost all of *The Lie of the Land*. However, in the last instance the binary ceases to be one between different protagonists in a marriage (since Quentin and Lottie have the same opinions on Brexit and the same general set of cultural and political values). Instead, when they stay together after their divorce this gesture has the effect of re-inscribing an overall mood of unsurpassable cultural difference between the metropolis and the regional South West, a categorisation which reunites them and remains unchallenged as a result.

* * *

As suggested above, Cornwall and the South West have, more than any other English region, been used by writers of Brexit fiction not just as a setting but as a controlling metaphor for the different values brought to the surface by the referendum campaign and the interim years between 2016 and 2020 when the genre of BrexLit emerged but in which the process of Britain leaving the European Union had not in fact occurred. It is very noticeable, for example, that Ali Smith's *Winter* uses Brexit as a device to symbolise a lifetime of diverging attitudes between two sisters, and is located almost entirely in Cornwall. Nevertheless, not only are Smith's protagonists not from the peninsula, they barely interact with anyone who is, and one of the remarkable features of it is that, for a novel set in Cornwall, there should be virtually no Cornish people present. The structure of the novel seems to imply that the best thing Smith can say about the Cornish natives is nothing at all.

Bernadine Evaristo takes a slightly different approach in her Booker Prize-winning *Girl, Woman, Other* (2019), a novel which has rightly been praised for its multifarious depiction of varieties of black female experience in Britain in the twentieth and twenty-first centuries through twelve linked monologues amounting to twelve character portraits. The best way in which Evaristo conveys this variety of experience is through the varieties of speech and language in which her characters think and speak: this is highly diverse, sometimes very street-based and youth cultural, sometimes more traditional and staid. To the extent that there is any unifying plot at all, it is provided by the opening night of Amma's play *The Last Amazon of Dahomey* at the National Theatre, which features both in the first monologue and the final chapter, 'The After-Party', thus sandwiching all the other monologues and bringing the other women together.

Amma's success as a playwright comes after years spent living in a squat in King's Cross and running a black women's theatre group with her friend Dominique who then left her to go and live in the USA with a domineering and controlling girlfriend, Nzinga, from whom it took years to free herself. Amma's daughter Yazz was fathered through sperm donation by the black intellectual Roland and is at university with a range of female friends – one very rural and cloistered, another, a rich and fashionable middle eastern Arab and a third who wears the hijab to embrace Muslim identity – and worries about what kind of future she will inherit as a result of Brexit. At the play's opening party Roland finds himself thinking about the EU debate and is happy to be called a part of the metropolitan elite because when his Gambian family tried to settle in the English countryside they were hounded out by racism and could only settle in the city. Besides, he pontificates, why should he, the son of working-class immigrants, not have the opportunity to rise in status and become part of such an elite?

Yet this, surprisingly, is not the plotline in which Evaristo most explicitly portrays the zeitgeist of the country, which she in fact ends up doing through historical indirection. One of Amma's guests at the theatrical party is her oldest school friend, Shirley King, whose Caribbean parents Winsome and Clovis did not support her when she was young because they were more interested in her brothers. Nevertheless, Shirley succeeded in doing a history degree and became a teacher in a deprived area where she mentors a few promising students every year in order to help them escape poverty through education. Carole, who was a recipient of this support, went on to Oxford and became a wealthy lawyer but the experience of doing so seems to have put a rift between her, her working-class Nigerian mother Bummi and her old school friend LaTisha. Carole's apparent ingratitude has thus made Shirley feel worn down and disillusioned by what she achieves in school, especially since she also has an antagonistic relationship with her colleague Penelope, who has very different views to her on how best to educate the students and who positively laments how multicultural her school has become.

When Shirley and Lennox take their daughters on a summer holiday to Barbados with her brothers and her parents Winsome and Clovis, her daughter Rachel asks Winsome about her own life story. Winsome remembers that when she and Clovis tried to get work in

Cornwall and even the Scilly Isles in the 1950s, although some people were kind to them, they were simply told they could not work there. Winsome also remembers that years earlier she had a love affair with her daughter Shirley's partner (now husband) Lennox. In other words, Winsome is not simply the ageing woman whom people see on the surface, but has a complex story and emotional life. Through her portrayal Evaristo squarely challenges the association of age, race and gender which frequently renders older black women marginal in British life. It is, however, unfortunate that she is not able to make the same challenge with regard to dominant negative assumptions about Cornwall. Her 1950s Cornwall, like Amanda Craig's in the twenty-first century, is thoroughly insular and racist. In this sense, though not directly about Brexit, *Girl, Woman, Other* passes on the same negative assumptions about Cornish insularity and xenophobia as many other overtly Brexit novels.

It also makes a related assumption about the sexual politics of another economically impoverished but culturally rich region, the North East. In a separate storyline Megan/Morgan, a transsexual living in Newcastle, decides not to have gender reassignment surgery, preferring to keep a range of identities in play, even though she only seems able to freely articulate any of them when she moves to London. In the North East itself, she feels that the only person who understands her sexuality is her great-grandmother, Hattie, who is ninety-three and whose maternal grandfather was an Ethiopian sailor, Wolde. But though this character is again effective in combating the invisibility of older black women in the wider culture, it has the effect of portraying the North East as a region whose values are fundamentally unlike those of London. Hattie has applied for (and been refused) an EU farming subsidy, which she suspects was declined because the visiting officials were surprised to see a black woman running a farm in the first place. This disillusion has resulted in her voting UKIP in the previous election and although the novel does not clarify which election is meant here (it could have been general elections in 2015 or 2017, or the referendum in between), the overall implication is clear: as a provincial region, the North East, like the South West, is opposed to the European Union as part of its general culture of hostility to otherness, which is also conveyed through Megan's transsexuality and Hattie's experiences of racism. It is unfortunate therefore that a novel so rich in combating cultural exclusion and marginality should nevertheless fully endorse the assumption of incompatible values and lifestyles between the metropolis and the provinces. Thus, although the final storyline (in which Penelope takes a DNA test and turns out to have Scandinavian, Irish and several different African ethnicities) serves as a corrective to the claims of the Brexiteers that Britain's culture could be entirely free from outside influence, it also fails to interrogate these wider assumptions about the differences between people in the city and the provinces, where the latter are starkly homogenised, thereby relaying and retransmitting precisely the kind of binary thinking that resulted in Brexit.

* * *

Implicitly, challenging such binary thinking is what Alan Kent does on behalf of Cornwall in his 2019 novel, *Turning Serpentine*. In the process, he succeeds in contesting and complicating the unnuanced association of Cornwall with racism and reactionary politics that we find in those other portrayals. Ostensibly, there is no contemporary context for *Turning Serpentine* at all since the plot concerns two twins, Davy Endean and Sefryn Penrose, separated at sea towards the end of the Second World War only to meet again as young adults and fall in love, with tragic consequences. However, *Turning Serpentine* is more than a conventional separated-twins plot with a Cornish flavour. Local monuments like the place where Marconi's company sent the first trans-Atlantic radio messages and the Earth Station at Goonhilly, which received some of the first ever satellite messages and retransmitted them all around the world, are key settings, so that although the plot is set in the 1940s, 50s and 60s, it is also narrated consciously from the satellite and internet age, thereby situating its history of global communication in a longer narrative and wider context. This means that, like Ali Smith's Scotland, Kent's Cornwall is most Cornish by belonging to, and being open to, the whole world.

Turning Serpentine opens with a highly poetic passage about the seven days of the Christian creation myth, playfully culminating with the creation of the Lizard peninsula. In turn this myth is juxtaposed with another poetic passage about the voyage by the ancient Greek traveller Pytheas to the Lizard, where he met its people, the Pretanikke after whom the whole island of Britain is now named, thus reinforcing the impression of Cornwall being part of a wider orbit both historically and geographically. Such a feeling is strengthened even further when the natural geography of the Cornish coast is narrated in terms that emphasise its physical connections to the European mainland, through a shared and deep-seated geological landscape that traverses national borders on the surface. In other words, through this emphasis on global connection and geographical evolution Kent endows the text with an implicit riposte to any idea of separation from Europe even though the plot is not in any simplistic way about it.

There is also a second reason why the Lizard setting provides an absolutely fundamental element rather than mere local colour, which is that, as with Kent's 2015 volume of poetry *Interim Nation*, one of the novel's themes is the gradual passing away of old Cornish customs and ways of life. After being rescued at sea as babies the twins had been rehoused by the artist Cressida Tonkin, herself courted by the local vicar, Peter Bodrugan. It is Peter and Cressida's discovery of the twins' true identity years later, after Cressida has suffered being raped while a student at the Slade School of Art and the subsequent blow of being treated like a provincial upstart by the savage critics and reviewers of her first London exhibition, which finally brings them together. By this time Peter has lost his Christian faith and suffers some sort of breakdown in which he vandalises the church altar at St Wynwallow's, a gesture of complex symbolism possibly representing the violent rejection of modern religion in favour of a return to a pre-Christian mindset and a reinvigorated commitment to Cornish cultural specificity. The twins' birth father, the Polish Count Bozenta, tells Peter that he should become a revolutionary leader for a Cornish national revival, and although Peter is no revolutionary in a political sense, he is a cultural nationalist who writes a book about the history of Lizard that documents many of its histories, natures and customs, which Kent, like his character, seems to affirm. Although the ancient handicraft of rock carving, or turning serpentine, is in decline and Davy's father closes his business down, the novel defiantly refuses to bow to a tragic history and rather than ending with the suicide of the twins finishes by proclaiming that one or two anonymous craftsmen still keep the old art alive – thereby refusing to let the culture of Cornwall pass entirely into history.

Thus, the rocks and stones of the peninsula which are symbols of Cornwall's geological connectivity to mainland Europe are also at the same time emblematic of Cornish custom, as if being connected to Europe is part of being Cornish. Compared to the fictional portrayals which simplistically equate Cornwall – or any other English 'region' – with an insular world-view and regressive cultural politics, Kent's depiction is much more dynamic and sophisticated. And this is why

Turning Serpentine is one of the most significant Brexit novels. So many, from *Winter* and *Middle England* to *A Stranger City*, and from *The Lie of the Land* to *Girl, Woman, Other* offer themselves as critical portrayals of the Brexit process but fail to interrogate the premise of a clash of cultures between an outward-looking metropolis and a taciturn, narrow-minded regional identity. *Turning Serpentine* cannot correct those portrayals, since to do so would be to re-inscribe the binary categories of right/wrong, true/false, in/out which is their main weakness. But by contesting the premises on which those representations are built, *Turning Serpentine* generates an alternative portrayal that eludes questions of correctness and accuracy altogether, moving beyond the blinkers of binary thinking and introducing into the genre a degree of aesthetic nuance and cultural complexity which from them was largely absent.

WELSH EUROPEANS?

Alan Kent studied at Cardiff University and Wales features prominently in his work as an example of a small nation which through a combination of political intervention and local practice has kept alive its language and feeling of nationhood within the UK whole. To a Cornish nationalist like Kent, this sense of Welsh cultural endurance appears to be an aspirational model for positive emulation. But although Wales's best-known public intellectual Raymond Williams described himself as a 'Welsh European' (1979a, 296) Wales in fact shares with Cornwall the fact that the majority of its electorate voted to leave Europe, giving rise to the potentially damaging tension explored in Chapter Two between its intellectuals and its people. In hindsight, it seems that Williams acknowledged this tension in the novel *The Fight for Manod* where he has the character Peter mock Tom for his overt enthusiasm for Europe: '"This is Tom Meurig," Peter said. "He lives in Llanidloes or in Europe, I can't remember which"' (1979b, 133).

A renewed version of that tension has re-emerged in updated form in two more recent novels from Wales, Robert Minhinnick's *Nia* (2019) and Niall Griffiths's *Broken Ghost* (2019), both of which are set in the aftermath of the 2016 referendum, although it should be said that the 'nation' as such is not the primary referent for either, since both are firmly situated in much more local contexts. Minhinnick's *Nia* (2019) is the story of a young woman's mission to explore Y Shwyl, an extensive and previously unexplored cave system below the Caib sand dunes in a tourist seaside town modelled on Porthcawl. She is to be accompanied by older former school friends Skye and Ike Pretty who have vast experience of travelling the world – although both have returned to where they are from – and this makes Nia feel that her own experience of the world is insignificant. For example, Skye has lived for a time in Saskatchewan, where she worked in a blues bar and was in simultaneous relationships with a male writer and an older black woman. One of her memories of the huge Canadian Wilderness is of a rundown church with a monument to seven Ukrainian children who died in a fire there. Ike has travelled even more extensively and considers the television travel journalist Johnny Tarr a nemesis; he is portrayed as an occasional bore for this reason. When he lived in Amsterdam Ike had a girlfriend, Niamh, who died of cancer, just as Nia's father John, a philandering poet but inspirational English teacher, has told her sick mother Siân that he is going away on a trip to Malta, leaving Nia to care for her.

Worldly experience, however painful, is associated with travel to other countries. Nia, by contrast, has not travelled and although on the one hand this might have shielded her from some of that pain it has also isolated her from the emotional experiences, close human relationships and rich life histories that it provided for the others. In contrast to their living and working abroad, Nia is portrayed as having stayed at home, selling cockles to tourists outside the town's slot machines when she was a teenager. But this seems to hint at a yearning for other kinds of experience in other places, not necessarily as a denial of her own place but as a growing awareness of how much more there is on the planet. For instance, in her mid-twenties she has befriended Rizmas, Petr and Virjilijs – Lithuanians working at the town's funfair – and feels at home among these people who ostensibly don't belong there. They live in caravans that are soon to be demolished, as if Nia's already limited global horizons are on the brink of contracting even further, however much she might wish otherwise. This feeling is made more explicit when Rizmas tells her that Virjilijs is considering going home to Lithuania since the referendum on Brexit; and Rizmas himself tells her he wants the people who planned Brexit to know how hard he works.

In other words, an open-minded global world-view is presented as a vanishing ideal for Nia who has never had a chance to experience other cultures and seems to fear that she now never will. She works in a Fairtrade shop, *Extraordinaria*, in a building that previously housed a nightclub. But the number of customers who come through the door is much lower in its current guise than in its previous, as if to suggest that the hedonism of the nightclub has a broader populist base than things like ethical consumerism and its implied relationship to global citizenship and questions of social justice, just as the photographs that Skye most often sells are images of the local lighthouse dwarfed by giant waves in a storm which have sparked a mini-industry of people coming to Porthcawl for 'hurricane tourism' (70) thereby voyeuristically converting the misery of others into mere entertainment.

Nia posits a critical relationship between consumer culture and Western civilisation, a critical portrayal that becomes more explicit through a conscious allusion to Conrad's *Heart of Darkness* (1899). During the three-day caving expedition at the centre of the narrative, Nia leaves her baby Ffresni with her co-worker Serene at *Extraordinaria*, but struggling through the claustrophobic, shadowy caves brings up a repressed memory of a time when, as a sixteen-year-old girl, she had been raped in the hills above the town. She had never told anyone about this or even apparently thought of it again until the cave expedition triggers the memory, and she is relieved to get back out of the cave, expelling the darkness of the memory by literally escaping from its heart. During the expedition, she had mused on the history of the place and wondered what unimagined animals or humans may once have sheltered in those caves, initiating the long history of human art and expression by first drawing lines in the sand. This use of a geographical metaphor to create a sense of relationship between people without regard to national borders parallels Kent's shift from daily sidereal time to long-term geological epochs as a means of positing connections between Cornwall and the continent in *Turning Serpentine*. Similarly, Nia's memory of the rape she suffered as a teenager is juxtaposed with her memory of a time when an ancient female skeleton was excavated from a burial cairn in the dunes: she feels a strange kinship with this wounded, vulnerable unidentified girl who once lived in the same dark spaces as her. The application of the archaeological metaphor to suggest forms of kinship with people before nation-states existed and whose identities were not straightforwardly defined by them recalls the unsettling, spectral elements in Smith's *Spring* and Moss's *Ghost Wall*.

All this suggests that through the allusion to *Heart of Darkness*, Minhinnick brings the dark heart of European civilisation that

Conrad juxtaposed with the brilliant white monuments of his sepulchral city even closer to home and with new resonance. Since the sepulchral city in Conrad is positioned at one end of a brutally exploitative colonial system whose opposite pole is in the Belgian Congo where forms of de facto slavery still operated, it can likely be identified as Brussels. Given that in 2019 Brussels was the administrative seat of the European Union from which Britain was on the brink of withdrawing, its association with symbolic darkness is subtly different from Conrad's: less now a matter of exposing the brutality of European imperialism and more about the new kinds of savagery unleashed by Brexit. In other words, where Brussels was a metonym for the corrupt centre of European civilisation as a whole to Conrad, in *Nia* it functions in the opposite way: symbolising Britain's fragmentation from Europe as a new kind of violence. Or to put it another way, to Conrad European culture depended on the barbarity that defined its dark underside, whereas to Minhinnick in 2019 Britain's severing of cultural ties with Europe is no less of a barbarism.

Perhaps for this reason Minhinnick follows a number of the other writers discussed in this chapter in assuming: (a) that opposing Brexit was a socially progressive stance; (b) that this form of progressive politics can be associated with forms of progressive politics in other areas of life; (c) that a pro-Brexit attitude is therefore reactionary and rebarbative; so that (d) those in favour of Brexit are likely to resist respect- and equality-based cultures in all other walks of life. These associations come together when Nia's friend Skye gets assaulted in the local pub by a thug, Cranv, in a hate crime apparently directed at her bisexuality. Nia herself is suspicious of forms of artificial intelligence, and when she plays chess against her computer does not allow it much time to think. Since we know from James Graham's film *Brexit: The Uncivil War* (2019) that the mining of big data through digital platforms played a key part in the victory of the Leave campaign in the referendum, this suspicion of artificial intelligence is implicitly constructed as one aspect of Nia's opposition to it. Again, the symbolism makes a direct association between the politics of Brexit and other repressive forms of social and political control. The more nuanced possibility that people might have been in favour of Brexit while also supporters of gay rights; or opponents of Brexit while also embracing the communicational possibilities enabled by new media and artificial intelligence, is not considered. For that we must look elsewhere.

* * *

Both technically and ideologically *Broken Ghost* by Niall Griffiths (2019) is a world away from all the other portrayals of Brexit discussed here. Although, as will be shown below, it is a work of considerable linguistic richness and social diversity, what mainly distinguishes it from them can be boiled down to the bare fact that Griffiths's protagonists – a 'slut and a junkie and a thug' (294) are not especially attractive people or even particularly pleasant ones. This means that whereas Kennedy, Smith, Coe, Grant and Craig people their narratives with conventionally articulate and university-educated characters, Griffiths sets out intentionally to do the opposite, eschewing the feeling of prissiness evinced by the rest and writing in the process a *Lionel Asbo* for Brexit Britain. As Gareth Kent found, not only is *Broken Ghost* 'rife with regional dialects' it also portrays the 'grit and squalor characterising – yet, often peripheral and vacant from the face most want to see – of British society' (2019).

For example, Adam reacts to the news that his rehab centre at Rhoserchan has closed by relapsing into drink and drugs and taking a job as the muscle man for a loan shark meeting a gang of bullies; and when he comes back he makes himself deliberately unkempt and obnoxious in front of a group of middle-class students in order to goad them into a fight. Emma neglects her son Tomos in order to devote her evenings to seedy encounters with men – a stranger in a bar; another up against his Land Rover; a third in his remote caravan, accompanied by half of his darts team – and an equally squalid encounter with a woman in a pub toilet. Cowley is the hardest to like of all: grumbling to his construction boss that his Polish co-workers (who are in fact Estonian) should have gone home by now; getting involved in a sexual threesome with his friends Bernie and Jack even though it makes them all miserable; attacking the darts captain Rang with a bottle; mugging students at knifepoint; violently beating the clergyman who had abused him and his brother Rhys as children; and taking part in an illicit prize fight for an Irish mobster.

Following an outdoor party on Pendam mountain above Aberystwyth, the three have a vision of a woman floating in the sky and appearing to speak to them. All three leave Aberystwyth for a time, but when they return they find that owing to Emma's blogpost about their experience the mountain has become a site for an unofficial commune. People of all genders, abilities, ages and backgrounds are camped out there apparently drawn by the feeling that epoch-making millennial change is about to happen. For this reason they are seen by the wider world as drop-outs and good-for-nothings and the mainstream media portray them as squatters, scroungers, unhygienic people with no regard to the safety of their children, harbourers of illegal immigrants and anti-Brexit 'remoaners'. By the time Adam, Emma and Cowley return to the site of the original vision, the commune is in full swing – but find it is none of these things. Whether their original vision was a real ghost or the meteorological phenomenon known as the 'Brocken' spectre (264) then becomes an irrelevant question: even when the denouement reveals that the ghost speaking to them was simply music projected by an iPod, what matters are the feelings and actions the vision inspires. Since it is duplicitously portrayed as a threat to law and order, the authorities are sent in to close the commune and remove its participants from the mountain with brutal force.

Coming at the end of a decade of austerity, the gradual demonisation of the working class, the dispossession and disempowerment of communities and a general shrinking in the public sphere, the Llyn Syfydrin commune symbolises a desire for something bigger and can be related to the creeping loss of hope on both an individual and a collective scale. To convey this desire, Griffiths deploys a polyphony of different linguistic idioms and different kinds of speech act which evoke a feeling of intersubjective experience. For example, when Cowley goes to the bridge construction site in Trefechan where he works, the fact that his Estonian colleagues have been given the better jobs (because they are more highly skilled) provokes his resentment and he waits until they go to lunch before committing the symbolically rebellious act of hanging from the half-built bridge by a winch over the river:

> Everythin' goin away, an me jes dangling yur. Gas bills, pikeys, still doin shitty jobs after twenty years' education ... It's all gone away. A feel meself driftin off, not asleep, more like Av jes smoked a fat spliff a size of-a fuckin pool cue. Like Am yur but *not* yur. But like A felt after A came down off-a mountain likes, after that party. After that glowing thing an after Ad found that eye-pod or whatever it is, a thought of which reminds me to pat me top pocket to check it's still yur, where A keep it, to see that it hasn't fallen out; it's still in yur. A feel it over me heart, which makes me think of them soldiers who were saved from bullets by silver ciggie boxes or Bibles n stuff – they'd be in eyr pockets an stop-a bullets from hittin

eyr hearts an keep em elive. Don't know why it makes me think-a this, A mean A don't even know how to use-a fuckin thing (93).

The inarticulacy of Griffiths's characters is rendered strangely articulate, in what Gareth Kent calls 'a distancing strategy emphasising their disassociation but also underscoring how people are easily moulded into caricatures when denied a voice' (2019). Cowley's ironic description of his adult life as twenty years of education that have got him nowhere carries a hint of regret and implies in retrospect a wish to have achieved more in his formal education – especially given that the immediate source of resentment has been the fact that his superiors are more skilled than him. The fact that they are Estonian is then an incidental reason for his scapegoating of them whereas his real frustration has much deeper causes relating to his social alienation, an alienation symbolised by the physical fact that he is swinging from a winch above the Rheidol river, breaking free, if only temporarily, from all the structures of authority that have trammelled his existence. The allusion to soldiers being saved by bullets hitting their Bibles carries a suggestion that his cultural literacy is more developed than it might appear, and by symbolically aligning himself with them he reveals a desire to discover and participate in forms of belonging that are bigger than himself. At the same time, checking his pocket for the iPod he found on Pendam mountain provokes a form of critical reflexivity: given that he cannot use, control or even sell it, what did he steal it for? In other words, the degree of introspection at work here is both profound and related to his search for transcendent meaning.

This search for meaning, and the material embodiment of that search in different varieties of language, are the main themes of *Broken Ghost*. 'What was it I wrote, a single paragraph?' Emma asks herself, when she realises her blog has started the commune (109). 'Is this what it feels like, to be, to be at the centre of something big?' (ibid.). In doing so, she too expresses a high level of critical self-consciousness, which Griffiths throughout the novel places in the mouths of characters who appear not capable of it on the surface, and in speech that is both more articulate and more poetic than it seems. Moreover, it also expresses a desire for something capable of transcending the individual. In this way, desire is shown to be socially structured even though it is subjectively experienced and the vehicle for expressing this interplay between individual desire and social structure is language, which is repeatedly shown to be multifaceted and intersubjective, so that relationships between people, ideas and experiences arise, evolve and develop in the spaces between individuals lives and in the interstices between the state and its subjects.

Arising out of his interest in how the state interpellates its subjects as such, what Griffiths really portrays in *Broken Ghost* is a competition over control of the technologies and apparatus of representation. So, when the text includes fictionalised excerpts from new media – Youtube, Blogspots, Twitter – as part of the wider conflict over the means of representation embedded in it, these are very carefully written in the particular linguistic codes appropriate to each. One reason that *Broken Ghost* is able to articulate a high degree of ethical complexity is because of how closely aligned all these different textual elements are. This does not mean that the many different narrators and voices say the same thing – far from it – but that they all contribute to an overall pattern of expression. The desire to find transcendent meaning through social participation is expressed in the overlapping and enmeshing of different intersubjective desires and attitudes which are themselves articulated through different linguistic structures corresponding to different subjectivities and diverse life experiences. For example, the blog created by Emyr Roberts in response to Emma's earlier blog:

> From *Pobl Annwyl*, **bilingual blogspot, Emyr Gwenallt Roberts, AKA Llewellyn Nesa, version saesneg**
>
> Knock. Fatima. Lourdes. Now we can add to that list: Llyn Syfydrin, Ceredigion.
>
> …
>
> The time has come. The choice between repent or rejoice has come at last but if you want my advice (and you wouldn't be reading this if you didn't) – do both (113).

In the economical language of the blogpost, Griffiths is able to convey several layers of signification, while also imbuing them with considerable irony. In giving Emyr the pseudonym Llewellyn Nesa (the next Llewellyn), he seems to align the blogger with the medieval princes and last dynastic leaders of an independent Wales. But that is not to say that Griffiths in any way endorses that feeling, since the blog itself bristles up against any number of other speech acts and hierarchies of representation so that none of them predominate and the concept of a single voice emerging to speak for the nation as a whole is revealed to be radically unstable and untenable. A similar counter-intuitive effect is achieved by the blog's name, *Pobl Annwyl*, which, although it is presented in the English version of the 'bilingual' blog, is not translated into the corresponding English ('Dear People') and which appears under a heading ('version saesneg') which uses the Welsh word for English, so that the English is in effect estranged from itself. Moreover, the very idea of an English version of the blog posits the existence of a separate and prior Welsh version, which presumably, since the blogger has allotted to himself the symbolic role of Welsh leader, is treated with a greater degree of priority. In this logic, the character Llewellyn is able to think that the Welsh language is more important because it came first, therefore offering to speak to and for the Welsh people with a higher level of authenticity than the English which is delayed and belated compared to it. But this assumption is undercut when he gives up the blog and signs off his last entry using a Welsh expression – '*Wrth ei draed cymerwch eich codwm yn deidi yn awr*' ('At his feet take your fall right now,' 294–5) – to recant his earlier belief that the vision of Emma, Adam and Cowley was tantamount to a religious sign. Thus, although Llewellyn is presented as both a linguistic and religious leader, his presence in a field of so many other representational technologies, languages, idioms and media renders this role provisional and relative.

There is an even greater irony, revealed in the tweets Griffiths includes as a response to Llewellyn's blog:

> @ListentoDawkins primitive taffs this is 21st century bet you don't have broadband over offas dyke #llewellynnesa #poblannwyl what does that even mean? #BVMshit

> @Enlightened #llewellynesa get a life, a modern life. Proof. Evidence. Grow the fuck up #MadonnaBollocks #BVMshite #trigger50now #hurryupandLeave (113).

Relative to conventional prose fiction, these tweets are difficult to read, requiring a distinct and separate media literacy. It might be that the linguistic patterns of Twitter effectively recreated by Griffiths are more directly mimetic of how people speak and therefore more demotic and more democratic than formal written English. But the irony is that though democratic in form, they are less democratic in content: the tone of the tweets is bilious, their cowardly authors hiding behind meaningless pseudonyms so that there is no chance of ever being held to account. In very short discursive space, their targets shift from the Welsh people in general ('primitive taffs'), to people of any religious faith ('MadonnaBollocks') and thence to a generic anti-European feeling ('trigger50now') which ironically peddles feelings of hatred and xenophobia in the name of scientific enlightenment. Then again, as we have seen, they are written in response to Llewellyn's blogpost, which though written in much more flowery and conventionally literate language is not a paragon of democratic expression, either. In other words, in the linguistic economy of the text we are not forced to take sides between Llewellyn's blog and those who tweet their responses to it; in fact, we are actively prevented from doing so. We cannot assume that a mistrust of the rhetorical claims made in the blog automatically places us unambiguously on the side of the tweeters because the text as a whole overrides the question of sides. Instead, what emerges is a feeling of different voices clamouring for attention and the act of clamouring itself ultimately signifies more than the content of any single communication.

The same can be said of the government spokesman's YouTube statement on the Llyn Syfydrin commune in the novel (292):

> As I said last night, as I think we're all aware, our, ah, the polite request that these people voluntarily remove themselves from what is essentially, what is lawful, ah, private property, well I'm sorry to say that this was met with abuse of the crudest sort. These people unfortunately will not listen to reason, I'm afraid to say. It was explained to them, clearly and civilly, that what they are doing constitutes a squatting offence and a breach of the law and moreover a safety hazard.

Whereas the tweets feel rebarbative, this official communiqué uses language that is more conventionally polished but nevertheless expresses sentiments that are almost exactly the same as them. The government spokesman condemns people at the commune as abusive, crude, uncivil and hazardous, while allotting to himself the virtues of polite civilisation. But when read alongside other excerpts, expressed in other vernaculars and other media, this can only have the effect of achieving the opposite: that is, drawing attention to the rhetorical gap between this official definition of what constitutes civilised behaviour and other definitions in circulation, thereby implicitly raising the question: who has the right to define these things?

As with the tweets in response to Llewellyn Nesa's blogspot, the government YouTube channel is portrayed by Griffiths as prompting a rush of tweeted comments:

@ThinBlueLine#battleofbeanfield#orgreave#2011riots & still they don't learn! Scum!

@PeopleofBritain#ThinBlueLine do it proper this time! Teach em a lesson! TRAITORS!!! No holding back

@KatieH#ThinBlueLine#PeopleofBritain to quote one of there hero's BY ANY MEANS NECESSARY #leftielibtards

@PeopleofBritain don't forget dale farm! DO IT RIGHT THIS TIME TEACH EM A LESSON ONCE FOR ALL LADS #dousproud

@Dionysus#lightindarkness#antifash fuck off
@KatieH@PeopleofBritain ignore ignore! Come and join! All welcome! Funfunfun! No bigot allowed #mynyddcariad (292)

A conjunction is made between authoritarianism in the present and both the class war of the 1980s ('orgreave') and the politics of austerity under the coalition government ('2011riots'). But, ironically, the senders of these messages are not opposed to state-sponsored violence, instead advocating and applauding it while also talking the language of liberation. In other words, there is a discursive gap between the propositional content of the tweets and their expressive meaning. Again, however, this discrepancy has the effect of transcending simple questions of for or against: the government spokesman who decried people as crude, abusive and impolite therefore presumably disdains these tweets which are all of those things even though their senders are his political ally. In other words, the logic of the narrative is a logic of incoherence, it cannot be made to make sense in simple terms. Words drift past, beyond and over the top of each other and refuse to cohere in a neat logic of either consensus or its opposite, while the parameters of language itself bypass the simple distinction between speaking for and speaking against. The resultant feeling of intersubjectivity is then consistent with the grammar of the tweets, a grammar in which there are no full stops or grammatical markers indexing the beginning of one clause or the end of another or the end of one voice and the beginning of another. The speakers flow into each other and meaning only minimally begins to emerge from the polyphony of expression and the whirlpool of semantic articulation: 'all welcome'. The tweets are thus not merely an interesting contemporary appendage to the novel but in and through their intersubjective grammar they synergistically embody the dynamics of expression which they carry. This inclusion of new media has the effect of taking a stage further the feeling of competing priorities in the conflict of definition that was already implicit in Emma's wondering about what it feels like to be at the centre of 'something big'.

In turn, this desire to feel something – anything – is a further component of the way *Broken Ghost* constructs meaning through intersubjective experience. For instance, when Adam travels with the loan shark Browne to Wolverhampton, he notices the increased number of St George's Crosses flying outside people's houses as soon as the train crosses the border from Wales to England because 'there's some fuckin thing going on, some royal bollox. Baby or a wedding or some such shite' (224). This is initially anathema to Adam, not out of any fully articulated political creed but precisely because he is portrayed as existing outside such creeds. Nevertheless, as the train journey continues, he realises that the people he sees happily waving their flags in celebration of the birth of the royal baby are expressing a hunger and a need somewhat congruent with the need for physical feeling and sensation which he himself had been used to satisfying through drugs: 'and for one sickening second he gets it: the dull and diffuse docility punctuated by moments of state-approved mass distraction and intoxication. The heady hits of nostalgia' (224). The nostalgia Adam thinks about expresses a deep-seated desire to merge the self with something external to it, reaching for a state where the difference between self and other is eliminated and thereby bringing about a form of communion and connection that is otherwise unavailable. In the desire for the eclipse of the self by some social or physical entity that is greater than it there are elements of yearning for atavistic regression and the Freudian death drive, which is simultaneously life affirming and potentially self-destructive.

This potential for violent self-immolation reaches its highest expression in Cowley's deliberation of the Irish gangster Aney Lavin's offer for him to take part in an illegal prize fight to the death. Travelling in a van from Aberystwyth to Cardiff, he remembers a previous journey on which his vehicle had run over a sheep: 'It was a *whomping* sound that the lamb made, not very loud ... not a sound of lethality, really. And the ease of transitioning that followed ... pantpantpant then nothing. That easy' (245). In turn, this makes him contemplate killing an opponent in a fight-to-the-death – '*Whomp* – just once. It'd be *that* fucking easy' (ibid.) – and the financial freedom the ill-gotten prize would bring him: 'Free not to be shunted and controlled. Free not to be chipped at so that the struggle to hold on to any kind of reliable structure in it becomes something to which every remaining cell must be devoted' (ibid.). The freedom from social structures that he imagines seems to recall the physical structure of the bridge from which he had suspended himself in tranquil isolation earlier in the novel, 'the newer bridge under which he once hung' (287), and metaphorically there is a connection between this bridge and the symbolic crossing he considers making into the dark netherworld of illegal fighting, which will carry him over 'not a small river but an abyss' (ibid.). That he never once considers the possibility that he might lose and die in such a fight comes across less as an example of hubris and more as a way of emphasising the potentially self-destructive nature of his desire to be free from social control. He is on the point of going to see the Lavins to accept their offer when a chance meeting with the taxi driver Stiff results in him going to the Llyn Syfydrin commune where he is able to channel the destructive tendencies of his instincts in a slightly differently direction. Watching birds thrashing in a puddle of dust in the mountains, we are told:

> Cowley wonders why they do that, as he has on rare occasions wondered before about the things with which he shares the world: the mangy dogs of the estate, the stabbing gulls with their stupid eyes. He wonders how he would be, *could* be, if he would, *could*, wonder about them more – whether there might be something apart from the dull frustration and numb anger (287).

Consistent with his earlier meditation while swinging from the bridge there is a high level of introspection invested with a meta-reflective quality. Cowley is shown to wonder what it would be like to wonder more often about other living things. What would this tell him about them? What would it tell him about himself? His thought process is both reflexive and implicitly self-critical, opening a new perspective for him with regard to the world around. Whereas contemplating mortal combat hinted at a self-destructive tendency based on the death drive of the ego, what he contemplates here is not so much the extinction of the self as the submersion of the self in the social world, a world that here includes awareness of and empathy for birds and dogs as well as other people.

Elsewhere in the novel, Adam is awe-struck by an osprey beating its wings against the side of the train carrying him to Wolverhampton. When Emma reaches the site of the Llyn Syfydrin commune she meets a little boy of her son's age who has found a snake and is worried that it will be frightened by the presence of so many people, so she helps him bear it to safety. When Adam says a moving farewell to his cat Quilty because he fears he can no longer care for it, Quilty takes up residence in the grounds of the now closed-down rehab centre which had cared for Adam, and where they are eventually reunited. Or again, Adam has a fond memory of seeing a woman taking her children to see the beautiful species enclosed in a butterfly house and is scornful of the children's father, who chose to stay outside washing his car. All of this has the effect of de-centring the human characters, as if to take to a logical extreme Emma's and Adam's and Cowley's desire to merge with the social environment and to transcend their own lives through communion with the living world.

The breakdown in distinctions between human speech and animal expression has the effect of rendering porous and semi-permeable the boundaries between different people and between people and other living creatures. Intersubjective language itself, in other words, is the real subject of *Broken Ghost*. Thus, at its conclusion, Emma, Adam and Cowley return to the mountaintop where they had had their original vision out of a deep-seated desire to communicate with each other and with others around them. In doing so, Emma is reconciled with the father of her son Tomos; Cowley gets a measure of closure for the childhood abuse he suffered by confronting his abuser; and Adam comes face-to-face with the counsellor, Sally, and her daughter Jess, whom in his earlier dissipated state he had felt too ashamed to face.

It is the first time he has met Jess since they had both attended a pro-Europe anti-austerity rally. This small detail retrospectively underwrites the whole text, showing that whatever forms of language are used in the novel and however inarticulate it may seem, he is both politically articulate and committed to social solidarity over and above individual self-interest. In the last instance, therefore, it is notable that in *Broken Ghost* Griffiths, an English-born writer of Irish ancestry writing about Wales took the binary us/them logic that typifies so many portrayals of Brexit Britain and converted them instead into an affirmation of love.

Afterword:
Brexit and Coronavirus

This book has critically identified a number of cultural developments that prepared the ground for Britain's withdrawal from the European Union while also placing the future relationship between the different nations of Britain in question. Chapter One showed that the replacement of subversive counter-cultures such as punk in the 1970s by politically non-dissenting ones such as Britpop and Cool Britannia in the 1990s undermined the capacity for culture to function as a site for political resistance. Chapter Two demonstrated that the festivals European Capital of Culture and UK City of Culture both employ the instrumentalisation of the arts that had been identified in Chapter One, while also suggesting that the latter represents a break-away movement with regard to the former and so amounts to a harbinger of Brexit. Chapter Three drew attention to how the widespread prevalence of Nordic noir film and television in Britain created an image pool that cultivated a feeling of disconnection between the North of Europe and the rest of the continent, at the same time that British imitators of the Nordic genre have increasingly generated a feeling of difference between the four nations of Britain. Chapter Four identified the free-market environment created by the European Economic Community as being a key context in which national book prizes historically arose, so that the growth of individual national book prizes in Scotland and Wales is a way of asserting national cultural specificity on the one hand, while on the other reaffirming a sense of solidarity with Europe – especially in the years after the

2016 European referendum. Finally, Chapter Five explored different responses to the referendum in literature to argue that the majority of writers of Brexit fiction were unable to transform the dominant ideological assumptions on which Brexit was premised and so remained trapped within them, while also widening national and regional differences between different parts of the United Kingdom.

With the election of Boris Johnson as Prime Minister in December 2019, almost four years of wrangling and prevaricating over whether, how and when to implement Brexit were crushingly ended. By the end of January Britain had left the European Union and the transition period that would last for the whole of 2020 was underway. With this development came a new phase in the evolution of the Brexit novel. No longer was it necessary for writers to project events forward into an imaginary future when they thought (or feared) Brexit would have taken place, simply because it now had. This development accounts for a subtle change in character in Brexit fictions published after 2019. The previous chapter showed how novels penned in the period 2015–19 were necessarily speculative and future-orientated and in this sense bucked the common critical trend to define contemporary culture through its characteristic feeling of coming after a long line of historical and cultural developments, with regard to which the contemporary is often described as self-consciously belated and stagey. From 2019 onwards, by contrast, Brexit fictions were no longer speculating about a future that had in fact arrived and ironically reverted to precisely this past-looking approach. In doing so, they tended to frame Brexit using a number of other, prior world-historical events.

Thus, for example, John Osmond portrays the politics surrounding the first referendum on devolution in Wales in 1979 in *Ten Million Stars are Burning* (2018), the first of a projected trilogy of novels that will end up in the present and raise many of the same questions about Wales's position in Britain and Europe as Griffiths's *Broken Ghost*. Ian McEwan's *Machines Like Me* (2019) situates the politics of Britain both joining and subsequently leaving the European Union within a counterfactual portrayal of the Falklands War (1982). John le Carré's penultimate novel *Agent Running in the Field* (2019) is a sceptical depiction of the populist politics of Brexit and the price paid by an idealistic individual who tries to stop it and who is crushed by the security forces. Yet its portrayal of Moscow Centre and the London Haven feel more akin to le Carré's output of the Cold War period, especially *Tinker, Tailor, Soldier, Spy* (1974), than contemporary

Britain. Deborah Levy also uses the context of the Cold War to frame her portrayal of Brexit Britain, impressionistically blending it with the authoritarian structures of the final days of Stasi-controlled East Germany in 1988 in *The Man Who Saw Everything* (2019).

Kate Atkinson takes a different approach in her Jackson Brodie crime novel *Big Sky* (2019), which sets the politics of Brexit in both regional and national contexts which complicate each other because nationally Brodie is fearful of the implications of Brexit but at regional level as a proud Yorkshireman he is drawn towards increased local autonomy. Moreover, the novel takes place against the backdrop of an investigation into historic child sexual abuse perpetuated by fictional entertainers and DJs apparently modelled on real life ones such as Gary Glitter, Rolf Harris and Jimmy Savile, who were convicted of those historic crimes. David Mitchell makes the representation of Savile explicit in his portrayal of an imaginary 1960s band in *Utopia Avenue* (2020), and although the novel does not allude specifically to Brexit, its final chapter leaps forward from the time of the lead singer's death in 1969 to the present day, remarking on things that had changed in between: the Arab Spring, the #MeToo movement and climate activism, in a catalogue of genuinely radical political movements where Brexit is conspicuous by its absence.

Possibly the fullest expression of the re-nascent use of the past in defining contemporary Brexit fictions can be found in the final volume of Ali Smith's *Seasonal* quartet of novels, *Summer* (2020), a novel which, like the third film in Krzysztof Kieślowski's *Three Colours* trilogy (1993–4), brings together characters from all the earlier works in the series. If Smith follows the approximate methodological approach of Kieślowski, however, it is perhaps sobering to note that the means of uniting plot and character from all three films in his case was through the portrayal of a cross-channel ferry disaster. It might be that this can be seen as a harbinger for what Smith clearly considers an equally disastrous separation from the continent in her later quartet.

In *Summer*, Smith revisits her earlier character Daniel Gluck: his memory of being interned on the Isle of Man during the Second World War because his father was German; and that of his sister Hannah who died while working for the resistance in France. In other words, the extended comparison of Brexit England to Nazi Germany that is familiar from Smith's *Autumn* recurs here without adding much to it. What is really new is that *Summer*, along with Sarah Moss's

Summerwater (2020), is among the first major novels to write about Brexit in a way that connects it to the other major global event of 2020: the coronavirus pandemic.

One of the poignant ironies of *Summer* is that the character Hero is released from detention along with various other migrants out of fear on the part of the authorities that they will all die of coronavirus in cramped conditions. In other words, the only reason the government starts releasing the migrants is that the detention centres have no openable windows and so there is a large risk of COVID-19 spreading, which would be a public relations disaster. The release is not the result of any innate care for the people themselves and the ageing radical Iris puts them up in her big house in Cornwall while lambasting a government too distracted by Brexit to care. It is quite interesting, however, that when Sacha writes to Hero in detention, her letters talk about how much she looks forward to the annual migration of swifts across 'Europe and Scandinavia' (119), thereby using a metaphor of mobility across national frontiers has tacit potential application to Smith's critical portrayal of Brexit Britain. At the same time, Smith repeats the error that was discussed in Chapter Three of treating Scandinavia as if it were somehow distinct from Europe, and of locating Britain in this separate orbit. In fact, in making an implicit connection between COVID-19 and Brexit, *Summer* ends up saying less about the latter than Smith may have expected when she started out on the quartet. In doing this, she takes a contrasting approach to that of Rachel Cusk, whose own trilogy of novels *Outline* (2014), *Transit* (2017) and *Kudos* (2018) takes on more of a Brexit context as each volume progresses.

If the return to understanding the contemporary through recourse to the past characterises the second phase of Brexit fiction, this method can also be found in critical and theoretical work. Nigel Culkin and Richard Simmons have argued in *Tales of Brexits Past and Present* that Henry VIII's decision to break from the papal authority of the Catholic church in 1532 (among other historic occasions) was tantamount to a '"Legal" Brexit, separating the English state from Roman ecclesiastical law' (2019, 65). Christian Schmitt-Kilb (2020) has retrospectively read Paul Kingsnorth's *The Wake* (2014) as a Brexit novel set during the Norman conquest; and Siobhan O'Connor (2020) reads Philippa Gregory's popular historical novels *The King's Curse* (2014) and *The Taming of the Queen* (2015) as expressions of a postcolonial melancholia incited by an alien (Tudor) usurpation of native English culture.

Moreover, the two phases that characterise writing about Brexit – the first speculative about the future, the second defined by what it comes after – can also be found in critical and theoretical writing about the coronavirus pandemic. Will Hayward's *Lockdown Wales: How Covid-19 Tested Wales* (2020) uses the techniques of investigative journalism to identify the political challenges raised by COVID-19 in Wales, and sees a number of intersections and complications between them and Brexit. But having been published before the pandemic reached its peak in Britain, it is again necessarily more predictive than it is a work of *post facto* analysis. By contrast, the New Zealand earth scientist and science communicator Rebecca Priestley made connections in an article in *Granta* in December 2020 between COVID-19 and earlier global challenges, in a way that directly recalls the filtering of the present through the experiences of the past that typifies the second stage of Brexit fictions: 'As a teenager in the 1980s I had thought we were heading for nuclear war, and as an adult that anxiety had transferred to climate change. Global pandemic? That'll do. It seemed to trip the "existential threat to humanity" switch that was hardwired into my psyche' (202).

It is too soon to anticipate precisely what the impact of either Brexit or the coronavirus pandemic will be on transforming the means and relations of cultural production in the future. One of the challenges for future analysis will be separating out these two things, which have coincided with each other so precisely and become so closely associated with each other in the zeitgeist that assigning causality for any future developments to one or the other is likely to be very difficult. For example, Coventry City of Culture Trust announced in October 2020 that the launch of its UK City of Culture programme (discussed in Chapter Two) would be delayed until 15 May 2021. The following month, the Saltire Society announced that it would have to cancel its Scottish Book of the Year awards (analysed in Chapter Four) for at least twelve months after failing to secure funding from Creative Scotland, ironically within days of Douglas Stuart becoming only the second ever Scottish winner of the Booker Prize (for *Shuggie Bain*). Both of these appear to be casualties of the pandemic. As a contrasting case, when it was announced in January 2021 that the leading classical conductor Simon Rattle was leaving London for Munich, the composer Michael Berkeley told BBC Radio 4's *Front Row* that this was partly because Rattle had become exhausted with the additional wrangling and bureaucratic procedures that had become necessary in bringing musicians to Britain as a result of Brexit.

Throughout the months of lockdown and semi-lockdown it became common to observe that there had been a relative upturn in reading because other forms of cultural activity had become unavailable. If this is true, it was also accompanied by an upturn in writing itself as actors, comedians, singers and musicians found themselves unable to tour or perform and found themselves turning to other forms of creative activity that could be performed in isolation. The need to do so, however, was clearly provoked by a nexus of causes including both the new administrative procedures imposed by Brexit and the coronavirus restrictions.

Arguably the most paradigmatic cultural form to have emerged as a result was Simon Evans's series of television plays, *Staged* (2020–1) featuring David Tennant and Michael Sheen playing fictionalised versions of themselves as performers forced out of work by the prevailing circumstances. In British drama, the two-hander had already been on the rise in theatres for a decade and this development can be attributed at least in part to the preceding period of austerity politics because the two-hander does not require a large cast or crew and thus can be produced with relatively low costs. Transplanting the two-hander format from theatre to television mainly for comic effect involved a portrayal of Tennant and Sheen talking to each other over the internet to keep themselves occupied during lockdown – thereby replicating the daily experience of millions of people and putting it on screen for the first time. Much is made in the script of their respective Scottish and Welsh identities, although these are clearly situated by the series firmly within the British whole. Whether this proves to be the first articulation of a new post-Brexit pan-British cultural consciousness or the end of the line for it, only time will tell.

References

Aaron, Jane and Chris Williams, eds. 2005. *Postcolonial Wales*. Cardiff: University of Wales Press.
Aaron, Jane and M. Wynn Thomas. 2003. '"Pulling You Through Changes": Welsh Writing in English Before, Between and After Two Referenda'. In *Welsh Writing in English*, edited by M. Wynn Thomas, 278–309. Cardiff: University of Wales Press.
Abasheva, Marina. 2012. 'The Literary Prize as a Means to an End. An Insider's Notes'. *Russian Studies in Literature*, 48 (4): 63–73.
Agamben, Giorgio. 2009. *'What Is an Apparatus?' and Other Essays*. Translated by David Kishik and Stefan Pedatella. Palo Alto, CA: Stanford University Press.
Agger, Gunhild. 2016. 'Nordic Noir – Location, Identity and Emotion'. In *Emotions in Contemporary TV Series*, edited by Alberto N. García, 134–52. Basingstoke: Palgrave Macmillan.
—— 2020. 'Realistic and Mythological Appropriations of Nordic Noir: The Cases of *Shetland* and *Ø*'. In *Nordic Noir, Adaptation, Appropriation*, edited by Linda Badley, Andrew Nestingen and Jaakko Seppälä, 17–36. Cham: Palgrave Studies in Adaptation and Visual Culture.
Alexander, Neal. 2009. 'Remembering to forget: Northern Irish fiction after the Troubles'. In *Irish Literature Since 1990: Diverse Voices*, edited by Scott Brewster and Michael Parker, 272–83. Manchester: Manchester University Press.
Amin, Ash. 2020. 'A Mediterranean Perspective on European Union and Disunion'. *Journal of the British Academy*, 8 (1): 1–4.
Anderson, Benedict. 1991. *Imagined Communities: Reflections on the Origin and Spread of Nationalism*. London: Verso.

Arac, Jonathan. 1997. *Huckleberry Finn as Idol and Target: The Functions of Criticism in Our Time*. Madison, WI: University of Wisconsin Press.

Archer, Neil. 2013. 'And then as farce: Globalization and ambivalence in Jo Nesbø and Morten Tyldum's Headhunters (2011)'. *New Cinemas: Journal of Contemporary Film*, 11 (1): 55–69.

Ashbridge, Chloé. 2020. '"It aye like London, you know": The Brexit Novel and the Cultural Politics of Devolution'. *Open Library of Humanities*, 6.1 (15): 1–29.

Atkinson, Kate. 2019. *Big Sky*. London: Doubleday.

Attree, Lizzy. 2013. 'The Caine Prize and Contemporary African Writing'. *Research in African Literatures*, 44 (2): 35–47.

Bala, Iwan. 2005. 'Horizon Wales: Visual Art and the Postcolonial'. In *Postcolonial Wales*, edited by Jane Aaron and Chris Williams, 234–47. Cardiff: University of Wales Press.

Balsas, Carlos J. L. 2004. 'City Centre Regeneration in the Context of the 2001 European Capital of Culture in Porto, Portugal'. *Local Economy*, 19 (4): 396–410.

Banks, Iain. 1987. *Espedair Street*. London: Macmillan.

Barry, Sebastian. 2008. *The Secret Scripture*. London: Faber & Faber.

BBC. 2020. 'Census 2021: Asian and Black Welsh terms to be added to survey'. Available at *https://www.bbc.co.uk/news/uk-wales-politics-51720344?ns_mchannel=social&ns_source=twitter&ns_campaign=wales_politics&ns_linkname=wales*. Accessed 29 October 2020.

—— 2021. *Today*. Radio 4, 19 January 2021.

Beer, Gillian. 1992. 'The Island and the Aeroplane: The Case of Virginia Woolf'. In *Virginia Woolf*, edited by Rachel Bowlby, 132–61. London: Routledge.

Bellamy, Richard, Dario Castiglione and Jo Shaw. 2006. *Making European Citizens: Civic Inclusion in a Transnational Context*. Basingstoke: Palgrave Macmillan.

Berger, Richard. 2016. 'Everything goes back to the beginning: Television adaptation and remaking Nordic noir'. *Journal of Adaptation in Film and Performance*, 9 (2): 147–61.

Bernardino, Susana, J. Freitas Santos and J. Cadima Ribeiro. 2018. 'The legacy of European Capitals of Culture to the "smartness" of cities: The case of Guimarães 2012'. *Journal of Convention and Event Tourism*, 19 (2): 138–66.

Bland, Sally. 2018. 'Multicultural reality. *Elsewhere, Home*. Leila Aboulela'. *Jordan Times*, 7 October 2018: 216.

Blandford, Steve, ed. 2000. *Wales On Screen*. Bridgend: Seren.

Blasco, Maribel. 2004. 'Stranger to Us Than Birds in Our Garden? Reflections on Hermeneutics, Intercultural Understanding and the Management of Difference'. In *Intercultural Alternatives: Critical Perspectives on Intercultural Encounters in Theory and Practice*, edited by Maribel Blasco and Jan Gustafsson, 19–48. Copenhagen: Copenhagen Business School Press.

Boland, Philip. 2007. 'Unpacking the Theory-Policy Interface of Local Economic Development: An Analysis of Cardiff and Liverpool'. *Urban Studies*, 44 (5/6): 1019–39.

—— 2010a. '"Capital of Culture – You must be having a laugh!" Challenging the official rhetoric of Liverpool as the 2008 European cultural capital'. *Social & Cultural Geography*, 11 (7): 627–45.

—— 2010b. 'Sonic geography, place and race in the formation of local identity: Liverpool and Scousers'. *Geografiska Annaler: Series B, Human Geography*, 92 (1): 1–22.

Boland, Philip, Brendan Murtagh and Peter Shirlow. 2019. 'Fashioning a City of Culture: "life and place changing" or "12 month party"?' *International Journal of Cultural Policy*, 25 (2): 246–65.

Boles, William C. 2014. 'Irvine Welsh And In-Yer-Face Theatre: From The Rise Of *Trainspotting* To The Fall Of *You'll Have Had Your Hole*'. *Review of Contemporary Fiction*, 34 (1): 35–53.

Braun, Rebecca. 2014. 'Prize Germans? Changing Notions of Germanness and the Role of the Award-Winning Author into the Twenty-First Century'. *Oxford German Studies*, 43 (1): 37–54.

Broster, Alice. 2019. 'Is "Shetland" Based On A Book? The Hit BBC Series That Started As A Thrilling Crime Novel'. Available at *https://www.bustle.com/p/is-shetland-based-on-a-book-the-hit-bbc-series-started-as-a-thrilling-crime-novel-15944753*. Accessed 25 May 2020.

Brumwell, Alison. 2019. 'The Carnegie and Kate Greenaway Medal'. *CILIPS: Scotland's library and information professionals*. 16 August 2019. Available at *https://www.cilips.org.uk/the-cilip-carnegie-and-kate-greenaway-medals-2/*. Accessed 16 June 2020.

Brunsdon, Charlotte. 2018. *Television Cities: Paris, London, Baltimore*. Durham, NC: Duke University Press.

Burns, Anna. 2018. *Milkman*. London: Faber & Faber.

Butchart, Pamela. 2015. 'What are the best Scottish children's books?' *Guardian*, 2 September 2015: n.p. Available at *https://link-gale-com.libezproxy.bournemouth.ac.uk/apps/doc/A427475075/STND?u=bu_uk&sid=STND&xid=ec3537a0*. Accessed 22 January 2020.

Butler, Patrick and Simon Parker. 2002. 'The official websites on UK bids for European capital of culture 2008'. *Guardian*, 30 October 2002. Available at *https://www.theguardian.com/society/regeneration/page/0,,774007,00.html*. Accessed 15 October 2020.

Butterworth, Susan. 2019. '*Elsewhere, Home.* By Leila Aboulela'. *Anglican theological review*, 101 (1): 169–71.

Cameron, Jean. 2019. 'Paisley's bid to be UK City of Culture 2021 is now Scotland's bid'. *Creative Scotland*. Available at *https://www.creativescotland.com/explore/read/blogs/guest-blogs/paisleys-bid-to-be-uk-city-of-culture-2021-is-now-scotlands-bid*. Accessed 15 October 2020.

Campagna, Desireé and Daniela Angelina Jelinčić. 2018. 'A Set of Indicators of Interculturalism in Local Cultural Policies: A Study of Three Croatian Candidates for the European Capital of Culture'. *Croatian and Comparative Public Administration*, 18 (1): 47–71.

Cartwright, Anthony. 2017. *The Cut*. London: Peirene Press.

Casanova, Pascale. 2004. *The World Republic of Letters*. Translated by M.B. DeBevoise. Cambridge, MA: Harvard University Press.

Christianson, Aileen and Alison Lumsden, eds. 2000. *Contemporary Scottish Women Writers*. Edinburgh: Edinburgh University Press.

City and County of Cardiff. 2000. 'Cabinet Proposal. Agenda Item: European Capital of Culture 2008'. 16 November 2000.

Clarke, John. 1975. 'Style'. In *Resistance Through Rituals: Youth subcultures in post-war Britain*, edited by Stuart Hall and Tony Jefferson, 175–91. Birmingham: Hutchinson, Centre for Contemporary Cultural Studies.

Clarke, John, Stuart Hall, Tony Jefferson and Brian Roberts. 1975. 'Subcultures, Cultures and Class: A theoretical overview'. In *Resistance Through Rituals: Youth subcultures in post-war Britain*, edited by Stuart Hall and Tony Jefferson, 9–74. Birmingham: Hutchinson, Centre for Contemporary Cultural Studies.

Clopot, Cristina and Katerina Strani. 2020. 'European Capitals of Culture: Discourses of Europeanness in Valletta, Plovdiv and Galway'. In *Heritage and Festivals in Europe: Performing Identities*, edited by Ullrich Kockel, Cristina Clopot, Baiba Tjarve and Máiréad Nic Craith, 156–72. Abingdon: Routledge.

Coe, Jonathan. 2001. *The Rotters' Club*. London: Viking.

—— 2004. *The Closed Circle*. London: Viking.

—— 2018. *Middle England*. London: Viking.

Colley, Linda. 1992. *Britons: Forging the Nation, 1707–1837*. New Haven, CT: Yale University Press.

Conran, Tony. 1982. *The Cost of Strangeness: Essays on the English Poets of Wales*. Llandysul: Gwasg Gomer.

Coulthard, Lisa. 2018. 'The Listening Detective: Thinking Music, Gender, and Transnational Crime's Affective Turn'. *Television & New Media*, 19 (6): 553–68.

Cox Clark, Ruth E., Maureen White and Nancy Bluemel. 2004. 'Using International Literature to Enhance the Curriculum'. *Teacher Librarian*, 31 (5): 12–15.

Craig, Amanda. 2017. *The Lie of the Land*. London: Little, Brown.

Craig, Cairns. 1999. *The Modern Scottish Novel: Narrative and the National Imagination*. Edinburgh: Edinburgh University Press.

Craig, David. 2019. 'When is Craith/Hidden Series 2 on TV? What's it about?' *Radio Times*, 13 November 2019. Available at *https://www.radiotimes.com/news/tv/2019-11-13/craith-hidden-season-2-release-date/*. Accessed 28 May 2020.

Crawford, Robert. 1992. *Devolving English Literature*. Edinburgh: Edinburgh University Press.

—— 2014. *Bannockburns: Scottish Independence and Literary Imagination, 1314–2014*. Edinburgh: Edinburgh University Press.

Creeber, Glen. 2015. 'Killing us softly: Investigating the aesthetics, philosophy and influence of *Nordic Noir* television'. *Journal of Popular Television*, 3 (1): 21–35.

Crooke, Elizabeth and Thomas Maguire, eds. 2018. *Heritage after Conflict: Northern Ireland*. Abingdon: Routledge.

Crump, Eryl. 2016. 'Aneirin Karadog is the chaired bard at the 2016 National Eisteddfod'. *North Wales Live*. Available at *https://www.dailypost.co.uk/whats-on/arts-culture-news/aneirin-karadog-chaired-bard-2016-11712198*. Accessed 20 July 2020.

Culkin, Nigel and Richard Simmons. 2019. *Tales of Brexits Past and Present: Understanding the Choices, Threats and Opportunities In Our Separation from the EU*. Bingley: Emerald Publishing.

Cusk, Rachel. 2014. *Outline*. London: Faber & Faber.

—— 2017. *Transit*. London: Faber & Faber.

—— 2018. *Kudos*. London: Faber & Faber.

Danbolt, Mathias. 2016. 'New Nordic Exceptionalism: Jeuno JE Kim and Ewa Einhorn's *The United Nations of Norden* and other realist utopias'. *Journal of Aesthetics & Culture*, 8: 1–16.

Davies, Grahame. 2011. *The Dragon and the Crescent: Nine Centuries of Welsh Contact with Islam*. Bridgend: Seren.

DCMS. 2015. 'UK City of Culture: Consultation Response'. Available at *https://www.gov.uk/government/consultations/uk-city-of-culture-consultation*. Accessed 16 October 2020.

De Glas, Frank. 2013. 'The Literary Prize as an Instrument in the Material and Symbolic Production of Literature: The Case of the "Prix Formentor"', 1961–1965'. *Quaerendo*, 43 (2): 147–77.

Deleuze, Gilles. 1989. *Cinema 2, The Time-Image*. Translated by Hugh Tomlinson and Roberta Galeta. Minneapolis, MN: University of Minnesota Press.

Drama. N.d. 'Shetland: The Books Vs The Television Series'. Available at *https://drama.uktv.co.uk/shetland/article/shetland-books-tv/*. Accessed 25 May 2020.

Eaglestone, Robert, ed. 2018. *Brexit and Literature: Critical and Cultural Responses*. Abingdon: Routledge.

Edwards, Rebecca. 2012. 'Cerys, Kelly & Cool Cymru: Wales, Pop and Performance'. Unpublished conference paper delivered at the Twenty-Fourth Annual Conference of the Association for Welsh Writing in English, *Performing Wales*, Gregynog Hall, 30 March–1 April 2012. Abstract available at: *https://www.awwe.org/uploads/3/9/0/7/3907975/awwe_2012_abstracts.pdf*. Accessed 21 February 2020.

English, James. F. 2002. 'Winning the Culture Game: Prizes, Awards and the Rules of Art'. *New Literary History*, 33 (1): 109–35.

Esser, Andrea. 2017. 'Form, platform and the formation of transnational audiences: A case study of how Danish TV drama series captured television viewers in the United Kingdom'. *Critical Studies in Television: The International Journal of Television Studies*, 12 (4): 411–29.

European Commission. 2010. 'Summary of the European Commission conference: Celebrating 25 Years of European Capitals of Culture'. Brussels: Education and Culture DG. Available at *http://ec.europa.eu/culture/tools/actions/documents/conclusions_ecoc_en.pdf*. Accessed 20 October 2020.

European Union Prize for Literature. 2018. 'What is the EUPL?' Available at *https://www.euprizeliterature.eu/what-eupl*. Accessed 3 July 2020.

Evaristo, Bernadine. 2019. *Girl, Woman, Other*. London: Hamish Hamilton.

Fitjar, Rune Dahl, Hilmar Rommetvedt and Christin Berg. 2013. 'European Capitals of Culture: elitism or inclusion? The case of Stavanger2008'. *International Journal of Cultural Policy*, 19 (1): 63–83.

Flood, Alison. 2012. '"African Booker" shortlist offers an alternative view of continent'. *Guardian*, 1 May 2010: n.p.

Flynn, Roddy and Tony Tracy. 2018. 'Waking the Film Makers: Diversity and Dynamism in Irish Screen Industries 2017'. *Estudios Irlandeses*, 13: 238–68.

Folk on Foot. 2020. *Front Room Festival 2*. Available at *https://www.folkon foot.com/festival*. Accessed 24 July 2020.

Freeman, Alan. 1996. 'Ghosts in Sunny Leith: Irvine Welsh's *Trainspotting*'. In *Studies in Scottish Fiction: 1945 to the Present*, edited by Susanne Hagemann, 251–62. Frankfurt: Peter Lang.

Frenkel, Ronit. 2008. 'The politics of loss: Post-colonial pathos and current Booker Prize-nominated texts from India and South Africa'. *Scrutiny 2: Issues in English Studies in Southern Africa*, 13 (2): 77–88.

Garcia, Beatriz and Tamsin Cox. 2013. 'European Capitals of Culture: Success Strategies and Long-Term Effects'. Luxembourg: Publications Office of the European Union. Available at *https://www.europarl.europa. eu/RegData/etudes/etudes/join/2013/513985/IPOL-CULT_ET(2013) 513985_EN.pdf*. Accessed 15 October 2020.

García Avis, Isadora. 2015. 'Adapting Landscape and Place in Transcultural Remakes: The Case of *Bron/Broen*, *The Bridge* and *The Tunnel*'. *International Journal of TV Serial Narratives*, 1 (2): 127–38.

Gardiner, Michael. 2004. *The Cultural Roots of British Devolution*. Edinburgh: Edinburgh Press.

—— 2006. *From Trocchi to Trainspotting: Scottish Critical Theory Since 1960*. Edinburgh: Edinburgh University Press.

—— 2012. *The Return of England in English Literature*. Basingstoke: Palgrave Macmillan.

Gardiner, Michael, Graeme Macdonald and Niall O'Gallagher, eds. 2011. *Scottish Literature and Postcolonial Literature: Comparative Texts and Critical Perspectives*. Edinburgh: Edinburgh University Press.

Gemzøe, Lynge Agger. 2013. '*Brødre* vs. *Brothers*: The Transatlantic Remake as Cultural Adaptation'. *Akademisk Kvarter*, 7: 283–97.

Germanà, Monica. 2014. 'Special Topic 1: The Awakening of Caledonias? Scottish Literature in the 1980s'. In *The 1980s: A Decade of Contemporary British Fiction*, edited by Philip Tew, Leigh Wilson and Emily Horton, 51–74. London: Bloomsbury.

Gifford, Douglas and Dorothy McMillan, eds. 1997. *History of Scottish Women's Writing*. Edinburgh: Edinburgh University Press.

Glanz, Berit. 2019. 'Icelandic Nature and Global Evils – Concepts of Nature in Romantic Poetry and Nordic Noir TV Series from Iceland'. *European Journal of Scandinavian Studies*, 49 (1): 128–40.

Goffman, Erving. 1963. *Stigma: Notes of the Management of the Spoiled Identity*. Upper Saddle River, NJ: Prentice Hall.

Graham, Brian. 2002. 'Heritage as Knowledge: Capital or Culture?' *Urban Studies*, 39 (5/6): 1003–17.

Graham, James. 2019. *Brexit: The Uncivil War*, directed by Tony Haynes. TV Film. Channel 4.

Grant, Linda. 2019. *A Stranger City*. London: Virago.

Gray, Alasdair. 1981. *Lanark*. Edinburgh: Canongate.

Gregory, Philippa. 2014. *The King's Curse*. London: Simon & Schuster.

—— 2015. *The Taming of the Queen*. London: Simon & Schuster.

Griffiths, Niall. 2019. *Broken Ghost*. London: Jonathan Cape.

Griffiths, Ron. 2006. 'City/Culture Discourses: Evidence from the Competition to Select the European Capital of Culture 2008'. *European Planning Studies*, 14 (4): 415–30.

Grydehøj, Adam. 2009. 'Historiography of Picts, Vikings, Scots, and Fairies and its Influence on Shetland's Twenty-first Century Economic Development'. PhD Thesis, Ethnology and Folklore, University of Aberdeen. Available at *https://digitool.abdn.ac.uk/view/action/nmets.do?DOCCHOICE=159220.xml&dvs=1589452321556~974&locale=en_GB&search_terms=&adjacency=&VIEWER_URL=/view/action/nmets.do?&DELIVERY_RULE_ID=4&divType=&COPYRIGHTS_DISPLAY_FILE=copyrightstheses*. Accessed 14 May 2020.

Gutiérrez-Sibaja, Alfonso. 2017. 'Abnormality and Stigmatization in Irvine Welsh's *Trainspotting*'. *InterSedes*, 18 (38): 3–13.

Hall, Sarah. 2002. *Haweswater*. London: Faber & Faber.

—— 2004. *The Electric Michelangelo*. London: Faber & Faber.

—— 2015. *The Wolf Border*. London: Faber & Faber.

Hall, Stuart and Tony Jefferson, eds. 1975. *Resistance Through Rituals: Youth subcultures in post-war Britain*. Birmingham: Hutchinson, Centre for Contemporary Cultural Studies.

Hames, Scott. 2015. 'Saving the Union to Death?' Available at *https://issuu.com/drouth/docs/scott_hames_saving_the_union_to_dea*. Accessed 7 January 2021.

—— 2019. *The Literary Politics of Scottish Devolution: Voice, Class, Nation*. Edinburgh: Edinburgh University Press.

—— 2020. 'Spitfire Britain and the Zombie Union'. Available at *http://www.thedrouth.org/spitfire-britain-and-the-zombie-union-by-scott-hames/*. Accessed 7 January 2021.

Hamilton, Jane. 2016. 'WE GO TO SOME DARK PLACES; CRIME WRITERS FINAL CONTENDERS FOR MCILVANNEY'. *Daily*

Record, 4 August 2016: 26. Available at *https://link-gale-com.libezproxy. bournemouth.ac.uk/apps/doc/A459874518/STND?u=bu_uk&sid=STND& xid=94a14be1*. Accessed 22 January 2020.

Hansen, Kim Toft and Anne Marit Waade. 2017. *Locating Nordic Noir: From Beck to The Bridge*. Basingstoke: Palgrave Macmillan.

Harris, John. 2003. *The Last Party: Britpop, Blair and the Demise of English Rock*. London: 4th Estate.

Harrison, Ellie. 2018. 'Where is BBC crime drama Hidden filmed?' *Radio Times*. Available at *https://www.radiotimes.com/news/2018-09-21/hidden-bbc-location-guide-filming-wales/*. Accessed 28 May 2020.

Hayward, Will. 2020. *Lockdown Wales: How Covid-19 Tested Wales*. Bridgend: Seren.

Hebdige, Dick. 1979. *Subculture: The Meaning of Style*. London: Methuen.

Heidemann, Birte. 2020. 'The Brexit within: Mapping the rural and the urban in contemporary British fiction'. *Journal of Postcolonial Writing*, 56 (5): 676–88.

Hewison, Robert. 1987. *The Heritage Industry: Britain in a Climate of Decline*. London: Methuen.

—— 2014. *Cultural Capital: The Rise and Fall of Creative Britain*. London: Verso.

Higdon, David Leon. 2004. '"Wild Justice" in the Works of Irvine Welsh'. *Studies in Scottish Literature*, 33 (1): 421–34.

Hirons, Paul. 2018. 'Review: Shetland (S4 E6/6)'. Available at *https://the killingtimestv.wordpress.com/2018/03/20/review-shetland-s4-e6-6-tuesday-20th-march-bbc-one/*. Accessed 25 May 2020.

Høeg, Peter. 1993. *Miss Smilla's Feeling for Snow*. Translated by Felicity David. London: Harvill Press. Originally published as *Frøken Smillas fornemmelse for sne*, 1992.

Hofmann, Michael. 2014. '*Other People's Countries: A Journey into Memory* – Review'. *Guardian*, 12 March 2014: n.p. Available at *https://www. theguardian.com/books/2014/mar/12/other-peoples-countries-patrick-mcguiness-review*. Accessed 24 July 2020.

Hook, Andrew. 2020. 'Rich in ideas, but certainly not reader-friendly. Review of *The Literary Politics of Scottish Devolution, Voice, Class, Nation*, by Scott Hames'. *Scottish Review*, 8 April 2020. Available at *https://www. scottishreview.net/AndrewHook519a.html*. Accessed 13 November 2020.

Horan, Jennifer. 2019. 'Scotland's Role in the Carnegie Medal'. *CILIPS: Scotland's library and information professionals*, 16 August 2019. Available at *https://www.cilips.org.uk/the-cilip-carnegie-and-kate-greenaway-medals-2/*. Accessed 16 June 2020.

Hudec, Oto, Paula Cristina Remoaldo, Nataša Urbanciková and José António Cadima Ribeiro. 2019. 'Stepping Out of the Shadows: Legacy of the European Capitals of Culture, Guimarães 2012 and Košice 2013'. *Sustainability*, 11 (5): 1–21.

Hudson, Christine and Linda Sandberg. 2019. 'Narrating the Gender-equal City – Doing Gender-equality in the Swedish European Capital of Culture Umeå2014'. *Culture Unbound: Journal of Current Cultural Research*, 11 (1): 30–52.

Huggan, Graham. 1994. 'The Postcolonial Exotic: Rushdie's "Booker of Bookers"'. *Transition*, 64: 22–9.

Hughes, Daniel. 2014. 'The Bridge: Nordic Noir Breaking Borders and Language Barriers with the British Television Audience'. MA Dissertation, Stockholm University. Available at *http://su.diva-portal.org/smash/record.jsf?pid=diva2%3A744442&dswid=-4315*. Accessed 7 April 2020.

Humfrey, Belinda. 2003. 'Prelude to the Twentieth Century'. In *Welsh Writing in English*, edited by M. Wynn Thomas, 5–46. Cardiff: University of Wales Press.

Hunt, Alex. 2017. 'Theresa May and the DUP deal: What you need to know'. Available at *https://www.bbc.co.uk/news/election-2017-40245514*. Accessed 7 January 2021.

Immler, Nicole L. and Hans Sakkers. 2014. '(Re)Programming Europe: European Capitals of Culture: rethinking the role of culture'. *Journal of European Studies*, 44 (1): 3–29.

Ivanova, Petya Tsoneva. 2019. 'The "Passing Clouds" of Nationalism in Anthea Nicholson and Kapka Kassabova: Cross-Border Recollection of Political Trauma'. *University of Bucharest Review*, IX (1): 75–82.

Ivona, Antonietta, Antonella Rinella and Francesca Rinella. 2019. 'Glocal Tourism and Resilient Cities: The Case of Matera "European Capital of Culture 2019"'. *Sustainability*, 11 (15): 1–12.

Jacobsen, Ushma Chauhan. 2018. 'Does subtitled television drama brand the nation? Danish television drama and its language(s) in Japan'. *European Journal of Cultural Studies*, 21 (5): 614–30.

Jenkins, Mike. 2004. *The Language of Flight*. Llanrwst: Gwasg Carreg Gwalch.

Jensen, Pia Majbritt and Ushma Chauhan Jacobsen. 2017. 'The "three-leaf clover": A methodological lens to understand transnational audiences'. *Critical Studies in Television: The International Journal of Television Studies*, 12 (4): 430–44.

Jermyn, Deborah. 2017. 'Silk blouses and fedoras: The female detective, contemporary TV crime drama and the predicaments of postfeminism'. *Crime Media Culture*, 13 (3): 259–76.

Jones, Glyn. 1968. *The Dragon Has Two Tongues: Essays on Anglo-Welsh Writers and Writing*. London: J. M. Dent and Sons.

Jones, Moya. 2017. 'Wales and the Brexit Vote'. *Revue Française de Civilisation Britannique*, 22 (2): 1–11.

Kelman, James. 1994. *How late it was, how late*. London: Secker & Warburg.

Kennedy, A. L. 2016. *Serious Sweet*. London: Vintage.

Kent, Alan. 2015. *Interim Nation*. London: Francis Boutle.

—— 2017. *Turning Serpentine*. Wellington: Ryelands.

Kent, Gareth. 2019. '*Broken Ghost* by Niall Griffiths'. *Wales Arts Review*, 8 October 2019. Available at *https://www.walesartsreview.org/books-broken-ghost-by-niall-griffiths/*. Accessed 29 October 2020.

Kidd, Colin. 2014. 'Independence day? Should Scotland go it alone?' *Guardian*, 19 July 2014: 2–3.

Kiguru, Doseline. 2016a. 'Prizing African literature: creating a literary taste'. *Social Dynamics*, 42 (1): 161–74.

—— 2016b. 'Literary Prizes, Writers' Organisations and Canon Formation in Africa'. *African Studies*, 75 (2): 202–14.

Kingsnorth, Paul. 2014. *The Wake*. London: Unbound.

Knight, Stephen. 2004. *A Hundred Years of Fiction: From Colony to Independence*. Cardiff: University of Wales Press.

Kostova, Ludmilla. 2009. 'Victimization and its Cures: Representations of South Eastern Europe in British Fiction and Drama of the 1990s'. In *Betraying the Event: Constructions of Victimhood in Contemporary Cultures*, edited by Fatima Fetić, 35–68. Newcastle: Cambridge Scholars Press.

Kumar, Krishan. 2003. *The Making of English National Identity*. Cambridge: Cambridge University Press.

Lähdesmäki, Tuuli. 2016. 'Politics of tangibility, intangibility, and place in the making of a European cultural heritage in EU heritage policy'. *International Journal of Heritage Studies*, 22 (10): 766–80.

Laird, Nick. 2017. *Modern Gods*. London: 4th Estate.

Larsson, Stieg. 2008. *The Girl with the Dragon Tattoo*. Translated by Reg Keeland. London: MacLehose Press. Originally published as *Män som hatar kvinnor*, 2005.

—— 2009. *The Girl Who Played with Fire*. Translated by Reg Keeland. London: MacLehose Press. Originally published as *Flickan som lekte med elden*, 2006.

—— 2009. *The Girl Who Kicked the Hornets' Nest*. Translated by Reg Keeland. London: MacLehose Press. Originally published as *Luftslottet som sprängdes*, 2007.

Latvian Publishers' Association. 2011. 'About us'. Available at *http://www.gramatizdeveji.lv/index_en.php?sx=parmums_en*. Accessed 3 July 2020.

Le Carré, John. 1974. *Tinker, Taylor, Soldier, Spy*. London: Hodder & Stoughton.

—— 2019. *Agent Running in the Field*. London: Viking.

Leask, Anna and Ivana Rihova. 2010. 'The role of heritage tourism in the Shetland Islands'. *International Journal of Culture, Tourism and Hospitality Research*, 4 (2): 118–29.

Leckey, Susan, ed. 2002. *The Europa Directory of Literary Awards and Prizes*. London: Abingdon.

Levin, Stephen M. 2014. 'Is There a Booker Aesthetic? Iterations of the Global Novel'. *Critique: Studies in Contemporary Fiction*, 55 (5): 477–93.

Levy, Deborah. 2019. *The Man Who Saw Everything*. London: Hamish Hamilton.

Linklater, Magnus. 2016. '"Scotland's profound change energises me": Kathleen Jamie, winner of the book of the year award, is passionate about the nation'. *The Times*, 26 November 2016: 19. Available at *https://link-gale-com.libezproxy.bournemouth.ac.uk/apps/doc/A471575751/STND?u=bu_uk&sid=STND&xid=3957ba76*. Accessed 22 January 2020.

Liptrot, Michelle. 2014. '"Punk belongs to the punx, not business men!": British DIY punk as a form of cultural resistance'. In *Fight Back: Punk, Politics and Resistance*, edited by Subcultures Network, 232–51. Manchester: Manchester University Press.

Lithuanian Writers Union. 2020. 'Literary Prizes and Awards'. Available at *https://www.rasytojai.lt/en/literary-prizes-and-awards/*. Accessed 3 July 2020.

Liu, Yi-De. 2015. 'Major event and city branding: An evaluation of Liverpool as the 2008 European Capital of Culture'. *Journal of Place Management and Development*, 8 (2): 147–62.

Luckett, Moya. 2000. 'Image and Nation in 1990s British Cinema'. In *British Cinema of the 90s*, edited by Robert Murphy, 88–99. London: BFI Publishing.

Luckhurst, Roger. 2012. 'In War Times: Fictionalizing Iraq'. *Contemporary Literature*, 53 (4): 713–37.

Lynch, John. 2017. 'Belfast in *The Fall*: Post-Conflict Geographies of Violence and Gender'. *International Journal of TV Serial Narratives*, 3 (1): 61–72.

Maas, Willem. 2007. *Creating European Citizens*. Lanham, MD: Rowman & Littlefield.

Macnab, Geoffrey. 1997. 'Made in Wales; But "Twin Town" isn't a film about male voice choirs or the death of the mining industry. And it's not a Welsh "Trainspotting" either. Even if Danny Boyle was executive producer.' *Independent*, 3 April 1997: 6.

Marklund, Anders. 2019. 'Foreign Influences on Nordic (Noir) Borderlands'. *European Journal of Scandinavian Studies*, 49 (1): 178–96.

Marrouchi, Mustapha. 1999. 'Fear of the *Other*, Loathing the Similar'. *College Literature*, 26 (3): 17–58.

Marsden, Stevie. 2019. 'Why Women Don't Win Literary Awards: The Saltire Society Literary Awards and Implicit Stereotyping'. *Women: A Cultural Review*, 30 (1): 43–65.

—— 2021. *Prizing Scottish Literature: A Cultural History of the Saltire Society Literary Awards*. London: Anthem Press.

Masterson, John. 2020. '"Don't tell me this isn't relevant all over again in its brand new same old way": imagination, agitation, and raging against the machine in Ali Smith's *Spring*'. *Safundi: The Journal of South African and American Studies*, 21 (3): 355–72.

Matless, David. 2005. 'Sonic geography in a nature region'. *Social and Cultural Geography*, 6 (5): 745–66.

McAtackney, Laura. 2018. 'Where are all the women? Public memory, gender and memorialisation in contemporary Belfast'. In *Heritage after Conflict: Northern Ireland*, edited by Elizabeth Crooke and Thomas Maguire, 154–72. Abingdon: Routledge.

McBride, Eimear. 2020. *Strange Hotel*. London: Faber & Faber.

McCann, Fiona. 2014. *A poetics of dissensus: confronting violence in contemporary prose writing from the North of Ireland*. Bern: Peter Lang.

McDermott, Philip, Máiréad Nic Craith and Katerina Strani. 2016. 'Public space, collective memory and intercultural dialogue in a (UK) city of culture'. *Identities: Global Studies in Culture and Power*, 23 (5): 610–27.

McEwan, Ian. 2019. *Machines Like Me*. London: Jonathan Cape.

McGavin, Patrick Z. 1996. '"Trainspotting" author "stumbled into writing"'. *Tribune*, 30 July: 52.

McRobbie, Angela and Jenny Garber. 1975. 'Girls and Subcultures: An Exploration'. In *Resistance Through Rituals: Youth subcultures in post-war Britain*, edited by Stuart Hall and Tony Jefferson, 209–22. Birmingham: Hutchinson, Centre for Contemporary Cultural Studies.

Minhinnick, Robert. 2019. *Nia*. Bridgend: Seren.

Mitchell, David. 2020. *Utopia Avenue*. London: Sceptre.

Monk, Claire. 2000. 'Men in the 90s'. In *British Cinema of the 90s*, edited by Robert Murphy, 156–66. London: BFI Publishing.

Mooney, Gerry. 2004. 'Cultural Policy as Urban Transformation? Critical Reflections on Glasgow, European City of Culture 1990'. *Local Economy*, 19 (4): 327–40.

Moore, Robert. 2016. 'Rebranding Belfast: Chromatopes of Post-Conflict'. *Signs and Society*, 4 (1): 138–62.

Morace, Robert. 2001. *Irvine Welsh's Trainspotting: A Reader's Guide*. London: Continuum Contemporaries.

Moretti, Franco. 2005. *Signs Taken for Wonders: On the Sociology of Literary Forms*. London: Verso.

Morris, Paula. 2020. 'The "leftovers of empire": Commonwealth writers and the Booker Prize'. *Journal of Postcolonial Writing*, 56 (2): 261–70.

Moss, Sarah. 2018. *Ghost Wall*. London: Granta.

—— 2020. *Summerwater*. London: Pan Macmillan.

Murphy, Robert, ed. 2000. *British Cinema of the 90s*. London: BFI Publishing.

Myerscough, John. 1990. 'Monitoring Glasgow 1990. A report prepared for Glasgow City Council'. Strathclyde Regional Council and Scottish Enterprise. Available at *http://www.understandingglasgow.com/assets/0000/5038/MONITORING_GLASGOW_ 1990_vpdf.pdf*. Accessed 15 October 2020.

Nairn, Tom. 1977. *The Break-Up of Britain: Crisis and Neo-Nationalism*. London: Verso.

Nancy, Jean-Luc. 2010. 'Art Today'. *Journal of Visual Culture*, 9 (1): 91–9.

National Assembly for Wales. 2002. 'Culture Committee – Minutes', 6 November 2002.

Nechita, Florin. 2015. 'Bidding for the European Capital of Culture: Common Strengths and Weaknesses at the Pre-Selection Stage'. *Bulletin of the Transilvania University of Braşov*, 8.57 (1): 103–18.

Nesbø, Jo. 2011. *Headhunters*. Translated by Don Bartlett. London: Harvill Press. Originally published as *Hodejegerne*, 2008.

Newman, Judie. 1990. 'Sexual and Civil Conflicts: George F. Kennan and *The War Between the Tates*'. In *University Fiction*, edited by David Bevan, 103–22. Amsterdam: Rodopi.

Nguyen Diem Tran, My. 2015. 'Capturing the effect of film production: A qualitative perspective on film tourism in Wellington, New Zealand'. *Pacific Geographies*, 24 (43): 21–6.

Nicula, Virgil and Cosmin Chindriş. 2017. 'Implications of Festival Culture in Tourism Development in the City of Sibiu'. *Revista Economica*, 69 (6): 120–7.

Nobel Foundation. 1965. 'Nobel Prize in Literature 1965'. Available at *https://www.nobelprize.org/prizes/literature/1965/summary/*. Accessed 2 July 2020.

—— 1995. 'Nobel Prize in Literature 1995'. Available at *https://www.nobelprize.org/prizes/literature/1995/summary/*. Accessed 30 July 2020.

Nora, Pierre. 1989. 'Between Memory and History: Les Lieux de Mémoire'. *Representations*, 26: 7–24.

Norris, Sharon. 2006. 'The Booker Prize: A Bourdieusian Perspective'. *Journal for Cultural Research*, 10 (2): 139–58.

Northern Ireland Book Award. 2015. 'About the Award'. Available at *http://www.nibookaward.org.uk/2014-15/about-the-award.php*. Accessed 5 August 2020.

Oancă, Alexandra. 2015. 'Europe is not elsewhere: The mobilization of an immobile policy in the lobbying by Perm (Russia) for the European Capital of Culture title'. *European Urban and Regional Studies*, 22 (2): 176–90.

O'Brien, Tom. 2003. 'To Read or Not to Read: A New Policy for Nobels and Pulitzers'. *Arts Education Policy Review*, 104 (4): 29–33.

O'Callaghan, Cian and Denis Linehan. 2007. 'Identity, politics and conflict in dockland development in Cork, Ireland: European Capital of Culture 2005'. *Cities*, 24 (4): 311–23.

O'Connor, Siobhan. 2020. 'Brexit and the Tudor turn: Philippa Gregory's narratives of national grievance'. In *The road to Brexit: A cultural perspective on British attitudes to Europe*, edited by Ina Habermann, 179–96. Manchester: Manchester University Press.

Ooi, Can-Seng, Lars Håkanson and Laura LaCava. 2014. 'Poetics and Politics of the European Capital of Culture Project'. *Procedia – Social and Behavioral Sciences*, 148: 420–7.

Osmond, John. 1996. *Welsh Europeans*. Bridgend: Seren.

—— 2018. *Ten Million Stars are Burning*. Llandysul: Gwasg Gomer.

Paris, Didier and Thierry Baert. 2011. 'Lille 2004 and the role of culture in the regeneration of Lille metropole'. *Town Planning Review*, 82 (1): 29–43.

Parveen, J. Jaya. 2019. 'The Politics Behind the Booker Prize and Oscar Award'. *Language in India*, 19 (2): 184–92.

Patel, Kiran Klaus. 2013. 'Integration by Interpellation: The European Capitals of Culture and the Role of Experts in European Union Cultural Policies'. *Journal of Common Market Studies*, 51 (3): 538–54.

Peach, Linden. 2008. *Contemporary Irish and Welsh Women's Fiction: Gender, Desire and Power*. Cardiff: University of Wales Press.

Perraudin, Frances. 2019. 'English people living in Wales tilted it towards Brexit, research finds'. *Guardian*, 22 September 2019. Available at *https://www.theguardian.com/uk-news/2019/sep/22/english-people-wales-brexit-research*. Accessed 9 February 2021.

Perret, Sally. 2015. 'In the name of the nation? The National Award in Narrative Literature, and the democratization of art in Spain (1977–2013)'. *Journal of Spanish Cultural Studies*, 16 (1): 77–93.

Perrins, Darryl. 2000. 'This Town Ain't Big Enough for the Both of Us'. In *Wales On Screen*, edited by Steve Blandford, 152–67. Bridgend: Seren.

Pimlott, Herbert. 2014. '"Militant entertainment"? "Crisis music" and political ephemera in the emergent "structure of feeling", 1976 – 83'. In *Fight Back: Punk, Politics and Resistance*, edited by Subcultures Network, 268–86. Manchester: Manchester University Press.

Pitcher, Ben. 2014. *Consuming Race*. Abingdon: Routledge.

Pittock, Murray. 2003. *A New History of Scotland*. Stroud: Sutton Publishing.

Popescu, Gabriela Virginia. 2017. 'Sibiu Between European Capital of Culture and Brexit: City Brand Perspective on Citizen.' *Ecoforum*, 6.3 (13): n.p.

Powell, Rachel and John Clarke. 1975. 'A Note on Marginality'. In *Resistance Through Rituals: Youth subcultures in post-war Britain*, edited by Stuart Hall and Tony Jefferson, 223–30. Birmingham: Hutchinson, Centre for Contemporary Cultural Studies.

Preuss, Stefanie. 2011. 'Occasional Paper: Now That's What I call a Scottish Canon!' *International Journal of Scottish Literature*, 8: 1–4.

Price, Karen. 2009. 'Mererid Hopwood: Spanish dramatist is my inspiration'. *Wales Online*, 15 May 2009. Available at *https://www.walesonline.co.uk/lifestyle/showbiz/mererid-hopwood-spanish-dramatist-inspiration-2105700*. Accessed 8 February 2021.

Priestley, Rebecca. 2020. 'Prepare to Be Kind'. *Granta*, 153: 193–210.

Rappas, Ipek A. Celik. 2019. 'From *Titanic* to *Game of Thrones*: Promoting Belfast as a Global Media Capital'. *Media, Culture & Society*, 41 (4): 539–56.

Rau, Petra. 2018. '*Autumn* after the referendum'. In *Brexit and Literature: Critical and Cultural Responses*, edited by Robert Eaglestone, 31-43. Abingdon: Routledge.

Rausing, Sigrid. 2019. 'Introduction'. *Granta*, 149: 10–12.

Redvall, Eva Novrup. 2016. '*Midsomer Murders* in Copenhagen: the transnational production of Nordic Noir-influenced UK television drama'. *New Review of Film and Television Studies*, 14 (3): 345–63.

Richards, Greg. 2015. 'Evaluating the European capital of culture that never was: the case of BrabantStad 2018'. *Journal of Policy Research in Tourism, Leisure and Events*, 7 (2): 118–33.
Richards, Greg and Lénia Marques. 2016. 'Bidding for Success? Impacts of the European Capital of Culture Bid'. *Scandinavian Journal of Hospitality and Tourism*, 16 (2): 180–95.
Roberts, Les. 2016. 'Landscapes in the frame: exploring the hinterlands of the British procedural drama'. *New Review of Film and Television Studies*, 14 (3): 364–85.
Romney, Jonathan. 1999. 'The Acid House, Bleak House'. *Guardian*, 1 January 1999: 6.
Rushdie, Salman. 2019. *Quichotte*. London: Jonathan Cape.
Sandbye, Mette. 2016. 'The New Nordic? A Critical Examination'. *Journal of Aesthetics & Culture*, 8: 1–3.
Santana, Mario. 2009. 'On Visible and Invisible Languages: Bernardo Atxaga's *Soinujolearen semea* in Translation'. In *Writers In Between Languages: Minority Literatures in the Global Scene*, edited by Mari Jose Olaziregi, 213–27. Reno, NV: Center for Basque Studies.
Sapiro, Gisèle. 2016. 'The metamorphosis of modes of consecration in the literary field: Academies, literary prizes, festivals'. Translated by Madeline Bedecarré. *Poetics*, 59: 5–19.
Sasaki, Shusaki, Hirofumi Kurokawa and Fumio Ohtake. 2019. 'Positive and negative effects of social status on longevity: Evidence from two literary prizes in Japan'. *Journal of the Japanese and International Economies*, 53: 1–17.
Schmitt-Kilb, Christian. 2020. 'A case for a Green Brexit? Paul Kingsnorth, John Berger and the pros and cons of a sense of place'. In *The road to Brexit: A cultural perspective on British attitudes to Europe*, edited by Ina Habermann, 162–78. Manchester: Manchester University Press.
Schoene, Berthold. 2007. *The Edinburgh Companion to Contemporary Scottish Literature*. Edinburgh: Edinburgh University Press.
Scully, Roger and Richard Wyn Jones, eds. 2010. *Europe, Regions and European Regionalism*. Basingstoke: Palgrave Macmillan.
Seargeant, Philip. 2012. *Exploring World Englishes: Language in a Global Context*. Abingdon: Routledge.
Shaw, Katy. 2018. *Hauntology: The Presence of the Past in Twenty-First Century English Literature*. Basingstoke: Palgrave Pivot.
Shaw, Kristian. 2018. 'BrexLit'. In *Brexit and Literature: Critical and Cultural Responses*, edited by Robert Eaglestone, 15–30. Abingdon: Routledge.

—— 2021. *Brexlit: British Literature and the European Project*. London: Bloomsbury Academic.

Sidwell, Nick. 2013. 'Heart of the Story: Mapping the Booker Prize'. *Guardian*, 11 September 2013. Available at *https://www.theguardian.com/books/booksblog/2013/sep/11/man-booker-prize-2013-map*. Accessed 7 July 2020.

Sinfield, Alan. 2004. *Literature, Politics and Culture in Postwar Britain*. London: Continuum.

Smith, Ali. 2007. *Girl Meets Boy*. Edinburgh: Canongate.

—— 2016. *Autumn*. London: Hamish Hamilton.

—— 2017. *Winter*. London: Hamish Hamilton.

—— 2019. *Spring*. London: Hamish Hamilton.

—— 2020. *Summer*. London: Hamish Hamilton.

Smith, Dai. 2010. *In the Frame: Memory in Society 1910 to 2010*. Cardigan: Parthian.

Snelling, Naomi. 2017. 'Director's bold vision of a counter-culture capital'. *Wales Online*, 17 May 2017. Available at *https://link-gale-com.libezproxy.bournemouth.ac.uk/apps/doc/A491829109/STND?u=bu_uk&sid=STND&xid=ec4ee313*. Accessed 30 January 2020.

Squires, Claire. 2004. 'A Common Ground? Book Prize Culture in Europe'. *Javnost – The Public*, 11 (4): 37–47.

—— 2013. 'Literary Prizes and Awards'. In *A Companion to Creative Writing*, edited by Graeme Harper, 291–303. Chichester: Wiley-Blackwell.

Steenberg, Lindsay. 2017. '*The Fall* and Television Noir'. *Television & New Media*, 18 (1): 58–75.

Stevenson, Deborah. 2004. 'Civic gold rush: Cultural planning and the politics of the Third Way'. *International Journal of Cultural Policy*, 10 (1): 119–31.

Stoke-on-Trent. 2019. *Together We Make the City: Stoke-on-Trent – Losing the Bid but Winning with Culture*. Stoke-on-Trent: Stoke-on-Trent City Council.

Stougaard-Nielsen, Jakob. 2016. 'Nordic noir in the UK: the allure of accessible difference'. *Journal of Aesthetics & Culture*, 8: 1–12.

—— 2017. *Scandinavian Crime Fiction*. London: Bloomsbury.

—— 2020. 'Criminal Peripheries: The Globalization of Scandinavian Crime Fiction and its Agents'. In *Translating the Literatures of Small European Nations*, edited by Rajendra Chitnis, Jakob Stougaard-Nielsen, Rhian Atkin and Zoran Milutinovic, 184–204. Liverpool: Liverpool University Press.

Subcultures Network, ed. 2014. *Fight Back: Punk, Politics and Resistance*. Manchester: Manchester University Press.
Suhr-Sytsma, Nathan. 2018. 'The Geography of Prestige: Prizes, Nigerian Writers, and World Literature'. *ELH*, 85 (4): 1093–122.
Theodoraki, Eleni. 2014. 'Evaluation and Legacy of the ECoC: Event Owners' And Event Hosts' Perspectives'. *Economia Della Cultura*, xxiv (2): 183–93.
Thomas, M. Wynn. 1999. *Corresponding Cultures: The Two Literatures of Wales*. Cardiff: University of Wales Press.
—— 2003, ed. *Welsh Writing in English*. Cardiff: University of Wales Press.
—— 2021. *Eutopia: Studies in Cultural Euro-Welshness, 1850–1980*. Cardiff: University of Wales Press.
Thomas, Ned. 1971. *The Welsh Extremist: A Culture in Crisis*. London: Victor Gollancz.
Thompson, Ben. 1997. 'Twin Town'. *Sight and Sound*, 7 (4): 54.
Thorpe, Adam. 2017. *Missing Fay*. London: Random House.
Thorup, Bjarne, ed. 2007. *Centring on the Peripheries: Studies in Scandinavian, Scottish, Gaelic and Greenlandic Literature*. London: Norvik Press.
Todd, Richard. 1996. *Consuming Fictions: The Booker Prize and Fiction in Britain Today*. London: Bloomsbury.
Tombs, Robert. 2021. *This Sovereign Isle: Britain In and Out of Europe*. London: Allen Lane.
Tretter, Eliot M. 2009. 'The Cultures of Capitalism: Glasgow and the Monopoly of Culture'. *Antipode*, 41 (1): 111–32.
Tursie, Corina. 2020. 'The unwanted past and urban regeneration of Communist heritage cities. Case study: European Capitals of Culture (ECoC) Riga 2014, Pilsen 2015 and Wroclaw 2016'. *Journal of Education Culture and Society*, 6 (2): 122–38.
Urbanciková, Nataša. 2018. 'European Capitals of Culture: What Are Their Individualities?' *Theoretical and Empirical Researches in Urban Management*, 13 (4): 43–55.
Varty, Anne. 2018. 'Poetry and Brexit'. In *Brexit and Literature: Critical and Cultural Responses*, edited by Robert Eaglestone, 59–65. Abingdon: Routledge.
Veličković, Vedrana. 2020. '"Eastern Europeans" and BrexLit'. *Journal of Postcolonial Writing*, 56 (5): 648–61.
Villa, Ilaria. 2019. 'Segnalazioni/Informes/Rapports/Reports'. *Altre Modernità: Rivista di studi letterari e culturali*, 22: 316–19.

Waade, Anne Marit. 2011. 'BBC's *Wallander*: Sweden Seen Through British Eyes'. *Critical Studies in Television*, 6 (2): 47–60.

Waade, Anne Marit and Gunhild Agger. 2018. 'Melancholy and Murder: Mood and Tone in Crime Series'. In *European Television Crime Drama and Beyond*, edited by Kim Toft Hansen, Steven Peacock, Sue Turnbull, 61–82. Basingstoke. Palgrave Macmillan.

Walford, Jessica. 2017. 'Bilingual Drama Going For Scandi-Noir Audience'. *Wales on Sunday*, 17 September 2017: 16.

Watson, L. 2016. 'Results and turnout at the EU referendum'. Available at *https://www.electoralcommission.org.uk/who-we-are-and-what-we-do/elections-and-referendums/past-elections-and-referendums/eu-referendum/results-and-turnout-eu-referendum*. Accessed 25 October 2020.

Welsh, Irvine. 1993. *Trainspotting*. London: Secker & Warburg.

Westall, Claire and Michael Gardiner, eds. 2013. *Literature of an Independent England: Revisions of England, Englishness and English Literature*. Basingstoke: Palgrave.

Whitehead, Andrew. 2020. 'The Documentary: The Hindu Bard'. BBC Sounds. 29 December 2020.

Whitfield, Agnes. 2016. 'Translations/Traductions'. *University of Toronto Quarterly*, 85 (3): 268–99.

Whyte, Christopher. 1998. 'Masculinities in Contemporary Scottish Fiction'. *Forum for Modern Language Studies*, 34(3): 274–85.

Williams, Raymond. 1964. *Second Generation*. London: Chatto & Windus.

—— 1973. *The Country and the City*. Oxford: Oxford University Press.

—— 1977. *Marxism and Literature*. Oxford: Oxford University Press.

—— 1979a. *Politics and Letters: Interviews with New Left Review*. London: New Left Books.

—— 1979b. *The Fight for Manod*. London: Chatto & Windus.

—— 1989. *Resources of Hope*. London: Verso.

Willis, Paul E. 1975. 'The Cultural Meaning of Drug Use'. In *Resistance Through Rituals: Youth subcultures in post-war Britain*, edited by Stuart Hall and Tony Jefferson, 106–18. Birmingham: Hutchinson, Centre for Contemporary Cultural Studies.

Wilson, Kerry and David O'Brien. 2012. 'It's Not the Winning ... Reconsidering the Cultural City: A report on the Cultural Cities Research Network 2011–12'. Liverpool: Institute of Cultural Capital.

Winterson, Jeanette. 2019. *Frankissstein: A Love Story*. London: Jonathan Cape.

Wollaston, Sam. 2014. 'Shetland: Original Drama – TV review: There's something of the Nordic about Shetland – but sadly no impressive knitwear on show'. *Guardian*, 12 March 2014: n.p.

—— 2016. 'Shetland review – wildness, beauty and a damn good yarn'. *Guardian*, 16 January 2016: n.p.

Worley, Matthew, Keith Gildart, Anna Gough-Yates, Sian Lincoln, Bill Osgerby, Lucy Robinson, John Street, Peter Webb. 2014. 'Introduction: from protest to resistance'. In *Fight Back: Punk, Politics and Resistance*, edited by Subcultures Network, 1–9. Manchester: Manchester University Press.

Zangen, Britta. 2003. 'Women as Readers, Writers, and Judges: The Controversy about the Orange Prize for Fiction'. *Women's Studies*, 32: 281–99.

INDEX

A
Aboulela, Leila 194, 197–98, 200–2, 211
Acorn Foundation Fiction Prize 185
Act of Union (1707) 9, 66, 189, 190
Adam, Pip 185
Akutagawa Prize 209–11
Albarn, Damon 21, 39, 40
Alps 109, 114, 242
Andersen, Hans Christian 113, 154
  Hans Christian Andersen Award 187
Anderson, Brett 39
Arab Spring 285
Artes Mundi Prize 206
Article 50 (of Treaty on European Union) 276, 277
Arts Council of Great Britain 32, 33
Arts Council of Wales 15, 37, 168, 203, 205, 216
Atkinson, Kate 191, 285
Atwood, Margaret 200
Azzopardi, Trezza 208, 209, 211

B
Baltic Centre, Gateshead 89
Barnett Formula 4

Barry, Sebastian 224
Basque culture 99, 103, 174, 207, 213
Bassey, Shirley 59
Belfast 12, 64, 80, 82, 84, 107, 140–3, 146, 148, 149, 218–20
Biden, Joe 226
Blair, Tony 21, 22, 34–6, 40–2
Blur 39, 40, 41, 46
Booker Prize 14, 16, 17, 167, 168, 169, 177–87, 192, 193, 194, 199, 201, 207, 208, 209, 211, 220, 221–3, 250, 263, 287
Bordertown (*Sorjonen*, 2016–20) 116, 122, 138, 140
Boyd, William 191, 192
Bragg, Billy 40
Brit Awards 19, 40, 41, 43, 44, 167
British Broadcasting Corporation (BBC) 40, 116, 127, 131, 143, 159, 160, 161, 209
  BBC Four 125, 126
  BBC National Short Story Award 208, 214
  BBC Northern Ireland 45, 143
  BBC Wales 150, 152, 157
  Radio 1 39

British Broadcasting Corporation
(BBC) (continued)
Radio 2 Folk Singer of the Year
225
Radio 4 287
Britpop 10, 14, 21–3, 37–46, 52, 56,
58, 283
Broadchurch 126, 161, 163–5
Brown, Gordon 6, 246
Burns, Anna 16, 169, 187, 220, 221–3
Burns, Robert 188, 189, 190
Burnside, John 192

C

Caine Prize 197, 200, 201
Cameron, David 1, 4, 5, 232
Cameron, James 141
Cardiff 37, 89, 90–2, 152, 156, 209,
211, 268
Cardiff Singer of the World 83
Carnegie Medal 187–8, 219
le Carré, John 284
Celtic Noir 134, 150, 152
Channel 4 23
Clarke, Gillian 235
Cleeves, Ann 131, 135, 136
Clegg, Nick 4
Climate Change 17, 139, 285, 287
Coalition Government (2010–15) 4,
106, 125, 234, 278
Cobain, Kurt 39
Coe, Jonathan 17, 246–52, 257, 272
Coetzee, J. M. 184, 201
Cold War 113, 114, 115, 178, 179, 180,
181, 182, 183, 230, 284, 285
Colman, Olivia 164
Connolly, Ríoghnach 224, 225
Conran, Alys 207
Cool Cymru 10, 58, 59
Cork 64, 80

Cornwall 18, 208, 239, 241, 258, 259,
261–3, 265, 266, 267, 268, 270, 286
coronavirus 150, 165, 283–8
Cosmopolitan (magazine) 28
Craig, Amanda 17, 231, 259, 261–2,
265, 272
Craith / Hidden 14, 111, 149–50, 157–9
Creation (record company) 38, 42, 43
Creative Scotland 197
Culloden, Battle of 245
Cummings, Dominic 251
Cusk, Rachel 286
Cultural Memory 16, 99, 218, 255

D

Dangor, Achmat 223
Daniel Owen Memorial Prize 203
Davies, Geraint Talfan 37
Davies, Grahame 205, 214
Davies, Peter Ho 208
Davies, Stevie 208
Democratic Unionist Party (DUP) 5,
148
Demos 43, 77
Department for Culture, Media and
Sport (DCMS) 12, 35, 43, 52,
80, 82, 90, 96, 104–5, 106
Derry Girls 23, 44, 45
Desai, Kieran 223
Deutscher Buchpreis 173
Devil's Bridge 154, 155, 157
Dharker, Imtiaz 235
Doctor Who 160
Dublin 11, 64, 77, 78, 80, 206
Duffy, Carol Ann 235
Dylan Thomas Prize 189

E

Elastica 39, 41, 46
EMI (record company) 39

English, varieties of 136–9, 161–3, 164, 263, 275
English Votes for English Laws (EVEL) 1, 5–6, 165
Euro (Currency) 11, 87, 96, 109, 127, 130, 165, 240
European Capital of Culture (ECOC) 9, 11–13, 36, 63–96, 98–101, 102, 105–8, 109, 127, 283
 Athens 65, 67
 BrabantStad (as candidate) 81, 87–9, 102, 103
 Bristol (as candidate) 12, 64, 80, 85, 86, 90, 91, 92, 99
 Cardiff (as candidate) 12, 64, 80, 82–6, 101
 Cork 77–80
 Glasgow 11, 36, 63, 64, 68, 70, 71, 73–6, 79, 85, 86, 87, 127
 Guimarães 72
 Istanbul 69, 107
 Leeuwarden 81, 89, 103
 Lille 88, 92, 94
 Linz 99
 Liverpool 12, 37, 64, 80, 85, 86, 89–94, 99, 104
 Marseille 99, 100
 Matera 70
 Newcastle (as candidate) 12, 64, 80, 86, 88, 89, 92, 103
 Porto 93
 San Sebastián 99
 Sibiu (Romania) 67, 93
 Stavanger 70, 79, 93, 107
 Turku 109
 Umeå 67
European Economic Community (EEC) 8, 14, 86, 127–8, 170, 171, 174, 175, 179, 181, 182, 250, 283

European Football Championship
 (1992) 127
 (1996) 41, 42
 (2016) 211–12
 (2020) 211
European Union (EU) 2–3, 9, 13, 14, 16, 53, 63, 65, 66, 68, 69, 77, 86, 92, 93–4, 95, 97, 99, 100, 107, 109, 128, 130, 132, 165, 168, 175, 176, 181, 182, 183, 212, 213, 225, 227, 229, 233, 239, 246, 252, 255, 257, 265, 271
European Union Prize for Literature 183
Evans, Caradoc 54
Evaristo, Bernadine 17, 199, 200, 263–5
Eyre, Richard 42

F

Facebook 244
Falklands/Malvinas War 284
Fearnley-Whittingstall, Hugh 118
Financial Crisis (2007–8) 118, 240, 261
Folk Music 97, 98, 224–5
Foster, Arlene 5
Frischmann, Justine 39
Frisian culture 103

G

Gallagher, Noel 8, 21, 40, 41, 42, 43
Galloway, Janice 192
Game of Thrones 140–3
Gay rights 17, 237, 246, 249, 255, 257, 258, 260, 261, 271
Glasgow 137, 138, 139
 2014 Commonwealth Games 79
Globalisation 109, 110, 115, 118, 119, 139, 160, 202

Golding, William 184
Good Friday Agreement 1, 16, 141, 144, 145, 169, 223, 253
Gordimer, Nadine 184, 201
Gorsedd of Bards 204, 205
Gorsedh Kernow (Cornish Gorsedd) 208
Grace, Patricia 178
Grade, Michael 42
Graham, Julie 137
Grant, Linda 17, 256
Granta 202, 229, 287
Gray, Alasdair 186, 193
Greater London Council 33
Gregory, Philippa 286
Griffiths, Niall 17, 18, 268, 272–81
Grunge 39, 40
Gunter, Chris 211

H
Hadley, Tessa 205, 208
Hall, Peter 42
Hall, Sarah 17, 208, 231, 231, 232, 235, 245, 246, 247
Halliwell, Geri 19, 20, 43, 44
Harries, Mali 155
Hay Festival 214
Heaney, Seamus 16, 169, 220, 221
Henshall, Douglas 136
Heseltine, Michael 37
Hinds, Ciaran 135
Høeg, Peter 115, 116
Holocaust 236, 237, 285
Holyer An Gof (Cornish book prize) 208
Hopwood, Mererid 206, 214

I
Ihimaera, Witi 178
IMPAC Dublin Literary Award 206

Interculturalism 15, 97, 98, 99, 100, 104, 107, 168, 184, 169, 197, 214, 256
Internal Markets Act (2020) 5, 225
Iraq War 230
Ishiguro, Kazuo 184, 209
Islam 94, 214, 241, 248, 249, 256, 261, 264

J
Jamie, Kathleen 192, 194, 195
Jenkins, Mike 217, 218
Johnson, Boris 5, 234, 250, 251, 284
Jones, Carwyn 212

K
Kane, Sarah 50, 51
Karadog, Aneirin 204, 215, 216
Kassabova, Kapka 194, 195–7, 202
Kay, Jackie 197–201, 211, 235
Keeping Faith 152
Kelman, James 7, 187, 193, 194
Kennedy, A. L. 17, 192, 231, 233–5, 246, 272
Kent, Alan 208, 213, 266–8, 279
Kerry Group Irish Fiction Award 226

L
Lalwani, Nikita 208
Lamacq, Steve 39
Larsson, Stieg 115, 116, 153
Leave Campaign 1, 16, 18, 65, 124, 196, 212, 228, 233, 235, 240, 244, 249, 251, 258, 260, 262, 268, 271, 277
Levy, Deborah 285
Lewis, Caryl 205
Lewis, Emyr 204
Literature Wales 203, 214, 216
Liverpool 134, 208, 255, 256
  see also European Capital of Culture

Livingstone, Ken 35
Lord of the Rings (Tolkien) 142
Lucashenko, Melissa 185

M

Major, John 34, 35
Man Booker International Prize 181, 183
Manic Street Preachers 22, 58
Massie, Allan 191, 192
May, Theresa 4, 5, 249, 251
McBride, Eimear 17, 226, 252, 255
McCorley, Roddy 224, 225
McDermid, Val 192
McEwan, Ian 17, 209, 284
McGuinness, Patrick 205, 208, 215, 216
McIlvanney Prize 190
Mediterranean 109, 114, 126, 131, 162, 163
Merthyr Tydfil 217
#MeToo Movement 285
Midsomer Murders 160
Miles Franklin Award 185
Millennium Dome 37
Miners' Strike (1984) 30, 52
Minhinnick, Robert 17, 268, 270, 271
Morgan, Rhodri 84
Morris, Jan 207
Moss, Sarah 241, 285
Multiculturalism 17, 100, 119, 168, 184, 196, 256, 264

N

Naipaul, V. S. 184
Naoki Prize 209, 210
National Assembly for Wales (Senedd) 4, 37, 59, 82, 83, 84
National Eisteddfod 15, 203–6, 213, 214, 215
National Front 27
National Lottery 35, 36

Nationalism 2, 113, 130, 168
  English 186, 250
  Irish 225, 227
  Scottish 8, 15, 168, 193
  Welsh 15, 16, 37, 168, 213, 216
Nesbø, Jo 116, 121
New Public Management 35
No Alibis (Book store) 219
Nobel Prize for Literature 16, 169, 178, 179, 183, 184, 201, 220, 221
Nordic Noir 13, 14, 109–18, 120, 121, 122–7, 129, 131–5, 138, 140, 142, 143, 149, 151, 152, 153, 154, 157, 160, 162, 164, 165, 283
Northern Ireland Book Award 16, 219, 220

O

Oasis 40, 41, 42, 56
Obama, Barack 246
O'Donnell, Alison 137
Olympic Games 11, 86, 87, 88, 89, 209, 246
Orange Prize (Women's Prize for Fiction) 208, 209, 210, 211
Orwell, George 30, 194
Osmond, John 213, 284

P

Palme, Olof 114
Plaid Cymru 1, 4, 212
Poetry Wales 206
Police Service of Northern Ireland (PSNI) 145, 147
Populism 212, 243, 251, 284
Post-conflict societies 12, 16, 17, 43, 97–8, 99, 100, 140, 141, 143, 144, 145, 148, 169, 218, 219, 220, 221, 223, 224, 225, 227, 228, 252, 255

Prix Formentor 175–9, 183
Prix Goncourt 170, 173, 177, 182, 183
Punk 10, 19, 21, 23–9, 42, 43, 44, 45, 46, 49, 61, 283

Q
Queen Elizabeth II 19, 30, 140
Queer Theory 17, 237, 238, 246, 249, 255, 257, 258, 260, 261, 271

R
Rattle, Simon 287
Ravenhill, Mark 50, 51
Red Wedge 38, 40, 41
Rees-Mogg, Jacob 251
Rees-Mogg, William 32, 33
Reese-Williams, Sian 157
Referendums
  for North Eastern Assembly 35
  on Scottish devolution 22, 46, 54, 58, 190, 193
  on Scottish Independence 1, 6, 132, 190, 191, 192, 195, 232, 233
  on UK membership of EU 2, 4, 6, 12, 15, 16, 69, 107, 169, 190, 194, 197, 202, 212, 215, 216, 229, 230, 231, 233, 234, 235, 236, 238, 239, 241, 246, 249, 250, 255, 257, 258, 263, 265, 268, 271, 284
  Welsh 22, 37, 54, 58, 60, 190
Reynolds, Idris 204
Robertson, Robin 191, 192
Robertson, Steven 137
Rough Trade 38
Rowling, J. K. 191
Rubens, Bernice 184, 187, 207
Rugby 54, 55, 58
Rushdie, Salman 185, 186, 212

S
S4C 150, 157
Saatchi, Maurice 42
Sage, Gateshead (music centre) 89
Salisbury, Eurig 204
Salmond, Alex 233
Saltire Society 15, 168, 188, 189, 287
  Scottish Book of the Year 193, 195–202, 211, 219
Sansom, C. J. 191, 192
Saville Report (2010) 97
Scott, Bob 86
Scottish Mortgage Investment Trust Book Awards 197, 198, 200, 201
Scottish National Party (SNP) 1, 3, 4, 5
Scottish Parliament 4, 6, 46, 232, 236
Sex Pistols 19–21, 29, 41
Sheen, Michael 288
Shetland 14, 111, 130–40, 157, 164
Shine (production company) 163
Sinn Féin 148
Smith, Ali 17, 231, 235–45, 246, 263, 266, 270, 272, 285, 286
Smith, Chris 35, 36, 52
Soyinka, Wole 201
Spice Girls 10, 19, 43
Steffan Ros, Manon 207
Stereophonics 22, 58
Stormont Assembly 148
Stuart, Douglas 186, 287
Sturgeon, Nicola 4, 5
Suede 39, 41
Super Furry Animals 22, 58
Swansea 60, 189

T
Tate Modern 34
Tennant, David 164, 288

Thatcher, Margaret 30, 35, 38, 40, 57, 120, 180
The Bridge (*Bron/Broen*, 2011–18) 116, 119, 122, 133, 134, 151, 153, 154, 163, 164
The Fall 14, 111, 140, 143–7, 149
The Killing (*Forbrydelsen*, 2007–12) 115, 116, 122, 124, 125, 126, 133, 134, 135, 147, 151, 153, 154, 161, 163
The Tunnel 14, 111, 129, 151, 159, 161, 163, 164, 165
Third Way (New Labour) 22, 35, 77
Thomas, Dylan 54, 60, 189
Titanic Belfast 140–43
Trainspotting 10, 22, 45–53, 54, 55, 57, 58, 60, 193
Transgender 212, 241, 248, 265, 271
Trapped (*Ófærð*, 2015–21) 116, 122, 138, 140, 149
Trezise, Rachel 209, 210, 211
Troubles (Irish) 5, 22, 44, 45, 96, 97, 141, 144, 145, 146, 148, 221, 222, 225, 227, 252, 253
Truth and Reconciliation Commission (South Africa) 223
Twin Town 10, 22, 53–60, 101
Twitter 244, 275, 276, 277–8

U

UK City of Culture 11–14, 16, 44, 65, 68, 94–8, 100–8
  Coventry 101, 103, 104, 287
  Derry / Londonderry 12, 16, 44, 65, 96–8, 100, 107, 252
  Hull 12, 65, 100, 105, 106
  St Davids (as candidate) 101
  Swansea (as candidate) 12, 101–3

United Kingdom Independence Party (UKIP) 260, 265
United Nations Convention on the Rights of the Child 188

V

Vanity Fair 42
Vietnam War 262–3
Visit Sweden 119
Visit Wales 214

W

Wales Book of the Year 15, 168, 169, 187, 203–11, 214, 215, 216, 219
Wales Millennium Centre 89, 155
Walford Davies, Jason 205
Wallander 14, 111, 116, 125, 126, 153, 159–61
Walter Scott Prize 189, 190, 191, 192
Warner, Alan 192
Waters, Sarah 208
Westwood, Vivienne 26
Whiley, Jo 39
Wigan Heritage Centre 30
Williams, Raymond 3, 24, 34, 120, 156, 213, 230, 231, 268
Winterson, Jeanette 212, 213
Wood, Leanne 4, 212
Woolf, Virginia 194, 239

Y

Y Gwyll/ Hinterland 14, 111, 121, 126, 149–54, 157, 158, 164
Yellow Bird (production company) 122, 123, 126
Yentob, Alan 42